About Island Press

Island Press is the only nonprofit organization in the United States whose principal purpose is the publication of books on environmental issues and natural resource management. We provide solutions-oriented information to professionals, public officials, business and community leaders, and concerned citizens who are shaping responses to environmental problems.

In 2002, Island Press celebrates its eighteenth anniversary as the leading provider of timely and practical books that take a multidisciplinary approach to critical environmental concerns. Our growing list of titles reflects our commitment to bringing the best of an expanding body of literature to the environmental community throughout North America and the world.

Support for Island Press is provided by The Nathan Cummings Foundation, Geraldine R. Dodge Foundation, Doris Duke Charitable Foundation, Educational Foundation of America, The Charles Engelhard Foundation, The Ford Foundation, The George Gund Foundation, The Vira I. Heinz Endowment, The William and Flora Hewlett Foundation, Henry Luce Foundation, The John D. and Catherine T. MacArthur Foundation, The Andrew W. Mellon Foundation, The Moriah Fund, The Curtis and Edith Munson Foundation, National Fish and Wildlife Foundation, The New-Land Foundation, Oak Foundation, The Overbrook Foundation, The David and Lucile Packard Foundation, The Pew Charitable Trusts, The Rockefeller Foundation, The Winslow Foundation, and other generous donors.

The opinions expressed in this book are those of the author(s) and do not necessarily reflect the views of these foundations.

Ecotourism
& CERTIFICATION

Ecotourism
& CERTIFICATION

Setting Standards in Practice

EDITED BY
Martha Honey

ISLAND PRESS
Washington • Covelo • London

Library of Congress Cataloging-in-Publication Data
Ecotourism and certification : setting standards in practice / edited by Martha Honey.
    p.   cm.
  Includes bibliographical references (p.).
  ISBN 1-55963-950-4 (hardcover : alk. paper) — ISBN 1-55963-951-2 (pbk. : alk. paper)
    1. Ecotourism—Certification. 2. Eco-labeling. I. Honey, Martha, 1945–
G156.5.E26 E35 2002
338.4'791—dc21   2002005940

British Cataloguing-in-Publication Data available

Book design by Brighid Willson

Printed on recycled, acid-free paper ✹

Manufactured in the United States of America
09 08 07 06 05 04 03 02   8 7 6 5 4 3 2 1

To Tony

for once again providing encouragement, good humor,
and great meals throughout this project.

Contents

Preface

This book grew out of the common experience I shared with most of the other authors at the Ecotourism and Sustainable Tourism Certification Workshop held at Mohonk Mountain House in New Paltz, New York, in November 2000. That three-day gathering turned out to be an extraordinarily productive and congenial event. It brought together some forty-five participants from twenty countries, many of whom have been involved in creating, running, and evaluating socially and environmentally responsible tourism certification programs. As these practitioners shared their experiences, it became clear that we had sufficient theoretical analysis and firsthand experience to formulate the basic principles and components that should be part of any sound sustainable tourism and ecotourism certification programs. The resulting Mohonk Agreement was unanimously approved by the workshop participants, along with a proposal, presented by the Rainforest Alliance, for a feasibility study examining the possibilities of creating an "International Accreditation Body for Sustainable and Eco-Tourism."

After meeting with and listening to these experts, it seemed to me that a wider audience could benefit from a volume that included the history, theory, evolution, and implementation, as well as the challenges and problems, of some of the leading tourism certification programs. A number of those who participated in the conference agreed. In the end, twenty-one authors based in nine different countries were involved in writing the chapters in this book.

The introduction and the first three chapters provide an overview and conceptual framework for analyzing the current proliferation of socially and environmentally responsible tourism certification programs. In the introduction and chapter 1, we examine the rise of the ecotourism movement, its place within the tourism industry, how ecotourism and the 1992 Earth Summit spawned the development of certification and ecolabeling schemes, and two ways to analyze certification programs—by their methodology or by the sector of the tourism industry they address. Chapter 2 covers the nuts and bolts of a certification program. Its author, Robert

Toth, is a highly respected engineer who for decades has consulted on certification programs in a variety of countries, including Costa Rica's Certification for Sustainable Tourism (CST) program. Chapter 3 situates sustainable tourism and ecotourism certification programs within the wider world of "green" certification initiatives. It is written by Michael E. Conroy, an economist and senior program officer with the Ford Foundation, who has been deeply involved in the creation and evolution of the Forest Stewardship Council and has studied other certification initiatives led by nongovernmental organizations (NGOs).

The eight case studies are all written by experts who have been personally involved in certification initiatives. While they vary in their abilities to assess their particular programs with a dispassionate and critical eye, the writers all bring hands-on, real-life experiences that are essential for understanding the complexities of creating socially and environmentally responsible certification programs. Chapter 4, on Central America, for instance, is written by Amos Bien, a transplanted New Yorker who has put down deep roots in Costa Rica. He is both founder and owner of the country's original ecotourism lodge, Rara Avis, and has worked as a consultant for various certification programs in Latin America. Similarly, Guy Chester and Alice Crabtree, coauthors of chapter 5 and two of the founders of the Nature and Ecotourism Accreditation Program (NEAP) in Australia, collectively bring expertise in business, academia, and nature tourism as well as the day-to-day experience of running, evaluating, and revising this pioneering certification program.

The author of chapter 6, Herbert Hamale from Germany, is not tied to any one certification program, but he has studied and catalogued scores of "green" tourism certification schemes, particularly ones for accommodations in Europe, and is considered one of Europe's leading experts in this field. The authors of chapter 7, academics Xaviar Font, a Brazilian based at Leeds Metropolitan University, and Tanja Mihalič, who teaches at the University of Ljubljana, Slovenia, have both been directly involved in two of Europe's leading tourism certification programs for beaches and parks.

Chapters 8 and 9, on Africa and Fiji, detail efforts to create new certification programs to measure the impacts of tourism in poorer countries. In these areas of the world, issues of how rural communities can be involved in and benefit from nature-based tourism are central to certification initiatives. The South African trio—Eddie Koch, Peter John Massyn, and Anna Spenceley—are professionally involved in efforts to help citizens of rural communities acquire skills and obtain legal rights so that they can benefit from ecotourism. American Kelly Bricker, author of the Fiji chapter, was president of the Fiji Ecotourism Association and, despite the volatile political climate, worked effectively with Fiji's several governments to push forward community-based ecotourism initiatives and lay plans for establishing a certification program. Chapter 10, on Green Globe, the only worldwide program examined in this book, is written by a team of five led by Graeme Worboys, who participated in the Mohonk workshop and is the chief executive officer of Green Globe Asia Pacific. The Asia Pacific division is spearheading Green Globe's efforts to build a more credible and vigorous system based in part on performance standards, third party assessment, and an alliance with NEAP.

The final case study, chapter 11, details an initiative led by the Rainforest Alliance to do a feasibility study for an accreditation system for sustainable tourism that would, in essence, evaluate and certify auditors based on a set of internationally recognized standards. In this chapter, Ronald Sanabria, a Costa Rican industrial engineer who is the main staff person on this accreditation study, outlines why an over arching accreditation system is critical to any sound certification program.

As these brief descriptions indicate, all of these authors are busy professionals with multiple responsibilities. I am grateful that they also embraced this book project as an important venture, handed in drafts (nearly always) on time, and addressed suggested edits seriously.

This book would not have gotten out of the starting gate if I had not had the assistance of Emma Stewart, whom I found through a chain of fortuitous e-mail contacts. Emma, who is completing a Ph.D. in environmental studies at Stanford University, has a particular interest in ecolabeling programs, having helped while an undergraduate at Oxford University with the important Synergy study on tourism certification programs that was commissioned by World Wide Fund for Nature-United Kingdom. I managed to entice Emma to modify her summer plans and come to Washington, D.C. to work on this book. Emma turned out to be not only easy and enjoyable to work with but also a quick, probing, and thorough researcher and writer with a keen sensitivity toward issues of conservation and local communities. Emma managed to pull together an extraordinary amount of material and do the initial drafts of the first two chapters, as well as assist with the organization and early edits of other chapters.

I am gratified as well that Island Press agreed to undertake a book on this important subject. Once again it has been a privilege and pleasure to work with senior editor Todd Baldwin, who combined his sound editing skills and clear conceptual and organizational judgment with enough polite pressure to keep the project moving forward. Michael Conroy not only agreed to write a chapter but also helped to secure financial support from the Ford Foundation. Finally, I am grateful to my colleagues at the Institute for Policy Studies and Foreign Policy in Focus for giving me time and space to write and edit. Special thanks go to IPS Director John

Cavanagh for giving me time to do this project and to Erik Leaver, who competently and calmly sorted out numerous formatting, endnote, and computer glitches that resulted as we zipped the various chapters around the world. I hope that the contributors and collaborators are, one and all, as pleased with the outcome as I am.

Acronyms

AAA	American Automobile Association
ARC	Airline Reporting Corporation
ASTA	American Society of Travel Agents
ATIA	Australian Tourism Industry Association
ATON	Australian Tour Operators Network
AV	Alianza Verde (Green Alliance)
BEST	Business Enterprises for Sustainable Travel
BETA	Belize Ecotourism Association
BMP	Best Management Practices
CANAMET	National Chamber of Tourist Microbusinesses
CAST	Caribbean Alliance for Sustainable Tourism
CCA	Conservation Corporation Africa
CEC	Commission for Environmental Cooperation
CI	Conservation International
CPPPs	community private public partnerships
CRC	Cooperative Research Centre for Sustainable Tourism
CREM	Consultancy and Research for Environmental Management
CRT	Centre for Responsible Tourism
CST	Certification for Sustainable Tourism
DEA&T	Department of Environmental Affairs and Tourism
DEHOGA	German Hotel and Restaurant Association
EAA	Ecotourism Association of Australia
EAST	Environmental Audits for Sustainable Tourism
ECEAT	European Centre for Eco-Agro Tourism
ECOTRANS	European Network for Sustainable Tourism Development
EEA	European Environmental Agency
EIA	environmental impact assessment
EMAS	Eco-Management and Audit Scheme
EMS	environmental management system
EPPO	Executive PAN Parks Organization

ESOK	Ecotourism Society of Kenya
ESP	ecotourism sub-program
EU	European Union
FEAC	Fiji Ecotourism Advisory Committee
FEE	Foundation for Environmental Education
FEEE	Foundation for Environmental Education in Europe
FEEE-S	Foundation for Environmental Education in Europe-Slovenia
FEMATOUR	Feasibility and Market Study for a European Eco-label for Tourist Accommodations
FETA	Fiji Ecotourism Association
FSC	Forest Stewardship Council
FTTSA	Fair Trade in Tourism South Africa
GDP	gross domestic product
IAC	International Advisory Council
IATAN	International Airlines Travel Agent Network
ICCL	International Council of Cruise Lines
ICT	Costa Rican Tourism Institute
IDB	Inter-American Development Bank
IFC	International Finance Corporation
IGTOA	International Galapagos Tour Operators Association
IHEI	International Hotels Environment Initiative
ILO	International Labour Organization
ISEAL	International Social and Environmental Accrediting and Labeling Alliance
ISO	International Organization for Standardization
ISTC	International Sustainable Tourism Commission
IUCN	World Conservation Union
IYE	International Year of Ecotourism
IYHF	International Youth Hostel Federation
KTDC	Kenya Tourism Development Corporation
NAFTA	North American Free Trade Agreement
NEAP 1	National Ecotourism Accreditation Program
NEAP 2	Nature and Ecotourism Accreditation Program
NEVP	National Ecotourism and Village-based Policy and Strategy
NGO	nongovernmental organization
NTC	National Tourism Council
NZODA	New Zealand Overseas Development Assistance
OAS	Organization of American States
PATA	Pacific Asia Travel Association
PPMs	production and process methods

PROARCA/	Regional Environmental Program for Central America/
CAPAS	Central America Protected Areas System
QTC	Quality Tourism for the Caribbean
SANP	South African National Parks
SATW	Society of American Travel Writers
SDI	spatial development initiative
SLH	Small Luxury Hotels of the World
SME	small and medium enterprises
STDS	sustainable tourism development strategy
STI	specialty travel index
STSC	Sustainable Tourism Stewardship Council
TAG	Tourism Action Group
TCA	Tourism Council of Australia
TIA	Travel Industry Association of America
TIANZ	Tourism Industry Association of New Zealand
TIES	The International Ecotourism Society
TOI	Tour Operators' Initiative for Sustainable Tourism Development
TRINET	Tourism Research International Network
TUI	Touristik Union International
UNCED	United Nations Conference on Environment and Development
UNCSD	United Nations Commission on Sustainable Development
UNEP	United Nations Environment Program
USAID	United States Agency for International Development
USTOA	United States Tour Operators Association
VISIT	Voluntary Initiatives for Sustainable Tourism
VTOA	Victorian Tour Operators Association
WESSA	Wildlife and Environment Society of South Africa
WSSD	World Summit on Sustainable Development
WTO	World Tourism Organization (acronyms in this book refer to this)
WTO	World Trade Organization
WTTC	World Travel and Tourism Council
WWF	World Wide Fund for Nature (in U.S. & Canada: World Wildlife Fund)

Ecotourism
& CERTIFICATION

Introduction

Martha Honey and Emma Stewart

In the twilight years of the twentieth century, a revolutionary new concept, ecotourism, began taking shape within the world's largest industry, travel and tourism. It holds out the potential to transform the industry as only technology and legislation have done before. For many centuries, invention drove advances in travel, as sailing ships and ocean liners, trains and automobiles, wide-bodied airplanes and jet engines opened up vast areas of the earth to increasing numbers of travelers. In the first half of the twentieth century, government legislation in both the capitalist and communist countries of Europe, North America, the Soviet Union, Cuba, and China guaranteed workers paid vacations. This helped democratize travel, widening the spectrum of the social classes who could spend time on leisure activities. However, ecotourism may well be the most profound intellectual innovation ever to have occurred within tourism.

Today, ecotourism is an idea, a concept, that is challenging tourism as we have known it. Defined most succinctly as "responsible travel to natural areas, which conserves the environment and improves the welfare of local people,"[1] ecotourism fundamentally reshapes the basic precepts behind tourism, which is, quite simply, travel undertaken for pleasure. Nature tourism, which is frequently but erroneously considered the same as ecotourism, is defined as travel to unspoiled places to experience and enjoy nature. Its close cousin, adventure tourism, is described as nature tourism with a kick—with a degree of risk taking and physical endurance. Nature and adventure tourism focus on what the tourist or traveler is seeking. In contrast, ecotourism is qualitatively different: it focuses on what the traveler does, plus the impact of this travel on both the environment and the people in the host country. Ecotourism posits that this impact should be positive. Ecotourism is not, therefore, simply another niche market within the tourism industry. Rather, ecotourism is a philosophy, a set of principles and practices that, if properly understood and implemented, will transform the way we travel. It is argued here that ecotourism is a

1

multifaceted concept that involves travel to fragile, pristine, and usually protected areas. It strives to be low impact and (usually) small scale; helps educate the traveler; provides funds for conservation; directly benefits the economic development and political empowerment of local communities; and fosters respect for different cultures and human rights.[2]

The term *ecotourism* first entered the lexicon in the late 1970s, a decade that saw the rise of a global environmental movement and a convergence of demands for sustainable and socially responsible forms of tourism. Ecotourism grew, initially in scattered experiments and without a name, in response to deepening concerns about the negative effects of conventional tourism. Citizens and governments of less developed countries in Africa, Latin America, and Asia were becoming disillusioned with the economic leakage of tourist dollars and the negative social and environmental impacts of mass tourism. Citizen movements, spearheaded by church groups, particularly in Thailand, mounted the campaign for responsible tourism that sought to counter child prostitution and other social ills connected to mass tourism. At the same time, scientific, conservation, and other nongovernmental organizations (NGOs) were increasingly alarmed by the loss of habitat and species in Africa and Asia, especially destruction of the rain forest and of rhinos, elephants, and other threatened wildlife. They began to argue that protected areas would survive only if the people in or around these fragile ecosystems saw some tangible benefits from tourism.

In addition, a portion of the traveling public was increasingly turned off by packaged cruises, overcrowded campsites, and sun, sand, and surf beach holidays and began seeking less crowded and more unspoiled natural areas. Spurred by relatively affordable and plentiful airline routes, increasing numbers of nature lovers began seeking serenity and pristine beauty overseas. Simultaneously, the World Bank and other lending and aid institutions that had invested heavily in tourism resorts came to view mass tourism as a poor development strategy. In the late 1970s, for instance, the World Bank and the Inter-American Development Bank even closed their tourism departments and stopped loans for tourism projects.[3] In addition, the travel and tourism industry came to view protection of the physical environment, its income base, as in its own self interest and also began to see that there was a growing market for "green" tourism.

Gradually, these different interests began to coalesce into a new field that between the late 1970s and mid-1980s was labeled ecotourism. Beginning in the early 1990s, ecotourism (together with nature tourism) was being hailed as the fastest growing sector of the travel and tourism industry.[4] In 1999, Héctor Ceballos-Lascuráin, the well-known Mexican architect and conservationist, declared, "Ecotourism is no longer a mere concept or subject of wishful thinking. On the contrary," wrote Ceballos-Lascuráin, who claims to have first coined the term, "ecotourism has become a global reality. . . . There seem to be very few countries in the world in which some type of ecotourism development or discussion is not presently taking place."[5] As the twenty-first century dawned, the United Nations declared that 2002 would be the Year of International Ecotourism, a clear signal that ecotourism had indeed become a movement to be reckoned with.

But parallel to ecotourism's global reach and recognition have been concerns, most articulately and persistently voiced by those in the global South, that the radical tenets of ecotourism would not continue to take root and grow in the new century. There is ample evidence that in many places ecotourism's principles are being corrupted and watered down, hijacked and perverted by both "greenwashing" and "ecotourism lite" (as elaborated below). Over the last decade, it has become increasingly clear that if ecotourism is to fulfill its revolutionary potential, it must move from imprecision to a set of clear tools, standards, and criteria. Ecotourism needs to move beyond conceptualization to codification, and it is here that green certification programs are viewed as having a central role. Although ecotourism seeks to provide tangible benefits for both conservation and local communities, certification that includes socioeconomic and environmental criteria seeks to set standards and measure the benefits to host countries, local communities, and the environment.

Although tourism itself is thousands of years old and certification of hotels and restaurants based on quality and cost is a century old, the field of socially and environmentally responsible certification is just a little more than a decade old. Most of these green certification programs started in the mid- to late-1990s, but the groundwork for them has been laid over a longer period. During the last thirty years, global concern has gradually grown over how to ensure sustainable development and how to create an integrated approach to industrial development, including for tourism. In the 1970s, many governments, at both the national and local levels, began passing laws that required companies to comply with regulations for environmental impact and emissions, particularly into the air and water. In addition, environmental impact assessment (EIA) has become one of the most widely used techniques for examining the potential ecological effects of particular companies or projects before construction begins. In the 1980s, a few companies tried voluntarily to go beyond compliance, using technologies and practices that exceeded government requirements.

For a number of industries, certification has been viewed as a way to promote sustainable development. Certification programs across different industries have grown significantly. In 1965, there were an estimated 120 certification organizations, while by 2001, there were more than 1,600 certification and some 200 accrediting bodies in the United States alone.[6] The criteria and quality of these certification programs vary widely. As one expert told the American Society of Association Executives back in 1990, "Certification programs are similar to dandelions. First, there is one certification program. Overnight, a whole field of certification programs seems to spring up! Once dandelions get a hold in your yard, it is difficult if not impossible to eliminate them—the same is true of certification programs."[7]

Indeed, the decade of the 1990s saw a real flowering of green certification programs, for tourism as well as other industries. The United Nations Conference on Environment and Development (UNCED), or so-called Earth Summit, held in Rio de Janeiro in 1992, provided an important impetus for a variety of efforts to set environmental standards through voluntary compliance, governmental regulation, and international treaty. The Earth Summit's Agenda 21, approved by 182 countries, laid out a broad path and challenge for business to adopt the principles and practices of sustainable development. In the wake of the Earth Summit, dozens of new tourism certification programs were started with the aim of measuring environmentally and socially responsible practices.

Today certification and ecolabeling are among the hottest topics within the travel and tourism industry. Around the world, there are some 260 voluntary initiatives, including tourism codes of conduct, labels, awards, benchmarking, and "best practices." Of these, 104 are ecolabeling and certification programs offering logos, seals of approval, or awards designed to signify socially and/or environmentally superior tourism practices.[8] These certification programs cover tourism professionals (guides and tour operators), businesses, products, attractions, destinations, and services. The majority of programs to date have focused on accommodations, but there are a growing number of certification and ecolabeling schemes covering other sectors of the tourism industry, including golf courses, protected areas, beaches, tour boats, naturalist guides, tour operators, and handicrafts.

Definitions

Certification

At different times, under different circumstances, and in various parts of the world, the term certification has been used in different ways. For many years, certification has been used by academics in the United States and elsewhere to measure whether an individual knows a certain body of knowledge.[9] Currently, in the United States, Europe, and Latin America, certification within the tourism industry refers to a procedure that audits and gives written assurance that a facility, product, process, service, or management system meets specific standards. It awards a logo or seal to those that meet or exceed baseline criteria or standards that are prescribed by the program. This is the definition used in this book. Certification programs themselves and the auditors who do the assessments may be either first, second, or third party, that is run and/or verified by the business itself, by an industry or trade association, or by an independent outside entity.[10] Third party is considered the most objective and therefore more credible. To date, all certification programs for the tourism industry are voluntary, although in other related industries, such as those involving food handling and construction, there are government-required certification programs.

As in other industries, there is wide agreement that customer satisfaction is the most reliable indicator of the success of any tourist business. Certification within the tourism industry has a long history of measuring visitor satisfaction by rating both quality and price, as well as health and safety conditions. More recently, certification programs have begun measuring visitor satisfaction based on qualities of sustainability, including economic, social, political, and cultural impacts. The three broad but interrelated categories of (1) quality and price, (2) health and safety, and (3) environmental and socioeconomic sustainability constitute what Robert Toth terms the three-legged stool of visitor satisfaction (see chapter 2).

Although sustainability indicators are the heart of the certification programs covered in this volume, there is as yet no universally accepted definition for this "leg." Further, these social and environmental indicators often affect visitor or customer satisfaction in less direct and more long-term ways than do quality, health, and safety conditions. They are, however, considered important to a sector of the traveling public, as well as to many host communities and countries, conservationists, social justice activists, development and aid agencies, and businesses, especially those based on a clean environment and adhering to the principles of ecotourism.

As detailed in chapters 1 and 2, certification criteria can be either performance- or process-based (or a mixture of both types). Performance-based certification programs involve using a set of externally determined criteria that are applied uniformly to all businesses seeking certification, while process-based programs use internally generated management systems for monitoring and improving procedures and practices. In addition to the process-performance distinction, certification programs for tourism can also be divided into three broad categories: those for conventional tourism, for sustainable tourism, and for ecotourism (see chapter 1).

To add to the confusion, currently Australia, New Zealand, Fiji, and Canada use the term *accreditation* instead of *certification* to refer to systems for rating products, such as accommodations, tours, and attractions. However, as used in this book, *accreditation* refers to the procedure by which an authoritative body formally recognizes that a certifier is competent to carry out specific tasks. In other words, an accreditation program certifies the certifiers[11] (see chapter 11).

Ecotourism

As outlined above, within the travel and tourism industry, the growth of the ecotourism movement has provided the foundation for the development of certification programs based on environmental and social criteria. Certification, in turn, is an important tool for setting standards that can help protect and promote real ecotourism.

The precise definition of ecotourism, however, has often remained vague. According to David Western, former director of the Kenya Wildlife Service and past president of The International Ecotourism Society (TIES), ecotourism "emerged like a phoenix from terms like nature tourism and wildlife tourism to become a universal conservation catchword, an exemplar of sustainable use. The reassuring prefix gave nature tourism the legitimacy and recognition it lacked. Few words have been adopted so quickly by a movement predisposed to catchwords or have offered so much promise. Ecotourism and biodiversity were popularized by a media hungry for a new, evocative and consoling jargon."[12]

In reality, there are today three trends within what is commonly labeled ecotourism. The most common trend is "ecotourism lite," which involves small, cosmetic, and often cost-saving steps rather than fundamental reforms that constitute socially and environmentally sensitive practices. Pushed mainly by the big corporations and trade associations, these sensible but token steps are often trumpeted as major innovations. For instance, in the mid-1990s, hotels that were part of the International Hotels Environment Initiative (IHEI) received the British Airways/ASTA (American Society of Travel Agents) annual ecotourism award for putting in energy-saving showers and the practice of laundering towels when guests requested, rather than daily. The press release announcing the award was headlined "Keep your towels—and help save the world!" This was obviously a gross exaggeration, especially because the biggest savings was certainly on the hotel's laundry bill. Although these and other cost-saving environmental reforms are commendable, they are not sufficient to green the industry and therefore do not constitute real ecotourism.

A second trend is toward "greenwashing," that is, projects or companies that claim to be involved in ecotourism but are merely using green language in their marketing in an attempt to ride on the crest of the ecotourism wave. Around the world, there are scores, undoubtedly hundreds, of such projects. International conglomerates have, time and again, adopted the "eco" label for their mass tourism resort projects. Next to one of Belize's finest coral reefs, a $50 million–venture billed as an "integrated and ecologically sound resort development" is constructing hotels, villas, polo fields, and golf courses that typically use 600,000 gallons of water per course per day. The Tourism Authority of Thailand, under the banner of sustainable tourism, is promoting privatization of thirteen national parks, and for one, Phu Kradung National Park, Japanese investors are discussing a possible cable car, hotels, and golf course on a mountain summit. In the ecotourism mecca of Costa Rica, there are numerous examples of greenwashing, including the Ecological Rent-a-Car company that rents the same gas-guzzling autos as Hertz or Avis; *Ecodesarrollo Papagayo* (Ecodevelopment), an enormous, controversial, Cancun-like beach development; and "Green Luxury," where, its architect promised, "ecotourism meets the high life in a luxury beach resort," but in reality, it is another disruptive beach resort along an ecologically sensitive beach used by nesting leatherback turtles. As Anne Becher, one of the developers of an early certification program in Costa Rica, put it, "The only thing 'green' about these places is the dollars they are earning." [13]

The third trend, the authentic form of ecotourism, is derived from the concept of ecosystems, and therefore includes the environmental and human (social, cultural, political, and economic) effects of tourism. Authentic ecotourism is closely linked to the concept of sustainable development. As defined by the 1987 Bruntland Commission, sustainable development is that which allows people "to meet the needs of the present without compromising the ability of future generations to meet their own needs." [14] This link between ecotourism and sustainable development is symbolized by the UN's decision to celebrate ecotourism in 2002, the tenth anniversary of the Rio Earth Summit on sustainable development. The meaning of authentic ecotourism can be reduced to the eight characteristics listed in Box 1.

Box I.I. Elements of Authentic Ecotourism

- Involves travel to natural areas.
- Minimizes impact.
- Builds environmental awareness.
- Provides direct financial benefits for conservation.
- Provides financial benefits and empowerment for local communities.
- Respects local culture.
- Is sensitive to the host country's political environment and social climate.
- Supports human rights and international labor agreements.

Source: Honey, *Ecotourism and Sustainable Development*, 21–26.

As the concept has evolved, many ecotourism proponents and practitioners have come to believe that the principles of ecotourism should not be limited only to fragile natural areas but should cover urban, beach, ocean, countryside, and mountain destinations, that is, all types of locations. "The tourism industry has to protect its destinations, and although we have a tendency to default to wildlife, urban renewal is just as important," says Thomas Keesling, former president of both the American Society of Travel Agents (ASTA) and its Environment Committee.[15] However, the World Tourism Organization (WTO), a United Nations–affiliated institution composed of 133 member coutries, argues that the term *sustainable tourism* is better suited as a guide and goal for tourism to all types of destinations, while *ecotourism* should be reserved for nature-based forms of tourism. "It is the position of the World Tourism Organization, that all tourism activities should be sustainable," said Eugenio Yunis, head of the Sustainable Development of Tourism Section at a WTO conference. "For ecotourism," or travel to fragile or protected areas, Yunis stated, "sustainability is a much stronger imperative than for other forms of tourism. The WTO is working to ensure that this [ecotourism] segment, more than any other, develops and operates in a sustainable fashion."[16] The International Year of Ecotourism, as defined by the WTO and United Nations Environment Program (UNEP), is, therefore, focusing on nature-based tourism.

However, when analyzing the origins, fundamental meaning, and ongoing role of the concept of ecotourism, the authors of this chapter take the broader view. We hold that ecotourism should be understood as more than a niche market within the tourism industry or a nature-based subset of sustainable tourism. Instead, the rise of ecotourism over the past two decades, with its roots in social movements for environmentally, economically, and culturally responsible travel, for improved protection of fragile and pristine ecosystems, for indigenous rights, and for community-based, locally driven, and sustainable development strategies, has offered a clear alternative to mass or conventional tourism. It is argued that the mass tourism industry has become unsustainable and a new paradigm is needed. Ecotourism charts this new direction. The fundamental challenge is to use the principles and practices of ecotourism to infuse and ultimately transform the entire tourism industry.

Size and Distribution of the Tourism Industry

By the late 1990s, the travel and tourism industry topped the list of the world's largest industries, reaping US$5.3 trillion in export earnings in 1998 alone,[17] equivalent to 11 percent of the global gross domestic prod-

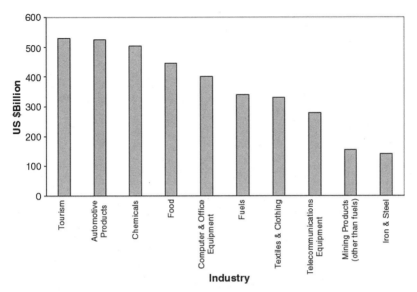

Figure 1.1. Top World Export Earnings Per Industry, 1998. *Source*: O. N'Diaye, World Tourism Organization (WTO) Regional Representative for Africa, "Global and Regional Tourism Trends," Seminar on Planning, Development and Management of Ecotourism in Africa, Maputo, Mozambique, March 5–6, 2001.

uct (GDP).[18] As Figure 1.1 shows, tourism rivals oil and ranks above automotive products, chemicals, and food in export earnings.[19]

If tourism were a country, it would have the second largest economy, surpassed only by the United States.[20] Tourism itself is the world's number one employer, accounting for approximately 200 million jobs, 11 percent of global jobs.[21]

Despite fluctuations in annual growth rates—and the nosedive after the September 11, 2001 terrorist attacks—global tourism growth has been running a net positive rate, ranging from 1 to 7 percent annually. Since 1950, the number of international tourists has increased nearly twenty-eight–fold, and between 1992 and 2000, the number of international tourists worldwide grew from 463 million to 698 million, a jump of nearly 50 percent, and has been projected to double between 1990 and 2010, according to the World Tourism Organization. One of the largest leaps occurred between 1999 and 2000, when international tourism arrivals grew by 7.4 percent and receipts rose by 4.5 percent.[22]

Most tourism takes place within or between developed countries. Citizens from wealthier nations, comprising less than 25 percent of the global population, account for 85 percent of the world tourist arrivals. Travel spending in the richer countries has increased at double or more the rate

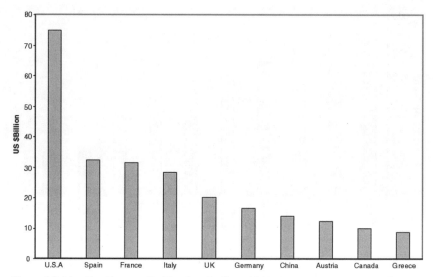

Figure I.2. Top Ten Earners for Tourism Dollars, 1999. *Source*: WTO statistics for 2000, adopted by Emma Stewart.

of GDP since 1945.[23] Europe as a whole captures 59 percent of international arrivals, with France the number one destination worldwide. The United States ranks second in numbers of arrivals, but ranks first in earnings from international tourism (US$74.9 billion in 1999), in part because tourists spend more in the United States (an average of $1000/tourist) than in other regions of the world.[24]

Although in total earnings, the industrial countries benefit most from tourism, this does not reflect either the impressive growth of tourism forecast for developing countries or their gains per capita. International tourism to the Third World is increasing at 6 percent annually, compared to only 3.5 percent to developed countries. About 80 percent of these foreign travelers come from just twenty developed countries, with destinations in Asia, Africa, and the Americas growing faster than those in Europe. Tourism already plays a major role in the economies of 125 of the world's 170 countries,[25] and tourism is the most important foreign exchange earner in a number of developing countries, including Kenya and Tanzania, Nepal, Costa Rica, Belize, and many Caribbean island nations. Particularly for countries in the global South, dependency on tourism is great and growing, despite the fact that their earnings and arrival numbers are far below those in the United States or Europe.[26] "Tourism is the only large sector of international trade in services where poor countries have consistently posted a surplus," stated the UN Council on Trade and Development.[27]

Structure, Growth, and Consolidation of the Travel Industry

More than other industries in which certification programs have been initiated, such as coffee, wood, and bananas (see chapter 3), the travel and tourism industry includes a wide variety of services and businesses, has multiple layers, and is located in virtually every country. It thus presents a number of unique challenges for certification and accreditation efforts.

In the country of departure, the tourism industry includes travel agencies (retailers), outbound tour operators (wholesalers), airlines, cruise lines, car rental agencies, credit card companies, public relations firms, advertising companies, tourist bureaus, and the media. In the host country, the industry includes inbound tour operators; ground transporters; guides; accommodations; restaurants; national and private parks; recreational activities, such as golf courses, ski resorts, and beaches; cultural and craft centers; and special concessions, such as balloon rides, whitewater rafting, aerial trams, horseback riding, biking, sailing, snorkeling, and fishing. The travel industry is supported by government policies and regulations; national tourism bureaus; roads, airports, and other infrastructure projects; and frequently, direct government subsidies, as well as by a wide array of commercial banks and international financial and aid institutions.

Since World War II, there has been an increasing consolidation within the tourism industry. Despite the fact that as much as 90 percent of tourist businesses are small and medium-size,[28] the industry's earnings overall are dominated by transnational corporations. In his book on the political economy of international tourism, Thanh-dam Truong writes that the "main economic agents in international tourism"[29]—hotels, airlines, travel agents, tour operators, and in regions such as the Caribbean, cruise lines—have all become increasingly integrated in terms of their services, financing, management, and research and development. Since the 1960s, both vertical and horizontal integration within the tourism industry has accelerated. As Thanh-dam Truong explains, "When expanding into developing countries, the industry has required mass production and the standardization of services and quality. Given their late entry into the field, many developing countries have limited possibilities to develop their own stock of knowledge and control over the business. They have had to adopt the established standards and therefore must rely on foreign firms to run major sectors of the industry."[30]

Polly Pattullo, writing about tourism in the Caribbean, says that the "key players in the tourist industry jigsaw . . . are largely owned, controlled and run from outside the region. Sometimes, through vertical integration, they are corporately linked, controlling every stage of the tourist's holiday."[31]

The increasing dominance of companies based in the global North means that most of the profits go to the country of departure. As ecotourism expert Kreg Lindberg states, "Given the realities of overseas travel, much of the trip cost, and thus the economic benefit, remains with outbound operators and source country airlines. To some extent, this simply is due to the nature of the tourism industry; substantial funds are spent on marketing, commissions, and transport before tourists even reach the destination."[32]

Accommodations

In the 1950s, Hilton Hotels, Inter-Continental, and Holiday Inns were among the first specialized hotel chains to invest abroad, before significant economic integrations were forged with air carriers and tour operators. Over the next four decades, more international chains expanded into developing countries, attracted by new investment opportunities for their excess capital, low cost labor, and increasingly, the potential offered through integration with other sectors of the tourism industry. By 1995, nineteen of the twenty largest hotel conglomerates were based in developed countries (the other was based in Hong Kong), and twelve of the top twenty operators were American multinational corporations. The leaders included U.S.-owned Sheraton, Holiday Inn, Hyatt, and Marriott Corporation, as well as Inter-Continental and Hilton International (UK), Accor (France), and Grupo Sol Melia (Spain). Between 1997 and 1999, hotel and restaurant mergers and acquisitions topped $19 billion, more than the previous seven years combined.[33]

In developing countries, affiliation with international chains has frequently been viewed as imperative in giving local investors a competitive edge over smaller, locally-owned hotels in the areas of marketing, bookings, technology, training, and standardization of services, as well as access to goods at lower marginal costs. Therefore, while only about 2 percent of the hotels in western Europe are linked to transnational chains through management contracts, in developing countries, this figure has been well over 50 percent: 75 percent in the Middle East, 72 percent in Africa, 60 percent in Asia, and 47 percent in Latin America.[34]

Airlines

With the growth of international travel, the biggest expense in a holiday is typically the airline ticket.[35] Although the percentage varies with the distance, group size, carrier, and season, in 1995, 61 percent of total U.S. travel agency sales went for airline tickets, 14 percent went for cruise lines, 10 percent for hotels, 7 percent for car rentals, and 8 percent for other sales.[36]

As with hotels, there has been an increasing consolidation among airline companies. In 1998, the top ten airlines were earning about two-thirds of the profits of the 270 airlines that belong to the International Air Transport Association (IATA).[37]

This was not always the case. Beginning in the late 1950s, most developing countries and newly independent colonies viewed setting up a national airline that carried the country's flag and was fully or partially owned by the government as an important symbol of sovereignty. Air Afrique, for instance, was created in 1961 by eleven former French colonies to signify African independence and unity and to capture travel dollars for their national economics. Air Afrique was emulated across the continent, as national or regional airlines, along with a new flag and a seat in the United Nations, became former African colonies' most visible sign of independence. During its first two decades, Air Afrique grew steadily, turning a profit, and acquiring a fleet of fifteen planes. By the early 1980s, Air Afrique had completed the "Africanization" of its staff, with nationals occupying all top administrative positions. That, many too facilely contend, marked the start of the airline's decline, as nepotism, corruption, and contraband dealings in tickets and cargo space became rampant. Today, Air Afrique is burdened with a $240 million–debt, has a fleet of just six planes, and is popularly known as "Air Maybe" because planes never come, arrive a half-day late, or surprise passengers by landing—and leaving—hours ahead of schedule.[38]

The demise of Air Afrique is not simply a matter of ineptitude. It mirrors what has happened around the world, in both developing and developed countries as airlines have gone under or been bought out. Today, a handful of first-world airlines dominate much of the international trade, while several former giants—United, Swiss Air, Sabina—hover on the brink of bankruptcy or have already collapsed. Back in the 1960s, the new national airlines in newly independent countries sometimes had a fleet of only two or three planes and were involved in a David and Goliath contest with the large international carriers. Many of the new airlines bought jet aircraft, navigation equipment, and services from Boeing and other U.S. companies. These deals were frequently financed by the U.S. Export-Import Bank, which both gave direct loans to foreign carriers and guaranteed loans made by commercial lenders. Other foreign airlines leased their planes and/or had management contracts with international commercial carriers, such as Pan Am, Air France, and British Airways.

As these nascent companies struggled to get a toehold in the international market, the big first-world airlines were acquiring wide-body aircraft with increased carrying capacity and decreased operating costs and were rapidly linking up with international hotel chains, travel agencies, tour operators, and car rental agencies for sales and promotional purposes and to offer discount tour packages. Inclusive tour packages given by air charter companies also siphoned passengers away from these new national airlines.[39] This shift from national airlines also affected visitor experience. Although national airlines have offered travelers from overseas a bit of the flavor of the destination and thus became part of the holiday experience, today's big carriers provide increasingly homogenized service and ambiance.

During the 1990s, as economic liberalizations and deregulation took hold, international carriers, with hefty marketing budgets, name recognition, and partnerships with other sectors of the tourism industry, increased their business in the most lucrative foreign markets in developing countries. Without protective trade barriers to keep out competition and control fares, computer systems and other technological innovations, and integration with hotel chains, car rental agents, and tour operators, many small national airlines could not compete and so were sold to foreign carriers.[40] By 1992, foreign airlines carried nearly three-quarters of passengers to the Caribbean, with American Airlines controlling more than half the seats. Meanwhile, the nine Caribbean regional carriers got only "a tiny slice of the schedules"[41]—29 percent of seats from the United States, 19 percent of those from Canada, and 15 percent from Europe. "These small, underequipped, state-owned regional airlines," writes Pattullo, "are not only outclassed by the international carriers but, in their struggle to survive, they lose phenomenal amounts of money."[42] In 2001, Air Afrique's fate was put into the hands of the World Bank. The bank offered financial support, a reorganization, and a new CEO—a retired American airline executive who spoke no French, had never visited Africa, and boasted that his mission was to "slash the workforce in half."[43] From the viewpoint of many in the global South, the downward slide of Air Afrique and other national and regional carriers is being orchestrated by the major airlines and their international financial institutions. "Everything that's happening at Air Afrique is a well-planned death by the West," says Karim Nana, who has worked as an airplane mechanic since 1975.[44]

Cruise Ships

Cruise ships, a cross between accommodations and transport, are perhaps the most rapidly expanding sector of the tourism industry. Cruises are a $12 billion a year industry and have been experiencing an explosive 8 percent annual growth rate. The worldwide cruise ship fleet included 223 ships by 1998, with about half of the fleet operating in North American waters, mainly the Caribbean. Caribbean cruises total between $4 billion and $6 billion annually and carry over 4.5 million Americans on some 130 ships. The industry is dominated by three companies, Carnival Corporation, Royal Caribbean International, and Princess Cruises, which carry nearly half of all passengers worldwide. [45] "A direct competitor to sun and sand holidays, the cruise industry has an enormous momentum and it is believed that North American and European demand will surpass 12 million passengers by the end of 2010," states a report by Oceans Blue Foundation, a Vancouver-based nonprofit organization promoting environmentally responsible tourism.[46]

Yet, because cruises involve travel mainly in international waters by foreign-owned and registered fleets, they are largely unregulated and untaxed. Under international maritime laws, cruise lines are exempt from many national regulations, other than those of the country of registry of their ships, which are typically tax havens such as Liberia and Panama. Cruise companies, even though they carry many U.S. passengers and are based or call at U.S. ports, are largely exempt from U.S. labor regulations, profit and income taxes, safety standards, sales taxes, and environmental standards. [47] Similarly, they have been exempt from most taxes and laws of the twenty-odd island countries, colonies, and dependencies in the Caribbean. According to Earth Island Institute, cruise ships pay less than 1 percent in taxes.[48]

Although tourism is the Caribbean's main industry and unemployment in many of the islands tops 20 percent, most of the 50,000 employees on board cruise ships plying the waters between the United States and the Caribbean are neither West Indians nor Americans. Many of these low wage workers are recruited by specialized labor contractors from depressed markets such as those in Eastern Europe and Asia and many work only for tips or commissions.

Not only does the cruise line business bring little income to the Caribbean, but it also has caused environmental damage by anchoring on coral reefs and dumping untreated waste into the ocean. Every day, an average cruise passenger generates 3.5 pounds of dry garbage and food waste and disposes of four cans and bottles—six times as much as a person on shore. The largest cruise ships, carrying more than 5,000 passengers and crews, have been characterized as floating cities. Experts have calculated that cruise ships dump some 20 million pounds of raw sewage and refuse into the world's oceans every day.[49] Approximately 77 percent of all ship waste comes from cruise ships.[50]

The Marpol Convention, the international treaty that prohibits sewage dumping in coastal waters (up to fifty miles from shore) and dumping of plastics anywhere, must be signed by all Caribbean countries before it can be enforced in this area. Yet signing the Marpol treaty requires destination countries to provide waste disposal facilities for visiting cruise ships, something that is difficult for these islands, most of whose landfills and incineration systems are already overburdened. Nonratifiers can refuse to accept the waste of visiting ships, and because most cruise ships do not have onboard waste-processing facilities, this encourages illegal dumping at sea.[51] Many of these countries also lack sufficient monitoring capacity (and dumping at sea is inherently difficult to catch) and therefore are sacrificing their coral reefs, marine mammals, estuaries, and other potential tourism attractions because of the unfortunate consequences of international policy. Despite these problems, the cruise business continues to grow. By 2004, the cruise industry is expected to add fifty-seven new vessels, increasing its capacity by 35 percent.

The cruise industry is a powerful lobby, contributing $1.2 million to candidates for federal office between 1993 and 1998. Not surprisingly, it has been especially generous to candidates from Florida and Alaska.[52] In addition, the Cruise Lines International Association, founded by the major lines in 1976, works closely with travel agents to promote cruises as less expensive and more glamorous alternatives to land-based Caribbean hotels. Cruise line sales have become a bread-and-butter business for U.S. travel agents, bringing in earnings of close to $600 million in commissions each year. Airlines also earn over $650 million in ticket sales to cruise passengers flying to jump-off points such as Miami. But almost all the money is spent either before the cruise begins or on board; cruise passengers buy relatively little on shore, and port taxes and other cruise line fees are low.

Travel Agents and Tour Operators

Travel agents are retailers who sell airline tickets and off-the-shelf packages put together by overseas tour operators. These packages are featured in brochures and distributed through the national network of travel agencies.[53] The bulk of retail trade for travel agents is package tours. The package usually includes the airfare, ground and internal air transportation, accommodation, some or all meals, transfers from airports to hotels, visa and other fees and taxes, and often, park entrance fees and excursions. In short, all but incidentals, souvenirs, and tips are included. Packages have fixed departures, lengths, itineraries, and costs, and a minimum (and often maximum) number of tourists. Generally, the travel agent earns 10 percent of the cost of any package tour.[54]

There is wide variance in quality of travel agents because the training and licensing procedures are very weak. The only regulatory bodies are the Airline Reporting Corporation (ARC) and/or the International Airlines Travel Agent Network (IATAN), through which travel agencies are licensed to write airline tickets. There are several professional organizations and associations, the most prominent of which is the American Society of Travel Agents (ASTA), with some 20,500 members in the United States and 26,500 worldwide. Experts estimated that in the mid-1990s, there were between 35,000 and 50,000 travel agencies in the United States.[55]

In the mid-1990s, an estimated 75 percent of U.S. tourists were booking their vacations through travel agents, according to Yvonne Rodgers, executive director of the International Ecotourism Education Foundation based in Virginia.[56] However, by the late 1990s, use of travel agents was declining as airlines cut back on their commissions and passengers found it cheaper to book directly with the airline or via the Internet. Although the tourism industry was expanding, the number of travel agents was declining. In 1999, for instance, while international travel was up and U.S. travel agents processed a record $76.6 billion in airline ticket sales, the number of travel agency locations dropped 4 percent. ASTA's core membership also dropped sharply, from 11,000 in 1997 to 7,500 in 1999 and, in 2001, ASTA launched a major recruitment drive, offering free membership to try to counter this trend.[57]

Although far less centralized than the airline and cruise industries, there are a handful of big players among the tour agents, including Thomas Cook, Lunn Poly, Going Places, and A.T. Mays (formerly Carlson Travel Network) in England, TUI in Germany, Michelin in France, and AAA in the United States. In 2000, four European tour operators alone handled trips for 50 million tourists.[58] The largest travel agency in the United States is American Express, with offices in every financially important city around the world. Created in 1850, American Express is best known for pioneering traveler's checks. Writer Patricia Goldstone contends that this "was, coincidentally, the only completely original innovation American Express has devised in all its corporate history, but it was sufficiently lucrative to support all the company's other endeavors."[59] Today, in addition to selling traveler's checks, American Express handles hotel reservations and airline, cruise, and ground travel, and offers credit cards, financial and small business advice, computer services, guidebooks, passport-processing assistance, and real estate services.[60]

In response to travelers' demands for outdoor, nature-based holidays, mass-market travel agents started to sell ecotours or conventional tours that include "eco-experiences," such as a cruise with a day's hike in a rain forest, while others are choosing and selling packages from a few select ecotourism wholesalers. As early as 1991, there were nearly 500 U.S. tour companies (agents and operators) offering trips with environmental themes. However, according to travel agent Marie Walters, although many agents claim they can handle ecotourism, "some are more professional than others."[61] Megan Epler Wood of TIES is more blunt, arguing that travel agencies lack the time, expertise, motivation, or training to sell specialty products such as ecotours. A former president of ASTA agrees: "Travel agencies do not have a profit bottom line that allows them to do much in this area financially. They are best-trained to pass on information"[62]

In contrast, tour operators in the United States and elsewhere offer more customized and hands-on services than travel agencies. Classified as wholesalers, although they sell to both travel agents and directly to the public, these companies market their own exclusive package tours and/or they resell packages put together by tour operators in the host countries. Known as "outbound tour operators" or "outfitters," they package the trips, oversee creation of itineraries, select and contract with inbound tour operators in the host countries, arrange airline tickets, and handle travel insurance and liabilities. They sell tour packages to the general public via either travel agents or special interest organizations, such as environmental groups, alumni associations, and museums. Some market directly through magazine or newspaper ads or through catalogues, brochures, videos, CD-ROM disks, and websites. Tour operators charge a 15–40 percent markup, depending on how customized the tour is. Competition is very stiff, and tour operators try to lure travel agents to carry their packages by offering higher commissions, incentive programs, glossy advertising, news articles, contests, and free or reduced-rate trips.[63]

Standards for tour operators are lacking: there is no accrediting body or licensing procedure for U.S. tour operators, and because little capital is required to get started, virtually anyone can hang out a shingle. The United States Tour Operators Association (USTOA), with membership restricted to well-established operators, requires the posting of a $250,000 bond, which is applied to a consumer protection plan for tourists and travel agents using these companies. However, the USTOA evaluates tour operators only on the basis of their financial worthiness, not on whether they are promoting high-quality or socially and environmentally responsible travel.[64]

The number of outbound operators in North America promoting nature-oriented and adventure tourism has been growing at 10–20 percent per year, according to Canadian ecotourism consultant Carolyn Wild.[65] In 1901, the Sierra Club was the only one in the United States, and in 1970, there were only nine.[66] By 1996, the Specialty Travel Index stated that the number had jumped to 219 U.S. tour operators offering ecotours to developing countries.[67] Serious ecotourists, in contrast to conventional vacationers, often plan trips on their own or turn to specialist nature tour operators rather than generalist travel agents. These outbound operators are usually located in the same country as the tourist, but they have an intimate, frequently firsthand knowledge based on having lived in or traveled frequently to the destination country. They are, therefore, the ecotraveler's most important source of expertise and information; choosing the right outbound ecotour operator can make or break a vacation. According to TIES, "This may require extensive work with their in-bound operators to insure that guiding, business and conservation practices, as well as relations with local communities are in line with ecotourism guidelines."[68]

Will Webber, director of Journeys International, an ecotourism operator based in Michigan, has committed himself to developing long-term relationships with operators and destinations through multiple visits and personal interaction. When researching new destinations, he sends an exploratory tour of travelers to test out the location and various local companies. He calls these "no promises" trips for the tourists but says that only by testing to see if visitors' expectations are met can he judge a location's suitability for future collaboration. Journeys International, like most tour operators, relies heavily on repeat customers and word-of-mouth, so without customer satisfaction, "we would have died out long ago."[69]

Host Country Tourism Operations

As outlined above, the mass tourism industry, both in terms of tourists and the industry, is largely based in the global North. Ecotourism, as a tool for sustainable development for poorer countries, seeks to alter this balance by maximizing the amount of tourism dollars that enter and stay in the host country. As ecotourism expert Héctor Ceballos-Lascuráin writes, "[T]ourist travel is still very much the privilege of people of the industrialized world. . . . Nevertheless, the shift in favoured tourism destinations—from developed to developing countries—indicates that international tourism could become a means of redistributing wealth 'from north to south.'"[70] But this will happen only if host countries are able to stop the leakage of profits from the South to the North.

Tourists, travel agents, and tour operators can help maximize the benefits to developing countries by utilizing, as much as possible, environmentally sensitive, socially responsible, and locally-based companies and facilities in developing countries. They often have no choice but to use multinational airlines. However, within the host country, inbound tour and ground operators are the most important component to insuring high-quality ecotourism, including the use of locally owned businesses. As Bryan Higgins puts it, inbound operators are the essential link, making "upstream connections to industrialized countries" and "downstream economic ties to local businesses within a particular country."[71] Outbound operators usually subcontract with inbound operators in host countries. The inbound operators are responsible for arranging all details of the trip, including assembling a network of lodges close to or in the nature viewing areas.

They meet the travelers at the airport (or port or border); provide transport throughout the trip; select local businesses; hire staff; and arrange accommodation (lodges, tented camps, inns, etc.), visits to parks, and specialty activities. The majority of inbound tour operators are concerned narrowly with price, quality, and compliance with health and safety standards, and they may be owned by or contractually linked to outbound travel agencies catering to the mass tourism market. However, in virtually all countries today, there are inbound operators who claim to be concerned with the environmental and social impacts of tourism and to be following the principles and practices of ecotourism.

Over the last decade, there has been an upsurge in environmentally sensitive, low-impact lodge construction, as well as a range of ownership and profit-sharing models intended to ensure that local communities are involved in and benefiting from tourism facilities. Although ecofacilities run the spectrum from basic backpacker tents and cabins to small, exclusive, high-end luxury resorts, most ecolodges fall in the midprice range. Inbound ecotour operators also select locally owned restaurants featuring authentic cuisine and the best artisans and cooperatives selling local crafts or displaying local culture.[72]

With the exception of Cuba, where inbound tour companies are government owned, in most countries, inbound operators are all now private or in the process of being privatized. The majority of the inbound operators involved in ecotourism are, like their counterparts in the United States, owned by their founders, who are either nationals or long-time foreign residents who keep most of their profits within the country.[73] Many companies espouse a common operating ethic of close involvement with their travelers as well as the destinations they are visiting.[74]

The Travel Press

When planning a vacation, many travelers rely on guidebooks, specialty travel magazines, newspaper travel supplements, radio programs, as well as TV documentaries, travelogues, and nature channels. Over the last two decades, there has been an explosion of travel information, particularly about nature and adventure travel. But this proliferation of media covering various aspects of the travel industry should not be equated with a breath of freedom of expression or better service of the public's right to know. Competition has not necessarily bred more independent and inquiring journalism. The travel industry, though the world's largest, has more successfully than its financial peers—oil, guns, and narcotics—largely managed to duck the spotlight of serious press scrutiny, exposés, and analysis. The reasons are several.

One is the travel industry's image as a service profession devoted to pleasure, fun, and relaxation. It is harder to take such an industry seriously. Indeed, tourism writing has developed as a genre devoted to good news— weekend getaways, divine dining, cozy mountain lodges, exotic wildlife adventures, breathtaking vistas from balconies of luxury suites, and so on. But the human need for escapism is just part of why tourism has escaped press scrutiny. There are systemic and institutional reasons as well.

Travel writers say that advertising works to keep the travel press tepid. Increasingly, travel ads are helping underwrite entire publications. Some guidebooks go so far as to require places to pay a fee to be listed, sometimes letting the proprietor write the copy, while some magazines refuse to list establishments that don't advertise. [75] Although travel sections in the *Washington Post*, *New York Times*, and other major newspapers do carry travel advice, including articles warning, for instance, about airport luggage theft, the dangers of traveling to certain parts of the world, and even the impact of subsidized "familiarization" trips on the accuracy of guidebooks,[76] they rarely pan specific companies, tourist attractions, restaurants, or lodgings. Writers say some criticism is permitted if it is balanced with positive comments.

It is perhaps the industry practice of giving the media familiarization or "fam" trips that has worked most directly to cloud the critical eye of many travel writers. Edie Jarolim, who has written Foder's and Frommer's guidebooks, calls fam trips and other complimentary items ("comps") "the dirty little secret of the industry."[77] These all-expense–paid or highly subsidized trips to tourist destinations in the United States and overseas are underwritten by national or local tourist boards, airlines, resorts, inns and lodges, hotel chains, restaurants, and tour operators. Fam trips are usually organized by tourist offices or public relations firms in the United States that have been hired by the destination. Although the public may look to the travel press for evenhanded insights of prospective vacation spots, the travel industry views these reporters as "flacks," as part of the in-house public relations arm. In return for offering journalists free or discounted excursions, the industry seeks publicity that is low on cost and high on flattery. Fam trips are intended to garner good news in return for a good time. An article in *Adventure Travel Business*, a monthly magazine that bills itself as "The Voice of the Adventure Travel Industry," is explicit about how to use the press: "Press trips are an important part of a public relations program as there is no substitute for the in-depth coverage that is generated by a media visit. It is the best 'advertisement' you can buy." The article goes on to give guidelines on how to "entice a journalist to cover your story" and "increase the chances that you'll get a return on the cost of hosting a journalist, in the form of a long, flattering article."[78]

For the travel press, especially its large stable of freelance writers and photographers, fam trips are standard operating procedure. "Unless you're writing for *National Geographic* [which pays well, plus expenses], you can't travel and survive without subsidized trips,"[79] says Diann Stutz, a public relations official who has been organizing fam trips since the late 1970s. Freelance writers are normally paid a pittance for travel articles and guide books: newspaper supplements generally pay only a few hundred dollars for a piece, while publishers typically pay a flat fee of $10,000–$15,000 for writing a guidebook from scratch, a project that could take a year or more.[80] Given these realities, fam trips become imperative, but the obvious danger is that travel writers lose their independence.

The issue of fam trips and comps has long been debated by travel writers and editors. Many of the largest circulation newspapers have officially stopped accepting articles by writers on subsidized trips. These include the *New York Times, Washington Post, Los Angeles Times, Philadelphia Inquirer, Miami Herald,* and *Newsday.* Some publications, such as *Conde Nast Traveler* and *National Geographic Traveler,* require their writers to travel incognito and show up unannounced to prevent their being given the red-carpet treatment.[81] But writers say that in practice, the policy is often "don't ask, don't tell": many editors and publishers will turn a blind eye if they like the writer or the article.

In addition, the professional travel writers associations often work to protect their members, at the cost of objectivity. The most important of these groups is the Society of American Travel Writers (SATW), with 1300 members, about half of whom are freelance writers, while the rest are public relations officials with resorts, tourist boards, airlines, and other parts of the tourism industry. Although SATW's Code of Ethics states that "no member shall deliberately misrepresent his or her participation in a press trip in order to secure an editorial assignment" and that "no member shall accept payment or courtesies in exchange for an agreement to produce favorable material about a travel destination," there is no enforcement.[82] These rules are routinely bent, travel writers say. One writer characterized SATW as a "closed shop," intentionally designed to keep people out because it is through SATW that journalists can secure fam trips.

Conclusion

Within the tourism industry, there are two contradictory crosscurrents. One is among the big players and is towards consolidation in the hands of fewer corporations, based mainly in the global North and catering largely to the mass tourism market. The other, less powerful trend is toward a proliferation and decentralization of businesses, many in host countries in the global South and based on the principles of ecotourism. Although the focus of the mass or conventional tourism industry has historically been on visitor satisfaction as defined by rating cost, quality, and health and safety standards, the rise of ecotourism also requires tourism businesses to measure environmental and socioeconomic impacts and consider the satisfaction of the host community, as well as the traveler. Coming out of the ecotourism movement, certification programs help to create coalitions among different stakeholders and use the power of information to distinguish and reward responsible tourism. Certification systems should, however, be viewed as only one in a combination of tools, both voluntary and regulatory, that are needed to promote social equity and a sustainable environment.

The following three chapters provide an overview of the growth of environmentally and socially sensitive certification programs during the 1990s, an analysis of the major components of sound certification programs, and a comparison of tourism certification with several of the best known, NGO-led certification programs. These chapters help delineate both the problems as well as the promise of certification initiatives within the tourism industry. The next eight chapters include contemporary case studies of environmentally and socially responsible tourism certification programs and initiatives in various countries and regions around the world. The final case study also details efforts to explore the feasibility of creating a worldwide accreditation system for sustainable and ecotourism certification programs. Despite the geographical diversity of these initiatives, there are many similarities in the mix of stakeholders involved in devising and implementing the programs, their standards, criteria, and blend of process- and performance-based systems. As the concluding chapter describes, these certification programs all face major challenges, including financial self-sufficiency; marketing; credibility; and consumer confusion, ignorance, and buy-in. There are as well some more fundamental debates over certification; the most significant is being articulated by activists and NGOs in the global South and can be characterized as part of the "North-South divide." This debate centers around whether tourism certification is simply another technique for strengthening the hand of powerful and largely foreign-owned corporations at the expense of businesses, communities, and countries in the South or whether certification can be shaped into a tool for setting standards and criteria that promote and protect the interests and welfare of those in the South.[83]

This volume is intended to help practitioners and academics understand the historical connections between ecotourism and certification, to clarify the distinctions between certification and other forms of setting standards (awards, EIAs, best practices, etc.), and to better interpret and analyze the current divisions and trends within the tourism certification movement industry. This volume also seeks to provide conscientious travelers with a richer appreciation of the workings of certification programs, as well as the importance of certification to ensuring long-term sustainability within the travel and tourism industry. Although recognizing that there are serious challenges that need to be addressed, it is hoped that this volume will help move forward efforts to establish more universal criteria for certification schemes, as well as an international accreditation program.

Notes

1. First crafted in 1991 by The International Ecotourism Society (formerly The Ecotourism Society), this is still the most commonly quoted definition. *The Ecotourism Society Newsletter* 1, no. 1 (spring 1991), 1, cited in Katrina Brandon, *Ecotourism and Conservation: A Review of Key Issues*, Environment Department Papers, Biodiversity Services No. 033 (Washington, D.C.: World Bank, 1996), 1.
2. Martha Honey, *Ecotourism and Sustainable Development: Who Owns Paradise?* (Washington, D.C.: Island Press, 1999), 25.
3. Ibid., 14–16. While the World Bank came under political pressure not to invest in large-scale tourism resorts which brought scant benefits to developing countries, IDB officials say they closed down their lending largely out of concern that these projects were not being carefully enough planned to ensure environmental protection. Honey's interviews with various World Bank and IDB officials, 1997–2002.
4. World Tourism Organization statistics for 2000 as cited in "TIES Ecotourism Statistical Factsheet," The International Ecotourism Society, http://www.ecotourism.org; Klaus Toepfer in United Nations Environment Programme (UNEP), "Tourism and Environmental Protection," Addendum C, Contribution of UNEP to the *Secretary-General's Report on Industry and Sustainable Tourism for the Seventh Session of the UN Commission on Sustainable Development* (New York: UNCSD, 1999).
5. Héctor Ceballos-Lascuráin, "A National Ecotourism Strategy for Yemen," speech at meeting hosted by World Tourism Organization, UNDP, and Government of Yemen; Madrid, Spain, 1999.
6. *Gale Research Directory*, as cited in NCCA Standards Review Project, National Commission for Certifying Agencies and National Organization for Competency Assurance, www.noca.org/ncca.htm (July 23, 2001).
7. A. Tourigny, "Certification: What, Why, and How," *Proceedings of the American Society of Association Executives, 8th Annual Management Conference* (Washington, D.C.: American Society of Association Executives, 1990), 206–212.
8. World Tourism Organization, *Voluntary Initiatives for Sustainable Tourism* (Madrid: World Tourism Organization, 2002).
9. A 1992 definition by the American Society of Association Executives defines this more narrow use of certification as "a process by which an individual is

tested and evaluated in order to determine his or her mastery of a specific body of knowledge, or some portion of a body of knowledge." Alistair M. Morrison, Sheauhsing Hsieh, and Chia-Yu Wang, "Certification in the Travel and Tourism Industry: The North American Experience," *The Journal of Tourism Studies* 3, no. 2 (December 1992), 33.

10. In chapter 2, Toth uses slightly different terminology for first- and second-party assessment or auditing. Toth defines first party as certification or assessment by the "supplier" (hotel, tour operator, etc.) and second party as by the "purchaser," a term that for the tourism industry most often refers to as a trade or industry association, such as the Automobile Association of American, American Society of Travel Agents, or World Travel and Tourism Council. In contrast, Gereffi and his coauthors divide the third party category in two, describing third party as an external group, often an NGO, and "fourth party" as involving "government or multilateral agencies." In practice, many certification programs within the tourism industry involve a combination of second, third, and fourth parties, that is, many involve multiple stakeholders. In contrast, there is a growing tendency, even among certification programs run by industry or industry associations, to use independent private, for-profit auditing firms, that is, third-party auditors. Gary Gereffi, Ronie Garcia-Johnson, and Erika Sasser, "The NGO-Industry Complex," *Foreign Affairs* (July–August 2001), 57–58.

11. The confusion is compounded because even these geographical differences do not always hold up. The Virginia Tourism Accreditation Council, for instance, sponsors an "accreditation program" for destinations, which is, in reality, a second-party certification program. John Watt, Tourism Accreditation Department, Virginia Tourism Council, interview by Emma Stewart, July 3, 2001 and http://www.vatc.org. In Australia, the Victorian Government Purchasing Board uses *certification* as it is used in the United States and in this book, that is, to refer to "official acceptance of an accredited certifying body that an organisation's quality systems and/or products conform to the requirements of particular standards of performance." Rosemary Black, "Professional Certification: A Mechanism to Raise Guiding Standards," chapter 3, draft, Ph.D. thesis (Melbourne: Monash University, August 2000).

12. David Western, "Ecotourism: the Kenya Challenge," in *Ecotourism and Sustainable Development in Kenya*, Proceedings of the Kenya Ecotourism Workshop, Sept. 13–17, 1992, eds. C. G. Gakahu and B. E. Goode (Nairobi: Wildlife Conservation International, 1992), 15.

13. For a full discussion of these three trends or tendencies, with examples, see Honey, *Ecotourism and Sustainable Development*.

14. World Commission on Environment and Development, *Our Common Future* (Oxford: Oxford University Press, 1987). Known as the Bruntland Commission after its chair Gro Harlem Bruntland, this commission was established by the United Nations General Assembly in 1984 to study the connections between the environment and development. Its definition of sustainable development has been adopted by the UN and a number of other bodies and organizations.

15. Thomas Keesling, former president of ASTA and former chair of the ASTA Environment Committee, interview by Emma Stewart, July 25, 2001.

16. Eugenio Yunis, "Conditions for Sustainable Ecotourism Development and Management," speech at Seminar on Planning, Development and Management of Ecotourism in Africa, Regional Preparatory Meeting for the International Year of Ecotourism, 2002, Maputo, Mozambique, March 5–6, 2001.

17. WTO, Statistics for 2000.

18. Töepfer in UNEP, 1999.

19. O. N'Diaye, "Global and Regional Tourism Trends," Presentation by WTO regional representative for Africa, Seminar on Planning, Development and Management of Ecotourism in Africa, March 5–6, 2001.

20. Editorial, "Exploring Tourism," *The Nation* (Oct. 6, 1997), 3; The Ecotourism Society, "Ecotourism Statistical Fact Sheet," http://www.ecotourism.org/textiles/stats.txt (1997).

21. World Tourism Organization, *Yearbook of Tourism Statistics*, 49th ed. vol. 1 (Madrid: WTO, 1995); "Exploring Tourism," *The Nation*; The Ecotourism Society, "TES Statistical Fact Sheet," http://www.ecotourism.org/textfiles/stats.txt (July 25, 1997); Patricia Goldstone, *Making the World Safe for Tourism* (New Haven: Yale University Press, 2001).

22. WTO Statistics for 2000; Lisa Mastny, *Traveling Light: New Paths for International Tourism*, Worldwatch Paper 159 (Washington, D.C.: Worldwatch Institute, December 2001), 10–11.

23. Leonard J. Lickorish and Carson L. Jenkins, *An Introduction to Tourism* (Oxford: Butterworth and Heinemann, 1997), 12, as quoted in Goldstone, *Making the World Safe*, 46.

24. "Facts and Figures 2001," *Travel Industry World Yearbook 2001*, http://www.travelbigpicture.com, August 2001.

25. David Nicholson-Lord, "The Politics of Travel: Is Tourism Just Colonialism in Another Guise?" *The Nation* (October 6, 1997), 14; Héctor Ceballos-Lascuráin, *Tourism, Ecotourism and Protected Areas* (Gland, Switzerland: IUCN, 1996), 9; Barbara Crossette, "Surprises in the Global Tourism Boom," *New York Times*, April 12, 1998, p. 6.

26. This is due to a number of factors, including higher spending per tourist in the United States and European countries and leakage of tourism dollars from the global South to industrialized countries.

27. UN Council on Trade and Development, as quoted in Goldstone, *Making the World Safe*, 46.

28. Mastny, *Traveling Light*, 16.

29. Thanh-dam Truong, "The Political Economy of International Tourism," *Sex, Money and Morality: Prostitution and Tourism in South East Asia* (London: Zed Books, 1990), 116.

30. Ibid.

31. Polly Pattullo, *Last Resorts: The Cost of Tourism in the Caribbean* (Kingston, Jamaica: Ian Randle Publishers, 1996), 15.

32. Kreg Lindberg, "Economic Aspects of Ecotourism," draft obtained from author, 1997, 12.

33. Samuel R. Waters, *Travel Industry World Yearbook: The Big Picture-1996–97*, vol. 40 (New York: Child & Waters, 1997), 153; Mastny, *Traveling Light*, 16.

34. Stephanie Thullen, "Ecotourism and Sustainability: The Problematic Role of Transnational Corporations in Ecotourism," Master of Arts thesis, American University, May 1997; Truong, *Sex, Money, and Morality*, 109–116.

35. Despite declines in total net profits (from $3.1 billion in 1998 to $1.9 billion in 1999), the number of airline passengers worldwide grew by 3.8 percent in 1999. U.S. travel agents processed a record $76.6 billion in airline ticket sales in 1999, while U.S. travel agency locations dropped by 4 percent in 1999 and 6.8 percent in 2000 due to reductions in major airlines commission and increased Internet purchases, *World Yearbook 2001*, July 2001.

36. Waters, *World Yearbook: 1996–97*, 150; International Resources Group, *Ecotourism: A Viable Alternative for Sustainable Management of Natural Resources in Africa* (Washington, D.C.: U.S. Agency for International Development, June 1992), 63; Lindberg, "Economic Aspects of Ecotourism," 12.

37. Mastny, *Traveling Light*, 17.

38. Norimitsu Onishi, "Troubles Tarnish a Once-Shining African Airline," *New York Times*, June 20, 2001.

39. Truong, *Sex, Money, and Morality*, 104–105.

40. Honey, *Ecotourism and Sustainable Development*, 34–37.

41. Pattullo, *Last Resorts*, 16.

42. Ibid.

43. Onishi, "Troubles Tarnish," *New York Times*.

44. Ibid.

45. Waters, *World Yearbook: 1996–97*, 165; Earth Island Institute, Bluewater Network Cruise Ship Campaign Activities, "Cruise Ship Factoids," http://www.earthisland.org/bw/cruiseships.shtml.

46. http://www.oceansblue.org, December 2001.

47. By 1997, cruise lines had to comply with new Safety of Life at Sea regulations and were spending millions of dollars installing fire doors, sprinklers, and other safety devices. Waters, *World Yearbook: 1996–97*, 77, 150, 164–165; Russell Nansen, "Hungry? Out of Work? Eat a Cruise Ship!" *Contours*, 7, no. 10 (June 1997), 4–8.

48. Earth Island Institute, "Cruise Ship Factoids."

49. Ibid.; Global Education, "Tourism: Paradise in Peril" (Church World Service, Baltimore), 4 pp.; Pattullo, *Last Resorts*, 111–112.

50. Earth Island Institute, "Cruise Ship Factoids."

51. Pattullo, *Last Resorts*, 111–112.

52. Earth Island Institute, "Cruise Ship Factoids"; "Facts and Figures," *World Yearbook 2001*.

53. Although travel agencies are primarily categorized as corporate and leisure agencies, the focus here is on leisure. International Resources Group, *Ecotourism*, 23.

54. Packages put together by overseas operators normally include a 30 percent markup so that wholesalers, tour operators, and outfitters in the U.S. get 20 percent and the travel agent 10–15 percent. In addition, large travel agencies

and tour operators can make significant commissions from airlines and hotels by selling large blocks of tickets. Honey, *Ecotourism and Sustainable Development*, 41–44; Karen Ziffer, *Ecotourism: The Uneasy Alliance* (Washington, D.C.: Conservation International and Ernst & Young, 1989), 21.

55. Honey, *Ecotourism and Sustainable Development*, 42–43; authors' interviews with various ASTA officials, September 1998 and July–August 2001; M. J. Kietzke, "The Role of Travel Agents in Ecotourism," *Earth Ways* (January 1996), EW4; http://www.astanet.com, July 2001.

56. Yvonne Rodgers, International Ecotourism Education Foundation, Falls Church, VA, telephone interview by Martha Honey, May 1996. Barbara Crossette, "Surprises in Global Tourism," *New York Times*, April 12, 1998, 5.

57. "Facts and Figures," *World Yearbook 2001*; Tricia Holly, "Worried about Its Member Ranks, ASTA Works to Lure New Recruits," *Travel Agent* (April 2, 2001), 4.

58. Mastny, *Traveling Light*, 17.

59. Goldstone, *Making the World Safe*, 9, plus other parts of the first three chapters.

60. Honey, *Ecotourism and Sustainable Development*, 35.

61. Marie Walters, interview by Martha Honey, Sept. 1994; E. Weiner, "Ecotourism: Can it Protect the Planet?" *New York Times* (May 19, 1991), cited in Anita Pleumarom, "The Political Economy of Tourism," *The Ecologist*, 24, no. 4 (July–August 1994), 144, ftnt. 21.

62. Megan Epler Wood, interview by Martha Honey, September 1994; Thomas Keesling interview with Emma Stewart, July 2001.

63. International Resources Group, *Ecotourism*, 25; TES materials produced for training course, "The 5th Annual Ecotourism Planning and Management Workshop," George Washington University, Washington, D.C., June 17–21, 1996.

64. Honey, *Ecotourism and Sustainable Development*, 43; International Resources Group, *Ecotourism*, 27–28.

65. Marie Walters and Carolyn Wild interviews.

66. Bryan Higgins, "The Global Structure of the Nature Tourism Industry: Ecotourists, Tour Operators and Local Business," *Journal of Travel Research*, 35, no. 2 (fall 1996), 14.

67. Honey, *Ecotourism and Sustainable Development*, 67. In an interview with Martha Honey, Specialty Travel Index (STI) publisher Steen Hansen said that some 550 tour operators, or about half the specialty companies in the United States, advertise in STI, which is distributed to all travel agents. Hansen estimated that there are between 11,000 and 12,000 tour operators in the United States (May 1997).

68. TES packet of materials produced for training course, Ibid, 1996.

69. Will Webber, director, Journeys International, interview by Emma Stewart, July 11, 2001; http://www.journeys-intl.com, July 2001.

70. Ceballos-Lascuráin, *Tourism*, 6, 9.

71. Higgins, "Global Structure," *Journal of Travel Research*.

72. TES packet of materials prepared for training course, Ibid, 1996.

73. Adventure Travel Society, Colorado, http://www.adventuretravelagents.com (August 2001).

74. Honey, *Ecotourism and Sustainable Development*, 41–44, 52–55.

75. Honey, *Ecotourism and Sustainable Development*, 44–47. Tom McNicol, "Misguided," *Washington Post* (April 19, 1998), E6–8.

76. In its "Misguided" piece, which critiques guidebooks, the *Washington Post* stated that its "Travel section does not permit contributors to accept any complimentary or discounted accommodations or meals, and our reporters usually travel incognito. We pay our writers' expenses or they pay their own." (April 19, 1998), E6–8.

77. Ibid.

78. Deborah Cooper, "Turning Press Trips into Client Trips," *Adventure Travel Business* (October 1997), 22.

79. Quoted in Honey, *Ecotourism and Sustainable Development*, 44.

80. McNicol, "Misguided," *Washington Post*, Ibid, 44–45.

81. Honey, *Ecotourism and Sustainable Development*, 45–46; "Writer Guidelines, 2001," *National Geographic Traveler*, http://www.nationalgeographic.com/traveler/, July 2001. In 2001, *National Geographic Traveler* stopped taking articles from freelance writers.

82. Society of American Travel Writers, "Code of Ethics," faxed copy received by author in 1997.

83. The Web site Planeta.com has been carrying on lively forums and debates around certification, sustainable and ecotourism tourism, the media and other important issues. www.planeta.com.

Part I

CONCEPTS

C h a p t e r   1

The Evolution of "Green" Standards for Tourism

Martha Honey and Emma Stewart

Before 1970, little attention was given by businesses, governments, or NGOs to the environmental and social impacts of tourism, which was benignly described as the "smokeless" industry. The oldest of the modern-day tourism certification programs were established by industry associations and were aimed at measuring quality and cost along with health, hygiene, and safety of tourism accommodations, sites, and attractions (see chapter 2) or at measuring the qualifications of tourism professionals. However, in the 1990s, the global environmental movement and rapid expansion of ecotourism stimulated the development of scores of new certification programs that incorporated environmental and increasingly socioeconomic criteria. These newer programs can be categorized and analyzed both by their methodology—as performance or process based—and by the sector of the tourism industry they cover—conventional tourism, sustainable tourism, or ecotourism. It is argued that although conventional tourism certification programs encompass the major parts of the tourism industry, they are typically too weak to provide standards for long-term sustainable development. Rather, it is the sustainable tourism and eco-tourism certification programs that offer the most promise, and it is these that are the main focus of the subsequent chapters in this volume. But first, it is useful to sketch a historical overview of the roots of these modern socially and environmentally responsible certification programs.

Michelin

Beginning in the early twentieth century, the automobile began offering many vacationers an introduction to independent travel over longer distances. So it is not surprising that Michelin, the company that patented the first removable car tire in 1895, was the pioneer of an early hotel and restaurant rating system via travel guides for the road. Michelin Red Guides, first published in 1900, initially covered hotels in France and gradually expanded across Europe, mapping road travel itineraries while campaigning for better highway sign posting. Michelin guidebooks developed a certification prototype, using information contributed by travelers. Through its *bureau d'itineraire*, Michelin provided vacationers with route descriptions, travel tips such as where to find gas stations and mechanics, and a cost and quality rating system for accommodations, based on visitor feedback. In 1926, Michelin also began a three-tiered Gastronomy Star rating system for restaurants in France.

Since 1945, Michelin's Red Guides have used on-site inspectors, including guidebook editors, to rate the overall quality and comfort of restaurants and hotels in Europe. According to Jean-Frédéric Douroux, a Michelin external relations official, hotels and restaurants are selected after "one or several visits of our full-time inspectors, who pay their bills anonymously, and only then may announce themselves as being there to make an inspection."[1] Michelin also continues to solicit traveler feedback by e-mail and by questionnaires located in the guidebooks.[2]

With the boom in mass tourism beginning in the 1950s, Michelin launched a variety of new types of guides, each with a three-star rating system based on "the overall interest the sights might have for our readers," said Douroux. He declined to provide the list of criteria used for inspection, arguing that this information is proprietary.[3] Although Michelin does not permit inspectors to accept subsidized meals or overnight stays, Elizabeth Siegal of Michelin Travel Publications acknowledged that it is "becoming increasingly usual for [travel guide] editors to go on media trips organized by PR firms and accept 'comps'" from businesses they are rating.[4]

American Automobile Association

Currently, AAA is both the largest leisure travel agency covering the U.S. market, with more than $3.5 billion in travel sales annually, and the largest federation of automobile clubs in the world, with a membership close to 44 million.[5] In 1902, AAA began building a federation of motor car clubs throughout the United States, which, like Michelin, has campaigned for a better quality road system to encourage independent automobile travel. In 1905, AAA produced its first maps, and since then, it has published guidebooks for road travel and, in recent years, for ship, air, and overseas travel. Today, AAA publishes about 200 travel titles each year, including the AAA tour books (free to members on request), as well as more specialized guides for both U.S. and non-U.S. destinations.

Accommodations and restaurants included in these guides are rated for quality and price. AAA maintains that objectivity in its rating program is assured because no business can pay to be listed and the granting of AAA discounts is not a requirement of listing. A property's general manager first completes an application about the facilities and services, and then, if AAA's basic requirements appear to be met, a field inspector makes an unannounced on-site inspection. The manager is notified only when the inspector is ready to leave. Evaluations are updated annually.

To handle these on-site visits, AAA employs a team of sixty-five tourism editors, who inspect approximately 41,000 lodgings and restaurants each year. This means that each editor must visit, on average, three sites a day. In addition, tourism editors are required to keep AAA up-to-date on new attractions and tourism sites in their territories. Jane Graziani, manager of public relations at AAA, said that "no attractions, lodgings, or restaurants are reviewed by non-AAA personnel."[6] However, in practice, this means that the evaluation process cannot be very rigorous or that AAA inspectors are using local club representatives to do some of the inspections.

Properties listed in both AAA and Michelin guides generally fall within the mass or conventional tourism market. Graziani says that AAA's criteria—which are updated based on input from consumers, members, lodging and restaurant professionals, and industry representatives and reviewed by AAA officials—have focused only on environmental questions "to the extent that truly effective green programs maintain quality standards of guest comfort." She explained that, for example, AAA supports the American Hotel & Lodging Association's Good Earthkeeping program, a modest "green" bed linen and towel reuse program, "as long as guests are not charged for requesting daily laundering."[7] Any deeper commitment to sustainable tourism is also circumscribed because AAA, like Michelin, remains wedded to promoting travel by car. AAA's governmental lobbyists advocate the expansion of highway systems, not building more mass transportation, to relieve congestion. Despite global warming and price hikes at the pump, U.S. consumption of gasoline and car rentals increased between 1999 and 2001.[8]

Qualmark

Other automobile-related associations have similar cost and quality certification programs, such as the star rating system run by the Mobil Travel Guide, in the United States and elsewhere. In New Zealand, for instance, the Qualmark Accreditation Program was launched in 1994 by the private sector (the Automobile Association), two NGOs (Adventure Tourism Council NZ and Tourism Industry Association NZ), and the government's tourism organization (Tourism New Zealand). Qualmark rates and certifies both accommodations (hotels, holiday parks, and backpacker, self-contained, and service facilities) and retail tourist shops, and awards one to five stars. Trained, independent auditors carry out annual audits based on a list of facilities, quality, service, and cost. Certification is valid for one year. Companies pay a fee to be certified and, in turn, receive publicity via guidebooks, brochures, a website, and visitor bureaus. However, unlike AAA, Michelin, and Mobil, Qualmark is backed by a variety of stakeholders who bring interests and concerns beyond the profitability of the certification program and promotion of conventional tourism. Qualmark has begun making a transition to incorporate environmental and sociocultural criteria, including rating a business's natural area focus, interpretation, contribution to conservation, work with local communities, cultural components, and responsible marketing. Qualmark has also formed an alliance with the international certification program, Green Globe[9] (see chapter 10).

Other Accommodation and Restaurant Programs

Today, there are a wide variety of certification programs for hotels, resorts, lodges, and restaurants, a number of which are linked to guidebooks or directories but not tied to the automobile. Some are owned and run as for-profit businesses and operate as exclusive membership clubs rather than as independent, impartial, and transparent rating systems. For instance, both Relais & Chateau and Small Luxury Hotels of the World (SLH), created in 1975 and 1991, respectively,[10] vet luxury properties that join their programs and purport to offer a type of certification. They accept membership of hotels and lodges around the world based on recommendations by other members in that region. The establishment must apply for membership, and on-site visits check a series of quality standards for hospitality, how long the establishment has been in operation, its track record, and management turnover. These programs charge a fixed entrance fee—SLH's rate is $13,000 per annum for a twenty-bed hotel—plus additional fees to participate in various special events, and a percentage of all reservations made through their central registration systems. In return, member hotels are promised market advantage. They get to use the Relais & Chateaux and SLH labels and are listed in their directories, which are distributed widely around the world. They are also promoted on the organizations' Web sites and via various systems used by travel agents. SLH members also receive a 45 percent discount when they advertise in *Conde Nast Traveler* magazine.

These programs are intended to assure visitors luxury and high standards of service and guarantee hotels and lodges branding and marketing. However, they have an inherent conflict of interest because they are rating only those accommodations that have paid to become members of these exclusive clubs. Although the brand these programs offer relies on consistent quality, they are not disinterested certification schemes using independent auditors who have no financial incentive to increase the number of members. In addition, even though some of these luxury lodges are located in game parks, on tropical islands, or in or near other protected or ecologically fragile areas, these programs are not focused on environmental or community impacts.[11]

Tourism Professionals

By the early 1990s, there were over a dozen voluntary programs in the United States to certify tourism professionals, up from only about two in 1980. These programs certify a range of professionals within the tourism and travel industry, including hotel administrators, tour professionals, meeting professionals, hotel sales executives, festival executives, incentive travel executives, and exhibit managers. The oldest program, the Certified Travel Counselor (CTC), was introduced in 1966 by the Institute of Certified Travel Agents as a voluntary program to rate and recognize the competence of individual travel agents.

In Canada and Europe, as well, there was by the early 1990s, a growth in the number of similar certification programs for tourism professionals.[12] These types of certification programs were designed to demonstrate professional competence and performance and to promote self-assessment and improvement.

Unlike the medical, legal, accounting, and other professions that have both academic and licensing requirements, in the United States, there is no compulsory academic track or license for travel and tourism professionals. Writing in 1992, Morrison argued that although U.S. colleges and universities were offering "a cornucopia of curricula" in the field of travel and tourism, there was little indication that these specialized degrees played a significant role in employment decisions. Rather, Morrison suggested that professional certification programs "may have filled a void by providing an alternative route to achieving professional status to studies towards specialized travel and tourism degrees."[13] Although these certification programs help to attest to the integrity of individuals, they are not linked to setting or measuring environmentally or socially responsible criteria for the industry. Further, like the automobile association and luxury lodge programs described above, they are all second-party certification programs, that is, ones run by industry trade organizations. As Morrison noted, the danger is that these industry-run certification schemes are "more interested in creating an additional source of income and members than in advancing their professions."[14]

Greening the Tourism Industry

In recent years, efforts to green the travel and tourism industry have taken a variety of forms. Industry associations, travel magazines and guidebooks, environmental and community-based NGOs, governments, international financial institutions, and the World Tourism Organization (WTO) and United Nations Environmental Program (UNEP) have adopted a wide variety of initiatives designed to set standards and give awards for environmentally, and in some instances socially, responsible practices. These efforts have included a range of government regulations and legislation; international forums and covenants; creation of new national and international business forums, such as the World Travel and Tourism Council (WTTC), and the founding in 1991 of The International Ecotourism Society (TIES) and, subsequently, a score of national ecotourism societies. Green initiatives have also included statements of definition and principle, codes of conduct, best practices, awards, ecolabels, ecotourism travel programs, and self-help guides and manuals. Taken together, these diverse initiatives seek to (1) set standards within the industry; (2) promote environmentally and often socially, culturally, and economically responsible practices; and (3) provide travelers with information on the best companies, services, and attractions.

For industry associations, another less publicly stated reason for promoting voluntary self-regulation is to avoid international or government directives or legislation. The WTTC's Environmental Guidelines, for example, offer a clear call for preemptive action to stave off outside regulation. Issued in 1997, the guidelines state, "Travel and Tourism companies should seek to implement sound environmental principles through self-regulation, recognizing that national and international regulation may be inevitable and that preparation is vital."[15] Talking the talk of environmental responsibility, the WTTC, which represents many of the world's largest tourism corporations, promotes only self-monitoring, while vigorously opposing any types of government or international regulation. Similarly, the Travel Industry Association of America (TIA), while applauding the growth of environmentalism, including ecotourism, opposes "governmental initiatives that would impede travel by discriminating against the traveler or the travel industry."[16]

Despite efforts to avoid regulation and push deregulation, travel and tourism, like other businesses and industries, is subject to certain government oversight. Every country sets standards intended to balance human and environmental health with economic development and technological sophistication. Licenses and/or permits and monitoring are used to ensure that enterprises meet the standards. In the last three decades, environmental impact assessment (EIA) has become one of the most widely used techniques for examining the potential ecological impact of particular companies or projects. This front-end approach is now typically required by governments and international development and lending agencies, such as the World Bank and the United States Agency for International Development (USAID) for both new and upgraded or expanded projects ranging from dams, highways, and factories to hotels and lodges. In practice, however, EIAs may be poorly performed and the results not made public, and government monitoring may be lax, standards weak, and officials susceptible to influence.

Another tool, popular with industry, is the environmental management system (EMS). This voluntary procedure helps management conduct baseline studies, put together a program plan, conduct staff training, and set up systems for ongoing monitoring and attainment of environmental targets, such as pollution and water and electricity use reduction.[17] As Toth describes (see chapter 2), the most widely recognized EMS standards are the International Organization for Standardization (ISO) 14000 series, one of several industry responses to the increasing public interest in sustainable development that came in the wake of the 1992 Rio Earth Summit.

Although the ability of government regulatory powers, particularly in less developed countries, has been weakened in recent decades, the rising global environmental consciousness, activism, and global organizing have served as some counterweight. This has helped spawn NGO campaigns to create voluntary environmental and social standards, to promote government regulation and legislation, and to compel corporate responsibility. Over the last decade, various components of the tourism industry have been subjected to a range of compulsory and voluntary environmental standards.

Airlines

For airlines, most new and proposed environmental regulations relate to noise levels. Jet engines are now certified for noise volume,[18] some airports have "noise preferential routes" to minimize affects on residential areas, and noisier engines pay higher landing fees. In addition, a number of the international carriers have given a nod to conservation by adopting some green practices, including separating plastics and bottles for recycling, contributing passengers' donations to environmental organizations and social welfare charities, promoting ecotourism in in-flight magazines and movies, and taking steps to voluntarily reduce fuel consumption and emissions.

Of all the international carriers, British Airways appears most responsive to growing public environmental and health concerns. British Airways has undertaken a program to monitor emissions,[19] and its emissions per available seat-mile have improved. Since 1992, British Airways, with the endorsement of the American Society of Travel Agents (ASTA) and travel associations in Britain and Asia, has sponsored annual Tourism for Tomorrow Awards. These awards, covering tour operators, individually owned and chain hotels, national parks and heritage sites, and other tourism services, are presented each year by an independent judging panel headed by the well-known British botanist, environmental campaigner, and broadcaster David Bellamy at an event carried on British television. However, despite their prestige, the Tourism for Tomorrow Awards, like most ecoaward programs, are far from rigorous. Companies nominate themselves and there is no on-site inspection or clear set of criteria, so the ecoaward recipients have been a mixed bag of some exemplary ecolodges and some far less than green tourism companies. Interestingly, this lack of rigor can cut both ways by rewarding high profile, well-connected, but less than exemplary businesses while not giving enough recognition to outstanding awardees.

Take for instance, Turtle Island, a luxury honeymoon resort on one of Fiji's Yasawa Islands that has been a pioneer in both environmental restoration and economic and social welfare projects for poor, rural communities on neighboring islands. Turtle Island's Andrew Fairley, who in 1999 received the award, says that afterward, when David Bellamy came for the first time to see the resort, he raved that what he saw was even better than he'd expected. As Bellamy told Fairley, "As Chairman of the Committee, when I read the report and you came and made a presentation, I thought, well, it can't really be quite that good. Now, having seen it, it's even more amazing. I don't really think you did yourself justice."[20] Fairley argues that these awards programs—and Turtle Island has won many—are the ones not doing justice to businesses that are really trying to uphold high ecotourism and sustainability standards. He, among others, contends that the value of such awards is watered down because the pool of recipients is so uneven. Awards programs would have much more credibility with the public if they included on-site inspections and precise guidelines and criteria for nominees.

Cruises

Perhaps more than any other sector of the mass tourism market, Caribbean cruise lines are most anathema to the concepts and practices of ecotourism and most difficult to green through environmental and socioeconomic reforms. These high volume, prepaid, packaged holidays, with their celebration of sun-and-fun consumption, self-indulgence, and brief ports of call to buy souvenirs or duty-free first-world luxuries are a mirror opposite of the small-scale, locally owned, culturally sensitive, environmentally low-impact, and educational precepts of ecotourism.

In recent years, however, the cruise industry has come under closer scrutiny by both the U.S. and Caribbean governments and environmental organizations. Caribbean countries have begun to organize an effort to impose some taxes and set some standards for cruise ships. These include increasing port taxes, prohibiting anchor drops on coral reefs, limiting the number of cruise ships in port, and recruiting and training more islanders for shipboard work. Nothing, however, has raised more public and government ire against the cruise industry than their illegal dumping of untreated waste and garbage into the open ocean. In the early 1990s, Greenpeace "ecowarriors" aboard inflatable dinghies secretly videotaped a cruise ship emptying its waste at sea. In the wake (literally) of this scandal, the cruise lines sought to clean up their image and, in some instances, their practices. In 1993, when Princess Cruise Lines was fined $500,000 for illegal dumping that had been videotaped by a passenger, Princess quickly paid up and, through a combination of concrete reforms and aggressive public relations, went on the offensive to repair its reputation. In 1995, Princess executives invited ASTA's Environment Committee to tour one of its ships. The ASTA newsletter carried a glowing report of the visit: "Princess has proven itself a leader in the movement to integrate ecotourism principles into their overall management policy. . . . We applaud the strength of their convictions, and urge all travel agents to support Princess for their efforts."[21] The following year, in 1996, the ASTA committee awarded Princess Lines the annual ASTA/*Smithsonian Magazine* Environmental Award for its "strong corporate commitment towards protecting the environment to which they bring passengers and guests."[22] Although the award was given largely for Princess Lines' "Save the Waves" campaign, a public relations effort targeting its customers, the company also took some concrete steps to improve its environmental track record. In the mid-1990s, officials at the watchdog group Center for Marine Conservation (now The Ocean Conservancy) praised Princess Lines for adopting a zero discharge program, which has become an industry standard, as well as for promoting waste reduction and recycling.[23]

Yet illegal dumping is still widespread. According to a General Accounting Office report, between 1993 and 1998 alone, 12 cruise lines, including Princess, were involved in 104 detected and confirmed cases of illegal discharges of oil, garbage, and hazardous wastes and paid more than $30 million in fines.[24] In 1999, Royal Caribbean Cruises, the second largest cruise line, was given a record $18 million criminal fine in a twenty-one-count felony plea agreement for dumping waste oil and hazardous chemicals. Recently as well, the environmental group Earth Island Institute filed a petition regarding cruise dumping and other matters with the U.S. Environmental Protection Agency (EPA), and the EPA has launched an initiative to examine various environmental impacts of cruises.[25] In June 2001 in Alaska, where the numbers and sizes of cruise ships have been increasing rapidly, Alaska took strong action, passing a bill to regulate and monitor waste discharge from cruise ships and finance the program with a per passenger fee.[26]

Cruise lines find these efforts at government regulations "a frightening prospect," says Russell Nansen, who worked for Royal Caribbean Lines for more than two decades.[27] This may explain why the International Council of Cruise Lines (ICCL), made up of some of the largest passenger lines in North America, has adopted mandatory waste-management practices. In 2001, the sixteen cruise lines that belong to the council began testing and installing wastewater treatment systems to "prevent the discharge of chlorinated dry-cleaning fluids, sludge, and contaminated filter material,"[28] all of which have historically been surreptitiously discharged into the oceans by cruise lines. More promising perhaps is the ICCL's stated willingness to incorporate new technologies and environmentally sensitive design and construction into new cruise ships.[29]

In addition to the watchdog role played by environmental NGOs such as Earth Island, Greenpeace, and The Ocean Conservancy, a Canadian NGO, Oceans Blue Foundation, is developing a certification program for cruise ships. This Cruise Ship Stewardship Initiative, still in its infancy in 2001, is "endeavouring to advance socioenvironmentally responsible tourism and informed cruise passenger choice."[30]

Hotels

In response to consumer demand for environmentally sensitive products and services, many conventional hotels, ranging from independent properties to major chains, had by the mid-1990s begun reusing and recycling programs, introducing towel laundry choices for guests, and installing low-flow toilets, showerheads, energy-efficient lighting, and amenity dispensers to replace individual plastic bottles.[31] Some major chains, such as Inter-Continental Hotels and Resorts, Holiday Inn, and Fairmont Hotels &

Resorts (formerly Canadian Pacific Hotels & Resorts), have taken steps of one sort or another to green their operations. In 1992, the chief executives of twelve multinational hotel companies, including Hilton International, Inter-Continental, Marriott, Accor, and The Taj Group, founded the International Hotels Environment Initiative (IHEI) "to increase general environmental awareness and to establish valid guidelines within the global hotel industry."[32] IHEI's list of "six good reasons for going green" includes cost savings through improved energy efficiency, anticipating consumer awareness and "market pressure," and preempting "legal requirements." On this latter point, IHEI notes, "The tourism industry is probably more aware than any of the inevitable increase in environmental regulation at a national and international level." By "taking a lead on self-regulation," IHEI argues, "the hotel industry can prepare in advance and avoid expensive remedial measures. It can also position as leading the field on responsible environmental practice and maybe even help to shape new legislation."[33]

IHEI publishes the magazine *Green Hotelier* which has carried serious articles on "green" innovations, ecotourism, and, in its May 2002 issue, certification.[34] In 1996, IHEI, the American Hotel & Motel Association (since renamed American Hotel & Lodging Association), the International Hotel Association, and the United Nations Environment Program (UNEP) produced the *Environmental Action Pack: Practical Steps to Benefit Your Business and the Environment*,[35] a set of environmental management benchmarking tools, practical suggestions, checklists, and forms, as well as a ten-point "Hotels' Environmental Charter." Addressed to hotel managers, the *Action Pack* states that its aim is "to help you introduce environmental management as an extension to the daily operation of your business." It is not a certification program because it does not involve an audit or an award. Rather the *Action Pack* and other similar packets developed by IHEI are intended to help hotels develop environmental management systems. The *Action Pack*, for instance, stresses that the EMS should be tailored to the needs of each hotel: "Manage it at a pace which is right for your hotel, and bring it into your normal working schedules from now on." This guide includes a "Green Health Check" covering six areas: (1) energy, (2) solid waste, (3) water, (4) effluents and emissions, (5) purchasing, and (6) business issues. Managers are asked to answer a list of yes/no questions in each category and if the score is five or more, the hotel is rated as performing well; four or less "you may need to consider that area as a priority for action." Many items are also cost-saving measures, as can be seen from the energy checklist (box 1.1).

There is ample evidence that using an EMS can save a hotel money. IHEI reports that the Inter-Continental in Sydney saved $24,000 in one

---

Box 1.1. Environmental Checklist: Energy

Does the staff switch off appliances & lighting when not in use?	Yes	No
Are energy services shut down when & where parts of the building are unoccupied?	Yes	No
Have temperature settings, timers, lighting levels, etc. been adjusted to ensure minimum energy use for given comfort levels?	Yes	No
Is hotel energy use regularly monitored?	Yes	No
Is consumption of energy going down year to year?	Yes	No
Have targets for reducing energy consumption been set?	Yes	No
Has energy use been compared with energy benchmarks?	Yes	No
Have you checked that the cheapest fuel rate is being used for each purpose?	Yes	No
Is all of your energy plant/equipment less than 10 years old?	Yes	No
Have low-energy lights been fitted where cost-effective?	Yes	No
Has an energy audit been undertaken in the last three years?	Yes	No

Source: American Hotel & Motel Association, *Environmental Action Pack*, 1996, p. 10.

---

year by reducing the temperature of its laundry water.[36] The FEMA-TOUR (Feasibility and Market Study for a European Eco-label for Tourist Accommodations) study in Europe collected similar types of data. In 1999, Grecotel in Athens reported that since starting its environmental and cultural programs in 1992, it had cut water consumption by 30 percent and oil consumption by 40–55 percent. The Ritz Hotel in London has reduced gas consumption by 40 percent since 1988 through its energy-efficient space heating and hot water project.[37]

Managers also view all of these green programs and practices as marketing strategies that can improve sales and increase occupancy rates for hotels. The Sol Elite Falcó, part of the Sol Meliá chain in Spain, reported a 15 percent increase in business after it adopted environmentally responsible practices in 1994.[38] One industry survey found that travelers are more likely to chose a hotel if, for instance, it provides recycling bins for guest use (67.5 percent of those surveyed said yes), has energy-efficient lighting (69.4 percent), turns off lights not being used in occupied guestrooms

(65.6 percent), changes sheets only upon request (58.9 percent), and uses in-room displays printed on recycled paper (65.1 percent).[39]

The tourism industry has certainly sought to market its often rather modest environmental reforms as major innovations. In 1996, for instance, IHEI hotels received the British Airways' Tourism for Tomorrow Award for their efforts to "think green" by installing energy-saving showers and laundering towels only when guests requested. The press release announcing the award trumpeted these useful but token green steps as major reforms. The headline, which read "Keep your towels—and help save the world!" was clearly an exaggeration.[40]

Travel Agents and Tour Operators

ASTA, to which most travel agents in the United States belong, is potentially a strong mechanism for educating travel agents, developing ecotourism standards, and helping to monitor implementation. In 1991, ASTA set up an environment committee composed of travel agents who volunteered to participate. The committee drew up the "Ten Commandments on Eco-Tourism" aimed at sensitizing travelers, and created, together with *Smithsonian Magazine*, an annual ecoaward to select two exemplary companies, countries, or individuals to show, according to committee member Marie Walters, that "the travel industry [was] really moving in a good direction to help preserve the environment."[41]

However, in 1998, ASTA cut its ties with the Smithsonian because of a dispute over the magazine's advertising policy, and the following year ASTA's environment committee was disbanded. ASTA continues to give the annual award, but interviews suggest that ASTA's current leadership does not see promoting environmental programs and practices as a real priority. Former environment committee chair and ex-ASTA president Thomas Keesling lamented that the demise of the committee marks "a big step backwards for environmental issues in the travel agent industry."[42]

In reality, the environment committee's functions had been quite minimal and, like other awards programs, the ASTA/*Smithsonian Magazine* Environmental Award and the reconstituted ASTA Environment Award lack clear standards, on-site inspections, and rigor. Applicants, for instance, must explain their nomination in 175 words or less, plus supplemental materials.[43] This type of nonjuried nomination process, based primarily on self-nominations, can easily be manipulated by companies submitting glossy brochures and inflated descriptions of their "green practices." The result, in ASTA's case, has been an incongruous assortment of recipients, including Intercontinental Hotels for its environmental management model, the people of Bermuda for their quality of life, and the Brazilian environmental activist and martyr Chico Mendes for his work in the Amazon basin.[44]

More rigorous than ASTA's efforts have been the travel programs run by a number of environmental, educational, and scientific organizations that offer nature, adventure, study, and service tours to their members. Among the leading conservation organizations, Sierra Club, The Nature Conservancy, Smithsonian Institution, National Audubon Society, World Wildlife Fund, Earthwatch Institute, and National Geographic Society all run travel programs. The main purposes of these trips are to promote educational and professional development among members, provide fun and relaxation, raise revenue, give members a tax break, and, in some cases, showcase the organization's overseas projects. Tour planners from many of these travel programs attend the annual Educational Travel Conference (formerly Non-profits in Travel) run by Travel Learning Connections.[45] Under the rules guiding nonprofit organizations, these trips cannot themselves be classified as fund-raising activities, but they can solicit voluntary charitable contributions from participants.

Most of these travel programs claim that they follow ecotourism principles, although they tend to use the larger, best-advertised U.S. nature tour operators and overseas ground operators, which are sometimes not the most socially and environmentally responsible companies. A tour planner at The Nature Conservancy, which runs about 40 international trips each year, said that they strive to find the most responsible inbound and outbound operators: "We check The International Ecotourism Society's rating of operator practices, we look at operator contributions to conservation, and we are in the process of finalizing our own green guidelines for use by our trip escorts in order to help them evaluate operators on the ground."[46] Several other environmental organizations are also experimenting with variants of this type of in-house rating program. Clearly, these environmental organizations, whose reputations and incomes depend on upholding sound environmental standards, are interested in promoting high-quality ecotourism.

In Europe, many tour operators have developed codes of conduct, and several have at least quasi-certification programs. Europe's largest tour operator, TUI (Touristik Union International), based in Germany, has had an environmental department since 1990; it has created both a statement of corporate principles and an environmental checklist for the accommodations, destinations, and transport companies its tour operators use. TUI owns some of the hotels to which it sends visitors and therefore has both more incentive for and control over any ecolabel program. TUI does annual on-site inspections of its destinations, particularly Mediterranean beaches, to monitor bathing water and beach quality, and its hotels to check on sewage treatment plants and waste disposal sites, among other factors. It also checks on environmental initiatives being taken, such as use of renewable sources of energy, reforestation, species preservation, and nature conservation. TUI gives each destination an environmental evaluation and those businesses that do not meet the minimum standards are assisted in improving their environmental performance. Selected hotels receive an Environmentally Sound Hotel Management designation and recognition in TUI's catalogues, which have a green box listing environmental findings for each destination. TUI is currently preparing to launch its own ecolabel, Green Thumb, beginning with destinations in the Alps, Cyprus, and Egypt.[47]

In Great Britain, many tour operators started to address issues of environmental responsibility after the 1992 Earth Summit, according to a study by the relief and development agency Tearfund. The Association of Independent Tour Operators began working in 2000 to produce "a responsible tourism code" for its members. In November 2000, the Association of British Travel Agents published a detailed study of the "ethical preferences" of their clients. In January 2000, market research done by Tearfund concluded that "the majority of tourists want a more ethical tourism industry, and would be willing to pay for it."[48] A subsequent Tearfund study, done a year later, looked at how the industry was responding to consumer demands. Based on a survey of sixty-five U.K.-based tour operators, the study "highlights examples of their good practice in ethical tourism and suggests ways in which they can be replicated and built upon."[49] In particular, this study found that most of these British tour operators were involved in a variety of programs to bring benefits to local communities, three-quarters of the companies were giving money to charities in the destinations, most were involved in partnership and training programs with their suppliers in the destination countries, and half the companies had responsible tourism policies for the operations of the company, the supply chain, or the tourists themselves.

In the mid-1990s, The International Ecotourism Society, in a sort of precursor for a full-blown certification program, carried out what is perhaps the earliest effort to monitor the environmental performance of inbound tour operators. They conducted a survey of tourists based on a set of guidelines TIES had compiled in consultation with stakeholders from industry, academia, and NGOs and published in a twenty-page booklet, *Ecotourism Guidelines for Nature Tour Operators*.[50] In 1995, TIES launched its Green Evaluations program in Ecuador to test how well tour operators were meeting the guidelines.

But, as TIES later recognized, this project suffered from a number of design faults. Because the Ecuadorian tour operators themselves distributed and in some cases collected the surveys from the tourists, there was no real independent monitoring.[51] A number of companies never returned a sufficient number of responses for statistically valid results. In addition, although tourists are an important component of a green evaluation or certification process, there are many areas of environmental, as well as sociocultural and economic, impact that they are not qualified to judge. They cannot, for instance, accurately assess a company's relationship with the community or even with its own employees or its waste disposal and other "gray" environmental areas.[52]

In March 2000, the WTO, UNEP, and United Nations Educational, Scientific and Cultural Organization (UNESCO), together with fifteen tour operators (including TUI) from various parts of the world, launched the Tour Operators' Initiative for Sustainable Tourism Development (TOI) at a meeting in Berlin. Although not a certification program, TOI is a network of tour operators whose "aim [is] to make their businesses reflect the 'best practice' in sustainable tourism." This includes "not only their internal company operations, but also the design of tours and external business relationships with partners, suppliers and sub-contractors."[53] By late 2001, TOI had twenty-four members and had produced a list of best practices by sixteen of these companies, including the Japan Travel Bureau, Finnair Travel Services, and British Airways Holidays, covering environmental, sociocultural, and economic aspects, including "co-operating with local communities and people" and "utilising local products and skills."[54] Described as "a work in progress," the list includes "good examples" of how tour operators are adopting practices that can "help tackle sustainable development in three main areas: the supply chain, within their own organizations, and at destination."[55]

TOI's activities include holding workshops and conferences, development of guides and manuals, implementation of management systems, training and education programs for staff and local partners, "building partnerships with local authorities and other stakeholders," and creation of "a database for the exchange of good practices." TOI also aims to "promote and assist member-to-member activities such as voluntary audits of members' operations."[56]

Although described as "developed by and for tour operators," TOI is bolstered by the expertise, administrative, and financial support of three United Nations organizations, and especially by the experience of UNEP in establishing similar voluntary initiatives in a number of other industry sectors. The initiative is self-funded, voluntary, nonprofit, and open to all tour operators, regardless of size or location, as well as to others who can join as associate members. Membership costs between $500 and $5,000 per year, depending on the tour operator's size. It has a twelve-member governing body and holds annual membership meetings.[57]

Travel Press

Although the travel press is frequently compromised by "fam" trips and other gifts (as described in the introduction) and circumscribed by advertising and professional associations that keep it tethered to the industry, during the 1990s there was tremendous growth travel guides and magazines catering to the nature, adventure, and backpacker markets and, to a lesser extent, to ecotourism and sustainable development. Although guidebooks continue to be cheaply produced and lack clear standards, a number do contain sections on environmental issues, projects, and ecotourism, as well as more thoughtful comments by their writers and editors. In addition, several of the ecoawards programs linked to magazines are undergoing makeovers.

Some of the changes are largely cosmetic. The *Let's Go!* guide series, for instance, strives to elevate its literary profile by hiring Harvard University students to travel around and send back their thoughts. However, as one writer complained, the budget and schedule were still too tight to allow any close evaluation of sites.[58] *Lonely Planet*, the guidebook popular with youthful and budget travelers, strictly prohibits its writers from accepting discounts. "If any of our authors were ever caught taking payment for inclusion, they'd be fired," said Eric Kettunen, *Lonely Planet* general manager in the United States.[59] Although *Lonely Planet* does not have a policy regarding ecotourism, their ethic of the "independent and involved travel" tends to attract writers who are interested in these issues. Its Costa Rica guide contains a page on the complexities of ecotourism, and this may be the only travel guide series to donate a portion of its profits to grassroots groups in the host countries.

Moon Publications takes a similar approach to travel. Its *Costa Rica Handbook* gives extensive coverage to conservation issues, volunteer organizations, and awards and then devotes a full chapter to "ethical tourism."[60] However, Beatrice Blake, the founder and long-time author of *New Key to Costa Rica*, the original green guide that pioneered Costa Rica's first ecotourism certification program (see chapter 4), believes travel guide writers and publishers, herself included, could do a more professional and systematic job if they collaborated rather than competed with one another. "Our rating list tends to get thrown on the cover of my book, 'Now With Eco-Ratings!!' by well-meaning editors and publishers. It's a green selling tool for the book, even though it is far from a perfect list. Why don't we work together to make it perfect?" She adds, "I do feel that there is room for guiding readers of my guidebooks to ecosensitive establishments. Guidebooks are one of the only and one of the best marketing tools that small or locally run places have."[61]

Over the last few years, the number of ecotourism award schemes have grown in the travel press, most without any independent auditing or clear criteria. Frequently, these awards do little to promote lesser known or locally owned projects that are struggling to break into the international market. Many recipients of the awards are either industry giants or the already well-popularized ecotourism projects.

Only recently have some of these award programs begun to address the issue of standards. According to Joan Tapper, editor-in-chief, *Islands Magazine*'s Ecotourism Award, which focuses on the Caribbean, is now cosponsored by the Caribbean Tourism Organization, which, she contends, allows it to be more "codified," have more formal criteria, and make better use of judges "on the ground."[62] The eligible applicants pool has also been narrowed to only those nominated by the ministries of tourism in their respective countries.

In 2001, *Smithsonian Magazine*, having earlier ended its awards program with ASTA, announced a new partnership with the United States Tour Operators Association (USTOA) and the Travelers Conservation Fund to give an annual conservation award to an outstanding project or person in the travel and tourism industry. The project has gotten off to a promising start with a solid list of well-qualified and independent-minded board members drawn from tour companies, a grassroots NGO, the World Bank, and business associations. Yet the evaluation process has not been modified from the ASTA format of a 175-word essay plus references.[63]

The voluntary NGO programs, governmental regulations, and industry initiatives described above represent a sampling of efforts begun over the last decade to improve environmental and social practices within the tourism and travel industry. These efforts parallel and complement the scores of environmentally and socially responsible certification programs that have begun during this same period. However, ecolabels, codes of conduct, awards, ecotourism societies, and EIAs and various other national legislation and international covenants are not substitutes for certification programs. Rather, certification should be viewed as an important instrument in the mix that, along with other tools, rules, and regulations, seeks to reshape tourism toward sustainable principles and practices. There are, however, several reasons why certification is an essential tool for setting standards and reforming the practices of the tourism and travel industry.

Certification: A Tool for Our Time

Certification is a tool uniquely suited to our current age. The prevailing notion for much of the twentieth century was that social, economic, and environmental problems should and could be solved by government intervention. However, over the last several decades, the role of the state has been rolled back, as corporations have moved outside national boundaries, developing new institutions for global corporate governance, including the World Trade Organization, North American Free Trade Alliance (NAFTA), and the Asia Pacific Economic Cooperation (APIC), and pushing a new ideology, known as the Washington Consensus, that trumpets free trade, privatization, deregulation, and economic globalization. Under the terms of the World Trade Organization, for instance, countries cannot exclude imports or foreign investment for environmental, labor, economic, or other reasons (see chapter 3).

In response, a dynamic global justice movement has taken to the streets in Seattle, Washington, D.C, Prague, Davos, Quebec City, Genoa, Ottawa, Porto Alegre, and elsewhere to protest the World Trade Organization, World Bank, and other institutions dominated by the wealthiest countries and corporations. The 1990s saw the rise of socially and environmentally responsible labeling and certification initiatives in many of the major industries, including chemicals, timber, coffee, bananas, mining, and transportation; these efforts can provide some lessons for certification programs within the travel and tourism industry. Tourism certification campaigns were spurred by increasing consumer awareness and expressions of consumer preference for socially and environmentally responsible products. As academics Gary Gereffi, Ronie Garcia-Johnson, and Erika Sasser argued, "While certification will never replace the state, it is quickly becoming a powerful tool for promoting worker [host country, and local community] rights and protecting the environment in an era of free trade." These authors correctly conclude that as "voluntary governance mechanisms," certification programs are "transforming traditional power relationships in the global arena."[64]

Certification programs provide an effective tool because, unlike many of the other initiatives described above, they can meet and balance the needs and interests of a variety of stakeholders. While, for instance, EIAs and other types of government regulation typically involve discussions between a developer and a government or a financial lending agency, certification schemes often involve—or at least purport to involve—a wider spectrum of stakeholders. Successful certification programs, particularly (as discussed below) those for sustainable and ecotourism, in contrast to those for the conventional tourism market, bring together and balance a mix of stakeholder interests, some complementary and some conflicting. These may include:

1) *Environmentalists*, park managers, and others concerned about the negative ecological impacts of traditional tourism, who view certification

as a way of raising the bar and holding tourism enterprises to standards that minimize environmental impact and help protect the long-term health of the ecosystem.

2) *The tourism industry*, which sees voluntary certification programs and ecolabels as a way to help companies evaluate their practices in relation to established standards, receive technical advice, and develop targets for improvement, as well as to gain market distinction, win consumer recognition, and increase business. In addition, self-audits or industry-run certification programs can be seen, particularly by some of the bigger players in the tourism industry, as a way to stave off further government regulation or independent, third party audit programs. Others view it as a way to undertake some cost-saving reforms that can also be marketed as green innovations.

3) *Host countries*, that look to certification as a way to raise their international image and sell tourism to the global market, as well as a way to measure compliance with government standards and encourage businesses to improve their environmental, sociocultural, and economic practices.

4) *Host communities* located near tourist attractions or facilities, that see certification as a way of measuring and improving the environmental and sociocultural impacts of the project. Certification can also help to assess financial benefits to both the country and the local community by, for instance, requiring local ownership or local partners, local hiring of staff, and use of locally made products. Therefore, it can be a tool to gain increased local equity and to help communities level the playing field in negotiations with investors, developers, and managers of tourism facilities.

5) *Consumers*, who view certification programs and ecolabels as a way to identify and select products and services that demonstrate their commitment to protecting the environment and respecting the social, cultural, economic, and political concerns of residents in host countries and near tourist destinations.

6) *International funding agencies*, that view certification as a tool to help ensure higher quality projects and compliance with existing regulations. Certified projects are more likely to win international recognition and encounter less trouble with both government regulators and host communities.

How these frequently conflicting stakeholder interests are mixed helps to determine the character and rigor of a particular certification program. As Gereffi, Garcia-Johnson, and Sasser noted, "Linking together diverse and often antagonistic actors from the local, national, and international levels, certification institutions have arisen to govern firm behavior in a global space that has eluded the control of states and international institutions." As the three authors conclude, "The contrast between industry-led certification and the NGO variety is stark."[65]

In analyzing the nature of different certification programs within the travel and tourism industry, two broad types of categories can be discerned. The first is based on methodology—process versus performance. The second is based on the three main divisions within the tourism industry—conventional tourism, sustainable tourism, and ecotourism.

Methodology: Process vs. Performance

Broadly stated, what are characterized as green tourism certification programs can be divided into two methodologies: (1) process-based using environmental management systems, or (2) performance-based using environmental and usually sociocultural and economic criteria or benchmarks. Increasingly, certification programs include a mix of both process and performance standards. In general, these two methodologies are implemented in similar ways: both can involve first, second, or third party audits and both award logos for those that achieve certification. However, understanding the process vs. performance distinction is vital to any analysis of the integrity of certification programs within tourism and travel, as well as those in other industries. As a major report commissioned by World Wildlife Fund in England and done by the consulting group Synergy, suggested, "For the credibility and effectiveness of tourism certification schemes, both consumers and the travel and tourism industry must understand and recognize this process-performance distinction."[66]

Process-based Programs

The process-based certification programs are all variations of environmental management systems (EMS). There are various types of EMS—ISO 14001, ISO 14001 Plus, Eco-Management and Audit System (EMAS), life cycle assessment, The Natural Step—as well as regional and national variations of the standards. The most widely known in certification programs is ISO 14001, the standard in the ISO 14000 family that contains the specifications for the EMS against which a business, regardless of its size, product, service, or sector, is certified. ISO 14001 can be used by tourism companies or any other type of business and can be applied corporate-wide, at a particular site, or to one particular part of a firm's operations. The exact scope of ISO 14001 is up to the discretion of the company.

Certification to ISO 14001 means that a business's environmental management system conforms to specifications as verified by an audit process.

ISO does not do auditing; it simply facilitates the development of EMS standards. Businesses often elect to use an outside firm because they believe that an EMS audit confirmed by a qualified, neutral, third party will be more credible. In addition, certification to ISO standards is based on having an acceptable process for developing and revising the EMS; it is not based on implementation of the EMS. Once a company is certified and registered to an ISO standard, it receives a certification that is valid for a maximum of three years.

A number of individual hotels and hotel chains (such as the Spanish chain Sol Meliá Hotel) have certification programs according to ISO 14001. Several of the largest international certification programs including Green Globe and several programs in Europe (Green Flag for Green Hotels, ECOTUR in Spain, The Nordic Swan, and Green Key in Denmark) are based on or have incorporated ISO 14001 or other EMS standards. The number of hotels certified to ISO 14001 standards is, however, small: only sixteen hotels in 1998 (including thirteen in Germany, Portugal, and Sweden and three in Hong Kong and Mauritius) and sixty-six hotels and restaurants in 2000.[67]

Proponents of EMS contend that it has the advantage of being versatile and applicable across industries and with different industry sectors. Critics argue that this is a drawback because it is too broad to accurately measure the environmental impacts of different businesses and industries. There are other problems as well. One is its high cost. According to one study, ISO 14001 certification, not including compliance, runs between $500 and $15,000, making it prohibitively expensive for all but the largest hotels.[68] Certification expert Robert Toth says the real out-of-pocket cost, if travel, staff training, and consultation is included, is typically between $20,000 and $40,000 for a medium-size company.[69] In addition, the ISO process is complicated and heavily engineering-oriented, it contains no social or economic standards, and the audit for ISO 14001 certification produces an internal document intended for senior management that cannot be compared with other similar business.

Because ISO 14001 allows a company to draw up its own environmental policy against which its management system is designed, the firm may become certified based on a weak or narrowly defined policy. There is no requirement under ISO 14001 for a company to exceed existing laws should these regulations be deficient. Further, because it measures process, not performance, what a business does is not important, only how it does it. "Following this logic," noted authors Krut and Gleckman, "a company making weapons for biological warfare can be certified to ISO 14001."[70] It is possible, as well, for a company to meet ISO requirements and gain certification, while at the same time it is in litigation and in conflict with environmentalists and local communities.[71]

In addition, ISO and other EMS standards do not fully meet consumer needs because they focus on what are known as "gray" environmental characteristics—consumption of water and energy and waste disposal, for example—while surveys show that tourists are more interested in "green" environmental aspects in the surrounding areas, such as beautiful and pristine surroundings, clean and healthy air and water, and peace and quiet (see chapter 7). To be marketable, certification programs and ecolabels must evaluate and satisfy consumers' broader green concerns.[72]

Today within the field of tourism certification, debate continues around ISO 14001, with efforts on some fronts to have it adopted as the standard both in Europe and worldwide. ISO and other forms of process-based certification have the advantage that they fit well with how large companies are organized, can operate globally, and can be used across tourism sectors. However, as detailed in box 1.2, there are a number of serious drawbacks to the ISO-type management system.

In sum, ISO 14001 and other process-based management systems are insufficient, by themselves, to generate sustainable tourism practices. As the Synergy study concluded, effective certification within the travel and tourism industry has been hampered because many of the older and larger programs have been wholly or largely process-based and therefore award certification to companies when they set up an environmental management system, rather than when certain standards are met.[73] EMS-based programs therefore cannot guarantee that companies are performing in environmentally and socially responsible ways. There is a growing aware-

---

Box 1.2. Drawbacks to Process-based Certification Programs

- They are insufficient to guarantee sustainable practices;
- They are less applicable to small business;
- The environmental aspects they address may ignore those that are important to host communities, to conservation, and to tourists;
- They can permit a company to earn a logo for setting up a management system, even though its performance record may be less sustainable than that of other companies;
- Their path to implementation and certification is not self-evident, resulting in additional expenses to hire consultants and trainers;
- Companies certified cannot be compared to one another because there are no common standards, so they are less useful to consumers.

ness about the shortcomings of this methodology and agreement that to be credible certification programs must include performance-based standards.

Performance-based Programs

Performance-based programs are based on a set of externally determined environmental and usually sociocultural and economic criteria or benchmarks. Although most authors in this book delineate only a process and performance division in certification methodologies, Toth, in chapter 2, subdivides performance standards into two categories, performance and prescriptive. This is a useful refinement, but it does not alter the broad distinction accepted by other analysts between process and performance methodologies.[74]

While process-based programs set up a system for monitoring and improving performance, performance-based methodology states the goals or targets that must be achieved to receive certification and use of a logo. These same performance criteria are then used to measure all companies or products seeking certification under that particular program. Blue Flag (see chapter 7), for instance, requires that any beach it certifies comply with a list of essential criteria, including that it meet or surpass official plans and legislation, have no discharge affecting the beach, and provide microbiological monitoring. Most programs, including Blue Flag, contract an independent auditor to inspect businesses or products to determine if the criteria are met. Following this audit, the applicant is awarded a logo that may have several different levels to indicate current status and to encourage improvement in fulfilling more or higher criteria.

Costa Rica's Certification for Sustainable Tourism (CST) is among those programs that have several levels and award logos based on the score an applicant obtains (see chapter 4). The CST certification questionnaire for hotels contains 152 questions that applicants, usually the hotel's owner, must answer. These questions are divided into four different areas: 1) physical and biological environment, 2) infrastructure and services, 3) external clients, and 4) socioeconomic environment. Each answer, in turn, is weighted in importance from one to three, with three the most important. For instance, one question under the socioeconomic environment asks if the hotel has a private reserve. If it does, the applicant gets two points. The total points received in each category are then calculated, translated into a percentage, and then given a rating, based on a scale of zero to five. Costa Rican officials say this graded system, like the traditional star rating used by AAA, Mobil, and Michelin, helps to promote improvement.

Performance-based certification programs are easier to implement because they do not require setting up complex and costly management systems. They are therefore more attractive to small- and medium-size enterprises. In addition, although EMS programs are typically devised by management and outside consultants, the most effective performance-based programs are created and implemented by a range of stakeholders (including representatives from industry, government, NGOs, host communities, and, often, academies) and can solicit and integrate tourist opinions. This type of certification program has proved most useful on a national or subnational basis in which the goal is to judge and compare businesses within a particular geographic area.

Performance-based programs do, however, present some challenges, particularly because many standards and criteria are qualitative, subjective, and imprecise and therefore difficult to measure. Many sustainability targets are undefined. There is no agreed upon methodology for measuring, for instance, carrying capacity or weighing the benefits and negative impacts for host communities. Despite these difficulties, certification programs must strive to cover these and other areas that fall broadly under the sustainability umbrella. As the Synergy report stated, "Only where universal *performance* levels and targets that tackle sustainability (environmental, social and economic) are specified within and by a standard, and where criteria making their attainment a prerequisite are present, can something akin to sustainability be promised by certification."[75] There are, as box 1.3 summarizes, numerous advantages of certification programs that use a performance-based methodology.

Increasingly, however, many of the newer or revamped programs represent a hybrid of process-based environmental management systems and per-

---

Box 1.3. Advantages of Performance-based Certification Programs

- They measure achievement, not intent, and therefore can promote sustainable development;
- They are less expensive and more applicable to small and medium businesses;
- They can include checklists that are easily intelligible to both businesses and consumers;
- They allow comparison among businesses or products;
- They typically involve a range of stakeholders;
- They better meet consumer demand because they can measure performance inside and outside the business and include social, cultural, and economic as well as environmental criteria;
- Programs that offer different levels encourage competition and continual improvement.

formance standards, benchmarks, or requirements. The Nordic Ecolabels for Hotels, for instance, combines both performance benchmarks with a process (management system) approach. The performance measures include that toilets use no more than six liters of water per flush, that rainwater is collected and used, and that all valves are economy flow. The environmental management criteria include that a plan of action for water-saving measures be drawn up, that appropriate staff should be trained once a year on how and why water should be saved, and that water consumption be controlled and measured twelve times per year. (The Nordic Ecolabels, however, is limited in scope to only environmental questions.) The Synergy study concluded that this combined approach is useful because it "encourages businesses to establish comprehensive environmental management systems that deliver systematic and continuous improvements, include performance targets and also encourage businesses to invest in technologies that deliver the greatest economic and environmental benefits within a specific region."[76] This type of hybrid system is certain to be the preferred methodology in the future.

Three Types of Certification Programs: Conventional, Sustainable, and Ecotourism

As outlined above, a central division among tourism certification programs is between two distinct methodologies: (1) environmental management systems based on process, and (2) externally determined criteria or standards based on performance (and prescriptions). Although this process-performance distinction is important, certification programs can be categorized with a wider lens than methodology. In terms of developing public policy, model programs, and international standards, as well as tourism accreditation systems, it is helpful to distinguish three fundamental types of certification programs: those covering the conventional (sometimes called mass) tourism, sustainable tourism, and ecotourism markets.

Conventional Tourism Certification

Conventional tourism certification programs cover companies within the mass or traditional tourism market, that is, the large sectors of the tourism industry that have been built without following ecotourism principles and practices. They generally include airlines, car-rental agencies, hotel chains, and often package tours such as cruises, Cancun- or Caribbean-type beach resorts, and other high-volume destinations that are typically marketed by travel agents. Although traditionally, certification programs within the mass or conventional tourism sector focused on quality, health, and safety, these newer green programs focus on monitoring and improving environmental efficiency within the business by setting up management systems. They involve an emphasis on adopting environmentally friendly, usually cost-saving, procedures and renovations. Certification and a logo are awarded for setting up the process, not for achieving certain standards or benchmarks. Some allow certification at a corporate level (a hotel chain or tour operator) or for a whole destination rather than for each site-specific individual unit or product. Green Globe (until at least its most recent transformations) and others based on ISO 14001 (or its derivatives) are the best known of the conventional tourism certification programs.

One example of such a program is the Committed to Green certification program developed in 1997 by the European Golf Association Ecology Union. Golf courses are notorious for their enormous consumption of water, liberal use of pesticides, preference for nonnative species of grass, bulldozing of forests, and filling of estuaries and wetlands, all in quest of the perfect fairway. As the popularity of golf has soared—a new course is constructed in Thailand every ten days and 350 new courses are built in the United States each year—so have public concerns about their environmental impacts. The golf industry has been relatively responsive to these public concerns. Currently, about 15 percent of U.S. golf courses participate in programs to monitor their environmental impact. Like the Audubon Cooperative Sanctuary Program in the United States, the Committed to Green program in England is based on a three-step program for developing and implementing an EMS aimed at setting up systems for reclaiming and recycling water, planting native grasses, creating buffer zones, and using integrated pest management. Certification is awarded once this EMS is in place.[77]

These golf course certification schemes, like most others for the conventional tourism market, do not include criteria to adequately measure the socioeconomic impacts of the tourism business, either internally or on the surrounding environment and community. Although these programs focus on the physical plant or the business, they may include sections on both staff training and community outreach. However, these "social" concerns concentrate on teaching the staff to implement the environmental management system; the community outreach may be little more than donations of surplus items, minimal efforts that are often advertised as best practices.

In essence, this type of certification program for the conventional market entails taking useful, but minimal, "ecotourism lite" measures that fall far short of sound practices and principles for sustainable development. Although it is important that certification programs seek to cover the major sectors of the tourism industry, the reality is that many of these sectors—cruise ships, beach resorts, airlines, golf courses, city hotels, car rentals—can, once they are in operation, only be "greened" so much. As TIES President Epler Wood likes to describe it, much of the existing mainstream tourism industry suffers from "hardening of the arteries," making difficult compliance with sound ecotourism principles or rigorous, broad-spectrum, performance-based certification programs.

Rather than having wide stakeholder involvement, often these conventional tourism certification programs are developed and financed by the industry associations. They are implemented in-house by management, and the details of the EMS are kept confidential and viewed as proprietary information, part of the company's business plan. Even though third-party auditors may be used, typically all that is public is the award or logo itself, not the details of the company's compliance with the certification criteria. (In contrast, for instance, the results of the CST surveys in Costa Rica are posted on a public Web site.) In fact, many of these programs are viewed by management as sort of preemptive strikes aimed at getting industry off the block before government, NGOs, or local communities have created broader and more rigorous ecolabeling or certification programs. In contrast, the next two categories of certification programs do contain sufficient criteria to at least hold out the possibility that the businesses they certify are following sound environmental and social practices. As one recent study argued, "Progress towards sustainable tourism requires certification programmes to embrace more explicitly the concept of sustainable development (especially some of the equity aspects of this term) and promote it to their members."[78] Further, certification programs may work better in terms of promoting sustainable development if they differentiate between the broader category of sustainable tourism and a more specific category for ecotourism, either through different levels within the same program or through separate programs.

Sustainable Tourism Certification

This type of program measures a range of environmental and at least some sociocultural and economic equity issues both internally (as pertaining directly to the business, service, or product) and externally (as pertaining to the surrounding community and physical environment). It involves consultation with a variety of stakeholders and uses primarily a performance-based system, third-party auditors, and a multifaceted questionnaire for management and, occasionally, staff and clients, that is, tourists. It may also include creating or implementing a management system to help establish better and more efficient environmental procedures within the business. Most often, sustainable tourism certification involves individual or site-specific businesses, such as hotels and lodges. The basic aim or motto of this type of program can be characterized as harm reduction.

Sustainable tourism certification programs can also cover distinct geographic areas or particular sectors of the industry, and their standards are tailored to fit these conditions. A number of the programs analyzed in this book, including Costa Rica's Certification for Sustainable Tourism (CST), fall most comfortably into this category. But the fit is not always perfect. Although CST has certified a range of sizes and qualities of Costa Rican hotels and lodges and has been adopted, in principle, as the model for certification in the rest of Central America, Amos Bien, who helped draw it up, admitted that the CST survey as originally formulated "doesn't work well for small and micro-businesses"[79] like his own Rara Avis. Bien says CST requires ISO-like management systems for the physical plant and has other design features more suitable to larger hotels. In addition, the CST survey gives only minimal attention to lodges that are involved in efforts to prevent logging, mining, poaching, and other environmentally destructive activities—all important environmental issues in Costa Rica (see chapter 4).[80]

Another interesting program, ECOTEL, which is not discussed in detail in the following chapters, is a hybrid between a conventional and a sustainable tourism certification program. Like Green Globe, ECOTEL was founded in 1994 as a for-profit, industry-affiliated, global certification program catering mainly to luxury hotels and chains scattered around the world. As is typical of conventional tourism certification programs, its criteria are considered proprietary and confidential and focus on measuring internal environmental standards. It is designed to encourage and assess environmentally responsible practices; its criteria do not include sociocultural or economic equity issues. But here ECOTEL's similarities with conventional tourism certification end. ECOTEL's Christopher Balfe spoke scathingly of EMS programs, especially ISO 14001. "We think EMS is a completely backward movement for environmental protection and education in the hotel industry, and ISO 14001 is the major culprit," Balfe said. He is particularly critical of Green Globe for "trying to be everything" through its various makeovers.[81]

ECOTEL has, instead, a set of stringent performance-based standards, a three-level mathematical scoring system, and five different categories of logos: environmental commitment, employee education, solid waste management, energy management, and water conservation and preservation. Hotels must apply for certification in at least two of these five categories and must pass all of the primary criteria and at least half of the secondary criteria. In addition, the hotel, together with ECOTEL, designs a set of tertiary or bonus criteria, which includes programs and environmental efforts above and beyond those in the first and second categories. According to the ECOTEL application, "This allows hoteliers to custom design their environmental program to fit their style of hospitality, all within the boundaries created by the ECOTEL Criteria."[82] ECOTEL-approved auditors carry out unannounced, on-site inspections every two years, which on occasion involve experts from environmental NGOS. ECOTEL has withdrawn certification and use of its logo from a number of hotels that have failed to comply or to pay for renewal.

Managed by a hospitality industry association, HVS Eco Services, ECOTEL was designed by experts from the U.S. Environmental Protection Agency and the Rocky Mountain Institute, an environmental think tank in Colorado.[83] Most of the hotels it has certified, such as a number of Hilton Hotels in Japan or The Benjamin in New York, are located in cities and could fall within the conventional tourism market. Balfe argues that ECOTEL is unique because it centers on "education and training for the staff. We're much more than not changing sheets and towels every day. We want to motivate and build teams of super-employees [known as Green Teams] and give them a program that sets higher standards than the guys across the street. And we want no guest to leave one of our hotels without knowing that it is ECOTEL-certified."[84]

Although ECOTEL has helped to pioneer a rigorous environmental certification program that specifically targets urban hotels and hotel chains, it does have limitations and challenges. One is that it is expensive, especially for smaller, less high-end hotels. The cost of certification and inspection ranges from $7,500 to $25,000 per hotel for two years. Second, ECOTEL has certified few hotels: only thirty-six by December 2001, although five hundred hotels had been inspected and some 1,200 had applied. The reasons are several: many hotels make the minimal up-front payment and receive ECOTEL assistance in creating Green Teams and doing self-evaluations of the various criteria. For some clients, this is more valuable than actually going through the audit and receiving an ECOTEL logo. In addition, ECOTEL itself is reluctant to actually conduct a surprise audit until they feel confident the hotel will pass. A third problem is that ECO-TEL has not established itself as a profitable, or even self-supporting, stand-alone operation. Rather, as part of HVS International, ECOTEL is subject, Balfe said, to wider corporate "business and political decisions" that make it difficult to lean on hotels to either follow through with certification or pay the full amount for certification.[85] Fourth, as mentioned above, ECO-TEL's criteria are almost exclusively focused on environmental issues within the hotel, although staff motivation and satisfaction is central to the program. But it does not adequately address the socioeconomic and cultural impacts of hotels on the surrounding community, even though these are less profound or apparent in large cities in developed countries than in rural areas or developing countries.

Ecotourism Certification

This third category of certification programs covers those businesses, services, and products that describe themselves (through their brochures, Web sites, etc.) as involved in ecotourism. They are invariably located in or near natural areas and involved in the protection of pristine and fragile ecosystems. Ecotourism certification includes individual or site-specific businesses, services, and products; involves a variety of stakeholders; and has standards tailored to the conditions of a particular country, state, or region.

Simple green standards for the mainstream or conventional tourism sector reduce energy consumption and waste. Ecotourism standards go beyond questions of ecoefficiency (i.e., those that are both cost-saving and environmentally better) and are more responsive to national and local stakeholder concerns. They look beyond the tourism entity itself and ask how ecotourism companies can contribute to conservation of protected areas and what mechanisms are in place to ensure that benefits reach local people. Because of the environmental and/or cultural sensitivity of these areas, the underlying goal of ecotourism certification programs is more than harm reduction; it is to strive to have the business improve or at least have near-zero impact on the area in which it is located.

Although ecotourism certification considers a company's internal and external impacts as equally important, in some instances, its role in the community and in conservation may be given even more weight than its internal business operations. For instance, although the first two types of certification make no distinction between locally owned and foreign-owned businesses, an ecotourism certification program would likely weigh local ownership as important because ecotourism strives to promote sustainable development partly through economic empowerment.

In a country like Costa Rica, whose tourism image is very clearly that of ecotourism, it would seem important to evaluate separately (either within the same program or in parallel programs) those businesses that claim to be involved in ecotourism. Costa Rica's original ecolabeling program, the Sustainable Tourism Rating, which is run by the *New Key* guidebook, is among the oldest ecotourism certification programs (see chapter 4). Today, the NEAP program in Australia, with its three-tiered division, is the best known example of an ecotourism certification program. Two of its three levels distinguish and rate those enterprises involved in ecotourism; the third category rates nature tourism enterprises or those more properly involved in sustainable tourism (see chapter 5).

In evaluating and comparing these three broad types of conventional, sustainable, and ecotourism certification programs, it is important to both review the methodology each uses and to assess what each does to satisfy the needs of the principle stakeholders: industry, consumers, NGOs, the host country, and local communities. The responses serve to highlight the differences among these types of certification programs:

- Conventional tourism certification programs generally satisfy the needs of business by providing cost-saving changes, technical assistance, and continuous improvement through creation of environmental management systems. Often, they also offer market distinction and advertising. But they amount to ecotourism lite, providing, through the tool of EMS, minimal standards and little transparency on what is behind the certification. They do not take into account the needs of host governments (particularly in relatively underdeveloped countries), local communities, and NGOs for cultural sensitivity, long-term economic equity, and environmental protection beyond the business's immediate footprint. They therefore fail to offer a framework that ensures sustainable long-term development.
- Sustainable tourism programs do better in satisfying, although not completely, the needs of various stakeholders—businesses, consumers, host governments, NGOs, and communities. They generally have a mix of both performance standards, which permit comparisons across businesses, and some type of management system to help implement the certification program. The downsides are that such programs do not adequately distinguish those businesses operating in or near natural areas, may be relatively expensive for small- and medium-size businesses, may not have adequate funding or sufficient marketing to consumers, and may still marginalize the needs of local communities and NGOs.
- Ecotourism certification programs tend to favor small and medium businesses, to be most respectful of the needs of local communities and conservation, and to help the public distinguish businesses, geographical areas, and even whole countries committed to the principles and practices of ecotourism. These programs often are spearheaded by NGOS. But they frequently suffer from insufficient funding for audits and promotion, thereby not adequately meeting the needs of either the businesses they certify, the host governments, or the ecotourism public.

Of the three types of certification program, sustainable tourism seems to offer the best option in terms of developing global standards and a model program that promotes socially and environmentally responsible practices. That was the conclusion of the first international conference on certification programs held at Mohonk Mountain House in November 2000. The forty-five participants came from twenty countries and some dozen certification programs. At the end of the three-day meeting, they reached unanimous agreement on the framework and universal components for creating a two-tiered program for sustainable tourism and ecotourism certification (see appendix). Under the so-called Mohonk Agreement, the criteria for sustainable tourism certification are broad enough to encompass various sizes of businesses and types of tourism, including niche markets such as nature, historic, and cultural. At the same time, it recognizes that this framework will need to be tailored to fit the realities of particular parts of the world. Further, it recognizes that there is need for a specific set of criteria for fragile and pristine areas and that these constitute a unique type of program for ecotourism certification.[86]

Vexing Issues and Areas of Debate

The following chapters will help to highlight a number of areas of intense discussion among certification advocates and critics. There are, in fact, a half dozen or so central concerns that confront most certification programs in the tourism industry. None have easy answers and all are currently hot topics at international forums, in publications, and on the Internet. These vexing issues, which are addressed at more length in the concluding chapter, are:

- *North-South Divide*: A central issue that has been brought into sharp relief by organizations and activists located in the global South or working with indigenous communities is whether certification is being used to further enfranchise the most powerful tourism companies rather than to help level the playing field by bolstering locally owned companies and protecting the rights and resources of local and indigenous communities. The challenge is how to create credible and rigorous certification programs that do not simply set environmental, labor, and other standards so high that they favor the wealthy and foreign-owned businesses and exacerbate rather than help alleviate the economic divide within and across countries.
- *Consumer Demand*: The success of certification programs hinges on consumer buy-in. However, there is debate and somewhat conflicting evidence over how strong the public demand is for environmentally and socially responsible tourism businesses and products and whether consumers will choose certified products, especially if they are more expensive. In addition, there is discussion, drawing on lessons learned from other certification programs, over the role of NGOs in building consumer demand.
- *Consumer Awareness and Confusion*: Surveys show that, at present, the traveling public is both unaware of many programs and confused by the proliferation of schemes, particularly in Europe. A central challenge is how to build consumer awareness and decrease confusion through merg-

ing and rationalizing existing programs, while creating new ones that
conform to general principals and standards.

- *Whom to Certify*: Most certification programs are for accommodations,
  and expansion into other tourism sectors has often proven more difficult.
  There is considerable debate over what sectors are most important,
  whether certification programs should target the biggest players, such as
  airlines and cruise ships, or whether they should concentrate on those
  operating in the most fragile ecosystems, targeting, for instance, naturalist tour guides and operators and national parks and other protected
  areas. There is also debate over whether an entire destination, a hotel
  chain, or even a tour company can be certified or if each part must be
  certified separately.
- *Marketing*: All certification programs must be marketed in two directions:
  to the travel industry to enroll businesses to be certified and to the traveling public to build patrons who use the certified products. Both efforts
  are costly and time-consuming, but some lessons have been learned
  about using the Internet, guidebooks and magazines, government
  tourism departments, and major environmental and other NGOs to promote certification programs. However, there is no magic bullet, and all
  certification programs realize that successful marketing will be a central
  factor in whether they succeed or fail.
- *Financial Viability*: Many experts contend that certification programs
  should be administered by reputable, independent, not-for-profit organizations. Yet how to make these programs financially self-supporting
  is one of the most difficult challenges. As Robert Toth puts it, "When
  you talk about cost and financing, that's where the rubber hits the road."
  Part of the answer is to build cost-effective programs that do not rely on
  high-priced, international consultants and assessors and utilize universities and other local resources instead. There is considerable debate over
  whether to accept government and industry funding and how to build
  in mechanisms that can maintain the independence and integrity of such
  programs.
- *Private vs. Government Sector*: Industry-run programs have been widely
  criticized for lacking vigorous standards and credibility with other
  stakeholders. To date, all tourism certification programs are voluntary,
  in part because of the weakening role of government over the last several decades. Yet in a number of places—Costa Rica, Australia, South
  Africa, and the European Union—governments are helping to finance,
  staff, and market certification programs. Although there is a growing
  consensus that certification programs should not be either wholly private sector or government-operated, there is ongoing debate over the
  best mix.

Notes

1. Emma Stewart correspondence with Jean-Frédéric Douroux, Relations Exterieures, *Michelin Editions des Voyages*, July 12, 2001.
2. "It's surprising how many people write to us when they have a problem with a hotel," says Elizabeth Siegal of Michelin Travel Publications, "because they think we can mediate." Siegal interview by Emma Stewart , Michelin Travel Publications, South Carolina, July 27, 2001.
3. Correspondence with Douroux, July 12, 2001.
4. Siegal interview.
5. Emma Stewart correspondence with Janie Graziani, manager, public relations, AAA National Office, July 21, 2001.
6. Ibid.
7. Janie Graziani interview; American Hotel & Lodging Association, Good Earthkeeping Program with Project Planet, www.ahma.com/ahma/proj_planet/ (August 2001).
8. Travel Industry of America (TIA), "Current Travel Indicators," http://www.tia.org (August 2001).
9. Mobile Travel Guide, Web site: http://www.exxonmobiletravel.com; Martha Honey and Abigail Rome, *Protecting Paradise: Certification Programs for Sustainable Tourism and Ecotourism* (Washington, D.C.: Institute for Policy Studies, October 2001), available on Institute for Policy Study Web site: http://www.ips-dc.org/ecotourism/protectingparadise/index.html; Tourism Industry Association New Zealand, Web site: http://www.tianz.org.nz; Qualmark, Web site: http://www.qualmark.co.nz/ (September 2001).
10. Relais & Chateaux Web site: http://www.relaischateaux.com/site/fr/home; Small Luxury Hotels of the World Web site: http://www.slh.com/media (November 2001).
11. Mafisa Research and Planning, "Sustainable Ecotourism: Proposition for a Global Programme to Brand and Certify Ethical and Responsible Nature-Tourism Enterprises," Johannesburg, January 2001. This was a draft feasibility study prepared for National Geographic Society, Washington, D.C. According to Mafisa, a recent survey of SLH members in South Africa suggested fatigue and resentment with additional fees for ongoing marketing and advertising campaigns.
12. Alistair M. Morrison, Sheauhsing Hsieh, and Chia-Yu Wang, "Certification in the Travel and Tourism Industry: The North American Experience," *The Journal of Tourism Studies*, 3, no. 2, (December 1992), 32–33.
13. Ibid., p. 36.
14. Ibid., p. 38.
15. World Travel and Tourism Council's, "Environmental Guidelines" (Oxford: WTTC, 1997); Martha Honey, *Ecotourism and Sustainable Development: Who Owns Paradise?* (Washington, D.C.: Island Press, 1999), 32–33.
16. TIA, "Travel Industry Association of America" (Washington, D.C.: TIA, n.d.); U.S. Travel Data Center, *Discover America: Tourism and the Environment: A Guide to Challenges and Opportunities for Travel Industry Businesses* (Washington, D.C.: TIA, 1992).
17. Leslie Wildesen, "The Natural Step to Sustainable Environmental Excellence:

EIA, EMS and TNS," presentation at International Association for Impact Assessment Conference, Hong Kong, June, 2000; Honey and Rome, *Protecting Paradise*, 23–25.

18. Convention on International Civil Aviation (1944) and International Civil Aviation Organization (1995), as cited in "Legislation, British Airways Community and Environment," http://www.britishairways.com, July 2001.

19. British Airways, "British Airways Emissions from Aircraft Model (BEAM)" and "Community and Environment," http://www.britishairways.com/responsibility/ (July 2001).

20. British Airways, "Tourism for Tomorrow," Web site: http://www.britishairways.com/tourism/index.shtml. Martha Honey's visit to Turtle Island in December 2000 and correspondence and conversations with Andrew Fairley, June–September 2001.

21. "Planet Princess' Cruises with an Environmental Plan," *ASTA Environment Committee News*, 3, no. 1 (November 1995).

22. Honey, *Ecotourism and Sustainable Development*, 39–41.

23. Ibid., Polly Pattullo, *Last Resorts: The Cost of Tourism in the Caribbean* (Kingston, Jamaica: Ian Randle Publishers, 1996), 111, 156–175.

24. United States General Accounting Office, GAO/RCED-00-48, *Marine Pollution: Progress Made to Reduce Marine Pollution by Cruise Ships, but Important Issues Remain* (Washington, D.C.: Government Printing Office, February 2000).

25. Earth Island Institute, Bluewater Network, "Cruise Ship Campaign Activities," http://www.earthisland.org/bw/cruiseships.shtml (June 2001).

26. Bill McAllister, "Cruise Rules 'Mesh Nicely'; Industry also invests in anti-pollution tools," *Juneau Empire* (June 2001).

27. Russell Nansen, "Hungry? Out of Work? Eat a Cruise Ship!" *Contours*, 7, no. 10 (June 1997), 4.

28. Environmental News Network (ENN), "Cruise Lines Raise the Shipshape Stakes," http://www.enn.com (June 19, 2001).

29. Ibid.

30. Martha Honey's correspondence with Coralie Breen, president and CEO, Oceans Blue, December 2001; http://www.oceansblue.org/bluetourism/chartacourse/cruiseship.html (December 2001).

31. Elaine Yetzer, "Companies offer products that conserve water, labor," *News & Trends*, Hotel and Motel Management (H&MM), http://www.hmmonline.com (July 2001).

32. IHEI, which represents over 8,000 hotels worldwide, is a program of The Prince of Wales Business Leaders Forum in England. IHEI, "International Hotels Environment Initiative," http://www.ihei.org (July 2001).

33. Ibid.

34. "Environmental Labels and Certification Schemes," *Green Hotelier*, Issue 25 & 26, May 2002, 12–19; Correspondence with editor Claire Baker, January–April, 2002.

35. American Hotel & Motel Association, International Hotel Association, United Nations Environment Program, *Environmental Action Pack: Practical Steps to Benefit Your Business and the Environment*, UNEP Industry and Environment Technical

Report No. 31, North Americas version (Washington, D.C.: American Hotel & Motel Association, 1996).

36. International Hotels Environment Initiative, http://www.ihei.com.

37. Consultancy and Research for Environmental Management (CREM), "Best Environmental Practices," chapter 5, *Feasibility and Market Study for a European Eco-label for Tourism Accommodations (FEMATOUR)*, draft version of a study commissioned by the European Commissions (Amsterdam: CREM and CH2MHILL, August 2000, no page numbers); In addition, Todd Comen, professor of tourism, Johnson State College, Vermont, provided information on hotel cost-savings. Personal correspondence, 2001–March 2002.

38. FEMATOUR, 2000.

39. Frederic Dimanche, "Greening Traditional Hotels," *Tour & Travel News*, (August 29, 1994), G29; Kirk Iwanowski, *Taking the Black and Blue Out of Being Green: Developing Hotel Environmental Programs* (Mineola, New York: HVS Eco Services, October 1994).

40. "Keep Your Towels—And Help Save the World!" *News From British Airways*, (May 22, 1996); http://www.british-airways.com/inside/comm/tourism/tourism.shtml+&hl=en.

41. Honey, *Ecotourism and Sustainable Development*, 49–50.

42. Thomas Keesling, former president of ASTA and former chair of the ASTA Environment Committee, interview by Emma Stewart, July 25, 2001; ASTA Environmental Awards, "Call for Nominations 2001," "Nomination Form," and "Criteria for Selection of 2001 Winners," http://www.astanet.com/about/awardapplication.pdf (July 2001).

43. Ibid.

44. Barbara O'Hara, vice president for government affairs and Jerry Brown, government affairs, interviews by Martha Honey and Emma Stewart ASTA Headquarters, Alexandria, VA, June 2001 and January 2002; "Past Recipients," ASTA awards, http://www.astanet.com/about/awardapplication.pdf.

45. Sara Swan, program coordinator for "Educational Travel Conference," Travel Learning Connections, interview by Emma Stewart, July 19, 2001; http://www.educationaltravelconference.com.

46. Jill Bernier, tour program manager, The Nature Conservacy, interview by Emma Stewart, July 2001.

47. Touristik Union International http://www.TUI.com (July 2001); "Best Environmental Practices," FEMATOUR, 2000.

48. Graham Gordon, *Tourism: Putting Ethics into Practice* (Teddington, Middlesex, UK: Tearfund, January 2001).

49. Ibid; Graham Gordon, *Worlds Apart: A Call to Responsible Global Tourism* (Teddington, Middlesex, UK: Tearfund, January 2002).

50. The International Ecotourism Society, *Ecotourism Guidelines for Nature Tour Operators* (Burlington, VT: TIES, 1995).

51. William Norman, "Green Evaluation Program and Compliance of Nature Tour Operators," http://www.ecotourism.org/textfiles/sirak.txt (February 1997).

52. Ibid.; Martha Honey's interviews with Bryan Higgins and other TIES personnel involved with Green Evaluations (April 1997).

53. Martha Honey, correspondence with Giulia Carbone, United Nations Environment Program, Paris; UNEP Tourism program Web site, http://www.unepie.org/tourism/; Tour Operators Initiative (TOI) Web site, http://www.toinitiative.org/ (November–December 2001).

54. TOI Web site, http://www.toinitiative.org (December 2001).

55. Ibid.

56. Ibid.

57. Ibid.

58. Leyla Sturdy, Harvard student and *Let's Go* writer for Britain, interview by Emma Stewart, June 1999, Oxford, England.

59. Eric Kettunen, general manager, Lonely Planet Publications, interview by Emma Stewart, July 19, 2001.

60. Christopher Baker, *Costa Rica Handbook*, 4th ed., Moon Travel Handbooks (Emeryville, CA: Avalon Travel Publishing, 2001).

61. Beatrice Blake, "Response to obstacles for guidebook writers," Planeta.com: Eco Travels in Latin America, http:///www.planeta.com/planeta/01/0103integrate.html; Martha Honey's correspondence with Beatrice Blake, 2000–2001.

62. Joan Tapper, editor-in-chief, *Islands Magazine*, interview by Emma Stewart, July 18, 2001.

63. Julie Coney, *Smithsonian Magazine*, interview by Emma Stewart, July 19, 2001; *Smithsonian Magazine*/USTOA Travelers Conservation Fund, Conservation Award, 2001 winners, Travelers Conservation Fund Web site: http://www.tcfonline.org/whatsnew.html#anchor880111 (January 2002).

64. Gary Gereffi, Ronie Garcia-Johnson, and Erika Sasser, "The NGO-Industrial Complex," *Foreign Affairs* (July–August 2001), 64–65.

65. Ibid., 61, 64–65.

66. Synergy, *Tourism Certification: An Analysis of Green Globe 21 and Other Tourism Certification Programmes*, Report prepared for WWF-UK (London: WWF-UK, August 2000), p. 10.

67. Hagler Bailly, *Assessment of Voluntary International Environmental Certification Programs*, report prepared for Jamaican Hotel and Tourist Association (Arlington, VA: Hagler Bailly, December 1998), 6; International Organization for Standardization, *The ISO Survey of ISO 9000 and ISO 14000 Certification-Tenth Cycle*, ISBN 92-67-1033-9 (July 2001).

68. Hagler Bailly, 1998, 5.

69. Martha Honey's communications with Robert Toth, September 2000.

70. Riva Krut and Harris Gleckman, *ISO 14001: A Missed Opportunity for Sustainable Global Industrial Development* (London: Earthscan Publications, 1998), 8.

71. Ibid., 8, 16.

72. "Consumer demand regarding tourism and environment," chapter 3, FEMATOUR, 2000.

73. Synergy, 2000; WWF-UK, "Tourism Certification Schemes Still Leave Much to be Desired," press release, August 29, 2000, http://www.wwf uk.org/news/news148.htm (September 2000).

74. Both the FEMATOUR and Synergy studies implicitly, though not explicitly, include prescriptive standards under performance-based standards.

75. Synergy, 2000, 10.
76. Synergy, 2000, 19–20.
77. Chris Reuther, "Towards a Greener Game: A New Environmental Awareness is Slowly Taking Hold of the U.S. Golf Industry," *Environmental Associates* (Philadelphia, PA: The Academy of Natural Sciences, August 1999), available on The Academy of Natural Sciences Web site: http://www.acnatsci.org/erd/ea/golf.html; http://www.golfecology.com; http://www.audubonintl.org/programs/signature/.
78. Synergy, 2000, 16.
79. Amos Bien, interviews and correspondence with Martha Honey, 2000–2001.
80. Bien and Beatrice Blake, interviews and correspondence with Martha Honey, 2000–2001.
81. Christopher Balfe, divisional president, ECOTEL, HVS International, Mineola, New York, interview by Martha Honey, December 2001; http://www.hvsinternational.com/eco.htm (December 2001).
82. ECOTEL, "The ECOTEL Certification Application & Inspection Process," confidential memo from HVS International provided by Balfe.
83. Honey and Rome, *Protecting Paradise*, 52; HVS Eco Services, http://www.hvsercoservices.com/ecotel.htm (December 2001).
84. Balfe interview; HVS Eco Services, http://www.hvsecoservices.com/ectel.htm (December 2001); Press releases and confidential documents on application and inspection process and criteria for certification.
85. According to Balfe, among the reasons why so few have fully completed the full process is that a company seeking certification is only charged between 15 and 50 percent of the total fee before an inspection. Many hotels conclude, after working with the ECOTEL staff and going through a self-audit, that they cannot comply with all the standards and so do not proceed. HVS International appears to view ECOTEL more as a kind of social service provided to its clients and is reluctant to vigorously enforce payments, particularly from long-standing clients who are using other HVS services. In a number of instances, HVS has compelled ECOTEL to refund hotels that do not complete the certification process. Balfe interview.
86. Abigail Rome and Martha Honey, "Summary Minutes: Ecotourism & Sustainable Tourism Certification Workshop" (Washington, D.C.: Institute for Policy Studies, December 29, 2000); Honey and Rome, *Protecting Paradise*. Both available on "Ecotourism and Sustainable Development" Web site, http://www.ips-dc.org.

Chapter 2

Exploring the Concepts
Underlying Certification

Robert Toth

Discerning hotels, tour operators, and destinations recognize that no single aspect of their services, facilities, or site determines success, and measures of success can be difficult to define and hard to quantify. However, just as retailers, automobile manufacturers, airlines, and others have found, there is general agreement that the most reliable, monitorable indicator is customer satisfaction. In a service sector such as tourism, customer satisfaction directly correlates with repeat visits, longer stays, and referrals, all of which have direct impact—for better or worse—on revenues and profits. The impressions that tourists take home from their vacations are the aggregate of a number of factors or experiences encountered during their vacation. These can be categorized in three areas:

1) **Quality**: Tourists' needs and expectations are determined principally through personal interactions with service providers. Staff in maintenance, housekeeping, food preparation, and others whose processes affect the customers and the appearance and functioning of facilities and furnishings also affect the guests' overall vacation experience.

2) **Health, hygiene, and safety conditions**: Vacations can be ruined when tourists experience food poisoning, encounter infectious diseases, are concerned about safety and security, or encounter inadequate pest control, sewage treatment, and the like.

3) **Sustainability**: Experienced tourists and tourism professionals recognize the need to reduce or prevent the adverse impact of tourism to ensure a future for a destination. In addition to the environment, tourists today are more aware of socioeconomic and cultural issues and protecting and conserving nature.

Figure 2.1. . The tourism industry's three-legged stool of customer satisfaction

There can be considerable overlap within these areas, but each is sufficiently distinctive to warrant attention, and a special set of tools has developed to address the challenges in each area. Distinctive as they may be, from the standpoint of customer satisfaction, these areas are totally interrelated. They can be viewed as a three-legged stool (figure 2.1). If any leg fails, then the stool (customer satisfaction) collapses.

Certification schemes are widely used in commerce and industry to promote implementation of standards, to reward those who achieve specified objectives, and to enable customers to identify operations that comply with applicable standards. The oldest rating systems for hotels and restaurants (e.g., Michelin, Mobil, AAA, etc.) certify quality.

Most tourists take for granted that the second leg of the customer satisfaction stool—health, hygiene, and safety—will exist wherever the destination. In North America, Europe, and many other regions we can assume that unless otherwise specified, the water is safe to drink, the sewage system is functioning, we can swim at the beaches, and security measures are in place so tourists are not the prey of criminals. All of these services and many more are provided or monitored by government agencies with checks and balances complemented by infrastructure to see that the standards or regulations are met. Many of the local standards are based on international norms set by bodies such as the World Health Organization, and the International Organization for Standardization (ISO).

Certification is a major tool for achieving results. In many places, restaurants are regularly inspected for hygiene and food handling. Although in some jurisdictions, this is pass/fail, many have a grading system and the rating (a certificate) must be prominently displayed where customers can see it. The performance of many systems is dependent on the practices of individuals, such as food handlers, operators of sewage treatment plants, lifeguards, or pesticide applicators. Responsible government agencies usually require that such individuals demonstrate their knowledge and competence and be certified. Evaluation may be by a government agency or by specialized nongovernment organizations. In many parts of the world, however, there are no standards, regulations, or the infrastructure to enforce them. Often, where standards and regulations are in the statutes, there are insufficient resources to implement them. In a few parts of the world, the tourism industry has recognized that if it can not depend on government to address these issues, then the private sector must take action. Most of these initiatives are based on voluntary prescriptive and management system standards coupled with certification.

Regarding the third leg of the tourist customer satisfaction stool, there is as yet no universally accepted definition of sustainability. Other chapters in this book highlight various interpretations of the term and the components and priorities that should be incorporated in sustainable tourism and ecotourism programs. This chapter will use a very general definition: *Sustainable tourism* is about creating a balance between social, environmental, cultural, and economic interests. Worldwide, there are approximately 100 ecological programs that certify or grant awards to tourism operations—primarily hotels. Sixty of these are viable ongoing programs, while the others have limited applications, are retrenching, or are still in the planning stage. Five of these programs are being implemented on several continents, forty-five are in Europe, and the remaining ten are functioning outside Europe.[1] The large portion of the world's tourism certification programs focuses primarily on environmental matters—pollution prevention, environmental protection, and energy conservation—and does not address cultural and socioeconomic issues. Because no international standard exists for sustainable tourism, each program has developed its own standard.

These next sections describe the major elements of effective tourism certification systems, essential concepts that should be addressed in such systems, and lessons learned that should be heeded when establishing tourism-related certification programs. Although certification programs are relatively new to the tourism industry, other sectors have used standards and certification for many years. Some practices can be traced back many centuries. The Code of Hammurabi (1800 B.C.) set standards and certification practices for building materials, and since A.D. 1300, the Goldsmiths' Company has been independently testing and hallmarking (certifying) gold and silver articles to guarantee conformity to standards.

As a result, there is a considerable body of certification experience and proven practices that have been codified into standards. These standards are readily available and widely used in all types of industrial, commercial, and service sectors. There is little reason for the tourism industry to reinvent the wheel, grope for effective procedures, or develop new terminology. Tourism certification programs will be more readily understood and

Box 2.1. Accepted Standards and Guides for the Components of Conformity Assessment Systems

Any organization planning to establish a certification program should consider using the documents listed here to define the system, as well as its procedures and practices. Not only will this save considerable time and resources, but the resultant system will be recognized and accepted more readily by government agencies and NGOs.

There are thousands of existing standards that could be used in tourism certification programs. For example, there are more than 350 ISO standards defining products and procedures for monitoring such aspects as the quality of air, water, and soil. There is no reason to reinvent these; they already exist and just need to be cited in any tourism-specific standard. In the same vein, ISO 14001, Specification for Environmental Management Systems, provides a framework for identifying and addressing environmental obligations that could be adaptable to applications within tourism.

STANDARDS

Existing standards for writing standards have been prepared for highly technical applications. The Standards Engineering Society is in the process of releasing guidance intended for nontechnical applications, such as tourism.

SES-2: Simplified practice for designating and organizing standards

ISO/IEC Guide 7: Guidelines for drafting standards suitable for use for conformity assessment

ASSESSMENT

The International Auditor and Training Certification Association (IATCA) has harmonized the qualification requirements for auditors, the contents of training courses, and certification requirements of course providers. Although these initiatives focus on ISO 9000 and 14000, IATCA is a resource for criteria and procedures that could be adapted to tourism certification. Other resources include:

ISO Standard 14001: Environmental management systems—Specification

ISO Standard 14010: Guidelines for environmental auditing—General principles

ISO Standard 14011: Audit procedures—Auditing of environmental management systems

ISO Standard 14012: Guidelines for environmental auditing—Qualification criteria for environmental auditors

Standards 14010 through 14012 and their counterparts for auditing quality management systems (ISO 10011 series) are being combined into a single standard, ISO 19011. This standard provides more specific guidance for audit program management and qualifications of auditors. A committee draft is currently available, and a final approved standard is to be released in 2002.

CERTIFICATION

Guidance for establishing and managing certification systems can be found in the following:

ISO/IEC Guide 28: General rules for a model third-party certification system for products

ISO/IEC Guide 65: General requirements for bodies operating product certification systems

ISO/IEC Guide 67★: Fundamentals of product certification

ISO/IEC Guide 66: General requirements for bodies operating assessment and certification of environmental management systems

ISO/IEC Standard 17021★: General requirements for bodies operating assessment and certification of management systems

ISO/IEC Standard 17024★: General criteria for certification bodies operating certification of personnel

ISO/IEC Guide 23: Methods of indicating conformity with standards for third-party certification systems

ISO/IEC Standard 17030★: Marks of conformity assessment and their use

ISO Guide 27: Guidelines for corrective action to be taken by a certification body in the event of misuse of its mark of conformity

ACCREDITATION

Guidelines for operating accreditation programs are included in the following:

ISO/IEC Guide 61: General requirements for assessment and accreditation of certification bodies

ISO/IEC Standard 17011★: General requirements for bodies providing assessment and accreditation

ISO/IEC Standard 17040★: General requirements for peer assessment of conformity assessment bodies

RECOGNITION

Nearly all guidance on recognition exclusively addresses criteria and procedures leading to mutual recognition agreements. The following may be useful as background information or as a source of definitions for specialized terminology.

ISO/IEC Guide 68★: Agreements for the recognition and acceptance of conformity assessment results

Committees responsible for standards and conformity assessment within the Asian Pacific Economic Cooperation (APEC) and Free Trade Area of the Americas (FTAA) have developed model mutual recognition agreements.

(continues)

Box 2.1. Continued

OTHER CONSIDERATIONS

As most certification programs have the potential to restrict trade, World Trade Organization requirements must be taken into account.

Final Act, April 1994: Agreement on Standards and Technical Barriers to Trade (TBT Agreement)

WTO TBT Annex 3: Code of good practice for the preparation, adoption and application of standards

   A World Trade Organization code of good practice for conformity assessment (including certification) is currently being considered. ISO and IEC have published:

ISO/IEC Guide 60: Code of good practice for conformity assessment

*These guides and standards are in various stages of development. Check the ISO Web site (http://www.iso.org) for their status and availability.

---

adopted when they use the accepted principles and practices that are used and recognized worldwide. The standards and guides that are most relevant to sustainable tourism certification are listed in box 2.1.

Essential Concepts

Certification is one of a number of interrelated activities by which a product, process, service, or system is evaluated for conformance against a standard. These activities are illustrated in figure 2.2. The generic term for the process depicted in the figure is *conformity assessment*, which encompasses a wide range of sectors and techniques ranging from verifying the capabilities of testing laboratories to acceptance of critical aircraft parts; hallmarking jewelry; certifying the competence of computer technicians; determining the quality of care provided by hospitals; and ascertaining the effectiveness of fire extinguishers. Conformity assessment is important to suppliers, consumers, and regulators. It enables conscientious producers to distinguish their products from those made by less reputable ones. It provides consumers with a reliable means to select products in the marketplace and enables government agencies to enforce regulations that protect the public's health and safety.

   This broad application of conformity assessment in diverse sectors has resulted in the use of different terminology between sectors and different interpretations or applications of terms that are often synonymous. Such

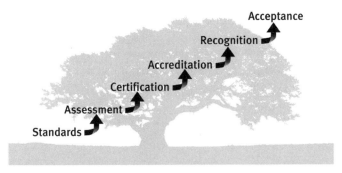

Figure 2.2. Essential components of conformity assessment systems

terms as "registered," "listed," "qualified," "validated," "verified," "approved," "rated," "accepted," "classified," "accredited," and "licensed" are used in various sectors to indicate that a product or service is "certified." Similarly, instead of "assessment" we find use of "audit," "inspection," "evaluation," "validation," and "assay." The terms listed in figure 2.2 are accepted as the primary terminology by the World Trade Organization. To improve readability, the term *product* will be used throughout to refer to a product, service, facility, process, or system. Similarly *supplier* will be used when referring to service providers, such as tour operators, hoteliers, or guides, or producers of products, processes, or systems. The reader will also note that the examples illustrate a variety of practices used in many industries, some of which may be particularly appropriate for adaptation in the tourism sector.

The conformity assessment process leading to certification can verify that a particular product meets a specified level of quality or safety or sustainable tourism model and provides explicit or implicit information about its characteristics. Conformity assessment can increase a buyer's confidence in a product, furnish useful information to a buyer, and help to substantiate a supplier's advertising claims. The quality and credibility of conformity assessment information conveyed by certification is dependent on the competence and impartiality of the auditor; the technical expertise of the certifier; the procedures that incorporate effective controls; and the adequacy and appropriateness of the standards against which the product is assessed.

Too many sustainable tourism and ecotourism initiatives appear to focus almost exclusively on the certification component and pay insufficient attention to the other components depicted in figure 2.2. Although the topic of this chapter is certification in sustainable tourism, it should be recognized that certification per se is one component of a system. To fully understand this component, it is important to understand the overall system and related components. The ultimate need is a cost-effective, credible sustainable tourism conformity assessment system, not just a certification program. A particular challenge is that unlike sectors with long-established conformity assessment practices, the tourism sector does not yet have in place some of the system components or infrastructure that would expedite implementation of certification.

Standards

Products, facilities, and services are assessed by measuring their level of conformity to prescribed requirements or achievement of specified objectives. These requirements or objectives are specified in standards that also spell out how to measure conformance. The critical difference between many standards is how requirements or objectives are specified. Within tourism, these standards are often classified as either performance or process methodologies (see chapter 1), however, more accurately, there are essentially three different approaches. No single approach is appropriate for every type of application; each one has its strengths and weaknesses.

"Prescriptive standards" describe the way required characteristics can be achieved by prescribing how a product will be made and used or how a process will be accomplished. Usually, there is no test of the final product as long as the prescribed components are used. The entire building construction industry functions on this basis. A typical prescriptive requirement in a tourism standard might read: "Each guest room shall have a master switch so that all electrical circuits are activated only by insertion of the guest's key and are turned off when the guest departs with the key." One advantage of prescriptive standards is that although the specified solution may not be the best or most cost-effective, everyone knows what is required to comply with the standard. Prescriptive standards have many drawbacks, most significantly in the way they restrict innovation and alternative solutions.

"Performance standards" describe what functional or operational characteristics are to be achieved but not how to accomplish them, for example, "Provision shall be made to turn off all electrical circuits automatically when a room is unoccupied." This requirement allows for alternatives such as acoustic and motion detectors, sensors in the door lock, or some new technology introduced in the future. But the hotelier has the burden of demonstrating to the certifier that the selected solution fully complies with the intent of the standard. Performance standards are subject to a greater degree of ambiguity and imprecision, which raises questions of the intent of the specified requirement. This in turn can lead to delays, debate, and additional costs. Certification programs based on performance standards need efficient communication channels so that applicants and auditors can quickly obtain authoritative interpretations.

"Management system standards" specify the elements and processes of a model management system on the premise that such a system demonstrates the capabilities of a supplier. Such standards specify the processes, not how specific characteristics are to be achieved, as in prescriptive standards or the functional or operational characteristics of a performance standard. A management system standard for tourism might specify that "The hotel shall undertake a detailed assessment of energy use throughout its operations, establish the type and amount of energy required for all activities, and monitor and review use on a regular basis." Management system standards do not set minimum levels of performance but provide a framework for achieving levels set by customers or the organization itself. Although benchmarking may be a requirement, as illustrated in the example, there are seldom requirements to improve on that performance level.

The most widely recognized management system standards are ISO 9000 for quality and ISO 14000 for environmental management. The twenty-one standards, guides, and technical reports that make up the ISO 14000 family are designed to assist companies in managing and evaluating the environmental effectiveness of their operations. The standards and guides are intended for organizations of any size or type on the premise that the requirements of an effective environmental management system are the same, whatever the business. At the end of the year 2000, quality management systems at more than 408,000 facilities, including 1,187 hotels and restaurants, had been certified to ISO 9000, and 22,900 facilities, including sixty-six hotels and restaurants, had ISO 14000-certified environmental management systems.[2]

Unlike Michelin, Mobil, and AAA, assessment and certification of a quality management system does not evaluate the quality of the product or service offered to the customer. The ISO 9000 certification provides some assurance that once the supplier has demonstrated that its processes yield a particular level of quality subsequent deliveries will be at that same level. Similarly, certification to the ISO 14000 environment management system standard does not ensure that the supplier does not pollute, waste energy, etc.; it verifies that the supplier has systems in place that should enable the supplier to avoid such problems. Because these standards are intended for all types of applications, they are necessarily generic and written very broadly. Suppliers planning to implement these standards have many questions as they read through the requirements, and often it is not self-evident what methods would constitute compliance at their operations. As a result, a whole subsector has developed, providing consultation, training, and self-help books. Many businesses are deterred from pursuing certification to management system standards because of the need for such support.

Each of the three approaches has its strengths and weaknesses. Many of the standards for newer certification programs, particularly those concerned with sustainability, combine the best features of each. To differentiate performance and prescriptive standards from the process-based management system standards, these standards are often called *performance-based standards* because they usually specify qualitative and quantitative criteria or benchmarks that establish minimum acceptable performance levels. Many certification programs for the tourism industry are really hybrids because they also include management system requirements regarding processes as well as specific solutions that characterize prescriptive standards. This is exemplified in these excerpts from the standard for the Rainforest Alliance's Smart Voyager certification program for tour boats:[3]

- **Performance**: "Noise levels to which a worker can be exposed must not exceed 85 decibels for a maximum period of 6 continuous hours."
- **Management systems**: "An environmental education program for all employees in the craft must be in place and designed in a way that allows for regular monitoring and evaluation."
- **Prescriptive**: "The operation must use recycled, bleach-free paper for printing at least 50 percent of its promotional or informational literature."

Hybrid standards, particularly those specifying a series of graded criteria or benchmarks, are particularly adaptable to systems that award certificates reflecting achievement of increasingly higher levels of performance.

Standards can be classified in numerous ways. One classification distinguishes between voluntary standards, which by themselves impose no obligations regarding use, and mandatory standards. A mandatory standard is usually published by a government regulatory body and imposes obligations to conform on specified parties. The distinction between voluntary and mandatory standards may be lost when voluntary consensus standards are referenced in government regulations, effectively making them mandatory. Voluntary standards may also become quasi-mandatory due to conditions in the marketplace. One example is the wide adoption of ANSI Z80.3, Requirements for Nonprescription Sunglasses and Fashion Eyewear. There is no market among large U.S. retailers for glasses that do not conform to the standards. Another demarcation among standards is between those developed by recognized standards-developing organizations, which are designated "formal" standards, and those developed by consortia, ad hoc groups, and individual organizations, which are characterized as "informal" because they ignore or short-cut traditional standards-development procedures and do not usually reflect a broad-based consensus.

Standards are also categorized by their range of usage (i.e., local, national, regional, global), or the status of the standards developer (e.g., industry, national, regional, international). International and global standards have the widest acceptance and recognition. Although the 13,000 standards of the International Organization for Standardization (ISO) are probably the best known international standards, more than 175 international organizations (seventy-five government/treaty bodies; 100 voluntary organizations and federations) also publish international standards.

Assessment

The crux of conformity assessment is determination of the level of conformance to a particular standard and the validity of findings. These are directly related to the method and level of investigation required for adequate assurance that findings are representative and correct, and the competence and professionalism of the agent performing the assessment. For products, the agent is usually a testing laboratory or inspection service. For facilities and management systems, the agent is an individual or team of specialists. For reasons that are lost in time, individuals who assess laboratories and management systems are called *auditors* not assessors.

There are three types of assessment:

- **First-party assessment** or self-assessment is the process by which a supplier declares conformance with a particular standard. In some cases (e.g., ISO 14000, environmental management), self-audits are components of the standard and are the basis for a supplier's declaration of conformance.
- **Second-party assessment** is accomplished by the purchaser, who mandates that potential suppliers and/or their products will be assessed by the purchaser prior to entering into a transaction. The nature of these programs varies greatly and may involve delegation of assessments to a trade association of purchasers or a commercial inspection service. Second-party assessment has always been common practice in the mass tourism markets dominated by major tour operators/wholesalers. These are the organizations that assemble package tours by contracting for hotel rooms, transportation, and guides. Most of the major wholesalers have their own standards and auditors or contract with inspection services. Recent action by the European Union that facilitates law suits by tourists has motivated European tour operators to intensify these assessments to demonstrate compliance with their obligation for "due diligence."
- **Third-party assessment** is carried out by a party other than the sup-

plier or the purchaser, an organization that is independent of buyer or seller. Third-party assessments may be mandatory or voluntary. Reliance on a third party may be required by a government agency or specified by the customer. Often, the supplier may seek it as a means of market differentiation or to obtain independent feedback on the effectiveness of the supplier's internal programs.

The level of uncertainty inherent to the assessment process has a direct bearing on findings and conclusions, their reliability and credibility, and to a large extent, the cost. The level of uncertainty is determined by the standard against which the product is evaluated and assessment methods specified in the standard. For example, a pressure test of a water pipe is very straightforward. It either passes or fails. Most standards specify unambiguous finite limits and explicit performance requirements that can be readily measured on-site or in a laboratory. A few standards, particularly those for management systems, depend on the personal judgment and interpretation of the auditor. Although product tests are replicable worldwide, subjective assessment may not be uniformly rigorous and consistent from country to country or among the auditors used by a certification organization. For these reasons, certifiers and their accreditors have established comprehensive requirements for auditors and checks and balances to forestall complaints of lax or overly rigorous audits. These are listed in box 2.1. Accredited certifiers must use certified auditors. A certified auditor must demonstrate detailed knowledge of the applicable standards and their application and possess professional and personal attributes to ensure there are no conflicts of interest or biases.

Certification of an auditor's qualifications is usually done by the accrediting organization. This is based on:

- an appropriate level of formal education;
- specified work experience involving accountability and the exercise of judgment;
- specified experience in the particular field (e.g., environmental management) in which the auditor will function;
- satisfactory performance under the supervision of a senior certified auditor; and
- successful completion of an auditor training course approved by the accreditor.

Because specialized auditor training is so critical, accreditors either provide training themselves or specify course content and certify training courses that comply with the accreditor's requirements and utilize the accreditor's examinations. Although few certifiers provide initial auditor training, most certifiers (and some accreditors) periodically hold workshops to enable auditors to share experiences and to promote uniform interpretations.

Certifiers seldom maintain a staff of auditors but engage freelance certified auditors. One reason is that full-time staff requires full-time funding. Another is the need to utilize auditors with experience in the sector being assessed, for example, pharmaceuticals, financial services, or hotels. Most certifiers offer services to many sectors but cannot justify retaining certified auditors to accommodate all of them. Similarly, tourism certifiers may need auditors with specialized training or experience. Auditors trained to assess hotels, for example, probably would need additional training and experience to qualify as auditors of tour operators or cruise ships.

Certification

The process of providing documented assurance that a product or management system conforms to a standard or that a person is competent to perform a certain task is called *certification*. The documentation may be through a certificate, a label, a listing in a publicly accessible register, or all of these media. Depending on requirements specified in the relevant standard or standards, the certificate may be awarded on the basis of compliance with a specific criterion, a minimum number of criteria, or achievement of a minimum score. An alternative to this pass/fail approach is a grading system. The applicable standard provides a baseline of prerequisite criteria and a rating system that awards additional stars, leaves, or qualifiers (good, choice, and prime) to products that exceed specified thresholds.

The use of certification in the marketplace goes back to earliest times, and until recently, has been used primarily for products affecting health and safety, as well as precious metals and gems. Most of these certification programs were established by government regulators (e.g., drugs and building materials); some were instituted by insurance underwriters with the introduction of new technology (e.g., electrical wiring devices, steam boilers); and others were established by associations of manufacturers to promote acceptance and confidence in their products by the public (e.g., gas appliances, civilian aircraft). Certifying the qualifications of personnel goes back to the ancient guilds, and to this day, most personnel certification programs are managed by professional societies.

A common way to categorize certification programs is based on the way a product, facility, or service is assessed.

1) **First-party certification** or supplier's declaration of conformance is more common than generally realized. Manufacturers of computer peripherals and telecommunications equipment self-certify confor-

mance with interoperability standards. Many trade associations enable their members to apply the association's certification mark. Most of these merely certify compliance with the association's code of business practices or commitment to the environment. Some trade associations do provide checks and balances, such as for manufacturers of room air conditioners, which self-certify cooling capacity. In the event of a complaint by a competitor or other party, units are tested at a recognized laboratory. If the units fail, the manufacturer is liable for all costs and relabeling. If the units pass, the complainant is responsible for the costs of testing.

2) **Second-party certification** is commonly used by major corporations when central purchasing departments certify that products from certain suppliers meet specified standards. Local operations or franchisees are required to purchase certified products from these suppliers. This practice is quite common among food and hotel chains to maintain a uniform level of quality as well as benefit from economies of scale. Certification of its members by a trade association is second-party certification whether the assessments are by contracted freelance auditors or the association's own auditors.

3) **Third-party certification** is a type of certification in which the producer's claim of conformity is validated by a technically competent organization not controlled by or under the influence of the supplier or buyer. Some trade association certification programs that claim to be third-party schemes do not meet this last criterion of arm's length neutrality and are more properly classified as first- or second-party programs. The certifier may perform tests to collect data, collect data from the supplier, and/or conduct assessments. The certifier may delegate all or part of these assessment activities to another party or parties, but the certifier is responsible for reviewing results and making a final determination on conformance or lack of conformance. The degree of confidence that can be placed in third-party certification programs varies greatly depending on:

   • the scope of the standard(s) defining requirements; these should address relevant characteristics that correlate with expected performance;

   • the assessment methods used to determine conformance;

   • the adequacy of the producer's quality control system to ensure consistent performance between assessments; and

   • the competence and reputation of the certifier.

4) **Supplier's audit confirmation** is a type of certification that involves elements of both first-party and third-party certification. In this

approach, a third party assesses the effectiveness of the supplier's internal audit program. It aims to reinforce the credibility of the supplier's declaration of conformance based on first-party assessment. Australia's Nature and Ecotourism Accreditation Program (NEAP) currently uses this approach. Award of certification is based on a "desk audit" of an applicant's self-assessment questionnaire. Certified operations respond each year to a paper audit on one set of NEAP criteria and receive an on-site audit on all criteria at some stage during the three-year period of certification.[4]

Certification programs mandated by government regulations are usually much more rigorous and expensive than voluntary private sector programs. A primary reason is that government programs are usually limited to matters of health, safety, and the environment in which the consequences of noncompliance can be catastrophic. Many government certification programs specify use of the agency's laboratories or auditors, but many are starting to use private sector certified auditors or accredited laboratories to acquire data. Evidence of conformance then results in certification by the agency. The increase of regional trade pacts and mutual recognition agreements, together with pressure from citizen groups to address environmental and socioeconomic issues, has resulted in more government involvement in setting criteria for assessment, certification, and accreditation.

Voluntary certification programs have many variants. Many certifiers are standards developers and assess conformance only to their own standards; others will assess against any standards, including those of competing certification programs. To provide global recognition for their certifications, certifiers in less-developed countries will enter into joint venture arrangements with one of the dozen or so multinational certifiers. An auditor from the multinational participates with its local partner in the initial audits, and the client receives a joint certificate or certificates from both certifiers. The local certifier then handles periodic reassessments and recertifications. The Rainforest Alliance and its Ecuadorian partner, Conservacion y Desarrollo, exemplify this approach, as described in chapter 11.

Accreditation

Not all certification programs are equally thorough or rigorous, and not all certifiers are equally competent. Accreditation is a process for certifying the certifier. One of the criticisms of first-party self-certification is that producers do not have a third party checking competence and the integrity of results. Many third-party certification programs also do not have anyone looking over their shoulders to ensure the quality of their programs. Like a supplier, a certifier can self-certify compliance with applicable ISO/IEC (International Electrotechnical Commission) guides and standards, or users of certification results can validate a certifier's compliance through second-party assessment. The accepted and most efficient practice, however, is through an accreditation program conducted by a third party independent of the certifier and the purchasers or users of the certification. Certification program accreditation indicates that the certifier is capable of performing specified certification procedures correctly, not that the certifier has competently certified all products or facilities in each and every instance. Accredited certifiers can be expected to achieve at least a minimal level of performance with greater consistency in the services they offer and uniformity in the results they produce.

Accreditation is an important element of decentralized third-party systems in which many certifiers are awarding certification to the same standard. For example, ISO itself does not award certification to the ISO 14001 environmental management system standard; nearly five hundred certifiers award their own certificates. ISO does not accredit these certifiers; nearly fifty national accrediting organizations fill that function. There are many examples of international certification programs with wide recognition and acceptance that do not delegate certification to organizations outside their control. These international certification programs support a wide range of sectors, including agriculture, electronics, textiles, sporting goods, electrical equipment, and seeds. Because they take full responsibility for certifications, there is no need for the complexities and expense of accrediting others. There are no questions about credibility, consistent interpretation of requirements, or the qualifications of auditors that are the *raison d'être* for accreditation. To date, there is no international accreditation program for tourism, but, as described in chapter 11, a study is underway to determine the feasibility of creating one.

Certifiers participate in accreditation programs in expectation of some type of economic return for their investment in obtaining accreditation, such as new business opportunities. Some may want to distinguish themselves from their competitors by having an impartial evaluation of their competence based upon internationally recognized criteria. The underlying reason in most cases is to use their status as an accredited certifier to enhance credibility with clients and the public.

Most accreditation bodies contract with specially trained freelance auditors, and the process of accreditation follows the same practices as certification, with the one notable alternative of utilizing peer review. Typically, a peer review process includes (1) self-evaluation by the certifier, (2) an on-site assessment by a team of auditors, and (3) judgment by an accreditation body that the certifier complies with applicable standards and guidelines. The two to five auditors of the assessment team come from other peer certifiers. Reciprocal assessments between peers are prohibited.

In most cases, the accreditation body is a primary unit within a national, regional, or international association or cooperative. Accreditation confers membership in the association. To ensure that the interests of users and other stakeholders are addressed, the association usually includes representatives of these groups on their policy board.

Accreditation bodies are often the developers or custodians of the technical standards against which products, services, processes, or systems are assessed by certifiers. Standards development, revision, and interpretation are usually accomplished by a separate operation parallel to the accreditation activity within an umbrella association or cooperative structure. Other accreditors leave responsibility for technical standards to well-established standard developers. Standards used by accreditors for assessing the professional qualifications of certifiers usually include the following criteria:

1) The certifier should have no conflict of interest. If the process is to be credible, no relationship should exist between the operation being certified and the certifier or its auditors that might influence the objectivity of the process. This precludes certifiers or auditors from providing training or consultation services to organizations that they would certify.

2) Procedures should be published and readily available. They should cover all aspects of granting and withdrawing certification, confidentiality of proprietary information, and conditions under which the certification mark can be used.

3) The certifier should have sufficient financial resources to satisfactorily perform its functions and allow it to refuse certification should that prove necessary.

4) The certifier should be able to demonstrate that its personnel are qualified. Each staff member's and auditor's training should be kept current and documented.

5) The certifier should have a quality system appropriate to the type and number of certifications performed. A comprehensive, up-to-date quality manual should be maintained and internal audits should be conducted periodically.

6) The certifier should demonstrate thorough understanding of applicable standards and channels for obtaining authoritative interpretations, should there be questions.

7) The certifier should have means of ensuring fair and equitable auditor selection and assignment and verification of their competence and impartiality.

8) Responsibility for certification decisions should not be delegated by the certification body to another party and should be based on all the evidence collected during the certification process.

9) The certifier should have a system for periodic reassessment to ensure that those certified and/or their products continue to comply with all certification requirements.

10) The certifier should have procedures in place that minimize the potential for fraud or deception by those certified regarding their certification status or the meaning of that status. There should be a system to enforce requirements for use of the certification mark, including swift withdrawal of certification from products and operations that fail to comply with the terms and requirements for certification. Appropriate action should be taken against uncertified producers that misrepresent their certification status.

11) The certification program should have an impartial appeals mechanism to handle disagreements that cannot otherwise be resolved. Procedures should be documented, with minimal limitations on their timing and on who may file.

With only minor changes, these criteria are applicable to accreditors as well and are incorporated in the bylaws and operating procedures of most accreditation bodies. It is important that all parties, particularly customers, understand the scope of a particular accreditation program. Some accreditation programs just evaluate compliance with a code of conduct. Others also evaluate the certifier's technical operations.

Recognition

The ultimate objective of the process outlined above is not only to improve competence and capability within a sector but also to enable those who deal with the sector to make decisions with confidence. They may not have the special knowledge or insight of those within the sector, but they can rely on the certificate and the way in which the certificate was granted. Certification and accreditation systems earn acceptance in the marketplace on the basis of their credibility and reputations of the certifiers and accreditation body. In many cases, a prominent nongovernmental organization or a governmental body at the national, regional, or international level may endorse or officially recognize that an accreditation program is competent or that a conformity assessment system fulfills objectives established by the NGO or government body.

Over the past decade, growth in international trade has highlighted the proliferation of different standards and regulatory requirements. Alleviating problems resulting from this proliferation has been concentrated in two areas: (1) harmonization of existing standards and preferential adoption of international standards, and (2) agreements to recognize the results of assessments, or certificates of conformity by responsible authorities located in two or more nations. Both approaches are cited in the World Trade Organization's Agreement on Technical Barriers to Trade, and all member nations are obligated to implement these policies. Harmonization and mutual recognition are divided into two areas. For regulatory matters, negotiation is being accomplished government to government. In areas involving voluntary standardization and conformity assessment, a wide range of private sector players are involved. Negotiations have proven to be contentious and time-consuming because each accreditation body has had slightly different requirements in areas such as auditor experience and training, time between reassessments, conditional certifications, and breadth and depth of internal quality controls.

After many years and a countless number of person-hours, the first mutual recognition agreements are emerging within and between regional blocs in both the regulated and nonregulated (voluntary) areas. Individual accreditation bodies or accreditors within a region are recognized as equally competent under the umbrella of an international recognition agreement. This is the pattern for the International Laboratory Accreditation Cooperation (ILAC) and the International Accreditation Forum (IAF). There is no international accreditation forum for all sectors or areas of conformity assessment. As a result, sectoral accreditors are organizing alliances and consortia patterned on ILAC and IAF to promote recognition and wider acceptance of their programs. A number of accreditors of sustainable development and social accountability have organized the International Social and Environmental Accrediting and Labeling (ISEAL) Alliance. Members include the Forest Stewardship Council, Social Accountability International, Fairtrade Labeling Organizations International, International Federation of Organic Agriculture Movements, International Organic Accreditation System, Conservation Agriculture Network, and the Marine Stewardship Council.

It is noteworthy that truly international conformity assessment systems do not need multilateral agreements to achieve recognition because from the beginning these systems used a common set of standards and procedures worldwide that assured consistency and uniformity.

These recognition initiatives and dozens of successful international and regional certification programs for industrial and consumer products provide insights that warrant consideration by the global tourism industry.

1) It is easier and more cost-effective to establish a single worldwide con-

formity assessment system than to organize a number of similar programs into a harmonized, cohesive system.

2) Government agencies, NGOs and other affected interests more readily
   recognize certification and accreditation procedures documented in
   international standards and guides, such as those in box 2.1, than systems that do not have this kind of documentation.

3) Availability of a single accepted set of technical standards against which
   products are assessed not only facilitates worldwide implementation
   but also recognition. The corollary is that accreditation of certifiers
   applying a multitude of technical standards is not only problematic, but
   may not garner adequate recognition or acceptance.

4) The level of recognition and acceptance of a certification system is
   directly proportional to the number of certificates in effect and their
   dispersion throughout a wide geographic area.

5) International and regional organizations readily recognize conformity
   assessment systems that support the objectives of these organizations or
   assist their constituents.

Acceptance

In the regulated areas of safety and health, government recognition of a
conformity assessment system confers automatic acceptance by all affected
interests and, in many cases, a monopoly to manage conformity assessment
in a particular field. In other areas, general acceptance of a certification
mark and the system that granted it does not automatically result from
recognition. Users and producers need to be convinced of the benefits
each will derive, as well as the credibility of the mark and the certification
process. Accreditation and recognition effectively address concerns about
credibility, but producers and their customers need to be educated on the
benefits each party can derive from certification.

Successful certification programs take into account the various factors
that motivate suppliers to become certified. A significant underlying consideration is that most enterprises (and some government agencies) prefer
voluntary certification programs based on realistic voluntary consensus
standards rather than government regulation, which often means inflexible
enforcement of broadly written legislation. Acceptance of certification
schemes can be facilitated when government agencies work together with
the sponsoring organization to achieve common goals. For example, certified tour operators can be given preferential access to wilderness areas or
marine parks. When governments support incentives or preferences for
certification, suppliers find it much easier to weigh the pros and cons of
certification and whether to do it now or later. The benefits and incentives

Box 2.2. Certification Benefits and Incentives

There are many factors that can motivate a hotel to seek certification of its operations. Realizing tangible return for the investment of time and resources to comply with applicable standards is often the primary motive, but intangible benefits are also influential. The more significant motivating factors are listed here.

- **Satisfaction**: Many hoteliers feel the need to conserve energy and protect the environment and to be responsible community members. Certification standards provide guidelines that indicate how they can contribute back to the surroundings that provide such rich benefits by reducing ecological impacts and improving health and safety.
- **Sustainability**: Hoteliers with vision want to ensure a future for their businesses. Their objectives include cost reduction, income growth, superior management practices, and continuity of tourism in the region. Certification programs help hotels to improve their management techniques and to find the best route toward sustainability.
- **Maintenance of Markets**: Certification enables hoteliers to focus on the primary factors affecting customer satisfaction. Achieving a requisite level of performance decreases complaints from clients and from clients to their travel agents and tour operators, with long-term direct benefits to all parties. Certification distinguishes operations and products in the market, making them increasingly more competitive.
- **Profitability**: Achieving certification requires implementation of practices that conserve resources and reduce direct and indirect costs while improving performance.
- **Public Image**: Certification improves the image of a hotel in the eyes of clients, friends, suppliers, government, and the general public. Certification results in prestige, pride, and publicity.
- **Dialogue**: Certification programs motivate hoteliers, health professionals, and environmentalists to work together in the search for equitable solutions to problems and permits sharing of information and ideas.
- **Credit Opportunities**: Certified hotels are viewed favorably by banking institutions. A hotel that effectively manages safety, health, and hygiene conditions, conserves resources, and takes into account security issues and disaster planning has competitive advantages when it comes to opportunities for credit.
- **Insurance Costs**: Insurers recognize that certification attests to a level of commitment and achievement that can have a positive effect on risk assessment, which translates into lower rates.
- **Reduced Liability**: The systematic assessment of procedures and upgrading of operations that characterizes certification programs can significantly reduce the potential for accidents, discharge of wastes, and other incidents. Insurers take this into account in calculating insurance premiums.

(continues)

Box 2.2. Continued

- **Capable and Dedicated Workers**: At certified hotels, workers receive adequate training, equipment, and motivation. This translates into worker pride and efficiency and thus a higher level of competitiveness.
- **Proactive and Participatory**: In contrast to government regulations, certification is voluntary, market-motivated, and independent. In this way, it allows hoteliers to participate actively in the search for solutions to health, environmental, and management challenges and permits citizens, scientists, and all other sectors to participate. Many times, it is more innovative and advanced than government regulatory processes.
- **Technology Transfer**: Certification programs facilitate technical discussions at all levels, strive for the best available technology, and provide incentives for the development of clean and innovative operating procedures.

---

associated with certification of hotels are listed in box 2.2. These benefits are also applicable to other tourism subsectors.

A critical ingredient found in successful, widely accepted certification programs is a complementary ongoing marketing initiative that alerts all affected interests to the program, promotes participation by producers, and encourages users to realize the added value inherent to certified products. At times, organizations that have endorsed or recognized a particular conformity assessment system help to promote acceptance of the system and its certification mark. Some conformity assessment systems spend as much on direct and indirect marketing as they do to operate the technical side of the system. Many systems do not achieve their full potential because they concentrate on procedures and practices but overlook the importance of marketing. This is especially true for tourism certification programs because tourism depends so much on public perception and image.

Lessons Learned

Due Process and Consensus

The image and reputation of a certification program are directly related to the adequacy and appropriateness of the standards against which the product, facility, or service is assessed. Certification enhances the value of standards by increasing the confidence of customers that products actually conform to the standards. The effectiveness of a certification program is determined by its technical standards. The best certification program in the world will not succeed if it does not assess against standards that reflect the requirements of the major stakeholders and unambiguously specify measurable levels of acceptable performance and not just goals or good intentions. If topics and criteria such as those listed in the appendix are not in the applicable standards, the certification program cannot compensate for the oversight. Special attention must be given to standards and the way they are developed if a certification program is to be successful. A few key points are:

Although the hundreds of private sector developers of formal voluntary standards have widely varied constituencies and charters, nearly all share two important features—due process and consensus. The American National Standards Institute (ANSI) supplies the following definitions:

"Due process means that any person (organization, company, government agency, individual, etc.) with a direct and material interest has a right to participate by: (a) expressing a position and its basis, (b) having that position considered, and (c) having the right to appeal. Due process allows for equity and fair play."[5]

Minimum acceptable requirements for due process are:

- *Openness*: Participation open to all persons who are directly and materially affected; no undue financial barriers or technical requirements; and adequate notice of any action.[6]
- *Balance*: There shall be balance of interests and no single interest category shall constitute more than one-third of the membership.[7]

"Consensus means substantial agreement has been reached by directly and materially affected interest categories. This signifies the concurrence of more than a simple majority but not necessarily unanimity. Consensus requires that all views and objections be considered and that an effort be made toward their resolution."[8]

Note that definitions of both due process and consensus limit participation to persons (i.e., organization, company, government agency, etc.) with a direct and material interest. The intention is to put decision making into the hands of those directly affected—not the consultants, the academics, or dilettantes. This principle is reinforced by the requirement for balance that is based on the number of participating representatives in what are called *interest categories*, or stakeholders. For ecotourism and sustainable tourism, these categories would be:

1) Suppliers, such as hotels, tour operators, tour boats;
2) Users, such as tourist and consumer associations and travel agents.;
3) Directly affected public, including indigenous people and local communities;
4) General interest, including conservation organizations, universities, consultants, and government.

The principles of consensus and balance make good sense because if the potential benefits of the standards are to be realized they must be accepted by as many "materially affected interests" as possible. A consensus among such parties during development of a standard clearly increases its prospects for broad acceptance. It should be noted that initial drafts of standards need not be developed from scratch by a full balanced committee. They may delegate preparation to task groups or even contract out, but the balanced full committee must consider the revised and final drafts.

Procedures that include due process and consensus, as well as an appeals mechanism, are also the prudent way to reduce exposure to litigation. Understandably, any organization that sponsors programs that dictate how businesses will operate, has the potential to restrict trade or increase prices, or establish criteria that affect safety and health eventually can expect to wind up as a defendant or codefendant in a legal action. Surprisingly, many NGOs considering establishing a standards or certification program are under the impression that somehow, as nonprofit organizations set up to promote worthy objectives, they are immune to such action. There is ample case law to demonstrate that this is a false assumption. Depending on the circumstances, a plaintiff may see fit to bring action against anyone or everyone in the supply chain, including the certifier and its accreditor. However, diligent implementation of procedures that foster equity and fair play and standards that represent a true consensus of balanced interests can be some of the best defenses, should there be a lawsuit. Potential legal problems can loom large as an organization considers establishing a certification or accreditation program, but the liability exposure is usually limited and the cost of liability insurance is reasonable. Hundreds of NGOs have weighed these issues and decided to establish certification programs. Nevertheless, experienced legal counsel should be consulted prior to initiating any program to develop standards, certify operations, or accredit certifiers.

Supply and Demand

There are many factors that prompt demand for certification, but any in-depth study will identify two characteristics that are common to all successful systems that are widely recognized and accepted:

1) They are demand-driven, that is the systems were established because of demands from major stakeholders, usually suppliers, and the systems continue to be responsive to the demands of the marketplace and stakeholders; and
2) They are self-supporting and financially stable.

Obviously, there is a cause and effect relationship between the two. Although some entrepreneurs have the attitude "Let's build it and customers will come," very few organizations can afford to invest in a conformity assessment system just on the hope that once it is established people will use it. If for no other reason, senior management and boards of directors have a fiduciary responsibility to see that the organization, its constituency, and sectoral stakeholders will realize tangible and intangible benefits as returns on the investment. Good intentions and expectations based on limited research are not enough. It is essential that the factors critical to supply and demand be identified and analyzed.

One of the most challenging tasks of tourism certification is to balance effective principles of sustainable tourism and ecotourism against criteria that tourists expect a certification program to address. To communicate effectively with tourists, it is important to understand which of the criteria in the appendix are of high interest and value to them. Although all these criteria should be included in the applicable standards, effective communication and marketing require a sharper focus. Creating awareness about certification among tourists is particularly challenging because tourism is worldwide. There is a plethora of ecolabels, and they continue to proliferate. As yet, however, there is no single, sustainable tourism certification mark that has achieved sufficient critical mass among tourists to elicit recognition. This problem is exacerbated in the global context of sustainable tourism certification. Ideally, a sustainable tourism certification mark will mean the same thing wherever a tourist goes, and tourists will have confidence that certifiers apply the same (or equivalent) criteria and that all assessments are equally rigorous. To make it easier for tourists, as well as to promote recognition, the same mark should be incorporated in certification of hotels and ecolodges, dive boats and tour buses, golf courses and jungle safaris.

The demand for some well-established sustainable tourism programs (e.g., in Australia, Costa Rica, Quebec) came from hoteliers and tour operators who were sincerely committed to sound sustainability, environmental, ecological, and socioeconomic practices. They faced what they perceived as unfair competition from "cowboys" or "greenwashers," who claimed similar practices but had taken no concrete action. The image and reputation of the entire tourism industry could suffer if tourists came away with the impression that sustainable tourism was just a marketing theme that was not really put into practice. Differentiating conscientious suppliers from less reputable ones has always been an objective of certification.

Field studies by the author have identified a key factor that determines whether hoteliers seek certification. They prefer to invest in a certification program with a grading mechanism rather than an absolute pass/fail decision. Truly committed operations that are willing to invest time and resources and motivate their staff have concerns that if deficiencies are found in a few areas they would be denied any indication of their commitments to sustainable tourism in a pass/fail system. This perceived risk can be decisive in choosing to seek certification. Hoteliers also report that a grading system is an incentive to address deficiencies and continually improve their operations. Motivation is particularly strong when a hotel with a four- or five-star quality rating merits a sustainable tourism rating of only two or three, or when a lodge that claims to have a comprehensive ecofriendly operation receives a low rating after third-party assessment.

The most critical factor on the supply side is cost. There are two types of costs. One is direct costs of assessment and certification and periodic reassessments. The second is implementation costs. These include time to learn about the certification program, its criteria, and what needs to be done to comply. Then there is orientation of staff, training of key people, working with suppliers, setting up mechanisms for monitoring performance, outreach to the community, and obtaining feedback. Up to this point, the supplier should have very limited out-of-pocket expenses. However, when equipment needs to be upgraded and new systems installed to handle wastewater, conserve energy, and other capital-intensive initiatives, the costs can be substantial. There has been little study of this aspect. Consultants glibly point out that investment in conservation of energy and water can soon pay for itself. Nevertheless, the supplier must somehow find the cash or credit to make these improvements so as to be certified. This is where a credible, recognized certification program can make a difference by showing government agencies, banks, and NGO lenders that supporting such investments is not only good business, but good for the community and the economy. Low-interest or subsidized loans, matching grant funds, tax credits, and waiver of taxes and duties on imported equipment are some possible approaches. Some jurisdictions already provide relief of taxes or duties on energy-efficient equipment, while others provide subsidies. A related need, particularly for smaller operations, is information on sources of equipment, suppliers, and services that can facilitate compliance with the sustainability standards, as well as authoritative interpretations of those standards.

Discussions of certification in the tourism sector often start with the premise that suppliers cannot afford the direct costs of assessment and certification. This has been repeated so often that the premise has become an accepted dictum even though there may be no information on the true costs of assessment and certification or pricing limits within the marketplace. But there is another way to look at these costs. The cost issue is related to the marketing advantages. If you pay $200 and do not get any exposure or more clients, it was an unwise expense. If you pay $350 and get exposure, tools to differentiate your business, a better image, and more clients, it was a sound investment and a good deal.[9]

The assumption that assessment and certification costs are unaffordable to most tourism operations appears to be based on the fees charged by multinational certifiers to ISO 9000 and ISO 14000 and fees charged by two of the earliest certifiers of hotels to their criteria for sustainability. In all these cases, the auditors were foreign-based and traveled long distances for preassessment surveys as well as the formal assessment. In addition, nearly all of these certifiers are for-profit organizations. One of the lessons learned is to use qualified local assessors who are paid fees prevailing in the area, not international rates. Another is to keep a flat management structure without numerous levels of indirect staff, who add to overhead. A recent study in Central America concludes that in some parts of the world it is more cost-effective to establish regional rather than country-specific sustainable tourism certification programs.[10] Centralized regional programs would make better use of trainers and auditors, and funding goes further for awareness and marketing within the industry and to tourists. This approach has the added advantage of exposing a larger pool of tourists to certified sustainable tourism, generating demand-side spillovers. Costs of assessment and certification for small suppliers can also be reduced when there is a mechanism enabling assessment teams to evaluate a number of applicants during a visit. Tourism-related trade associations, such as the Caribbean Hotel Association, have demonstrated that they are well-positioned to handle this and other aspects of scheduling, training, and orientation at very low cost.

To maintain their independence and credibility, certifiers must have a sound financial footing. Decisions on whether an applicant qualifies for certification should not be influenced by the need to maintain a positive cash flow. Although some certification programs start out with government support, trade association contributions, and donor grants, these sources of funding cannot be counted on for the long term. No one can guarantee that financial support will be maintained, and there are many examples of worthwhile, proven conservation programs that have collapsed when support was not renewed. Any organization establishing a certification program needs to shape the program so that it will be self-supporting. A widely used approach in conservation circles is user fees. As with national forests and coral parks, operating costs should be covered by the beneficiaries—in this case, the tourism industry and its customers.

Another side of certification that needs to be taken into account when considering demand factors is the negative attitude of many business people toward any initiatives that might be construed as a form of regulation. They question the value of management system standards and complain about the intrusiveness of auditors and the high direct costs of certification and actual and hidden implementation costs. Attempts to apply similar conformity assessment practices to other areas, such as occupational health and safety, risk management, and social accountability, have reinforced the view that assessment and certification are driven by the suppliers of these services, not by the users nor the marketplace.[11] Whether these attitudes are justified or not, such views and other doubts exist within the tourism sector. They must be weighed and addressed and factored into a certification program's business plan and marketing efforts.

Some Caveats

Certification is not the silver bullet that assures that all tourism facilities and services will magically implement best practices. Well before a certification program is introduced the affected jurisdiction must develop a tourism policy and plan. This is primarily a political process, and indigenous people and local communities must have the opportunity to participate. Standards and certification are not the drivers of this process but are tools that can facilitate implementation of policies and plans. Some of the biggest impediments to sustainable tourism are inadequate (or nonexistent) land use planning; ineffective enforcement of statutes on land use when they do exist; and failure to integrate environmental considerations into tourism policies. Voluntary standards and certification programs can help make some progress, but they may not be the complete answer when political will is lacking.

Stakeholders in sustainable tourism should not fixate on certification to the extent that more significant achievements become secondary. The primary objectives are to implement the principles of sustainable tourism and thereby improve environmental performance and the quality of life in local communities, to enable disadvantaged groups to share in the benefits of tourism, and to meet the expectations of tourists. Tangible results come from commitment, effective use of available resources, and striving to improve operations. Certification verifies that systems are in place, determines if improvements have been realized, motivates proprietors to participate in the program, and can be a strong marketing tool. But sustainable tourism certification should not be the end in itself.

Notes

1. Herbert Hamele, based on the ECOTRANS archive, http://www.eco-tip.org and World Tourism Organization, *Voluntary Initiatives for Sustainable Tourism* (Madrid: WTO, 2002).

2. International Organization for Standardization, *The ISO Survey of ISO 9000 and ISO 14000 Certification—Tenth Cycle* (Geneva: ISO Central Secretariat, 2001) or online: http://www.iso.ch/iso/en/iso9000-14000/pdf/survey10thcycle.pdf (July 2001).

3. Conservation & Development and Rainforest Alliance, *Environmental Certification for Tour Boat Operators in the Galapagos Islands* (Quito: Corporation for Conservation and Development, January 2001), available on Rainforest Alliance Web site: http://www.rainforest-alliance.org/programs/sv/sv-standards.pdf.

4. Nature and Ecotourism Accreditation Program, "Nature and Ecotourism Accreditation Program" (Brisbane: NEAP, August 2000).

5. American National Standards Institute (ANSI), *Procedures for the Development and Coordination of American National Standards*, section 1.2 (New York, ANSI, January 2002), available on American National Standards Institute Web site: http://www.ansi.org/public/library/std_proc/anspro.html.

6. Ibid., section 1.2.1.

7. Ibid., section 1.2.3.

8. Ibid., section 1.3.

9. Maurice Couture, "Introductory Message," Certification Workshop Summary, Planeta.com, www.planeta.com/ecotravel/tour/certsummary_reports.html, January 25, 2001.

10. Carol Jones et al., "Strategic Issues in the Design of a Green Certification Program for Tourism," in *Environment for Growth: Environmental Management for Sustainability and Competitiveness in Central America*, ed. Theodore Panayotou (Cambridge, MA: Harvard University Press, 2001), 292–321.

11. Robert B. Toth, "Conformity Assessment: The New Imperative," in *Proceedings, Second Interdisciplinary Workshop on Standardization Research* (Hamburg:VW Foundation, May 24–27, 1999), 228–249.

Chapter 3

Certification Systems for Sustainable Tourism and Ecotourism: Can They Transform Social and Environmental Practices?[1]

Michael E. Conroy

Tourism is arguably the world's largest industry. Present to some degree in every nation of the world, it employs millions of people in activities that serve the recreational desires of hundreds of millions of travelers every year.[2] Estimated total receipts from international tourism alone (i.e., not including global domestic tourism) exceeded $500 billion dollars in 2000 and grew by more than 7 percent that year over 1999 levels. Although this industry, like many others, suffered setbacks in the wake of the tragedies of September 11, 2001, tourism experts predict that the industry will recover its previous pace of growth in 2002.[3]

Tourism, that is, travel for pleasure, needs both a clean and healthy environment and vast quantities of low-skilled and high-skilled labor. As such, it is an industry that should be susceptible to the principles of sustainable development on both social and environmental grounds. Yet both tourism and travel are often criticized for their nonsustainable dimensions, including:

• The tendency of the industry to consume enormous quantities of petroleum products, thereby contributing to the generation of greenhouse gases, and to disperse petroleum residues worldwide at damagingly high altitudes;
• The tendency of the industry to involve foreign investors who take over a nation's most scenic natural resources, provide minimal training to local workers, and consume minimally from local production, while damaging and destroying the very resources upon which they depend; and
• The cultural conflicts under which tourists are isolated from local pop-

ulations in guarded enclaves, prey upon the local population for sexual and other services, or contribute otherwise to the degradation of local health and culture.

Can tourism be made sustainable? There is ample evidence that both industry and consumers are concerned with these issues. The tourism industry worldwide has developed no fewer than 250 voluntary initiatives, including codes of conduct, awards, best practices and benchmarking programs, labels, and seals designed to assure consumers that their services are provided in a more sensitive and more sustainable fashion.[4] Whether it is the private, for-profit Green Globe system or the government-supported system in Costa Rica, this cacophony of claims may be more confusing than helpful to the consumer who wishes to be selective in the use of his or her tourism funds.

In recent years, there has been enormous growth in programs that seek to certify to consumers that firms are practicing high levels of social and environmental responsibility. Bolstered by advocacy campaigns on the part of national and international nongovernmental organizations, this tendency is indeed a new movement for private, voluntary, market-based governance of corporate practices. This global growth in efforts to provide certification—that is, the development of systems that provide negotiated sets of standards and independent, third-party verification that those standards have been met—may offer an important opportunity to build consumer demand within the tourism industry for improved information and assurance to travelers that they are not damaging the communities whose recreational benefits they enjoy. The emergence of a certification movement is closely associated with the evolution of newly defined trading rules under the Global Agreement on Trade and Tariffs and the World Trade Organization. Understanding the origins and implications of these trading rules will help to visualize the potential strengths and weaknesses of private voluntary certification as an approach to corporate accountability and to distinguish it from strict regulatory processes.

The Global Context for Certification

World trade was brought under a dramatically changed set of rules in 1994 with the signing of the Marrakesh Treaty, which created the World Trade Organization as a new mechanism for governing the trade relations among its members. Membership in the World Trade Organization reached 142 nations in 2001 with the accession of both the People's Republic of China and the state of Taiwan. The World Trade Organization has drawn great international attention during its first six or seven years, partly because of the extensive debates over the implementation of its rules for governing international trade and partly because of the massive protests against its rules and regulations that occurred in Seattle in 2000 and in Genoa in 2001. The reach of World Trade Organization rules extends much further than most people realize.

Few consumers realize, for example, that the World Trade Organization prohibits placing any restrictions on products or services solely because of the way they were produced. Forest products, for instance, cannot be banned on the basis of the ways in which the timber is logged, no matter how egregious the denuding of whole mountainsides, no matter how much erosion or contamination of rivers may have resulted, no matter the labor conditions under which logging, milling, and finishing took place. Similarly, textiles and apparel cannot be banned because of the working conditions faced in factories abroad. Food products cannot be prohibited on the basis of the chemicals used in their production, not even when those chemicals are banned in the importing country.

For the tourism industry, the evolving World Trade Organization rules on trade in services such as airline transport and hotels have created conditions under which countries can no longer protect their national airlines from international competition, countries cannot build the tourism industry by extending preferential treatment to local, environmentally more responsible, or socially more rooted tourism firms, and government intervention in creating a healthy, sustainable tourism industry is sharply restricted.

The ways that products are produced, "production and process methods" (PPMs) in the language of trade negotiators, were deliberately excluded from the Uruguay round of trade negotiations that concluded with the agreement to create the World Trade Organization. At the time, negotiators representing the governments of all the nations involved in the modification of trade rules believed that countries might use their disapproval for the ways that products are made in other countries as a barrier to free trade that would bar their importation. For the services industries, such as tourism, negotiators from the advanced industrial countries sought to open tourism markets around the world for their investors, refusing to accept constraints on the social and environmental characteristics of the industry that might favor local groups, no matter how much better they might be in terms of sustainability.

The impact of this exclusion has been significant. No matter how high a local community or a nation chooses to set its own standards for social and environmental regulations, including minimum wage laws, environmental protection laws, or worker safety laws, that same government cannot impede the importation of items produced under much worse (and presumably less costly) conditions elsewhere in the world. Nor can they impose social or environmental regulations on international investors in service industries that are different from those required of national investors. This decision by the trade negotiators has unleashed a massive force for lowering social and environmental standards worldwide, under-cutting generations of legislative progress and hard-earned community and worker rights.

Concern about production and process methods, however, has increased rapidly since the creation of the World Trade Organization. This chapter outlines the origins and development of the movement to use voluntary, stakeholder-based, negotiated social and environmental standards to substitute for the inability of nations to exert control over the nature of products they import. This international movement toward voluntary standards previously has been described in terms of the pursuit of higher corporate accountability and the use of certification processes based on firms' altruistic behavior.[5] This chapter describes a more dynamic, advocacy-led process that is changing corporate practices more rapidly than altruism alone has done in the past and in ways that governments may no longer be able to undertake under current World Trade Organization rules. It outlines the strategies used by social and environmental advocacy organizations to target certain industries and bring about corporate compliance with sets of social and environmental standards, the reasons why some corporations are positively seeking to participate in standard-setting and certification processes, and the lessons for market-based citizen-led advocacy that can be drawn from these experiences. These are lessons that potentially can be applied to both tourism certification initiatives as well as to much broader areas of civil society. The conclusion, succinctly, is that advocacy-led certification processes, in the words of researchers at Duke University, "have arisen to govern firm behavior in a global space that has eluded the control of states and international organizations."[6] More explicitly, the processes represent an increasingly successful pursuit of alternatives to the downward pressure placed upon social and environmental responsibility by the refusal of the World Trade Organization to permit the use of PPMs as a basis for trade policy.

In the evaluation of the potential efficacy of this approach to the improvement of sustainability in the tourism industry, let us review the experiences of two early and relatively successful advocacy-led stan-dard-setting processes. The first is the Forest Stewardship Council, a small international, nongovernmental organization that has set the highest standards for social and environmental responsibility in sustainable forest management and has stunned the forest products industry by the speed of its growth. The second is the "fair trade" certification movement, originally established in Europe in the early 1990s, which has grown most rapidly since adopting advocacy-based processes in the United States in 1998.

Seemingly Improbable Recent Events

Who would have guessed that representatives of Greenpeace, the Natural Resources Defense Council, and other environmental groups would share the podium in June 1998 with the top executives of MacMillan Bloedel, the giant Vancouver-based timber and paper company, and would encourage consumers to give preference to "MacBlo" products? The environmental groups had long pilloried MacMillan Bloedel for its clear-cutting forest practices in Clayoquot Sound on Vancouver Island and elsewhere on the British Columbia coast. On that day, however, MacMillan Bloedel announced that it would cease clear-cutting practices in its British Columbia logging operations and that it would seek broader certification of its forest management under the principles of the Forest Stewardship Council. Commenting on this announcement, Lester Brown, president of Worldwatch Institute, noted:

> Under the leadership of a new chief executive, Tom Stevens, the company affirmed that clear-cutting will be replaced by selective cutting, leaving trees to check runoff and soil erosion, to provide wildlife habitat, and to help regenerate the forest. In doing so, it acknowledged the growing reach of the environmental movement. MacMillan Bloedel was not only being pressured by local groups, but it also had been the primary target of a Greenpeace campaign to ban clear-cutting everywhere...
>
> Among giant corporations that could once be counted on to mount a monolithic opposition to serious environmental reform, a growing number of high profile CEOs have begun to sound more like spokespersons for Greenpeace than for the bastions of global capitalism of which they are a part...What in the world is going on?[7]

The Greenpeace campaign had focused on a relatively novel "markets campaign" strategy: to lobby and demonstrate against the purchasers of MacMillan Bloedel forest products, pressuring them to cancel or threaten to cancel orders unless the firm implemented improved environmental practices.[8]

A second seemingly improbable event occurred on October 8, 1999, when the Rainforest Action Network (RAN) published a full-page advertisement in the *New York Times* urging consumers to shop at Home Depot,

Inc. The ad was unlikely for many reasons. RAN had campaigned actively against Home Depot for more than two years, orchestrating more than 700 demonstrations against the company's purchasing policies. RAN had organized activists who climbed into the rafters of Home Depot stores, dressed in grizzly bear costumes, and used megaphones to decry the destruction of grizzly bear habitat in British Columbia by firms shipping lumber to Home Depot. RAN had draped the Home Depot headquarters building with five-story banners decrying the logging practices of its suppliers, and it had filled billboards across the street from a Home Depot shareholder meetings with images of forest clear-cutting allegedly linked to Home Depot's wood purchases.[9] RAN also was alleged to have been behind other, less traditional means of placing pressure on the firm, including a somewhat scurrilous Web site. The paid advertisement in the *New York Times* that praised Home Depot resulted from a decision by the firm, announced on August 26, 1999, to end all purchases of wood products coming from old growth forests and to give preference in its purchases to products certified as arising from sustainable forest practices, such as under the standards of the Forest Stewardship Council.[10]

A third startling event of this sort occurred on April 13, 2000, when Global Exchange, a social activist organization in Oakland, California, turned threatened demonstrations against the Starbucks coffee chain in thirty U.S. cities into demonstrations in praise of its coffee purchasing practices. Starbucks is the largest chain of coffee houses in the United States, accounting for more than 20 percent of the total. Global Exchange had spent more than a year orchestrating a campaign against Starbucks because the firm refused to sell brands of coffee certified to provide higher prices and better conditions for small-scale coffee producers worldwide. This effort was part of a much longer, multiyear strategy to improve the benefits from trade for producers of a number of products in the global South through various mechanisms, including a certified "fair trade" system. Four days before the planned demonstrations, Starbucks executives signed a letter of intent with TransFair USA, a Fair Trade Certification organization, to sell certified coffee in all 2,700 Starbucks outlets in the United States. On October 4, 2000, certified fair trade coffee began to appear at Starbucks.[11] It wasn't the only coffee they sold, nor was it a coffee brewed for sale very frequently; but certified fair trade coffee became available to the U.S. public in many, many more locations than ever before. From that beginning, Starbucks' purchases of certified fair trade coffee have grown from a few thousand pounds per year to an anticipated one million pounds annually in 2002 and 2003.[12] Many other roasters in the United States began to follow the Starbucks lead.

Basic Concepts

What are the certification systems that have triggered these improbable events? They are market-driven processes designed to encourage and reward firms that choose to produce or trade in products that use the highest social and environmental standards in their production. Rather than requiring those standards by law (which is often politically difficult to achieve), and rather than trying to block the importation of products that do not meet the standards (which is not allowed under World Trade Organization rules), certification offers a positive alternative system designed to encourage compliance with voluntary standards and to reward those who do comply by offering increased market share and, at times, market price premiums. As applied to forest management, Upton and Bass have defined certification as "an economic market-based instrument which aims to raise awareness and provide incentives for both producers and consumers towards a more responsible use of forests." [13]

In theory, certification requires little more than an independent assessment of management practices. In reality, the creation of a credible certification system requires the development of standards by a diverse set of stakeholders in an inclusive process designed to build consensus. Without an agreed-upon set of standards, the meanings of certification can vary widely. The mere presence of standards, however, does not provide assurance that they are being fulfilled by producers. There is a need, therefore, to establish a set of third-party certifiers who are independent of the outcome of the certification process, as well as an accreditation system for the certifiers that assures the integrity of their application of the standards.

The Forest Stewardship Council

The Forest Stewardship Council (FSC), a nonprofit organization created by an international assembly of about 300 people in Toronto in 1993, has built a certification system whose aim is to transform the $50 billion worldwide timber industry. The FSC opened its offices in 1994 in Oaxaca, Mexico, partly because it wanted to be based in the global South and partly because of the personal preferences of its first executive director. From that original base, the FSC has grown to have operations in fifty countries; its international headquarters will be moved to Europe in 2002.

The governance of the FSC is structured around three "chambers": an environmental chamber, an economic chamber, and a social chamber. Each chamber represents a group that has a vested interest in—or are stakeholders in—the management of forests around the world. In addition, the FSC structures all of its international activities to include balanced representation from the global North and the global South. When people run for election to the FSC board of directors, for example, they run for a position in the "social chamber from the global North," or for the "economic chamber from the global South."

How does it work? The Forest Stewardship Council has developed a stakeholder-based set of forest management standards with ample participation of all three chambers, including timber and paper industry representatives, social and environmental nongovernmental organizations (NGOs), and local community representatives. The FSC does not undertake the certification itself; rather it accredits other organizations or firms to perform the certification. It assesses candidates to make certain that they have the capability and knowledge of the field to analyze the forest management practices of applicant timber companies. It monitors the certifiers, resolves any disputes that may arise in the application of the standards, and protects the integrity of the label that it creates. The certifiers themselves determine the eligibility of firms and other forest owners to receive certification, issue the FSC certificates, and then monitor compliance annually to assure continued eligibility.

There are two types of certificates issued by the FSC. The first is a "forest management certificate" based upon how the forest is managed; the second is a "chain-of-custody" certificate that tracks the wood from the forest to the consumer. To obtain chain-of-custody certification, a mill that is going to process certified wood is required to establish a system for keeping the certified wood separate from the noncertified wood. Only forest products derived from wood from certified forests and processed in a certified chain-of-custody mill or factory qualify to carry the FSC logo (figure 3.1).

The broad principles embodied in FSC standards for sustainable forest management embrace social as well as environmental characteristics, as exhibited in box 3.1. Detailed dimensions of each of these standards have been developed for worldwide application, and localized standards are being created for most of the countries (and for subregions within countries) where FSC is operating. The social standards are intended to secure and protect long-term tenure and use rights and the rights of indigenous

FSC   Figure 3.1. The FSC seal

Box 3.1. Forest Stewardship Council Principles (abridged version)

The Forest Stewardship Council principles state that to be certified, a forest operation shall:

- Meet all applicable laws.
- Have legally established, long-term forest management rights.
- Recognize and respect the rights of indigenous peoples.
- Maintain the economic and social well-being of local communities.
- Conserve the forest's economic resources.
- Protect biological diversity.
- Have a written management plan.
- Engage in regular monitoring.
- Conserve primary forests and well-developed secondary forests.
- Manage plantations so as to alleviate pressures on natural forests.

Source: Forest Stewardship Council-US, as quoted by Rose Gutfeld, in *Ethical Wood, Equitable Coffee: Big U.S. Retailers Give Certified Products a Major Boost*, Ford Foundation Report (Fall 2000).

peoples. The ecological standards specifically call for the conservation of old growth or primary forests and other high-priority conservation areas, a documented reduction in the use of chemicals such as herbicides, and a prohibition on the use of invasive or exotic species (including some genetically modified species) in tree plantations. FSC standards also call for the reduction of clear-cutting (the practice by which all trees and undergrowth are removed from large tracts of land), and they require the protection of the interests of local communities and forest industry workers. They allow for the certification of forest plantations so long as they comply with the other standards.

FSC Success

Since 1995, when FSC began certifying its first forests, the number of acres of forest certified around the world has grown to seventy million (as of mid-2002). To put this in context, there are approximately 1.1 billion acres (450 million hectares) of working forests worldwide. That suggests that the management of more than 6 percent of the world's working forests is now certified under the FSC standards. Similarly, more than 1,600 firms were certified for chain of custody of FSC-certified forest products as of mid-2002. The rates of growth are depicted in figure 3.2.

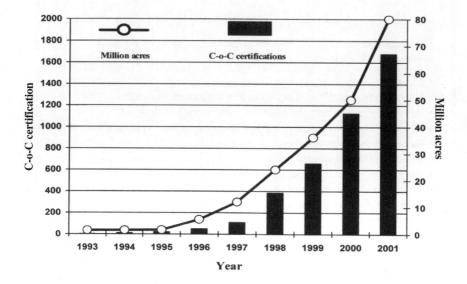

Figure 3.2. Growth in FSC Forest Management and Chain-of-Custody certifications

Success as measured by demand is even greater. The demand for FSC products has been growing far faster than supply. Price premiums are being paid for certified products, although this fact rarely is acknowledged publicly. Price premiums of 4–12 percent on softwoods in European markets are admitted by one of the largest European certified forest products firms. Premiums of 100 percent on certified teak have been paid to Malaysian exporters. One of Canada's largest forest products manufacturers has offered a 30 percent premium on FSC-certified timber delivered to its mills, even though its own forest lands are not yet certified.[14]

This demand is not driven directly by consumers of forest products who seek certified wood products in stores. It is driven, in fact, by the commitments of major producers of forest products, such as Andersen Windows, and by major retailers of forest products, such as IKEA and Home Depot in response to their own internal culture of social and environmental responsibility, a culture that is strongly encouraged by the pressure brought to bear by the advocacy networks' market campaigns. One indicator of these corporate commitments is the surging membership in the Global Forest and Trade Network (GFTN) and its U.S. member, the Certified Forest Products Council. More than 700 companies have now joined the GFTN, thereby formally expressing a preference for forest products certified under the FSC standards. The members include all five of the largest do-it-yourself retail chains in the United States, as well as major forest products manufacturers. The network also includes forest products business consumers, such as Nike (for paper and cardboard), The Gap (for flooring and shelving), and Kinko's (one of the largest purchasers of paper in the United States).[15]

The FSC also has major opponents. They are clustered in three rival forest management certification schemes in the global North. The first is an industry-created set of standards fashioned by the American Forest and Paper Association, the principal association of timber and paper companies in the United States. Its program, the Sustainable Forestry Initiative (SFI),[16] claimed to encompass 110 million acres of forests in the United States and Canada by the end of 2001. In Europe, where most large forests are now certified under the FSC, small-scale forest owners have set up a Pan-European Forest Certification system (PEFC), which in less than a year claims to have certified compliance with its standards on more than seventy-nine million acres (thirty-six million hectares).[17] Finally, a smaller rival certification scheme for forests is the Canadian Standards Association (CSA), a general purpose standard-setting organization with standards for more than 2,000 products.[18] The most complete comparative evaluation of the four systems to date reaches unambiguous conclusions. Using such criteria as transparency, stakeholder participation, and assessment procedures, the study concludes that:

> [T]he Forest Stewardship Council is currently the only independent and credible certification scheme in the [forest products] market. . . . This does not mean that the FSC scheme is perfect. Continued vigilance is required to ensure that its implementation lives up to its commitments.[19]

The report's toughest criticism focuses on the PEFC scheme, which was found to have substantial tracts of land certified as fulfilling PEFC requirements without ever being visited. Also, numerous tracts were included in the PEFC statistics without the landowners' knowledge or consent.

A further comparison of FSC and SFI has been published by the National Wildlife Federation, the Natural Resources Council of Maine, and Environmental Advocates.[20] It, too, found the following systemic differences:

- FSC sets more stringent guidelines in many areas of environmental protection, such as maintenance of older forest and reserve areas, use of chemicals, exotic and genetically modified species, and conversion of natural forest to plantations. These guidelines promote ecologically sound forest management.

• FSC is based on mandatory standards, and a required and consistently applied third-party audit; SFI is not.
• Most FSC standards emphasize on-the-ground field performance, but few SFI standards evaluate on-the-ground results.
• FSC requires public reporting of audit results and enforceable conditions; SFI does not.
• FSC has social criteria focusing on local communities and indigenous peoples; SFI does not.
• FSC has chain-of-custody certification and a product labeling system that allows processors, retailers and consumers to know confidently that their wood comes from a well-managed forest; SFI does not.

The battle will continue for the hearts and minds of consumers and retailers. The advantage rests with the FSC, however, precisely because of the strong support that it receives from many of the leading social and environmental NGOs. More importantly, perhaps, the creation and early success of the FSC has forced rival systems to improve their standards and their processes, emulating the FSC on many levels, and encouraging improvements, albeit lesser improvements, in the management of many other forests.

TransFair USA and Fairtrade Labeling Organizations International

A significantly different form of social certification is offered by the Fairtrade Labeling Organizations International (FLO International) and its U.S. affiliate, TransFair USA. The FLO was born of the Max Havelaar Foundation in the Netherlands and TransFair International in Germany, two groups that separately had begun to define criteria for fair trade and to label products that met those criteria. They joined into a common organization in 1998. The standards for certified fair trade coffee are quite simple (box 3.2). This certification system deliberately seeks to focus on improving the market conditions faced by small-scale family coffee farmers, many of them organized in cooperatives. Approximately 80–85 percent of the world's coffee farmers fall into this category.[21]

Fair Trade Certified coffee standards require buyers to pay a fixed minimum coffee price that was negotiated with small-scale producers in the 1990s. In mid-2001, that price was more than twice the prevailing spot market price ($1.26 per pound compared with about $.60 per pound) in a very depressed coffee market. Although twice the market price paid to farmers for green coffee at the point of production, the fair trade minimum

Box 3.2. Certified Fair Trade Criteria

Under TransFair USA's guidelines, coffee can be sold as Fair Trade–certified in the United States if importers agree to:

• Purchase from the family-farmer cooperatives included in the International Fair Trade Coffee Register.
• Guarantee cooperatives a minimum "fair-trade price" of $1.26 per pound for their coffee. If the world price rises above this floor, cooperatives will receive a small (five cents per pound) premium above the market price.
• Provide partial payment to farmers at the time they ship their coffee, against future sales, to help the cooperatives stay out of debt between harvest seasons.
• Develop direct, long-term relationships with producer groups, thereby cutting out middlemen and bringing greater commercial stability to an extremely unstable market.

And if coffee roasters agree to:

• Buy Fair Trade–certified coffee only from certified importers.
• Use the Fair Trade–certified label only on Fair Trade-certified products.
• Use the label only on blends that contain 100% Fair Trade-certified coffee.
• Submit quarterly reports to TransFair of all sales and purchases of Fair Trade products.
• Pay TransFair a licensing fee of 10 cents for each pound of green Fair Trade–certified coffee purchased from a certified importer.

price is still less than 15 percent of the price paid by consumers in retail markets in the global North.

Buyers of certified fair trade coffee must make available partial payment to the farmers at the time their coffee is shipped, when requested. This differs from the usual industry practice in which producers ship their coffee to brokers and are paid only if and when that coffee is eventually sold. The resulting delays in payments often force small-scale coffee farmers to fall back upon usurious credit systems because they must cover all the costs of harvesting and processing the coffee months before they are paid by the brokers. Finally, certified fair trade coffee encourages longer-term contractual relationships and discourages one-time purchases on the spot market.

Sales of Fair Trade–certified coffee in the United States have gone from virtually nothing in 1998 to an estimated seven million pounds in 2001; global sales of the entire FLO network in Europe and the United States are expected to exceed thirty million pounds in 2001. There are now more

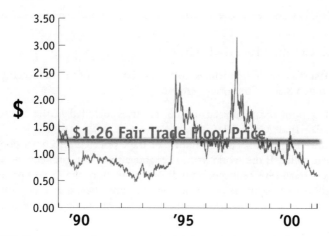

Figure 3.3. Spot coffee prices compared with Fair Trade-Certified minimum price

than 100 coffee companies selling Fair Trade Certified coffee in the United States, including the pioneer companies (Equal Exchange, Peace Coffee, and Cooperative Coffees); café chains such as Starbuck's, Peet's, and Tully's; food chains such as Whole Foods, Wild Oats, Andronico's, ShopRite, Stop 'n' Shop, some Safeway stores; and even most ExxonMobil convenience stores in New England.

The direct impact of this upon the coffee farmers is significant, especially in times of very low market prices paid to farmers for their green coffee. With the current $0.60 per pound difference between the spot price in mid-2001 and the minimum price of $1.26 paid for Fair Trade Certified coffee, sales of this level imply annual net gains for farmers of more than $18 million dollars per year for participating in fair trade certification.

But demand in this case, unlike the markets for certified forest products,

Figure 3.4. The Fair Trade-Certified label

remains well below supply. There are more than 400,000 farmers listed on the fair trade worldwide coffee producer registry; they produce an estimated 170 million pounds of coffee each year.[22] After growth in sales in Europe began to stagnate in the mid-1990s, growth in the U.S. markets has led the world. The growth of sales in the United States has been driven, more than anywhere else, by NGO advocacy, such as the Global Exchange campaign to convince companies to offer certified coffee to their customers.

Elements of a Theory: The Attraction of Certification for Transnational Corporations

Why would corporations willingly choose to participate in certification schemes? The logic can be established in a set of simple propositions:

1) **Branding**: Given the increasing importance of retail concentration and the top-level importance to firms of establishing their brands—for some firms, the majority of their investment is said to go toward branding—consumer awareness is the name of the game in terms of global production growth. The historical importance of branding has been the focus of countless studies. Marketing specialists look with envy upon global brands, "brands whose positioning, advertising strategy, personality, look, and feel are in most respects the same from one country to another."[23] This is a problematic strategy for smaller firms, reinforcing its importance and advantage for large firms.[24]

2) **Vulnerability**: The more successful a firm becomes in dominating a particular industry and the more successful it is in getting worldwide recognition of its product label or logo, the more vulnerable it becomes to pressure on social and environmental grounds. Every dollar invested successfully in strengthening consumer recognition of a global brand paradoxically also increases the firm's vulnerability to attacks on that brand.

3) **Risk reduction**: Certification systems can constitute a risk-reduction strategy for globally branded firms, a form of insurance against criticism of a firm's practices. Unsubstantiated or fraudulent attacks may be easy to thwart, but well-organized, well-documented acts of corporate engagement by NGOs are the marketing manager's nightmare. The best response is to search for a certification system to validate that the firm is, in fact, pursuing appropriate social and environmental practices.

4) **Credibility**: It is only natural for a firm to assert a code of conduct according to which it will perform. But the claims of individual firms have little credibility with consumers and less with advocacy groups. Often, an industry attempts to create a carefully controlled industry-wide set of standards to protect its members from charges of social or

environmental irresponsibility. The chemical industry was one of the first to develop such a scheme, the Responsible Care Program initiated after the disaster in Bhopal, India.[25] The Sustainable Forestry Initiative is another of these second-party certification attempts, wherein the industry association sets standards that are relatively easy for all of its members to meet. But such first- and second-party claims have weak credibility. Hence, no matter how sophisticated the process, they yield little risk reduction. It does not take long to realize that independent, third-party certification is the only road to credible certification, although hundreds of millions of dollars have been spent by firms as they have sought to avoid reaching that conclusion.

5) **Costs**: Previous economic analyses of the costs of certification tended to focus on the fixed costs of meeting minimum standards and obtaining certification, plus the variable costs of expanding the output of certified products.[26] It is equally important, however, to recognize the additional benefits, over and above sheer production economics, that businesses gain from engaging with certification systems. Businesses understand the value of reducing a risk, and they are normally willing to pay for that reduction. They pay for bonding of key management employees, and they insure themselves against exchange rate risk and casualties of all sorts. By the same logic, they are willing to pay for certification that their practices meet well-established standards. The costs of certification, furthermore, may be offset by savings associated with shortening the value chain. Chain-of-custody certification in forest products has tended to reduce the number of intermediaries, generating net benefits for both producers and retailers. Fair Trade Certified coffee, for example, is most often sold directly from producer cooperatives to roasters, again shortening the value chain and permitting a combination of higher prices for the producers (as warranted by the requirements for certification) without requiring the roaster or retailer to charge higher final market prices. Home Depot, a notoriously tough negotiator of prices for forest products, is paying a premium for most of the certified wood it purchases, yet it does not pass that premium on to the consumer.

6) **Protection from less responsible firms**: The firms in an industry that have chosen to implement higher levels of accountability and responsibility (or that have been required by local regulations to do so) may choose to seek certification of their practices to compete more effectively with those firms that are less responsible. Timber producers in states such as Oregon and Washington, for example, where state-mandated forest management practices are stricter than the national average, find that certification to FSC standards validates their more

responsible practices and lessens the price competition from producers in other states whose costs of production are lower because their practices are less responsible.

7) **Ancillary benefits**: There are additional benefits for industry leaders in certification. These can include the positive advantages of market differentiation brought about by early entry into a green or Fair-Trade–certified market. Some retailers have reported that employee satisfaction with their leadership in the shift to certified forest products has increased morale and reduced turnover, yielding immediate benefits in terms of labor costs. Financial markets are increasingly aware of environmental risks, and the so-called socially responsible investors networks often use FSC certification as a screen for the highest levels of social and environmental responsibility in the industry. The latest example of this is the June 2001 announcement of the creation of the Xylem Rainforest Fund, L.P., which is seeking to invest $500 million in forestry companies in the tropics and subtropics that adhere to the FSC standards for sustainable forest management.[27]

These propositions constitute the simple facts of why a firm would find certification systems to its benefit, so long as the costs imposed by meeting the standards were not excessive.

Elements of a Theory: Why NGOs Find Certification Systems Attractive

What leverage do certification systems offer to advocacy groups that seek to improve the social and environmental performance of firms? A parallel logic leads creative NGOs, from Greenpeace and World Wildlife Fund to Global Exchange and Oxfam, to find corporate engagement through certification systems a highly productive approach to reaching their goals.

1) **Global advocacy**: Over the past fifty years, there have been myriad campaigns focused on advocacy against certain corporate practices. Improved international communications have greatly increased the ability of advocates to orchestrate truly global sets of actions. Increased transparency in firms and changing governmental reporting requirements have increased further the ability of advocacy groups to launch market-focused campaigns. Networks of NGOs have begun to organize as never before to wield "sticks" against corporations and official global economic institutions, documenting and criticizing their practices and calling for changes in behavior.[28] However, when there is no agreed-upon set of changes that are being pursued, the resulting changes in corporate behavior may be difficult to document. More-

over, continued changes in practice may be costly to monitor, and the permanence of changes therefore may be questionable. Maintaining the energy of staff, volunteers, and contributors for such efforts may be difficult.

2) **Consolidating the gains of advocacy, plus an alternative**: Certification systems embody a specific set of alternative practices toward which advocacy campaigns can drive corporate and other international actors. Systems for verifying change and for monitoring it over time can be set up that are independent of both the advocacy NGO and of the target corporation or institution. These systems can be financially self-sufficient if the organization seeking certification pays the costs of the certification process. Success can be measured tangibly. Satisfaction with the changes produced can motivate staff and volunteers to continue the effort and can motivate financial supporters to continue to provide funding.

3) **Stakeholder-based standards**: Standards can be created out of whole cloth and superimposed on the subjects of the process, but direct engagement of corporations and other institutions in the standard-setting process increases the likelihood of reaching consensus on requirements that are both improvements over current practice and minimally acceptable to the target firms. Multiple voices can be incorporated; standards to meet all of their needs can be created; and advocacy can be used to encourage continued participation by the firms in the standard-setting process. Ownership of the resulting standards by the full range of stakeholders is much more likely to achieve the stipulated goals than could be expected with externally superimposed standards.

4) **Identification of industry leaders**: Just as labor unions select an industry leader on the basis of complex analyses of the firms with which to negotiate, NGOs can identify an industry leader on the basis of its vulnerability "on the ground." This may be a function of the evidence available with respect to its practices, or it may relate to its importance in the industry. MacMillan Bloedel was apparently selected by advocacy groups in British Columbia because of its paramount importance in the region. It also may have been selected because its president was in the middle of a turnaround, in which he took a firm that was losing more than $300 million per year and transformed it into one that was earning nearly $50 million per year. Starbucks may have been a target for advocacy in support of improved pricing practices for coffee farmers because of its national prominence and market share. It also may have been targeted because by promising to create a code of conduct for producers that sold to it, the firm had avoided a threatened

boycott in 1996 by the Guatemala Labor Education Project. Those promises later proved impossible for the small advocacy group to monitor, leading to negligible results.

5) **Positive imbalances**: The general public concedes greater credibility to advocacy groups than to firms or industry associations. This is a very important positive imbalance that NGOs can and do exploit. Firms and industry need very large marketing budgets to persuade the public that first-party or second-party sets of standards are worthy of consumer confidence. It takes far less resources for advocacy groups to counter those campaigns through well-organized press conferences, well-covered demonstrations, and the free publicity that these generate. The more attractive alternative for industry is to participate with advocacy groups in creating standards and certification systems that put both sides on the same track.

6) **Cumulative effects**: One reason given by coffee industry representatives for refusing to endorse certification of organic or sustainably harvested coffee (as revealed at a recent meeting of the Specialty Coffee Association of America) is their fear that consumers will see labeled coffees and ask "What's wrong with all the others?" Every successful certification scheme, every label well-placed before consumers, and every campaign that successfully raises consumer consciousness of production and process methods sows doubts about all unlabeled products on the shelf. Does this mean that full-fledged certification systems need to be created for every production dimension of every product? Not necessarily, for many production and process claims are already routinely used to distinguish environmentally preferable products. Chlorine-free and recycled paper products are examples. Requirements for the use of those labels have become codified in law, and government (presumably) monitors their appropriate use. The existence of dolphin-safe canned tuna has entered public awareness to the point that continued advocacy may be less necessary. More importantly, certification systems offer the possibility of raising public awareness to the point that unlabeled products will be increasingly resisted by consumers and laws to curtail repugnant environmental and labor practices will be pressed upon governments.

Certification and Poverty Alleviation

The movement for Fair Trade certification represents an explicit attempt to assure that the first level of producers, for example, the small-scale coffee farmers it is designed to serve, receive higher prices, more direct access to markets, and improved long-term contractual relationships with the buyers of their coffee. Consumers are encouraged to recognize that they are contributing to sustainable livelihoods for these farmers at a cost that may be only a few cents (and a very small percentage increase) in the price of the final product. Given that farmers are receiving as little as $0.60 per pound in mid-2001 for coffee that often retails at or above $10.00 per pound, the fair trade price to farmers of $1.26 per pound means an increase of 110 percent in the price that farmers receive. For the consumer, however, the increase is only about 6 percent, if, indeed, the full increase is passed on. This price premium is generally managed by the coffee cooperatives themselves, with some portion of it used to improve infrastructure of the co-op or to fund community projects, such as schools and clinics, and the remainder returned directly to the farmers.

The poverty alleviation impacts of certification of sustainably managed forests and chain-of-custody certification of forest products processors are less direct, possibly much greater, and generally less well documented. Livelihoods in the forest products industry may become more sustainable in certified forests, for managing forests sustainably most often implies a slower and more continuous rate of harvesting rather than the forty-year cycle of massive harvesting practiced by traditional commercial logging. The boom and bust history of temporary mill towns can be replaced, in theory, by a sustained balance between continuous harvesting of wood products and continuous processing of them over much longer periods of time, although the volumes harvested in any year would be well below the logging levels of typical commercial practices.

The ecological benefits of FSC standards help communities to build forest assets rather than destroy them, whether the forests are community-owned or privately owned. The use of variable retention harvesting techniques, as opposed to massive clear-cutting, is expected to reduce greatly the erosion that occurs and to retain forests of mixed age and species. It also contributes to the retention of greater biodiversity in fauna and flora, encouraging livelihoods based on nontimber forest products. Reductions in the use of chemicals diminish the damaging runoff into local streams, lessening the health consequences for local residents.

The chain-of-custody certification process also introduces or protects some aspects of the working conditions for workers in forest products mills. This certification requires that all local laws be followed, in addition to requirements for systematic management of certified products separate from uncertified products in a mill or factory. There have been examples in which worker safety conditions have been improved as a condition for chain-of-custody certification.[29]

Small-scale and community-based forests have had less success in penetrating the booming global market for certified forest products than large-scale industrial producers. But there is a growing number of successful community-based certification efforts that have reaped greater market access and, in some cases, significant market price premiums for their forest products that neighboring uncertified community forests were unable to obtain.

Applicability of the Theory to the Travel and Tourism Industry

The travel and tourism industries exhibit a number of characteristics in common with the forest products industry and the coffee industry, but the differences may be more significant. Some of the most important similarities are the following:

• There are major global retailers of travel and tourism services whose products are sold worldwide and who have the ability to specify the conditions that those products meet. American Express Travel Services, for example, could choose to book its clients only in those properties or on those tours where a minimum set of conditions are met. The shrinking of the number of global providers of air travel services and the acute competition that characterizes the industry offers opportunities for an industry leader to distinguish itself by the adoption of a set of travel standards that embrace sustainability better than its competitors.
• The major national and international associations of travel agents (such as ASTA in the United States) are analogous to the Specialty Coffee Association of America in their ability to call the attention of their members to the growing pressure for greater social and environmental responsibility and to assist their members in the development of adequate responses. As in the sustainable coffee industry, many tourism service providers are very small-scale producers, located in environmentally rich but economically poor areas; consumers will have well-founded concerns about the quality of the services that they might be provided.
• If, as in the forest products industry, small-scale providers have a competitive advantage in assuring the fulfillment of social standards, the establishment of distinct standards for sustainable tourism and ecotourism may provide a clear opportunity to privilege the contributions of the individuals and communities providing environmentally and socially sound services.

The differences between the tourism industry and the forest products and coffee industries begin with the fact that the travel and tourism industry provides a wide range of products and services without the unifying characteristics of a single commodity, such as forest products or coffee. This raises, as discussed in other chapters throughout this volume, a series of specific questions and challenges for certification programs in the travel and tourism industry. Among them:

- How does one establish a common set of standards that applies to air travel and cruise ship travel; hotels of all vintages, sizes, and descriptions; tourism products from skiing to scuba diving; and facilities in urban as well as remote rural locations?
- Given the existence of numerous tourism labeling schemes, how does one validate those that meet the resulting set of standards and verification criteria while demystifying those that have less credibility or less stringent requirements?
- How does one reduce consumer confusion over labeling processes without destroying the investment that has been placed in the strongest and most valid existing labeling schemes?
- Given the huge investments already in place for the big players in the tourism world, for example, the airlines, cruise ship lines, and car rental companies, how does one retrofit the industry to meet stringent new standards?

There are, on the other hand, advantages found in the tourism industry that one may not encounter in forest products or coffee. The Internet is not a vehicle for significant retail sales of coffee or forest products, but it is an important vehicle for the purchase of tourism and travel services. The importance of the Internet augurs well for the potential success of a new set of standards in the travel and tourism industry and the development of an accreditation system for both new and existing labeling schemes. It is much easier to provide the background information to consumers on the label or seal through hyperlinks directly on the vendors' Web pages than it is to provide point-of-sale information in grocery stores or lumber yards. NGO support for the seal could also be made more apparent through cross-posting of testimonials and cross-selling through the Web sites of the largest and strongest social and environmental supporters of the accreditation systems.

However, there are further important questions that need to be answered. Do tourists care enough about the social and environmental responsibility of their tourism service providers to seek out this information? Is there a sufficiently large proportion of consumers with these preferences to expect that attention will be paid to the setting of standards? Will consumers purchase socially and environmentally more responsible tourism and ecotourism services if they cost somewhat more? Can the market be moved to a tipping point beyond which less responsible service providers become isolated and their services identified as outlaw or less favorable?

It is important to remember that the growth in certification of forest management under the FSC has not been driven by consumers clamoring for FSC-certified products. It has been driven by the interaction of social and environmental NGOs and the major retail sellers of the forest products. The threat of damage to their global brand reputation is the prime mover of the retail industry, followed by the marketing advantages of taking the lead toward greater sustainability, especially when it is accompanied by testimonials from the advocacy groups that assist them in their efforts to distinguish themselves from their competitors.

It is not necessarily true that sustainably harvested forest products are more costly to produce over the long run. They are likely to be less profitable than forest products produced under less sustainable practices because timber firms can generate larger quantities of short-term profits from the unsustainable logging of public forest lands (by passing the costs to the public and to future generations) or even from their own timber lands, which they then often sell to insurance firms or developers after they have destroyed most of the forest resources. In similar fashion, the tourism industry can extract short-term profits from the unsustainable use of natural resources, including the dumping of effluents into the environment, overutilizing marine attractions by overbuilding facilities, destroying reefs or fisheries by excessive use, or by the "plastification" of facilities to resist heavy use, which destroys their natural qualities in the interest of short-term returns. Reducing destruction of environmental resources by controlling access through voluntary or legislative requirements is just as likely to generate higher profitability, through the marketing advantages that it brings to certified tourism properties and products, as it is to reduce profitability through lower volume. With both regulation or voluntary standards and certification, the longer run sustainable use of the environmental resources essential to the tourism opportunity can compensate for excessive short-term profits.

Voluntary market-based certification systems offer interesting intersections with government regulations, and they face complicated interactions with the emerging rule making of the World Trade Organization. To date, there has been no serious attempt at the level of the World Trade Organization to undercut the emergence of voluntary standards, whether of the ISO management systems type or the FSC performance-based standards. So long as they remain voluntary systems without official government sanction, they do not become official barriers to trade. Voluntary certification, however, can lead the development or accelerate the development, of higher regulatory standards. Higher regulatory standards facilitate the acceptance and implementation of certification systems. Bolivia, for example, is close to becoming the first developing country with most of its forest landscape certified under FSC standards. That result came about, in part, because the Bolivian government elected to establish some of the highest forest management standards in the world at precisely the same time that FSC certification was arising around the world. Forest concessionaires on government-owned land found that once they had met the Bolivian government requirements, it took relatively very little additional changes in their practices to qualify for FSC certification. Similarly, in states such as Oregon and Washington, which have very high forest management standards and requirements, FSC certification offers forest owners and managers a measure of validation of their high standards, access to specialized niche markets, and a degree of protection in the marketplace from the low-cost competition of timber harvesters who are not required to operate in such a stringent regulatory environment.

In the tourism and travel industry as well, one can expect that voluntary certification systems would establish criteria at levels that are higher than what one could normally expect in a legislative or regulatory process. Once the feasibility of meeting those standards is established (and industry participation in the development of the standards should assure that feasibility), it would not be surprising to find regulatory mechanisms that follow the lead of voluntary standards.

Conclusions

Citizen-led advocacy campaigns linked to the establishment of certification systems represent a new movement that is only now gaining major strength. The ability of advocacy groups to bring market pressures to bear upon firms offers a powerful alternative to simple invocations of corporate altruism and civic responsibility. In an increasingly privatized world, with restrictions on what the global trading system will allow local and national governments to legislate, these movements may be the only alternative to the competitive downgrading of social and environmental practices by firms worldwide.

There is evidence that financial markets are paying increasing attention to these dimensions of corporate practice, rewarding firms that become leaders and punishing those that lag behind. The incentives for corporate collaboration in the creation and management of certification systems appear to be growing. Struggles between NGOs and corporations can be expected to continue for many of the same reasons that firms also struggle against government regulations. In the twenty-first century, this dynamic new strategy for corporate engagement may become an important global force for "civilizing globalization" and for assuring that its environmental and social benefits exceed its costs. Although travel and tourism certification initiatives are less developed and less cohesive than in some other industries, there is every reason to believe that this NGO-led movement for improved corporate responsibility holds out the potential for transforming this industry as well in directions that are more socially and environmentally sustainable.

Notes

1. This paper has been adapted from a substantially similar paper by the author that was first distributed as a working paper of the Political Economy Research Institute at the University of Massachusetts, Amherst. The opinions in the paper are those of the author alone; they do not necessarily reflect in any way the perspectives of the Ford Foundation.
2. International tourist arrivals in 2000, as reported by the World Tourism Organization, were 698.8 million, up nearly 50 million over 1999. "World Tourism Highlights, 2001," http://www.world-tourism.org (August 2001).
3. World Tourism Organization, "Tourism after 11 September 2001: Analysis, remedial actions and prospects (updated November 2001)," (November 2001).
4. Martha Honey and Abigail Rome, *Protecting Paradise: Certification Programs for Sustainable Tourism and Ecotourism* (Washington D.C.: Institute for Policy Studies, October 2001) 11.
5. Christopher Upton and Stephen Bass, *The Forest Certification Handbook* (London: Earthscan Publications, Ltd., 1995).
6. Gary Gereffi, Ronie Garcia-Johnson, and Erika Sasser, "The NGO-Industrial Complex," *Foreign Policy* (July-August 2001), 56–65.
7. Lester R. Brown, "Crossing the Threshold," *World Watch* (March/April 1999).
8. For a history of the campaign, see the Greenpeace press release archive on forest campaigns at http://www.greenpeace.org. An analysis of the impacts of the market campaigns in British Columbia is provided by Sheldon Kamieniecki in "Testing Alternative Theories of Agenda Setting: Forest Policy Change in British Columbia, Canada," *Policy Studies Journal*, 28, no.1 (2000), 176–189.
9. This market campaign was documented in an article by Matt Biers-Ariel entitled "A Chanukah Forest Miracle," *Tikkun* (November/December 1999), 64–65. Home Depot's commitment to FSC-based certification is noted and explained on its Web site, under company info/ environment/forestry at http://www.homedepot.com.
10. A copy of the advertisement is available at Rainforest Action Network's Web site, http://www.ran.org/info_center/press_release.
11. Documentation of this market campaign may be found on the Global Exchange Web site, http://www.globalexchange.org/economy/coffee. Starbucks corporate analysis of certified fair trade coffee can be found at http://www.starbucks.com/aboutus/fairtrade.asp.
12. Starbucks, http://www.starbucks.com, press release, November 18, 2001.

13. Upton and Bass, *Forest Certification Handbook*, 42.
14. Documenting these market characteristics has proven difficult because it is in the interest of neither buyer nor seller to publicize the information. Buyers would prefer that sellers not expect a premium. Sellers receiving a premium have no interest in stimulating increases in supply by others, lest they lose their premium prices. So the evidence is largely anecdotal.
15. For a complete list of member firms, see the Certified Forest Products Council Web site: http://www.certifiedwood.org. Membership in the CFPC represents a commitment to the use of certified forest products; it does not, however, guarantee to consumers that member firms' practices in other areas, such as labor standards in nonforest areas, meet preferred levels of responsibility.
16. American Forest and Paper Association, http://www.afandpa.org/forestry/sfi/menu.html, August 2001.
17. Pan-European Forest Certification, http://www.pefc.org, August 2001.
18. TechStreet, http://www.cssinfo.com/info/csa.html, August 2001.
19. Nicole Gerard and Jess Wenban Smith, editors, *Behind the Logo: An Environmental and Social Assessment of Forest Certification Schemes* (Moreton-in-Marsh, UK: Fern, May 2001).
20. National Wildlife Federation, Natural Resources Council of Maine, and Environmental Advocates, "A Comparison of the American Forest & Paper Association's Sustainable Forestry Initiative and the Forest Stewardship Council's Certification System," (June 2001). National Wildlife Federation Web site, http://www.nwf.org/northernforest/auditprograms.html, September 2001.
21. International Trade Centre, UNCTAD (United Nations Conference on Trade and Development), *Coffee: An Exporter's Guide* (UNCTAD: Geneva, 1992).
22. TransFair USA Web site, http://www.transfairusa.org, August 2001.
23. David A. Aaker and Erich Joachimsthaler, "The Lure of Global Branding," *Harvard Business Review* (November/December 1999).
24. Jack Neff, "Rethinking Globalism," *Advertising Age* (October 9, 2000).
25. See Ronie Garcia-Johnson, *Exporting Environmentalism: U.S. Multinational Chemical Corporations in Brazil and Mexico* (Cambridge, MA: MIT Press, 2000).
26. See, for example, Michael B. Jenkins and Emily T. Smith, *The Business of Sustainable Forestry: Strategies for an Industry in Transition* (Washington, D.C.: Island Press, 1999); and Markhu Simula, "Economics of Certification," in *Certification of Forest Products: Issues and Perspectives*, ed. Virgilio Viana, et al. (Washington, D.C.: Island Press, 1996).
27. World Wildlife Fund Media Advisory, June 4, 2001.
28. There are many places where this logic has been explored, including: Naomi Klein, *No Logo: Money, Marketing, and the Growing Anti-corporate Movement* (London: Picador Press, 1999); Margaret E. Keck and Kathryn Sikkink, *Activists Beyond Borders: Advocacy Networks in International Politics* (Ithaca, NY: Cornell University Press, 1998); and Robert O'Brien, Anne Marie Goetz, Jan Aaart Scholte, and Marc Williams, *Contesting Global Governance: Multilateral Economic Institutions and Global Social Movements* (Cambridge, UK: Cambridge University Press, 2000).
29. See "Against the Grain: How Home Depot and Activists Joined To Cut Log-

ging Abuse—If a Tree Falls in the Forest, The Small, Powerful FSC Wants to Have Its Say—Sniffing the Cedar Lumber," *Wall Street Journal*, September 26, 2000.

Part II

CASES

Chapter 4

Environmental Certification for Tourism in Central America: CST and Other Programs

Amos Bien

Hanging midway up Masaya Volcano, impressed with the solitude and the extraordinary features of a scene upon which so few human eyes have ever rested, and the power of the great Architect who has scattered his wonderful works over the whole face of the earth, I could not but reflect, what a waste of the bounties of Providence in this favored but miserable land! At home this volcano would be a fortune; with a good hotel on top, a railing round to keep children from falling in, a zigzag staircase down the sides, and a glass of iced lemonade at the bottom. Cataracts are good property with people who know how to turn them to account...The owners of volcanoes in Central America might make money out of them by furnishing facilities to travellers.

—John L. Stephens, *Incidents of Travel in Central America, Chiapas and Yucatan*, 1841[1]

The history of environmental certification for tourism in Central America is closely tied to the development of national parks, private protected areas, and the growth of environmental consciousness in the region. The original tourist poles in Central America were Guatemala, for living cultures and archeological sites (such as Tikal) and Panama, for the Canal. Costa Rica was the pioneer in the development of nature-oriented tourism, starting in the late 1970s and early 1980s. Nature tourism in Costa Rica originated from more than 100 years of environmental research there and twenty years of conservation efforts. Because many of the early nature tourism projects grew out of scientific and conservation efforts, they considered environmental and ethical principles to be fundamental to their philosophy and success. Hence, later abuses of the concept of "ecotourism" were seen against a background of intrinsically sound industry practices and a great willingness by the industry itself to adopt environmental standards. The first codes of ethics and rudimentary environmental certification systems developed soon after an explosion in growth of the industry in Costa Rica as a response by the pioneers of the industry to what they perceived as a dilution of the ethical underpinnings of ecotourism.

Birth of Environmental Consciousness

National Parks

Costa Rica's interest in natural history and conservation dates to the late nineteenth century, when a small group of biologists and naturalists established the national museum and excellent field collections.[2] A small corps of dedicated naturalists maintained this tradition, training students and successors and making a hospitable environment for ecological research. In the 1950s and 1960s, private nature reserves and biological stations were quietly established, and a halfhearted effort was made to establish national parks at the summit of the country's volcanoes and along part of the Pan-American Highway. However, it was not until the arrival of Kenton Miller and his influence on his students Mario Boza and Alvaro Ugalde in the early 1970s that today's strong and healthy system of national parks began to be created.[3] Boza and Ugalde led a campaign that continues today to establish national parks and biological reserves in all the habitat types of Costa Rica.[4] This effort was very successful, and currently almost 13 percent of Costa Rica is securely protected by national parks and biological reserves. Other protected areas, such as "protected zones," forest reserves, and wildlife refuges, are largely under private ownership and are candidates for what is now called *sustainable development*, meaning, in most cases, ecotourism. Hundreds of undeclared private nature reserves also exist. Over 111 of these have ecolodges or other ecotourism activities. Most private nature reserve owners have been shown to be motivated by factors other than money to conserve their land.[5] This mosaic of large, pristine national parks with smaller private reserves with visitor facilities provided the fertile ground necessary for ecotourism to be born in Costa Rica.

Birth of Nature Tourism

In the early 1970s, the Organization for Tropical Studies (OTS) established biological stations and a series of courses in tropical biology stations in Costa Rica. Students spent time at La Selva Biological Station, Palo Verde National Park, and Monteverde Cloud Forest Reserve, as well as other national parks. A study by Jan Laarman in 1989 revealed that visits by family and friends of OTS researchers, as well as return visits of former students, was the principal source of the growth of nature-oriented tourism in Costa Rica at that time, concentrated in OTS research sites, especially Monteverde.[6] Word-of-mouth recommendations from these initial visitors to Costa Rica's natural areas may well have created the market for nature-oriented tourism and ecotourism in Costa Rica. OTS graduates, both Costa Rican and foreign, became the first naturalist guides and lodge owners, giving the industry a sophisticated, scientifically sound set of initial parameters for design and interpretation. This robust beginning set the stage for the high quality of Costa Rica's incipient ecotourism industry.

One of the key factors that motivated researchers, students, and tourists to come to Costa Rica in the first place is its unusual social and political history. Unlike most of Latin America, Costa Rica has been a democracy for most of its existence and almost continuously for the last 120 years. Its life expectancy and health statistics are comparable to those of the most developed countries.[7] This in turn is a direct result of the abolition of the armed forces of Costa Rica in 1948, allowing military funds to be redirected to health and education. All this has produced a country with a strong middle class, able to vacation within the country and without, and welcoming to foreign tourists. The preconditions for establishing a tourist industry thus were already in place: an educated workforce, a populace which itself was familiar with vacation travel, and reasonably good infrastructure. Complementing the magnificent system of national parks and intrinsic natural beauty is also Costa Rica's proximity to the United States, its principal market.

First Efforts to Develop Environmental Standards for Tourism in Central America

Historically, Central America was comprised of the five small countries of the Central American Federation, which was dissolved in 1848: Guatemala, Honduras, El Salvador, Nicaragua, and Costa Rica. Both social and geographic ties have kept these countries in close, usually friendly, but sometimes tense relations ever since. At the northern and southern extremes of the region, two additional small countries, Belize and Panama, form part of geographic Central America. Although they have had very different social and political histories, proximity and size have pulled them ever closer to the five core countries of Central America, and they are now considered full partners in recently revived efforts for regional economic integration.

During the mid-1980s, there was little tourism of any type to most of Central America because of political troubles or wars in every country except Belize and Costa Rica. Even Costa Rica was a staging area for the civil war in Nicaragua; hence, a few conventional tourist projects were delayed for several years. Nevertheless, at this time, visitation to Costa Rica expanded rapidly from a small initial base, in part as a substitute for Guatemala, but mostly because of the growth in nature-oriented tourism by word-of-mouth recommendations. Absolute numbers of visitors remained small, however, and limited to a well-educated, sophisticated market of nature connoisseurs.[8] This public was well able to choose among the small offerings of nature lodges and hotels, based on educated judgment of environmental compliance as an intrinsic part of the value of their tours.

At the end of the 1980s and the early 1990s, however, two events dramatically increased the general public awareness of Costa Rica. First was the awarding of the 1987 Nobel Peace Prize to Costa Rican president Oscar Arias for his Central American Peace Plan. Second was the surprisingly excellent performance of Costa Rica in the 1990 World Cup soccer tournament. Both these events served to focus the news media on this small, little-known country that was often confused with Puerto Rico, or if not, lumped with the rest of war-torn Central America. The paradoxical existence of an "ecological paradise" with no army, a Nobel-winning president, and a superb national park system became big world news, especially as Costa Rica had become the site for rest and recreation for Central America's war reporters. The world press, which had earlier started publishing extensively about Costa Rica's innovative and successful public and private conservation efforts and its orientation toward what became known as "sustainable development" and "ecotourism," now became enamored of Costa Rica. Tourists started visiting in large numbers, but they often lacked the sophistication of the earlier visitors, and facilities were developed to accommodate them. Almost any place with walls and beds could be filled because of the shortage of lodging.

The need to establish some sort of ethical standard for ecotourism became apparent quite early during the rapid expansion of the tourist industry in Costa Rica. By 1990, tourism was producing more income for Costa Rica than coffee production and by 1993, it had surpassed bananas, becoming the most important industry in the country.[9] As the trickle of sophisticated nature travelers in 1985 grew into a substantial volume of more naïve tourists by 1992, the ecotourism business community began to attract the attention of the mainstream business community, first local investors and financial institutions and then international investors and hotel chains. Many of these investors had little experience in nature, environmental issues, or even the tourist trade. The residual "founder effect" of an industry started by environmentalists, nature-lovers, and biologists served to give a solid ethical basis to the core industry and a sound model to copy, but an ever increasing number of new entrepreneurs entered the business without the ethical underpinnings of the founders. A classic example was a former director of the tourist board, a political appointee with no real knowledge of the industry, who discovered ecotourism on the job. Not having educated himself properly, however, he started a nature lodge on his cattle ranch, where one of the features he proudly showed his guests was the skin of a jaguar he had killed on the property, on the wall next to the caged macaws.

Devaluation of Term Ecotourism

This sort of abuse led to some accusations by the mid-1990s that Costa Rica had been oversold and over promoted as an ecological paradise. By then, the tourist industry itself had become convinced of the need for some sort of standards for quality and environmental compliance. The effects of noncompliance became obvious in 1995, when a highly visible kidnapping of a German tourist gave the German press a three-month period in which to take a close look at Costa Rica and loudly voice complaints about its environmental problems. The kidnapping and the press complaints led to the utter collapse of the German market for Costa Rica in less than six months. Although numbers of visitors from all other countries increased, the loss of German tourism, combined with the construction of new, unnecessary rooms, led to a serious decline in room occupancy.[10] Rather than let this become the pattern for a generalized decline of the industry, the private sector and the government became active in looking for ways to protect and promote nature tourism and Costa Rica's image. From this effort grew the official program of Certification for Sustainable Tourism (CST), intended as a general world standard. Today, this somewhat controversial system is competing with a number of other systems implemented or under development in Costa Rica, the rest of Central America, and the rest of the world, particularly Europe and Australia.

Code of Ethics for Sustainable Tourism

The earliest code of ethics for tourism was established by the Costa Rican Audubon Society and the Institute for Central American Studies in 1989. The code was introduced by the simple preface: "Ethical and environmentally sound tourism is a joint responsibility of professional tour operators and you, the traveler. Please join this partnership by reading through this code and then doing your best to abide by it."[11] The "Code of Ethics for Sustainable Tourism" itself consisted of eight simple points:

1) "Tourism should be culturally sensitive."
2) "Tourism should be a positive influence on local communities."
3) "Tourism should be managed and sustainable."
4) "Waste should be disposed of properly."
5) "Wildlife and natural habitats must not be needlessly disturbed."
6) "There must be no commerce in wildlife, wildlife products, or native plants."
7) "Tourists should leave with a greater understanding and appreciation of nature, conservation, and the environment."
8) "Ecotourism should strengthen conservation efforts and enhance the natural integrity of places visited."[12]

The code was neither widely accepted nor well-known because many members of the tourist industry at the time felt that it was unnecessary, given the high existing standards in most of the industry. By the time this sentiment changed, other instruments had been developed. The Institute for Central American Studies continued with the effort, however, and in 1994 ranked all known tourist lodgings in Costa Rica (approximately 300 businesses), based on compliance with the "Code of Ethics for Sustainable Tourism" in five categories: tourism facility, customer satisfaction, business practices, environmental practices, and social responsibility.[13] Compliance was to be monitored by the institute, an outside consulting firm, and consumer surveys. Although there are no published data on whether compliance was monitored under the original system, the document was published in *The New Key to Costa Rica*[14], then Costa Rica's most popular guidebook, and formed the basis for a more rigorous ecolodge survey in subsequent editions.

IYHF (Hostelling International) Environmental Charter

Between 1991 and 1994, the International Youth Hostel Federation (IYHF), with thousands of hostels in over 100 countries, developed an environmental code of ethics as part of an effort to confront increasing competition from other groups offering lodging for the youth and backpacker market. IYHF, after extensive market studies, identified environmental compliance and eventual certification, as a key element in attracting and maintaining market share. The European member countries emphasized the use of environmentally friendly cleaning materials and proper waste management. The Costa Rican Youth Hostel Association (Red Costarricense de Albergues Juveniles) participated in the development and implementation of this code, principally by adding recommendations with respect to the inclusion and protection of natural areas with lodging. This difference in orientation is typical of the differentiation between subsequent certification schemes developed in Europe versus those developed in Costa Rica. The Environmental Charter was adopted in 1994 and later became a fundamental requirement for IYHF hostels around the world.[15] The charter functions as a set of mandatory minimum requirements for the IYHF hostels, rather than as a voluntary certification system. However, auditing is irregular and is mostly based on criteria for quality of facilities and services.

The International Ecotourism Society

The International Ecotourism Society (TIES, formerly The Ecotourism Society), based in the United States but with membership all over the world, developed two standards for ecotourism, with substantial input from Costa Rica: "Ecotourism Guidelines for Nature Tour Operators" (1993)[16] and "Guidelines for Ecolodges" (unpublished results of the Second International Forum and Workshop on Eco-lodges, 1995).[17]

The guidelines for nature tour operators were published as a small, widely distributed pamphlet developed from surveys of tour operators, travel agents, consumers, and academics, mostly from the United States and Costa Rica, but including many other countries. The surveys were analyzed and synthesized by three groups of experts from the United States and Costa Rica. Guidelines were established for programs prior to departure, for guiding and monitoring tours, and for program management, as well as for the rudimentary evaluation of accommodations. The concise but clearly written guidelines have served as an important source for several subsequent certification systems, such as Green Deal.

The guidelines for ecolodges grew out of an international forum and workshop on ecolodges in Costa Rica in October 1995. The original results of the workshops and subsequent meetings were synthesized in a document that was published only in Spanish[18], but the widely circulated manuscript version of the ecolodge guidelines has served as a source of criteria for the development of other certification systems, such as Green Deal and CST. A set of guidelines under a different format was eventually developed in book form, entitled *The International Ecolodge Guidelines*. According to editor and architect Hitesh Mehta, "an ecolodge is a lodge that meets the following criteria:

1) helps in the conservation of the surrounding flora and fauna;
2) has minimal impact on the natural surroundings during construction;
3) fits into its specific physical and cultural contexts through careful attention to form, landscaping and color, as well as the use of vernacular architecture;

4) uses alternative, sustainable means of water acquisition and reduces water consumption;

5) provides for careful handling and disposal of solid waste and sewage;

6) meets its energy needs through passive design and renewable energy sources;

7) uses traditional building technology and materials wherever possible and combines these with their modern counterparts for greater sustainability;

8) endeavors to work together with the local community;

9) offers interpretive programs to educate both its employees and tourists about the surrounding natural and cultural environments; and

10) contributes to sustainable local development through education programs and research." [19]

Mehta concludes that "if nature-based facilities satisfy at least five of the above, they should be certified as 'ecolodges.'"

Neither of the sets of guidelines of The International Ecotourism Society is a certification scheme, but both have been widely used as international standards for designing such systems.

The New Key System

The first true certification system to be implemented in Central America was developed by Beatrice Blake and Anne Becher, the authors of the Costa Rican travel guide *The New Key to Costa Rica*, with the collaboration of Jane Segleau. The book was first published in 1978 as a simple guide to Costa Rica's small tourist offerings, mostly concentrated in the capital, San José. Starting in 1990, as the number of lodging facilities in Costa Rica exploded, the authors perceived the need to distinguish between businesses that respected the environment and those that did not. The 1993 edition of the book made an effort to measure "sustainability" in the lodging facilities evaluated. In the following edition, Becher and Segleau tried to establish an objective system for environmental evaluation and certification. The system, as it developed, was used to evaluate only facilities that claimed to be involved in ecotourism, that is, those with their own nature reserves or offering tours to nearby protected areas. In this sense, the instrument is clearly differentiated from systems designed to evaluate the sustainability of all kinds of hotels, lodges, and tour operators. Using current terminology, the *New Key* system is for "ecotourism certification," as distinguished from "certification of sustainability." This distinction is further discussed below.

The *New Key* system was the first to establish third-party qualification of objective criteria. Earlier systems, such as the Code of Ethics for Sustainable Tourism, the Environmental Charter of IYHF, or the Guidelines of The International Ecotourism Society, were all self-evaluative (first-party certification). The principal criteria used by the *New Key* system are environmental compliance, impact on the local economy, and sociocultural factors. As shown in box 4.1, the evaluation of each criterion was divided into three tiers, the first tier being most heavily weighted and the third tier having the least weight.

Box. 4.1. Facility Ratings Criteria Used in *The New Key to Costa Rica*

Environmental variables emphasizing environmental impact and energy and natural resource use

Tier One:
• Solid waste disposal
• Sewage treatment
• Does the lodging own a reserve; what percentage of total land owned is set aside as a natural reserve?
• What type of protection is given to the reserve (the lodge's own or a nearby public/private reserve used for tours)
• Participation in conservation projects

Tier Two:
• Real impact on the site by construction
• Number of persons per tour
• Erosion of trails
• Use of biodegradable cleaning products
• Energy conservation
• Construction materials
• Information for visitors
• Wild animals in captivity
• Employee training on environmental topics

Tier Three:
• Introduction of exotic species
• Water conservation
• Impact studies

Economic variables examining how much money stays in the local community and how much flees to the country's capital or international investors

Tier One:
• Employees' origin
• Owners' origin/residence

(continues)

Box. 4.1. Continued

Tier Two:
- Contracts with local providers
- Where are purchases made
- Are local handicrafts sold?
- Year-round employee contracts
- Employee incentives

Tier Three:
- Which major purchases for the lodging are imported directly?

Sociocultural variables, evaluating the owners' understanding and strengthening of local culture

Tier One:
- Takes action on culture questions
- Participates in community organizations

Tier Two:
- Makes donations (money, resources, time)

Tier Three:
- Identifies positive and negative cultural aspects

Because the evaluation is independent, verified on site, and crossed with information obtained in the neighboring communities, the instrument meets many of the generally accepted criteria for a certification system but not those applying to accreditation. The term used by the authors is *green-rating* of "eco-oriented lodgings that are practicing successfully what we call 'sustainable tourism' . . . to promote establishments that embodied our vision of how tourism should develop in Costa Rica. We wanted to do what we could to help the tourist industry avoid the pitfalls of traditional tourism."[20] In this sense, the instrument does not comply with one of the principal components of widely accepted certification systems: harmonizing criteria in consultation with all major interested parties, rather than imposing a top-down system written entirely by the proponents. In spite of this limitation, the system is well-respected by both end-users and the evaluated businesses. Because the guidebook is an important marketing tool with an assured audience and impeccable reputation, hoteliers have recognized a clear advantage to listing and recognition. This is not the case with any other certification scheme in the region, where the marketing of the certification system must be undertaken independently.

The authors themselves identified some additional limitations to their evaluation system, especially those relating to the time and cost of evaluation, the need for expert criteria in waste management, and the occasional conflict between their subjective opinion of each place evaluated for the guidebook and the objective evaluation of its sustainability for the green-rating. The substantial cost and difficulty of inspection and certification was assumed by the authors and the publisher, Ulysses Press. Although some guidebook publishers, such as Michelin or AAA, have found it cost-effective to institute and sustain complex proprietary evaluation schemes, in this case, the publisher was unwilling to assume the full cost of certifying all of Costa Rica's ecotourism industry, perhaps because of the small size of the market. Because of this burden, the authors expressed hope that another system, such as Certification for Sustainable Tourism (CST, discussed at length below), would assume the responsibility for certification. However, three years later, the authors rejected CST as unsuitable for small ecotourism businesses.[21]

Guaria

Guaria is the name of the orchid that is the national flower of Costa Rica. It is also the name of the quality seal of the National Chamber of Tourist Microbusinesses (CANAMET). It is oriented toward small and microbusinesses providing lodging, food, and beverages. Emphasis is far more oriented toward quality of service criteria than environmental ones, and in this sense has more in common with certification programs such as AAA than with the *New Key* system. Criteria include client service, cleanliness, occupational health, and employee appearance. CANAMET awarded twenty-four quality seals in 1999, the first year of its application. The program has had some difficulty in monitoring compliance after the initial certification, and it is not well known. It is a second-party auditing program run by an industry association whose principle goal has been to improve the quality standards of its members.[22]

BETA

During the period 1995–2000, it appeared that each Central American country would launch its own tourism certification system. The Belize Ecotourism Association (BETA) established a code of ethics in the early 1990s for ecolodges in Belize; the system was based on the posting of simple requirements in a visible place in each lodge and reporting of non-conformities to BETA by clients. According to BETA, its code of ethics "commits its membership:

- to support economic and social sustainability by encouraging small scale tourist developments, providing employment of local people, purchasing products made locally from sustainable resources and providing guidance to all guests to be environmentally and culturally responsible.
- to provide education in Belizean geography, customs and culture, creating opportunities for cultural, historical, environmental, and archaeological learning for visitors to Belize.
- to maintain and conserve the flora and fauna habitats in Belize by providing appropriate information to visitors, teaching them to avoid disturbing wildlife and flora, discouraging the sale of products or species on the endangered species list, helping to implement carrying capacities, and preventing the introduction of nonindigenous species.
- to promote the sustainability of all resources, both renewable and nonrenewable; conserving water and energy, and increasing awareness of the need for energy and water conservation.
- to reduce the amount of solid waste and climatic contaminants which pose a threat to the ecosystem; using durable, biodegradable, and renewable products instead of aluminum and styrofoam; disposing of all waste in a manner that is environmentally and aesthetically acceptable; and maintaining vehicles for maximum efficiency to decrease emissions and reduce fuel consumption." [23]

Because compliance is based on self-reporting and verification by clients who are so inclined, this system is not compliant with the modern requirements for a certification system but has apparently resulted in a good deal of psychological change by tourism property owners. The program had become inactive in recruiting new lodges in 2000.

Green Deal

Green Deal is a certification scheme for small tourist businesses in Petén, Guatemala (the Tikal region). It was developed by Alianza Verde, a nonprofit association of environmental organizations (particularly Conservation International) and Petén small business owners, with support from USAID. Begun in 1999, Green Deal is designed to rate small and micro tourist businesses in the region.[24] Evaluation criteria follow three axes: quality, environment, and social impact. The system is intended to cover hotels, community-based tourism, restaurants, tourist transport, travel agencies, tour operators, and guides. Stakeholder workshops with all these groups were used to establish the underpinnings of the system. These were then adjusted by field trials and expert criteria. Green Deal is a sophisticated instrument based on best practices guidelines in environmental and quality aspects of tourism, the best of other certification systems, and the International Organization for Standardization's ISO 9000 series. Its accreditation system is compatible with ISO/IEC (International Electrotechnical Commission) Guide 61, the generally accepted norms for certification and accreditation bodies.[25] Nevertheless, Green Deal is written in simple language for application by business owners with little access to capital, some of whom are unable to read or write.

As with many certification and evaluation schemes for small and microbusinesses, Green Deal considers the existence of basic business and economic tools to ensure the health and survival of the business being certified. These considerations are generally deemed superfluous in programs designed for larger businesses, because it is supposed that a medium to large business already has adequate administrative and accounting tools in place. In contrast, a microbusiness may not have them and might therefore fail, producing many serious environmental and social consequences.

Although Green Deal was designed for use in the Petén as a regional seal, it is applicable throughout the developing world for small and microbusinesses. To become economically self-sufficient and applicable at low cost, it must have economies of scale achieved by wide use and the inclusion of some larger businesses. Green Deal is designed to be complementary to Certification for Sustainable Tourism (CST). A business that complies in full with the simpler criteria of Green Deal would achieve a medium-level rating in CST. As the business grows larger, it would become increasingly cost-effective to comply with CST criteria and certification, which are more expensive to implement.

Best Practice Guidelines for Ecotourism in Protected Areas

The *Best Practice Guidelines for Ecotourism in Protected Areas*, by Ana Báez and Alejandrina Acuña,[26] is an innovative state-of-the-art guide covering all aspects of ecotourism practices in national parks, private reserves, and other protected areas. The guidelines are based on worldwide best practice guidelines from dozens of sources, compiled into one uniform format and instrument. It was developed for use in Central America but is sufficiently general that it is in wide use throughout Latin America. With the publication of the English edition, it is likely to become a standard work for all developing countries. Each aspect of ecotourism is described with a section on conceptualization, another on methodology, and a final one on verification criteria (which can be used for qualification or certification). As with the guidelines of The International Ecotourism Society, it is not a certification system, but it incorporates all the elements that a certification system should take into account.

Choice of Evaluation Systems

There is much overlap among evaluation and certification systems, as well as among categories of tourist businesses, but the appropriate certification or evaluation system depends on what is being evaluated: the *Best Practice Guidelines for Ecotourism in Protected Areas* (not a certification system but permitting evaluation according to the international state of the art) is designed for public nature reserves, the *New Key* system is for small ecotourism businesses, and Green Deal is appropriate for small and very small tourist enterprises of all types. In contrast, the Certification for Sustainable Tourism (CST), discussed below, is appropriate for medium to large lodges, hotels, and tour operators.

The Evolution of a Regional Standard for Central America: CST

As nature-oriented tourism grew from its small, obscure niche market, it became a major economic force and, by 1994, Costa Rica's main foreign exchange earner. In the year 2000, Costa Rica received a little over one million visitors, with average in-country expenditures of about $1000 each over an average stay of ten days. About 60 percent of the visitors were motivated primarily by ecotourism, and another twenty percent visited a national park or ecotourism facility, although it was not the primary motivator for their visit. More than $600 million dollars were received by Costa Rica for ecotourism and other nature-based attractions in 2000.[27] This trend is also beginning in Belize, Guatemala, and Panama, as well as parts of Honduras and Nicaragua.[28]

These visitor numbers and sums of money are attractive to conventional business operators and foreign hotel chains. Ecotourism and nature tourism in Central America is no longer limited to small dedicated ecolodges, as it was ten years ago. Therefore, the certification systems and best practice guidelines in use in the region have had to accommodate in recent years a much broader and less dedicated set of users (both businesses and their clients).

The market offerings can now be classified as (1) lodging in public and private nature reserves, (2) small to medium locally owned businesses (still 80 percent of the offering), and (3) a large variety of conventional or luxury accommodations on the beach, in the cities, or near natural areas. Nearly all of these businesses cater largely to clientele who visit a natural area or were attracted to Central America because of its reputation as a destination for nature, living cultures, or archeology, although many of these clients would not be classified as ecotourists. Nevertheless, the credibility of the destination as a whole depends to some degree on environmental and social compliance by even the largest city hotels.

As the gap grows between promotion of the region as a natural destination and the perception that many tourist businesses are lacking in environmental consciousness, industry leaders and the Central American governments have perceived an urgent need to assure credibility of the region's principal tourist attractions. As a result, the Certification for Sustainable Tourism (CST) was developed in the mid- to late-1990s and has since been proposed as a regional and international standard.

Certification for Sustainable Tourism (CST)

The Costa Rican Tourist Board (ICT) is not normally noted for innovation and creation. Nevertheless, when ICT officials Marco Picado and Rodolfo Lizano proposed the creation of a certification system for sustainable tourism around 1995, the idea was readily accepted. Lizano then spent over a year working with logistical support from the Central American Institute for Business Administration (INCAE, a close collaborator with Harvard Business School) to develop the theoretical framework of the system, to be called Certification for Sustainable Tourism (CST). In contrast to many systems then being proposed, Lizano felt that CST would be robust and able to place all tourist businesses on the same footing only if it were explicitly *not* an ecotourism certification program. At the same time, he felt that tourism in Costa Rica was increasingly moving away from small ecolodges and toward larger, more luxurious facilities. For Costa Rica to remain competitive internationally, with an image based on nature tourism, even the largest and most conventional hotels should abide by principles of environmental sustainability. In 1996, Lizano said, "Without exception, tourism develops in a physical space in which the attractions that are its marketable product are a fine mix of natural (natural resources), cultural, and social elements. For this reason, the activity cannot be isolated from its context, as often happens in industrial or agricultural activities, where negative externalities do not directly affect the quality of the product. In tourism, on the contrary, the quality of the product is highly dependent on environmental quality, natural resource conservation, the stability of ecological processes, and social development around it."[29]

The first edition of CST for hotels was released in 1997 and the first edition for tour operators in 2001. After an initial development phase, several stakeholder workshops refined the instrument. This was followed by field testing and final release. All rating criteria and scores for each certified business are publicly available on the CST Web site.[30] Evaluation is made by a team of assessors (auditors) with professional specialties in various aspects assessed by CST, who report the findings of their on-site inspections to a multidisciplinary certification and accreditation board. The board holds the copyright of CST and makes final decisions about certification, accreditation of auditors, and modifications of the system.

CST for hotels was designed to be applicable to all medium to large lodging facilities, whatever their market. It does not evaluate ecotourism criteria per se, and the documentation is clear that it measures sustainability, along three axes: environmental, social, and economic. The instrument evaluates and qualifies (1) biological and physical surroundings, (2) physical plant, (3) customers, and (4) socioeconomic context (see box 4.2). Questions are weighted by importance, and the final score achieved by a business is the lowest of the ratings in each of the four areas. A minimum score of 20 percent in each area is required to achieve the lowest qualification and be certified. Beyond that minimum level, there are four addi-

---

Box 4.2. CST Criteria for Hotels, Agencies, and Tour Operators

Hotels

A) Biological and physical surroundings
1) Policies and programs
2) Emissions and wastes
3) Green zones
4) Natural areas
5) Protection of flora and fauna

B) Physical Plant
6) Formulation of policies
7) Water consumption
8) Energy consumption
9) Commodity use
   –Food and beverages
   –Cleaning and cosmetics
10) Waste management
11) Training

C) External Client
12) Communication and participation
13) Guest facilities and instructions
14) Management of groups
15) Feedback

Agencies and Tour Operators

A) Biological and physical surroundings
1) Impact prevention
2) Protection of the natural environment
3) Emissions and wastes
4) Product consumption
5) Services offered
6) Environmental management
7) Policies and programs

B) Administration of services
8) Administration of personnel and training
9) Product consumption
10) Communication and participation
11) Product design
12) Service offerings
13) Direct economic benefits
14) Feedback
15) Policies and programs
16) Tour guides

C) Client
17) Mitigation of impacts
18) Emissions and wastes

D) Socioeconomic context
  16) Direct economic benefits
  17) Indirect economic benefits
  18) Contribution to cultural
     development
  19) Contribution to health
  20) Infrastructure and security

19) Communication and participation
20) Client persuasion
21) Environmental management
22) Policies and programs

D) Socioeconomic context
  23) Policies and programs
  24) Final product
  25) Service offerings
  26) Direct economic benefits
  27) Indirect economic benefits
  28) Protection of local culture

Source: Costa Rican Tourism Institute (ICT), *Certificación para la Sostenibilidad Turística CST: Manual de Categorización. Manual para Hoteles*, 1997; ICT, *Certificación para la Sostenibilidad Turística CST: Manual de Categorización. Manual para Agencia y Tour Operadoras*. Working draft document, 2001.

tional levels to be reached. The maximum rating, level five, can be achieved only by reaching that level in each of the four rating areas.

As of August 2001, CST had received requests for certification from over 100 hotels, had certified fifty-one (76 percent of which have fewer than fifty rooms), and was launching an effort to expand certification services to tour operators. Field use of the first edition of CST for hotels (on over 100 hotels over a three-year period) demonstrated that it needs modification of 2–5 percent of its 152 questions in order to be applicable internationally and to very small businesses. This modification is to be based on a series of stakeholder workshops, with results to be presented to the accreditation board for approval. In this author's opinion, the principal changes required are:

1) ISO-like requirements should be reduced for a large number of written registers of all manner of details of resource management for small and microbusinesses. As currently written, these requirements are onerous for small businesses and do not produce substantially improved environmental compliance. For example, hotels are asked to monitor the quantity and composition of their solid wastes and to record the results in a written register. The effort required to do this in a very small business without specialized employees exceeds the possible benefit, whereas this information is useful and important in a large hotel. Similar registers and official measurements are required for the quality and quantity of wastewater, which usually is processed by septic tanks for

small businesses. The modifications required to CST to correct this are few and simple.

2) Criteria for water and energy conservation are not based on absolute consumption (liters per guest per night; KWH per guest per night), which would level the playing field for hotels large, medium, and small, but rather on conservation devices. These would allow a big hotel with huge water consumption for swimming pools and golf courses, but elaborate mitigation devices, to score better than a hotel with extremely low consumption, one that does not need fancy devices to do so. Two heavily weighted questions can correct this problem in CST.

3) There is a statistical artifact in the design of "not applicable" questions that gives additional weight to nonconformities by smaller hotels. Instead of excluding the questions, hotels with N/A for swimming pools and golf courses should receive maximum scores.

4) CST does not take into account historical and archeological sites, living cultures, and habitats not found in Costa Rica (tundra, deserts, coral reefs, etc.). These fragile habitats must be taken into account in different regional versions of CST.

Response to CST has been favorable, although the problems cited above have caused some accusation of "greenwashing," a term that was developed to describe promoting goods, services, or businesses as environmentally friendly when they are not. The issue of greenwashing became important in environmental certification for tourism in July 2000, when WWF-UK released a document accusing Green Globe, until then the best known tourism environmental certification system, of misleading practices. In particular, Green Globe was accused of permitting hundreds of businesses to use their logo simply by paying a fee and signing an agreement to move toward environmentally friendly practices.

In August 2001, Beatrice Blake, coauthor of the *New Key* system, accused CST of greenwashing because the system does not reward the small businesses that are the heart of the ecotourism industry and Costa Rica's tourist industry in general. Blake wrote, "CST in its present form and presentation does not offer reliable information about which businesses really make an effort to offer a sustainable tourism product (because most sustainable businesses are not on it) and how it helps big tourism businesses compete with the visionary ecotourism businesses that have made Costa Rica famous. The CST has become another greenwasher itself."[31] However, Blake goes on to state, "Part of the problem stems from the confusion of the terms 'sustainable tourism' and 'ecotourism'."

In a conference in Mohonk, New York in November 2000, most of the principal actors in environmental certification in tourism agreed on a set of protocols, called the Mohonk Agreement, that clearly separated sustainable tourism and ecotourism. Under the Mohonk criteria, ecotourism is a restricted subset of sustainable tourism (see appendix). In other words, to be classified as an ecotourism business, a company must first comply with the basic requirements for sustainability and then comply with additional requirements. Under the Mohonk criteria, and especially with the changes proposed for CST in its second edition, the greenwashing accusation by Blake would appear moot.

Proliferation of Initiatives: 1995–2000

Since the publication and popularization of the ISO 9000 series of quality standards in the 1980s, there has been an explosion of voluntary certification initiatives of all kinds. In tourism, there is a long tradition of awarding stars for categorization based on quality of physical plant and service, but the voluntary certification of environmental performance and sociocultural behavior is a recent phenomenon, dating mainly from the 1990s. Currently, there are more than 100 social and environmental certification initiatives for tourist businesses, more than half of them in Europe.[32]

The multitude of certification initiatives has confused consumers to the point where a typical European client, well accustomed to using certification labels for choosing wine or organic vegetables, will not use the presence or absence or type of tourist certification for choosing lodging, even within Europe. To avoid this problem and increase the credibility of the environmental labels, there is an effort to establish a single environmental and social label for tourism in Europe.[33] This problem was already faced and resolved by organic food producers, who have established a supervisory and accrediting body for nearly all recognized seals. Mutual recognition and accepted standards demonstrably increased the credibility of the seals. Leading experts in the field of tourism agree:

> We are concerned about the proliferation of tourism certification processes—especially those based on paid membership in the certifying organization and self-evaluations. We worry that if the public sees that different certifying organizations recognize different lodgings, the general perception will be that all evaluation methods are subjective and any lodging can buy its way into a certification. Ideally, we believe that a sustainable-tourism umbrella organization should certify the certifiers, to prevent the misuse of this process. (Beatrice Blake and Anne Becher[34])

The proliferation of over 100 schemes worldwide offering logos and labels has made it difficult for the tourist to distinguish exactly what is being certified. This confusion has, in turn, led to a lack of consumer demand for certified holidays. Furthermore, less than one percent of businesses have joined up to these schemes. The failure to establish clear brand recognition could seriously undermine the potential of certification to bring about sustainable tourism. (World Wildlife Fund[35])

The majority of those interviewed are of the opinion that there are so many labels, that the overview is lost. . . . The 18 countries studied in FEMATOUR are acquainted with more than 50 different ecolabels for tourist accommodations. (FEMATOUR)[36]

This phenomenon has become a serious problem in Europe, and by 2000, Central America appeared to be on the same path. There has been longstanding worry that with each change of government in each of the seven countries, the new administration would try to establish its own national certification system, unaware of the enormous cost and many years that this would take.

There is deep concern as well that efforts to develop adequate systems for tourism certification, especially in environmental and social aspects, will fail in the marketplace if too many environmental labels are used. This has already occurred in Central America, with its twenty-six different labels for coffee production (organic, shade-grown, bird-friendly, and so on), leading the consumer to ignore them all.[37]

Furthermore, there is an additional danger stemming from the confusion between process-based certification systems (ISO 14001 and Green Globe) and the performance-based certification of results or final products (CST, Green Deal, and almost all others).

To resolve these problems of credibility, a vigorous international discussion has started in several venues. In Europe, FEMATOUR[38] has undertaken a study to assess the feasibility of establishing a single European standard. It has received the support of all surveyed sectors except HOTREC, the European Association of Hotels, Restaurants, and Cafes. In Australia, the predominance of a single green seal, NEAP, has effectively resolved the problem, as it enjoys substantial support and recognition by both businesses and clients. However, Green Globe is moving aggressively in Australia and elsewhere and is proposing to partner with or absorb NEAP.

In Central America, the outlook is promising for development of a single ecolabeling scheme. In spite of the widespread impression of rampant proliferation of national and local green seals and certification systems, there have been only four local systems effectively implemented: CST for hotels, the *New Key* system in Costa Rica, Green Deal, and Guaria.

Of the international systems, ECOTEL has a small presence in Central America. Green Globe does not yet have any certified businesses and very few noncertified affiliated businesses in Central America. ISO 14001 is being promoted in the region by AENOR, the Spanish assistance agency; however, the ISO norms prohibit using this type of process-based certification system for advertising a product (such as a hotel or tour) to consumers. Although AENOR claims the contrary, ISO/IEC Guide 61 specifies, "Where a supplier is certified/registered only with respect to its quality system, the symbol or logo shall not be used on a product or in any other way that may be interpreted as denoting product conformance."[39] Because the point of certification in tourism is generally to attract clients, this prohibition of using the logos of process-based quality systems makes the utility of ISO 14001 for tourism of dubious value.

In general, the tendency of a few years ago for each new government to try to establish its own national certification system appears to be waning, with general support by all the governments of Central America (including Belize and Panama) for the implementation of CST as a regional system.

Concentration on a Few Well-chosen Systems: 2000–2001

Integrationist Policy: Central America as a Development Pole

With the wars in Central America having ended by the early 1990s, the region was left in economic tatters, except for Costa Rica and Belize. Each of the countries of Central America has had an independent political and social trajectory since separating from the Central American Federation in 1848; however, there remains great cultural affinity and geographic dependence among Guatemala, Honduras, El Salvador, Nicaragua, and Costa Rica. Although Panama and Belize do not share this political history, they nevertheless share geographic dependence. All are small countries with small economies.

The concept of regional economic integration, along the lines of the original European Common Market, was in the process of implementation when the wars came. Afterward, just as Europe moved on to tighter integration, Central America as well has been following the model of ever tighter economic ties. Although the short and fragile existence of democracy in some of the countries has made others reticent to consider any sort of political integration, there are growing efforts toward economic cooperation, and these are paralleling cross-border efforts to link Central America's parks.

Mesoamerican Biological Corridor

Plants and animals are largely immune to political boundaries. Because of the small size of the Central American countries, it became clear that the existing systems of small national parks in each country would not be able to maintain viable populations of many plants and animals without international connection through a biological corridor. This idea evolved to become the Mesoamerican Biological Corridor.[40] Parts of it are now under execution in each of the seven countries, with the goal of establishing interconnections among as many as possible of the protected natural areas. The corridors are largely on privately owned land with undisturbed natural habitat, while the protected areas are state lands.

To maintain the corridor without the great and politically unacceptable expense of expropriating this land, existing owners must be given economically and environmentally acceptable land-use alternatives. Ecotourism in the Mesoamerican Biological Corridor is likely to become one of the principal tools for conservation. Because of the multinational supervision of the corridor, it is likely that an environmental certification system will be put in place to ensure minimal damage to the natural habitat.

Multinational Tourist Routes

As a corollary to the process of economic integration and biological corridors, at least four efforts are underway to establish multinational Central American tourist routes. These would allow visitors to travel through the seven countries, staying in facilities and using services that meet minimum and uniform environmental and quality standards.

Ruta del Maíz is the first of these routes to be consolidated. Using entry criteria for quality, extensive training, and environmental management systems based on Green Deal, over 100 businesses in the seven countries have been brought to similar levels of quality and environmental compliance. Funding has been by the eight member NGOs in the seven countries, USAID, and FODESTUR-GTZ. It is likely that a certification system of some sort will be applied to maintain standards in the future in Ruta del Maíz.

Ruta Verde, the Mesoamerican Trail, and the Mesoamerican Ecotourism Alliance (MEA)[41] are incipient efforts to promote transborder travel, consistent environmental and quality standards, and increased revenues for impoverished rural and indigenous populations. MEA, coordinated by the

RARE Center for Tropical Conservation, is an alliance of organizations that manage natural sites and protected areas and NGOs that provide technical support to the MEA member organizations.

Through the Regional Environmental Program for Central America in the Central American Protected Areas System (PROARCA/CAPAS), a U.S. Agency for International Development conservation initiative, several efforts took place in this region to bring these certifiers to a common forum. For example, PROARCA/CAPAS held the first regional workshop of certification programs in Central America in 1999.[42] Although these efforts certainly helped advance the concept of tourism certification, there still remains a lack of clarity in the definition of standards and an absence of harmonization and mutual recognition among certifiers. Currently, there is no forum in Central America to address the fragmentation among certification schemes. There is also no entity to internationally promote sound certification schemes among sustainable tourism suppliers and consumers that may want to contribute to biodiversity conservation and social welfare. In May 2001, the Central American Council of Tourism Ministers backed the adoption of the CST program for the region.[43] This effort may bring marketing advantages to certified operations in the region, but it does not address the fragmentation problems and lack of mutual recognition among certifiers.

An effort is underway to obtain first regional then international recognition of CST under an accreditation mechanism called the International Sustainable Tourism Commission (ISTC).[44] There have been some inconclusive discussions with the World Tourism Organization (WTO) to adopt CST as a worldwide model for sustainable tourism, but this is not likely to take place until after CST's adoption by all of Central America and some other countries.

Conclusion

Until a tourism certification scheme is recognized by a prestigious body and achieves real market recognition, it is unlikely to generate real demand either from business owners or from final clients.[45] The incentives for environmental certification are closely correlated with these market-driven economic motivations to conserve natural resources. The risk of proliferation of little-known certification schemes without credibility threatened Central America in the 1990s but appears to have been supplanted by the realization that one or a few credible schemes should be adopted throughout the region, with the goal being international recognition. At present, there has been little penetration of the region by external certification schemes because of credibility (and cost) problems. To the contrary, three of the schemes developed in Central America have potential to become international standards for the rest of the world:

- Certification for Sustainable Tourism (CST), for medium to large hotels and tour operators, applicable in any location with some minor changes,
- Green Deal, for small and micro tourist businesses in developing countries, and
- *Best Practice Guidelines for Ecotourism in Protected Areas*, as evaluation (not certification) criteria for protected natural areas.

The only well-established ecotourism standard for the region is the *New Key* system, but this has not been extended beyond Costa Rica. The developing consensus on regional environmental standards for tourism is being used as a principle qualifying and marketing criterion for international tourist routes in Central America.

Notes

1. John L. Stevens, *Incidents of Travel in Central America, Chiapas and Yucatan* (Mineola, NY: Dover Publications, 1969).
2. L. D. Gómez and J. M. Savage, "Searchers on that Rich Coast: Costa Rican Field Biology, 1400–1980," in *Costa Rican Natural History*, ed. D. H. Janzen (Chicago: University Chicago Press, 1983), 1–11.
3. David Rains Wallace, *The Quetzal and the Macaw: The Story of Costa Rica's National Parks* (San Francisco: Sierra Club Books, 1992), 13–16.
4. Randall García, *Biología de la Conservación y áreas Silvestres Protegidas: Situación Actual y Perspectivas en Costa Rica* (Heredia, Costa Rica: Instituto Nacional de Biodiversidad, 1997).
5. Jeffrey Langholz, "Economics, Objectives, and Success of Private Nature Reserves in Sub-Saharan Africa and Latin America," *Conservation Biology*, 10, no. 1 (1996), 271–80; Jeffrey Langholz, James Lassoie, and John Schelhas, "Incentives for Biological Conservation: Costa Rica's Private Wildlife Refuge Program," *Conservation Biology*, 14, no. 6 (December 2000), 1735–1743; Claudia L. Alderman, *A Study of the Role of Privately Owned Lands Used for Nature Tourism, Education and Conservation* (Washington, D.C.: Conservation International, 1990).
6. Jan G. Laarman and Richard R. Perdue, "A Survey of Return Visits to Costa Rica by OTS Participants and Associates," FPEI Working Paper No. 29 (Research Triangle Park, NC: Southeastern Center for Forest Economics Research, 1987); Jan G. Laarman and Richard R. Perdue, "Tropical Science as Economic Activity: OTS in Costa Rica," FPEI Working Paper No. 33 (Research Triangle Park, NC: Southeastern Center for Forest Economics Research, 1987).
7. Proyecto Estado de la Nación, *Estado de la nation en desarrollo humano sostenible:*

un análisis amplio y objetivo de la Costa Rica que tenemos a partir de los indicadores más actuales, 1996 (San Jose, Costa Rica: Estado de la Nación, 1997).

8. Instituto Costarricense de Turismo (ICT), *Plan Estrategico de Desarrollo Turistico Sustentable de Costa Rica (1993–1998)* (San Jose, Costa Rica: ICT, 1993).

9. Ibid.

10. Instituto Centroamericano de Administración de Empresas (INCAE), *Turismo en Costa Rica: El Reto a la Competitividad* (Alajuela, Costa Rica: Centro Latinoamericano de Administración de Empresas, 1996).

11. "Code of Ethics for Sustainable Tourism," San Jose, Costa Rica: Collaboration for Sustainable Tourism, 1992; Richard Leon Holland, "Ecotourism Without Monitoring Isn't Sustainable," n.d.; Richard Holland, "Ecotourism Project: Certification of Ecotourism Operators," Ecotourism Committee, San Jose Audubon Society, September 1992, and other documents Martha Honey received from Richard Holland.

12. Ibid.

13. Ibid.

14. Beatrice Blake and Anne Becher, *The New Key to Costa Rica,* (Berkeley, CA: Ulysses Press, 1994–2001); Martha Honey and Abigail Rome, *Protecting Paradise: Certification Programs for Sustainable Tourism and Ecotourism* (Washington, D.C.: Institute for Policy Studies, October 2001), 44–45.

15. "Minutes," Environmental Working Party, International Youth Hostel Federation, Hertfordshire, U.K., 1991–1994; European Union Federation of Youth Hostel Associations (EUFED), "Measures/Initiatives: Codes of Conduct: IYHF Environmental Charter and Implementation Guidelines," Web site: ECoNETT, http://www.greenglobe21.com/econett.code.code0033.htm.

16. The International Ecotourism Society (TIES), *Ecotourism Guidelines for Nature Tour Operators* (Burlington, VT: TIES, 1995), Web site: www.ecotourism.org.

17. The International Ecotourism Society (TIES), "Guidelines for Ecolodges," unpublished results of the Second International Forum and Workshop on Eco-lodges, Puntarenas, Costa Rica, October 1995.

18. Amos Bien, *Aciertos y Debilidades del Ecoturismo en Reservas Naturales: el Papel de la Certificación* (San José, Costa Rica: Universidad para la Cooperación Internacional, 2001).

19. Hitesh Mehta, *International Ecolodge Guidelines* (Burlington, VT: The International Ecotourism Society, 2001).

20. Ibid.; Anne Becher and Beatrice Blake, "Reflections on 'Green Ratings'" (August 1998). Web site: http://www.planeta.com/planeta/98/0898rating.html (August 2001).

21. Anne Becher and Beatrice Blake, "Hierarchy of Importance of Criteria for the New Key Sustainable Tourism Survey" (August 1998). Web site: Planeta.com: Eco Travels in Latin America, http://www.planeta.com/planeta/98/0898rating2.html (August 2001).

22. Amos Bien, "Estrategia de Certificaciones Turísticas en Centroamérica," FODESTUR-GTZ (Fomento al Desarrollo Sostenible Mediante el Turismo en Centroamérica—Gesellschaft für Technische Zusammenarbeit), Managua,

2000, on FODESTUR Web site: http://www.geprotur.com.ni/download/ estudio_abien.zip.

23. Belize Eco-Tourism Association, "Code of Ethics," www.belizenet.com/ beta/ethics.html, August 2001.

24. Amos Bien, "Análisis del instrumento de certificación Green Deal de la Aso- ciación Alianza Verde, Flores, Petén, Guatemala" (Guatemala: Alianza Verde, 2000).

25. Ibid.

26. Ana Báez and Alejandrina Acuña, *Best Practice Guidelines for Ecotourism in Pro- tected Areas* (Guatemala: PROARCA/CAPAS-USAID-CCAD, 2001).

27. Instituto Costarricense de Turismo, *Anuario Estadístico* (San Jose, Costa Rica: ICT, 1985).

28. Crist Inman, Jean Pierre Ranjeva, and Gustavo Segura, *Destination Central America: A conceptual framework for regional tourism development* (Alajuela, Costa Rica: INCAE, 1998).

29. Rodolfo Lizano, "Certificación para la Sostenibilidad Turística: Hacia una nueva ventaja competitiva, Instituto Costarricense de Turismo" (San Jose, Costa Rica: ICT, 1996).

30. Certificación para la Sostenibilidad Turística (CST), "Hoteles Aprobados por Tamaño," http://www.turismo-sostenible.co.cr/ES/directorio/estadisticas/ hotel_eval_tam.shtml (August 2001).

31. Beatrice Blake, "Comparing the ICT's Certification of Sustainable Tourism and *The New Key to Costa Rica's* Sustainable Tourism Rating: CST: Another Form of Greenwashing?" http://www.planeta.com/planeta/01/0104costa.html (August 2001).

32. World Tourism Organization, *Voluntary Initiatives for Sustainable Tourism* (Madrid: World Tourism Organization, 2002).

33. Ute Haak and Rolf Spittler, *Descripción y evaluación de las distinciones ambientales en el turismo* (Germany: Akademie für Umweltforschung und-bildung in Europa (AubE) and Bund für Umwelt und Naturschutz Deutshland (BUND), 1998; translated to Spanish by FODESTUR and PROARCA/CAPAS, 2000.

34. Becher and Blake, "Reflections on 'Green Ratings,'" (August 1998).

35. WWF-UK, "Tourism Certification: An Analysis of Green Globe 21 and Other Certification Programmes," *WWF-UK News* (London: World Wide Fund for Nature, August 29, 2000).

36. Consultancy and Research for Environmental Management (CREM), *Feasi- bility and Market Study for a European Eco-Label for Tourist Accommodations (FEMATOUR)*, commissioned by the European Commission (Amsterdam: CREM and CH2MHILL, August 2000).

37. Damaris Chaves; personal communication, Programa Ambiental Regional para Centroamérica (PROARCA), 2000–2001.

38. CREM, *FEMATOUR*, August 2000.

39. International Organization for Standardization, *ISO/IEC Guide 61, General Requirements for Assessment and Accreditation of Certification/Registration Bodies* (Geneva, ISO General Secretariat, 1991).

40. WWF Centroamérica-CCAD, "Corredor Biológico Mesoamericano: Logros Importantes" (Turrialba, Costa Rica: WWF Central America, 2001).
41. Christine Iffrig, "An Alliance for Ecotourism" in bulletin *Mesoamerican Ecotourism Alliance: El Circuito Verde* (Belize: Mesoamerican Ecotourism Alliance), I, no. 1, http://www.ecotourismalliance.org (January 2001), 1.
42. María Damaris Chaves, "Iniciativas Centroamericanas de Sellos y Certificaciones en Turismo," PROARCA/CAPAS, http://www.capas.org/iecotur0. htm (June 1999).
43. Certificación para la Sostenibilidad Turística (CST), "Centroamérica Preparándose para Promover la Marca CST," Archivo de Boletines http://www.turismo-sostenible.co.cr/ES/boletin/docs/20010817.00021.htm (August 2001).
44. Robert Toth, "Enhancing Credibility of Costa Rica's Sustainable Tourism Certification System," INCAE-CLADS Working Paper CEN-661, http://www.incae.ac.cr/ES/clacds/investigacion/pdf/cen661.pdf (October 1998). Robert Toth, "Implementing a Worldwide Sustainable Tourism Certification System," INCAE-CLADS Working Paper CEN-662, http://www.incae.ac.cr/EN/clacds/investigacion/pdf/cen662.pdf (June 2000).
45. Amos Bien, "Diagnóstico Institucional y Estructural Regional para el Programa de Certificación de Sostenibilidad Turística (CST) en Centroamérica," (1999) PROARCA/CAPAS, http://www.capas.org/iecotur0.htm (1999).

Chapter 5

Australia: The Nature and Ecotourism Accreditation Program

Guy Chester and Alice Crabtree

The Australian Nature and Ecotourism Accreditation Program (NEAP) is a well-established, voluntary certification scheme that was initially developed to recognize and reward "best practice" ecotourism products in Australia. Launched in 1996, NEAP is a program now administered and managed by the Ecotourism Association of Australia (EAA)[1].The team that initially developed NEAP included specialists in ecotourism, minimal impact practices, protected area management, licensing systems, environmental auditing, guiding, and management of certification (i.e., accreditation[2]) programs. Substantial input was solicited from an eclectic range of stakeholders that included the mainstream and ecotourism industry (both associations and individual businesses), conservation groups and other non-governmental organizations (NGOs), protected area managers, government officials, and academics.The number of products certified by NEAP grew from fifty-five in 1996 to over 300 by mid-2001, including nearly 250 tour, forty accommodation, and ten attraction products. In addition, the EcoGuide Program had certified over fifty individual guides.

The NEAP program has two broad objectives. The first is to provide nature and ecotourism businesses with the means to gain knowledge of best practice principles and to encourage continual improvement of their product. The second is provide both primary consumers—the tourists—and secondary consumers—protected area managers, tour wholesalers, and local communities—with a means of recognizing operators of genuine nature tourism and ecotourism products. In mid-2001, NEAP was further developed and expanded to include a new category, nature tourism, as well as the EcoGuide Program for nature and ecotour guides. In late 2001,

NEAP announced that in collaboration with Green Globe 21 (see chapter 10), it would produce an international ecotourism standard based principally on the NEAP criteria with conditions to conform with the Mohonk Agreement (see appendix 1) and elements from Green Globe's benchmarking system.[3]

Tourism and Ecotourism in Australia

Tourism, based on both domestic and international travel, is an increasingly important industry to Australia. In 1997–1998, tourism revenues totaled Au.\$58.2 billion (nearly US\$30 billion), with international tourism accounting for approximately 22 percent of the total.[4] With major government funding for international marketing, tourism has grown from a minor contributor to the Australian economy to now being one of the largest export industries, rivaling agriculture (beef, wool, sugar, etc.) and mining (iron ore, coal, etc).[5] The fastest growth is anticipated to come from travelers from Asia and Europe/North America. [6]

Australia's ancient landscapes, unique flora and fauna (a result of being an isolated island continent that provides an evolutionary refuge for marsupial mammals), range of ecosystems—from alpine snow-covered mountains to tropical coral coasts—and indigenous cultures have long formed the major drawing cards for international visitors. World Heritage areas such as the Great Barrier Reef on the northeast coast; Uluru (formerly Ayers Rock), a huge monolith in the central desert; and Kakadu National Park in the Northern Territory (made famous by the blockbuster movie *Crocodile Dundee*) are must-see attractions and honey pots for tourists. The hype and delivery of the 2000 Sydney Olympics helped to further propel Australia onto the world stage as a major tourism destination, despite the long haul it represents to most tourists.

The major natural attractions have long had well-established tourism industries that focused on nature—well before the term "ecotourism" was coined or ecotourism certification was established. With Australia's inbound and domestic tourism levels growing, there is an expanding market for nature and ecotourism products. The country's awesome variety of nature and ecotourism offerings includes:

- Accommodation ranging from small rainforest lodges to mountain and remote outback desert guest houses to large tropical island resorts.
- Major tour vessels visiting the Great Barrier Reef, ranging from smaller, ten to thirty–passenger dive boats to large catamarans that carry up to 440 passengers and are supported by pontoons, glass bottom boats, and semisubmersible underwater vessels for viewing the reef.
- Many other tour vessels in lakes, rivers, wetlands, estuaries, and coastal

areas that focus on a natural area and/or wildlife such as crocodiles, dolphins, whales, and whale sharks.
- Thousands of walking tracks, ranging from organized weeklong tours in wilderness areas to high capacity boardwalks in such areas as eucalyptus forests, mangroves, rainforests, wetlands, and coastal and sand dune systems.
- Four-wheel drive vehicle tours in landscapes including massive sand islands, remote savannah, the outback, coasts, deserts, rainforest, mountain ranges, and subalpine areas.
- Scenic air tours, ranging from weeklong trips through the remote deserts to short helicopter and fixed-wing scenic tours.
- Sea kayaking, river canoeing, and rafting tours ranging from a half-day to a week long.
- Visitor centers and nature (e.g., rainforest/local wildlife) theme parks with interpretive displays.
- Aerial gondola cable-ways and elevated treetop forest walks.
- Wildlife tours and attractions, including nocturnal spotlighting for elusive marsupials and glowworms, platypus viewing, and fairy penguin parades.

There is no recent published overall assessment of the ecotourism industry in Australia. Statistics from 1994–1995, however, indicate that there were some 600 companies advertising as offering ecotourism products. These were generating Au$250 million (US$125 million) a year and employing some 4,500 full-time equivalent staff.[7]

History and Philosophy behind the Development of NEAP

In 1991,[8] a pivotal conference laid the groundwork for development of the Ecotourism Association of Australia (EAA). Tourism businesses and other stakeholders argued that EAA was necessary to help consumers identify genuine ecotourism from the "cowboys." These "cowboys" were businesses not following sound ecological practices that had jumped on the "eco" bandwagon to gain a marketing advantage. Initially, many felt that developing a relatively simple ecotourism code of practice would suffice.[9] However, the 150 people who attended EAA's inaugural conference in 1993[10] expressed strong support for developing a certification scheme. These delegates represented a broad spectrum from industry, academia, NGOs (The Wilderness Society, Australian Conservation Foundation, World Wildlife Fund, etc.), protected areas, and government.

In hindsight, a major benefit of the development of NEAP was to clearly and concisely define ecotourism, in a single sentence: "Ecologically sustainable tourism with a primary focus on experiencing natural areas that fosters environmental and cultural understanding, appreciation and conservation."[11] Today, few tourism industry leaders question the concept of ecotourism, although some of its specifics continue to be debated.

At around the same time, the Australian government's Department of Tourism (DoT) was seeking strategies for implementing the principles of ecologically sustainable development in tourism development, planning, and management. Australia's national tourism strategy highlighted the need for sustainable tourism development and a balanced approach to economic, social, and environmental issues.[12] The government believed that a formulation of an overall policy framework for the development of ecotourism for both the international and domestic markets would contribute to achieving sustainable tourism in natural areas. In 1994, therefore, it released the national ecotourism strategy[13] and appropriated Au$10 million (approximately US$5 million) over 1994–1997 for its implementation through the National Ecotourism Program. The government's aim was to develop ecotourism through innovative projects that would increase Australia's international competitiveness, enhance visitor appreciation of natural and cultural values, and contribute to the long-term conservation and management of ecotourism resources. The National Ecotourism Program also funded a consultancy on developing an ecotourism certification program[14]. The consultants were guided by a steering committee that included a member of the EAA, the Australian Tourism Industry Association (ATIA),[15] the Australian Conservation Foundation, and the Commonwealth Department of Tourism. The final report was, however, heavily criticized (mainly by ecotourism businesses) for being overly bureaucratic, administratively top-heavy, cumbersome, expensive to administer, and unsophisticated, with criteria that did not address the needs of major stakeholders.[16] As a result, the Australian government decided to provide additional funds (approximately US$30,000) to create a more workable certification program, particularly for the smaller microbusinesses that dominate Australia's ecotourism landscape.

The net result was that eighteen months were essentially lost between the EAA workshop in 1993 and 1995, when the EAA decided to take the lead in developing a certification scheme. However, the failed process did have two important outcomes. First, it helped crystallize the EAA's conviction that tour operator ownership was a fundamental aspect of any ecotourism certification. Second, EAA concluded that any scheme must be "lean and mean," with little administrative overhead, if it were to have any hope of success. These two conclusions are still fundamental to NEAP today.

A new working party was set up to develop a more feasible ecotourism certification scheme. There was, however, a reluctance to rely solely on the EAA—then a small association of 100 or so members run by volunteers—

so the consultancy was awarded to Tourism Council Australia.[17] The council had little corporate interest in either ecotourism or certification but was prepared to manage the process. The grant conditions also forced an arranged marriage with the Victorian Tour Operators Association (VTOA),[18] which had established and were continuing to develop a tourism business certification[19] program. This certification program focused mainly on business development aspects, such as hospitality quality and risk management for accommodations, but rapidly expanded to include other sectors.

NEAP was launched jointly by the EAA and VTOA (through its new national arm known as the Australian Tour Operators Association or ATON) with an independent chair. This alliance with VTOA, although initially resented by the EAA,[20] is now widely acknowledged as being fundamental to NEAP's eventual success. It allowed EAA's ecotourism experts to concentrate on development of the criteria while the Victorian Tour Operators Association provided the much-needed expertise on how to administer and roll out a successful certification scheme.

Although many expected the new scheme to cover all sustainable tourism businesses, the working group[21] quickly resolved to limit the scope to ecotourism by defining ecotourism in the certification criteria to have a nature focus and include interpretation. However, other criteria—environmental sustainability, contributions to conservation, working with local communities, cultural issues, and returns to local communities—also defined best practices for sustainable tourism.

Once the framework for the scheme had been developed, a major pilot project was undertaken involving over forty tourism operators from a range of tourism business sizes, sectors (accommodations, tours, and attractions), and ecosystems. This was to ensure that the new program received feedback from and would be supported by the industry. This testing was invaluable in determining the practicality of the criteria and benchmarking the levels of Ecotourism and Advanced Ecotourism certification through setting both core and bonus criteria for scoring a product. This pilot study was used to revise the criteria so as to seek a balance between setting the criteria too high (and thereby reducing the number of ecotourism products that could be certified and risking being too exclusive) and setting them too low (and hence reducing the integrity of the program).

The working group proposed a two-tiered system, with the Advanced Ecotourism certification benchmarked so only a small minority (5–10 percent), the crème de la crème, state-of-the art products could achieve this level and the Ecotourism certification set deliberately low to encourage as many businesses as possible to step on. Although this was initially criticized, particularly by the conservation movement, the working party felt that once businesses got on the certification path, the continuous improvement required by the certification program through revision and ratcheting up of criteria every three years would improve Australian ecotourism standards. In hindsight, however, the score for Advanced Ecotourism certification was set too low, allowing a large percentage (> 80 percent) of products to be certified at the higher category under NEAP I. (In recognition of this, EAA moved in 2000 to considerably tighten criteria for the next generation of the program, NEAP II, while also putting in place bonus criteria.)

The program was finally and officially launched in October 1996 at the EAA's annual conference at Kangaroo Island, South Australia. In the rush to launch the program, all activity was focused on producing the application document, and the commercial arrangements between the EAA and the Australian Tour Operators Network (ATON) were not formalized. This "handshake deal" caused some concern and angst within EAA because ATON had a substantial role in the ecotourism certification process despite having little perceived expertise or interest in ecotourism products. In addition, the government's seed funding was exhausted, so the organizers had to move on a voluntary basis to actually administer the system, including developing checklists, marketing materials, media kits, logos, and a rudimentary brochure. EAA and ATON jointly appointed an independent chair, Tor Hundloe, professor of environmental management at the University of Queensland, as well as the panel[22] and assessors. In early 1997, the first twenty-five ecotourism products were certified amid lots of national and local media coverage. With this propitious start, NEAP quickly became widely known. While most Australia's mainstream tourism bodies took an initial wait-and-see attitude, one in particular, Tourism Queensland (the state-level agency responsible for tourism marketing and product development) gave huge support and continues to provide major marketing benefits to certified operators.[23]

NEAP II: The Next Generation

Integral to the NEAP program is the encouragement of continuous improvement of certified ecotourism products though the revision and toughening of criteria every three years. The first comprehensive review of the criteria was conducted during 1999, and the second edition of the program, NEAP II, was launched in 2000. The decision was made early in the redevelopment process to expand the program to include a third category of certification: Nature Tourism. This new category of certification was mainly introduced in recognition of the need for all tourism in natural areas, not just ecotourism, to be ecologically sustainable. The major improvements included in NEAP II are:

- introduction of the Nature Tourism category;
- an increased emphasis on the interpretation criteria to distinguish between Ecotourism Accreditation and Advanced Ecotourism Accreditation (i.e., certification);
- A comprehensive review and redrafting of the entire NEAP I certification criteria, including increased stringency in the criteria needed to achieve Advanced Ecotourism Accreditation;
- An improved introduction section, with a comprehensive background on the program and a clearer application procedure; and
- An expanded appendix section that provides operators with a glossary, information on innovative best practices and interpretation, suggested reading, and a comprehensive list of industry contacts.

The development of NEAP II was far more straightforward than NEAP I, with none of the organizational wrangling over responsibility and ownership. The now well-established NEAP panel invited some of the original working party members to assist. Without federal government support and with NEAP I only just self-sufficient, NEAP II was forced to look for other funding to help with the redevelopment process. Tourism Queensland offered a modest grant (approximately US$10,000) to cover the development of NEAP II. All members of the working party—many of whom are successful consultants and professionals in their own right—continued to offer their expertise on a voluntary basis.

It is conservatively estimated that by 2001, both phases of NEAP had cost around US$400,000 to develop. This is based on the actual consultancy costs, EAA, ATON/VTOA, and Tourism Council of Australia (TCA) contributions, and an estimate at modest commercial rates of the volunteer hours. The total cost of developing the certification program could never be passed on to the industry, given the modest fees currently charged for annual certification and assessment. Today, NEAP is self-funding for day-to-day administration, but it suffers from the lack of sufficient money for effective marketing, redevelopment, and a comprehensive audit program. NEAP has had to seek grants for ongoing marketing, development of revised administrative and auditing processes, and development of revised criteria, as well as the development of NEAP into an international certification program.

During its first five years, NEAP operated as a joint venture between the EAA and ATON. The NEAP panel, consisting of two members from each organization and an independent chair, usually meets monthly via teleconference to discuss certification applications and general management issues. It also meets face-to-face at least once a year. A team of fee-for-service assessors familiar with the NEAP process[24] reviews certification applications, which are then submitted to the panel for a final decision. An administrator (who is also the office manager for the EAA) coordinates the day-to-day running of the program. NEAP generally holds various industry workshops and a half-day session at the EAA's annual general meeting/conference to help ensure that those involved in the certification program do not lose touch with certified operators and the ecotourism industry.

NEAP's Basic Elements and Principles

Certifying Product, Not Business Entity

NEAP was developed through a long and somewhat tortuous route involving extensive debate over the guiding philosophy and principles. There was, in particular, much deliberation about what should be certified—the guide, the business, or the product.[25] Many argued that the spotlight should be on the operating entity, but this presented difficulties because this would exclude businesses such as tour companies that often have a range of ecotourism and non-ecotourism products. It was therefore decided that the most accurate approach would be to assess and certify individual products, such as a tour, rather than the whole business.

Once the decision had been made to certify products, not companies, it became a much more straightforward process to establish criteria for three types of nature tourism and ecotourism products:

- **Accommodation** is a facility that includes infrastructure and services designed to house visitors overnight in nature. Common examples of nature tourism and ecotourism accommodation include lodges, resorts, standing camps, and camping/caravan grounds.
- **Tours** are activities in which one or more guides take an individual or group on an excursion. Tours typically combine activities such as walking, driving, or riding with viewing and interacting with the environment. Tours may offer overnight accommodation via a camping site or built structure, but these are not assessed as part of the tour product. Common examples of nature tours or ecotours include bush walking, caving, and snorkeling.
- **Attractions** are facilities that combine a natural area (or natural area focus) with fixed infrastructure designed to help people explore and learn. Common examples include wildlife parks or sanctuaries, aquaria, and visitor centers. Tours or accommodations offered as separate ticketable items are assessed separately from the attraction product.

Process Versus Performance

During the development of the criteria for NEAP certification, the team also had to resolve the fundamental issue of whether to target the performance of a product or an operator's commitment to process[26] (see chapter 1). While keeping clear of theoretical debates over process versus performance, the team worked up the criteria from a core set of principles (discussed below). In the end, NEAP incorporated a mix of both performance-based (e.g., sewage treatment meets certain effluent standards) and process-based criteria (e.g., creating a system for assessing and encouraging training of interpretive guides as an indicator of interpretive quality). As such, the criteria are quite technically prescriptive (i.e., performance based) in some areas and more general in others, relying on a commitment by the operator to implement a process to meet the desired outcomes. A major concern was to ensure that NEAP did not become too technical but still set measurable and practical performance indicators.[27]

The Eight Principles of NEAP: The Criteria

The following section describes the eight major principles of the ecotourism program that are exhaustively detailed through specific criteria in the NEAP I and II application manuals. [28]

1) **Natural Area Focus.** The fundamental aspect that NEAP identifies for ecotourism is a focus on the visitor's personal experiences, leading to greater understanding and appreciation of nature. Fundamentally, the core (essential) criteria require that the majority of a customer's time is spent within a natural area with the opportunity to use at least three of our five senses—sight, sound, smell, touch, and taste—while experiencing nature. Other criteria address group size, quality of intergroup encounters, setting, and use of natural theme in marketing images.

2) **Interpretation.** For the Ecotourism certification, customers must have the opportunity to learn about natural and cultural heritage. For Advanced Ecotourism certification, interpretation must be a core component of the experience, and at least one interpretive opportunity must involve use of a trained guide (i.e., guided activities, lectures/talks, games, or theatre). There are additional detailed criteria and guidelines setting out the required standards for interpretation accuracy, planning, staff awareness and understanding, and staff training.

3) **Environmental Sustainability.** There are detailed criteria addressing performance and process aspects for ecological sustainability. In addition to criteria that are summarized below, there are specific minimal

impact codes for many activities ranging from, for instance, whale watching to camping, diving, and vehicle use. The criteria address:

- staff training, education, responsibility, knowledge, and awareness in environmental management;
- contingency planning and emergency preparedness (focusing on aspects of the ecotourism operation in which there is a risk of environmental harm);
- locally appropriate location, site layout, scale, and design (embodying a sensitivity toward sense of place);
- environmental planning and impact assessment, considering social, cultural, ecological, and economic impacts (including cumulative impacts and mitigation strategies);
- site disturbance, landscaping, and rehabilitation;
- drainage, soil, and water management;
- construction methods and materials (focusing on the sustainability of materials and supplies);
- visual impacts and lighting;
- sustainability of water supply and minimization of use;
- sustainability of wastewater treatment and disposal;
- noise (focusing on the concept of natural quiet);
- air quality (including greenhouse gas emissions);
- waste minimization and litter;
- sustainability of energy supply and minimization of use;
- minimal disturbance to wildlife.

4) **Contribution to Conservation**. The criteria require positive and active contributions to conservation of natural areas or biodiversity. This includes physical, financial, or in-kind assistance provided for rehabilitation of areas subject to visitor impact or feral animal/weed control, and/or simpler efforts, such as removal of litter. It also includes steps such as support for research and monitoring (financial or in-kind support for research personnel and participation in tourism impact monitoring) and donations and sponsorships of local and national conservation groups.

5) **Working with Local Communities**. The provision of benefits for local communities (employment, purchasing services, and materials, and local communities' access to ecotourist spending, for example, including local souvenir, food, and beverage outlets in tour itineraries) is required. Further requirements to minimize impacts on local com-

munities are established. Tourism businesses are also required to make contributions to the life of the local community.

6) **Cultural Component.** Although the focus of ecotourism in Australia is primarily on the natural values of an area, many of these sites also have significant cultural value, particularly indigenous cultural value. The criteria require minimal impact on and presentation of local (indigenous) culture, including involving indigenous communities in the delivery of the ecotourism product. This includes consulting about the nature and scope of the tourism business with traditional custodians, providing tourists with guidelines for behavior in culturally sensitive areas, and, where appropriate, restricting access to specific sites of spiritual significance.

7) **Client Satisfaction.** There are requirements for tourism businesses to obtain consumer feedback regarding quality of the tourism experience, with bonus criteria for responding to surveys and contracted third-party reviews by tourism professionals (such as other ecotourism businesses, product development and marketing officers from national, state, or regional tourism operations, etc.).

8) **Responsible Marketing.** These criteria address accurate, responsible marketing leading to realistic expectations by ecotourists. The criteria also address the content of marketing material to ensure that customers are provided with information that will increase their respect for the natural and cultural environments of destination areas.

Core and Bonus Criteria and Innovative Best Practice

In developing NEAP, the team faced the difficulty of how to set minimum standards across each of the principles that would allow for the great diversity of achievement within Australia's huge variety of ecotourism products. The solution was the identification of core criteria for each of the eight principles that every certified product must meet (see table 5.1). These core criteria measure a reasonable level of ecological sustainability and are relatively achievable for most tourism businesses with a natural area focus. They therefore form the minimum requirements a tourism product must fulfill to be certified as ecotourism—unless, under special circumstances, particular criteria do not apply. For example, a product may be exempted from the core cultural component if there are no remaining traditional custodians or cultural artifacts present.

However, to leave the certification system at this level would codify that just enough was good enough. The 1996 pilot study showed that ecotourism products often excelled in one area (nature interpretation, ecologically sustainable design, or cultural aspects, for example) but met only basic aspects of the other principles. The creators of NEAP therefore decided to award both basic Ecotourism certification and Advanced ecotourism certification (see categories below). They also recognized that there needed to be a mechanism to identify a reasonably high level of achievement under each principle, while acknowledging that most ecotourism products would not achieve the same level across all eight categories. The bonus category was therefore devised to allow operators to gain credit where they clearly achieved well beyond the core criteria. To achieve Advanced Ecotourism certification, an operator had to meet 80 percent of the bonus criteria under NEAP I; this was lowered to 75 percent under NEAP II.

In one final addition, the NEAP creators devised the concept of "innovative best practice" to award extra points to those who in a particular area achieve well beyond the bonus criteria. For example, an ecotourism business that supports the natural area visited by contributing a set amount annually to an independent research foundation is clearly superior to NEAP's specified bonus criteria, so the operator receives additional points toward the Advanced Ecotourism certification level. Those involved with NEAP are convinced that this framework of setting core and bonus criteria and innovative best practice has been a great success. It has encouraged innovation in areas such as energy generation/use/conservation, waste minimization, cultural involvement, contribution to the conservation of natural areas and local communities.

Certification Categories and Levels

Originally, NEAP addressed only the category of ecotourism certification with two levels: Ecotourism and Advanced Ecotourism. Later, under NEAP II, a new certification category for Nature Tourism was introduced. NEAP defines *Nature Tourism* as "ecologically sustainable tourism with a primary focus on experiencing natural areas."[29]

1) **Nature Tourism Certification.** To qualify for Nature Tourism certification, a product must meet core criteria for four principles of the program: those of natural area focus, environmental sustainability, responsible marketing, and client satisfaction. The provision of interpretation is not mandatory; however, where it is provided, it must satisfy core criteria. Operators undertaking Nature Tourism certification are encouraged to implement a continuous improvement program and, if desired, seek Ecotourism certification.

2) **Ecotourism Certification.** A product must meet all core criteria for the eight principles of the program to attain Ecotourism certification. In addition, the operator must include opportunities for customers to experience interpretation as part of their experience. Operators seek-

Table 5.1. NEAP's Three Categories of Certification

NEAP's 8 Principles	Nature Tourism	Ecotourism	Advanced Ecotourism
1) Natural Area Focus Focuses on directly and personally experiencing nature.	Core	Core	Core + Bonus
2) Interpretation Provides opportunities to experience nature in ways that lead to greater understanding, appreciation, and enjoyment.	Optional, but must meet criteria if it occurs	Mandatory but not necessarily core to experience	Core
3) Environmental Sustainability Represents best practice for ecological sustainable tourism.	Core	Core	Core + Bonus
4) Contribution to Conservation Positively contributes to the conservation of natural areas.		Core	Core + Bonus
5) Working with Local Communities Provides constructive, ongoing contributions to local communities.		Core	Core + Bonus
6) Cultural Component Is sensitive to and involves different cultures, especially indigenous cultures.		Core	Core + Bonus
7) Client Satisfaction Consistently meets customer expectations.	Core	Core	Core + Bonus
8) Responsible Marketing Is marketed accurately and leads to realistic expectations.	Core	Core	Core + Bonus

ing Ecotourism certification are encouraged to undertake a continuous improvement program that will allow them to seek Advanced Ecotourism certification.

3) **Advanced Ecotourism Certification.** A product must meet all core criteria for the eight principles of the program and meet, under NEAP II, 75 percent of the bonus criteria to be awarded advanced ecotourism certification. As stated above, this may be done either by meeting the set bonus criteria and/or being awarded extra points for demonstrating innovative best practice. To be eligible for Advanced Ecotourism certi-

fication, the operator must include interpretation as a fundamental component of the product.

The Certification Process

NEAP's rather complex certification process (see box 5.1) has been carefully developed through discussion, field testing, and continual modification. In late 2001, EAA announced "a new governance framework"[30] that includes creation of separate, independent working groups with responsibility for NEAP management, assessments, and audits. This revision addresses an ongoing concern that NEAP's structure contained a conflict of interest because the same team of experts were managing the program, assessing applications and issuing certification, and carrying out the paper and occasional on-site audits.[31]

1) **Self-Assessment Backed by Audits**. One of the longest running debates within NEAP has been whether or not to rely on self-assessment. Many felt self-assessment was worthless and on-site audits should be required prior to certification. However, both geographical distances and the small (often micro) size of most Australian ecotourism businesses made doing on-site, independent audits too expensive. Instead, NEAP's requirement that applicants provide two independent referees to verify the data serves to provide a check against fraudulent or spurious claims. Applicants must also send in examples of their marketing materials (which has turned out to be a surprisingly informative mechanism for verifying operator claims). Finally, where inaccuracies are suspected, NEAP does spot audits, both paper and physical on-site, to verify compliance.

   The scope of NEAP's criteria means that smaller operators do not always have all the necessary management practices in place to seek certification. By taking the self-assessment document back into their business for a period of months (or sometimes even years), operators can implement the necessary improvements according to their own time frame and budget before applying for certification.

   In completing the application, an operator may apply for certification of one or more Nature Tourism or Ecotourism products at the same time. Operators work through the manual's self-assessment criteria that apply to their products and then return the document to the administrator with the appropriate application and annual fees. Operators usually take at least eight hours to complete the 150-page application.

   The NEAP assessors review the applications, contact referees, and enter data against a checklist into a database. They make recommendations regarding the level of certification, points that may be claimed as innovative best practice, and, where necessary, request further information or referees or occasionally site inspections. The panel considers the assessors' recommendation and then certifies the products.

Referees have turned out to be a great mechanism to identify areas needing further investigation or, most commonly, to confirm that the product meets certification requirements. Under NEAP I, it was recommended that one referee be a protected area manager or from an environmental protection agency; with the launch of NEAP II, this has become mandatory. This helps to assure that the tour operator meets the local requirements for environmental compliance and licensing. However, because the NEAP administrators have found that many referees have no personal experience with ecotourism products, more specific guidelines for referees are being developed.

2) **Audits.** All products for certification are subject to paper audits, administered approximately once a year, that focus on selected criteria from one of NEAP's eight principles. The paper audit helps verify responses given in the original application. Although this audit is again based on self-assessment, the level of detail required is both extensive and objective. For example, the 1999–2000 audit, which focused on the principle of interpretation, solicited specific information on criteria such as interpretive themes and techniques, sources of interpretive content, and qualifications and/or methods of guide training.

In addition to the paper audits, a system of occasional on-site audits is also in place. Through 2000, on-site audits were administered on an ad hoc basis, undertaken by either a panel member or an assessor. Rather than being strictly random, these audits were implemented in response to adverse feedback, problems encountered during the assessment process, or requests from operators interested in improving their product. However, late in 2000, NEAP engaged the firm GHD Consultants to develop an audit protocol based on the NEAP II criteria, and an extensive schedule of on-site audits to test these protocols was rolled out in 2001.

Under the new protocol, the auditor must visit the site(s), experience at least one of the business's products[32] (assuming that the business entity has a number of certified products), and have permission to interview management, front of house and technical staff, and guides. Auditors also review records such as monitoring results, permits, licenses, and training qualifications. While this more formal audit process is being tested, the auditors are NEAP panel members or assessors, but revisions of the NEAP structure[33] mean that audits will move to an independent (of the NEAP management group) assessment/auditing group. Both assessors and auditors will be working for a fee-for-service and will be trained in NEAP protocols and assessment techniques. NEAP has set a target of conducting one random, physical on-site audit of every certified product within a three-year period. Because it is not practical to cover all aspects, these audits will target the following areas:

- innovative best practices claimed by the ecotourism business;
- elements of the bonus criteria claimed by the ecotourism business; and
- essential core criteria, including interpretive component, and compliance with permits and licenses issued to the ecotourism business.

An overall focus of the audit program is also to identify opportunities for improvement. Obviously, it is possible that an audit will uncover a product's noncompliance with the criteria that requires instant removal of certification. However, in most instances, audits identify practices and areas that can be improved to meet the criteria. Operators then must make the required improvements within an agreed time frame.

3) **Using the Logo.** If the application is successful, the operator is eligible to display one of the NEAP logos next to their certified product and is provided with a kit including a certificate, artwork, and decals to assist in promoting their product as a genuine ecotourism or nature tourism experience. Once certified, a product is eligible to display the NEAP logo for a period of three years, after which the operator must undergo a reapplication process. During the three years, those who have been certified must supply an annual statement of recommitment to the standard, declare any changes that impact upon their ability to meet the criteria claimed, and pay an annual renewal fee. Controlling use of the NEAP logo, in both print and electronic format, is seen as fundamental to the integrity of NEAP. For any single certified product (i.e., a single tour, attraction, or accommodation product), the NEAP logo may be included in any of its print or electronic marketing materials. In marketing a number of products, all of which are not certified, the NEAP logo may be located only alongside products that have gained certification. In all print, visual, audio, and electronic marketing materials, operators must not imply that all products are equally certified if that is not the case.

4) **Fees.** Fees cover the three-year certification period and are based on annual gross income. Fees range from about US$250 for operators with a turnover of less than US$50,000 to US$1,500 for operators with turnover in excess of US$1.5 million per year. The fees cover administration, assessment, and audit costs.

5) **Appeal, Suspension, or Forfeiture of Certification.** If certification is removed or an application refused, an operator or applicant has a right to appeal and to be assessed by an independent arbiter. Certification can be suspended or revoked by the NEAP panel if a certified product is found not to meet the nominated criteria. However, there is no right of appeal for applicants who dispute a panel decision that they do not meet core criteria.

If the NEAP panel receives a complaint or adverse consumer feedback, it will write to the operator, requesting a written response. If an adequate explanation is not provided, the operator will be given a certain period in which to change the practice in question. Failure to comply with the request within the designated period may result in the panel suspending or revoking certification. If this happens, then:

- the operator must return the current certificate of certification;

- the operator must cease representing his or her product as certified. This includes withdrawing all marketing material featuring the NEAP logo and notifying third parties (e.g., wholesalers, agents, etc.) who may be promoting the product as certified; and

- NEAP will distribute a notice of loss of certification status to relevant government agencies and key tourism industry organizations.

Over the years, NEAP has received a number of complaints regarding operations not meeting standards; these have been investigated. To date, there have not been any appeals needing the independent arbiter. By late 2001, no business had lost certification, although some needed to commit to improvement strategies.

NEAP officials believe that this structure ensures that the ecotourism industry can effectively self-regulate with a system that keeps up with the current state of improvement in the technology available for achieving ecological sustainability and the other principles of ecotourism. However, the scheme also embodies an independence: it involves both tourism and nature conservation experts, as well as tour operators, and has been accepted by almost all government tourism and conservation agencies throughout Australia. Further, there is a third-party aspect as each assessor and auditor is usually an ecotourism professional (academic, consultant, or public servant rather than a tourism operator). The NEAP panel is appointed for their knowledge of ecotourism. Conflict of interest is carefully managed; panel members, assessors, and auditors are not involved in decisions or actions where they have an interest.

Box 5.1. Snapshot of NEAP's Structure

- Certification based on eight principles that address focus on nature, interpretation, ecological sustainability, conservation, local communities, culture, customer satisfaction, and responsible marketing.
- The product rather than the whole business is certified, the products are divided into three major sectors—accommodations, attractions, and tour operations.
- Certification is provided for two categories: Nature and Ecotourism product. Ecotourism certification has two levels: Ecotourism and Advanced Ecotourism.
- Criteria are divided into "core" criteria, "bonus" criteria, and an opportunity to present "innovative best practice." Bonus criteria score a specified number of points; innovative best practices receive points at the discretion of the management panel.
- Certification for the different ecotourism categories and levels of ecotourism depend on meeting: (1) a subsection of the core criteria (Nature Tourism), (2) all core criteria (Ecotourism), and (3) all core criteria plus a percentage of bonus criteria and/or innovative best practice (Advanced Ecotourism).
- A panel of Ecotourism Association of Australia (EAA) members and an independent chair (plus co-opted expertise, if and when necessary) oversee the management of the program.
- Tour businesses complete an application, based on self-assessment of their product against the relevant criteria, supported by two referees. Application becomes a contractual commitment to meet the claims made in the application. A team of assessors reviews certification applications, which are then forwarded to the panel for ratification.
- Appointed auditors undertake paper audits of selected criteria on a yearly basis.
- Targeted physical on-site audits are undertaken when application documents, referee reports, consumer complaints, or interviews with business managers or staff indicate either a misunderstanding of the criteria requirements or blatantly fraudulent claims.
- A target of one random, physical on-site audit of every certified product within a three-year period is aimed for (but has not yet been reached).
- There is an appeals system in place for operators wishing to dispute a decision.
- Certification is valid for three years, based on an annual report that advises EAA of any major operational changes that affect the product's ability to meet relevant criteria and on an annual renewal fee.
- Operators may use logos in marketing; logos may be withdrawn by NEAP if a company is found not to be complying with the criteria.
- NEAP operates as a self-funding program, with administration, assessment, and auditing costs covered by application and annual fees paid by certified operators. Ongoing development of the program has been achieved through government grants.

NEAP's Successes and Challenges

One of the reasons for NEAP's continued success is that it provides a practical, measurable process for assessing the sustainability of nature tourism and ecotourism products. Rather than requiring participating operators to simply sign off on a voluntary code of conduct, the program obliges them to demonstrate that they actually have best practice management in place before they can be certified. However, because the first part of the application process is based upon self-assessment, NEAP also provides a non-threatening means for operators to determine the extent to which they comply with the standard. Thus, NEAP is an educational tool for nature and ecotourism operators.

From the outset, NEAP's creators sought to develop the program in close collaboration with protected area managers. In most national and marine parks in Australia, tour operators need to obtain annual licenses. NEAP has been successful in obtaining extended tenure for certified operators in three states, and plans are in place to include the rest of Australia's states and territories in this program in the near future. By cooperating with NEAP, protected area managers get assurance that operators meet requirements such as the ecological sustainability criteria and interpretation aspects.

The NEAP program has always had the philosophy of using the carrot rather than the stick. The aims are to provide such strong, tangible commercial and promotional benefits to businesses that they simply can't afford not to be certified. For more than one operator, this has meant that finance for expansion or to buy new vehicles has been far easier to obtain. As two business owners who have gone through NEAP certification have stated:

> "The ecotourism scheme provides a valuable checklist for self-assessment and improvement of operating standards, and it will do much to raise standards and improve customer perceptions of the industry." (Alan Roberston, Gipsy Point Lodge)
>
> "We believe accreditation [certification] will add credibility to our operation and assure our clients and tourism colleagues that they are dealing with a highly professional operator."(Karen and Brian Garth, Eco-Adventures Tours)

NEAP does, however, continue to face a number of challenges. There have been and still are very high expectations that NEAP actively promote the logo to consumers. Given the organization's very modest budget, it has not had the resources to directly promote the logo to the traveling public. Instead, NEAP has made numerous efforts to promote the logo at the industry distribution and supply chain level. Certified products are also promoted in NEAP's annual ecotourism guidebook that is increasingly used as the industry source for nature and ecotourism products in Australia. One initiative that suffered frustrating delays has been the creation of a Web site with pages for each certified ecotourism product and links to the operators' sites.

Tourism Queensland has been at the forefront of helping to market NEAP, providing major support for certified operators in that state. It has developed a range of logo promotion materials, including reception desk displays, in-room use displays, and stickers, as well as "familiarization" programs of certified products for journalists and travel agents. In addition, the Australian Tourist Commission has provided discounted marketing rates and pages dedicated to promotion of NEAP in their *Australian Tourism Source*, the major promotional guide to the country, distributed to tens of thousands of travel agents and wholesalers worldwide.

In reality, however, by 2001, NEAP was covering only a small proportion (estimated to be less than 10 percent) of the Australian ecotourism industry, and an even smaller proportion of the nature tourism products. NEAP administrators have attempted to compare the program against its stated objectives, similar standards and systems for certification, and codes of practice and best practice in relation to ecologically sustainable design, interpretation, etc. This process of comparison and evaluation (benchmarking) is considered vital to gauge the program's success. In 2000, for instance, Tourism Queensland undertook a survey[34] of NEAP-certified operators, and about two-thirds responded. Operators were asked what impact NEAP certification has had on their business. Half identified increased awareness and one-third reported increased business because of their certification. Further, when asked if they expected future benefits, 85 percent saw ongoing advantages with certification and 92 percent said they would renew. Importantly, the survey also probed consumer awareness by surveying tourists using certified ecotourism products. Only one-third reported that they were aware of the NEAP program, at least to the point of logo recognition. Just over two-thirds of those aware of NEAP said they use it to choose their ecotour products. Of all those surveyed, 60 percent said that after using a NEAP product, they would be more likely to use NEAP in their future travels. In addition, over two-thirds said they would be prepared to pay 5–10 percent more for NEAP-certified products.

The international certification conference held at Mohonk Mountain House in New York in November 2000 provided an opportunity for NEAP to evaluate its achievements against other programs and a template of universal standards, as incorporated in the Mohonk Agreement (see appendix). NEAP administrators provided major contribution to the wording of the Mohonk Agreement by including those aspects that NEAP has come to believe are vital to a sound ecotourism certification program.

However, the conference also highlighted a number of aspects that NEAP does not address in sufficient detail:

- mechanisms for monitoring and reporting environmental performance;
- impacts upon social structures, culture, and economy (on both local and national levels);
- appropriateness of land acquisition/access processes and land tenure;
- measures to protect the integrity of the local community's social structure;
- mechanisms to ensure that rights and aspirations of local and/or indigenous people are recognized;
- requirements for ethical business practice;
- mechanisms to ensure that labor arrangements and industrial relations procedures are not exploitative and conform to local laws or international labor standards (whichever are higher); and
- requirements to ensure contributions to the development/maintenance of local community infrastructure.

Recognizing the importance of these points, the NEAP program is currently integrating new criteria into an international standard and will be integrating these into NEAP III.

While NEAP is working to expand its coverage and improve its performance inside Australia, it has also been involved in assisting and forming alliances with other certification programs in the Asia Pacific region, as well as globally. Since 2000, NEAP has been providing support to the Fiji Ecotourism Association in its efforts to develop a certification and best practices program. In addition, NEAP has been working to support the Pacific Asia Travel Association (PATA) and the Asia Pacific Economic Cooperation's (APEC) Code for Sustainable Tourism, which was adopted in 2001. NEAP has also been involved in detailed negotiations about possible collaboration with Green Globe 21 through its Asia Pacific division.

Although NEAP officials have had concerns about the historical baggage the first Green Globe scheme brings, they developed increasing confidence in the administrative arrangement and implementation of the Green Globe 21 program, as it has been conceptualized and implemented by Green Globe Asia Pacific. In November 2001, EAA and Green Globe announced they would launch, during the International Year of Ecotourism in 2002, a new international "standard for Ecotourism" based on the NEAP system. In making the announcement, EAA president Peter O'Reilly stated that "this will be the first global ecotourism standard developed. We are proud that it is an Australian product—NEAP . . . that is being used to set the standard for the world."[35]

After six years gestation and five years in operation, NEAP had, by late

2001, achieved surprising success and growing respect and recognition within Australia and worldwide. The outstanding success of the NEAP program should not be measured simply by how many products have been certified but by the undoubted raising of nature and ecotourism standards through businesses using the program as a developmental blueprint and tool. NEAP has provided a much-needed model that, although far from perfect, helps nature and ecotourism businesses improve their products and helps tourists and other consumers make better selections. Further, NEAP has provided a standard definition of ecotourism and nature tourism that can (with some modification to suit local ecological, economic, and social conditions) be used globally.[36] The future lies in both expanding NEAP's coverage within Australia and in harmonizing this program with other initiatives under the umbrella of internationally recognized certification criteria and a global accreditation system.

Notes

1. Although the EAA now has sole ownership of NEAP, its initial development was through an arranged marriage, forced through federal government grant funding conditions, between two other tourism associations—the Victorian Tour Operators Association (VTOA), sometimes referred to interchangeably with its national counterpart, Australian Tour Operators Network (ATON), and the Tourism Council of Australia (TCA).
2. In Australia, the term *accreditation* was and mostly still is used universally for the recognition of business and products, with the term *certification* being used to recognize of individuals (i.e., guides). NEAP recognizes that there is a growing acceptance of the use of the terms *certification* for the recognition of individual tourism businesses/products and *accreditation* for formal recognition of a certification program by a higher body. We have "translated" the Nature and Ecotourism Accreditation Program terminology of *accreditation* to *certification* for this article, and plans by the NEAP administration to conform to international usage are on the drawing board, including changes to current logos.
3. Information on the EcoGuide Program can be obtained from the Ecotourism Association of Australia: GPO Box 268, Brisbane Qld 4001, Australia or from the EAA Web site: www.ecotourism.org.au; Ecotourism Association of Australia "Australian Ecotourism: Leading the World," press release and "Green Globe 21: NEAP Alliance in Principle Agreement" (November 2001).
4. According to "Impact: A Monthly Fact-sheet on the Economic Impact of Tourism," published by the Australian Federal Department of Industry, Science, and Resources based on the Australian National Accounts: Tourism Satellite Account 1997/98 (March 2001).
5. Australian Bureau of Tourism Research. FORECAST. Latest figures and addi-

tional data are available from their Web site: http://www.btr.gov.au (August 2001).

6. "Impact" (March 2001).

7. See Econsult, Commonwealth Department of Tourism, "National Ecotourism Strategy Business Development Program Report" (1995); and Blamey, R., "The Nature of Ecotourism," Occasional Paper No. 21 (Canberra: Bureau of Tourism Research, 1995).

8. "Ecotourism Incorporating the Global Classroom," Brisbane, Australia, 1991. Papers from this conference have been published under the same name by the Bureau of Tourism Research (1992), edited by Betty Weiler.

9. This code is published in early EAA brochures and can be seen in Betty Weiler, "Ecotourism Association of Australia" in *Sustainable Tourism: An Australian Perspective,* Rob Harris and Neil Leiper, editors (Sydney: Butterworth-Heinemann, 1995).

10. Ecotourism Association of Australia (EAA), "Evaluating Ecotourism Workshop" inaugural meeting held at Port Douglas, Queensland, 1993.

11. NEAP working party, *NEAP: Nature and Ecotourism Accreditation Program,* 2 ed. (Brisbane: EAA, 2000), p. 4.

12. Commonwealth Department of Tourism, *Tourism, Australia's Passport to Growth: A National Tourism Strategy* (Canberra: Australian Government Printing Service, 1992).

13. Commonwealth Department of Tourism, *National Ecotourism Strategy* (Canberra: Australian Government Printing Service, 1994).

14. Manidis Roberts Consultants, *An Investigation into a National Ecotourism Accreditation Scheme* (Canberra: Australian Government Printing Service, 1994).

15. ATIA was relaunched as the Tourism Council of Australia and was subsequently involved in the development of NEAP. However, this peak industry body went into receivership in 2001 but has reemerged into distinct state bodies.

16. See EAA, "Analysis of the Ecotourism Association of Australia's Members Questionnaire on the Commonwealth Government's Investigation into a National Accreditation Scheme," Ecotourism Research Paper No. 95/01 (Brisbane: EAA, 1995).

17. *Tourism Accreditation Program* (Melbourne: Australian Tourism Operators Network, 1995).

18. VTOA developed a national arm known as the Australian Tourism Operators Network (ATON) that was the formal partner in the joint venture that originally developed and administered NEAP.

19. Tourism Accreditation Program, ATON.

20. Australia is rife with state allegiances and politics: ATON was obviously Victorian, and the EAA suffers from being considered a predominantly Queensland-focused, rather than national organization.

21. The following working party and officials developed the initial NEAP program: Tony Charters (EAA), Guy Chester (EAA), Alice Crabtree (EAA), Jean-Pierre Issaverdis (ATON), Tony Lee (ATON), Simon McArthur (EAA), Cathy

Parsons (ONT), Isabel Sebastian (TCA), Peter Shelley (ATON), Tania Tear (ONT), Stuart Toplis (EAA), Cherise Walmsley (EAA).

22. Alice Crabtree and Guy Chester representing the EAA, and Tony Lee and Peter Shelley representing ATON.

23. This is partially because a large proportion of ecotourism products are based in Queensland but has certainly not been hindered by the presence of EAA committee influence within Tourism Queensland.

24. Assessors were initially EAA contacts that had relevant expertise, such as being members of the original working parties.

25. Most elements of guiding were considered vital to ecotourism and integrated under the major principle of "Education and Interpretation."

26. This debate ran concurrently with the evolution of many other environmental management frameworks in the mid 1990s, particularly the ISO 14000 standards.

27. ISO 14001, which addresses environmental management systems, and ISO 14002, which addresses auditing, were used as a basis for the development of NEAP II criteria and the audit protocol. However, we argue strongly that whilst all enterprises should address environmental management, ISO 14000 does not ensure ecological sustainability because its uses process based standards as the sole measure of any tourism business achieving ecological certification.

28. NEAP working party, *NEAP: Nature and Ecotourism Accreditation Program*, 2 ed. This document is also available on the EAA's Web site http://www.ecotourism.org.au as a downloadable pdf document.

29. Ibid, p. 4.

30. Ecotourism Association of Australia, *NEAP Corporate Governance* (Brisbane: EAA, October 2001).

31. Ibid.

32. For a complete short tour or selected section/day of an extended tour.

33. This followed the EAA obtaining sole ownership of the NEAP program in 2001 and consequent revisions of the management structure.

34. *National Ecotourism Accreditation Program (NEAP) Industry and Consumer Feedback Survey Reports* conducted by Enhance Management for Tourism Queensland (Brisbane: EAA, 2000).

35. "Australian Ecotourism: Leading the World," EAA media release (November 2001). At the time of press, NEAP had developed a preliminary standard for global ecotourism certification. NEAP intends to consult widely over its content during the International Year of Ecotourism with the hope of launching the standard in late 2002. NEAP has made an agreement "in principle" with Green Globe Asia Pacific that it will market and administrate the scheme.

36. The authors would like to acknowledge that from its inception, NEAP has been a collaborative and consultative effort. The initial and ongoing development of the program have drawn on the collective expertise of individuals involved in fields as diverse as protected area management, guiding and guide training, environmental consulting, business certification, and tourism marketing. As the authors of this chapter, we would like to acknowledge that we

were part of a dedicated team that has developed and administered NEAP II and I. Further, we have used text throughout this chapter taken from NEAP's literature and developed collaboratively. NEAP would not be the success it is without the dedicated working party members, panel, and assessors, or the many tour operators who participated in the original pilot of NEAP and came back for more with NEAP II. Many have provided advice, suggestions, and their time, and it is this effort that fundamentally makes NEAP a practical and relevant program. Financially, NEAP would not exist without the seed funding provided from the Australian government and the substantial direct and indirect support of Tourism Queensland.

C h a p t e r   6

Eco-labels for Tourism in Europe: Moving the Market toward More Sustainable Practices

Herbert Hamele

In 1982, the Bavarian poet Harald Grill characterized the careless behavior of tourists and host populations in destinations as follows:

> "We as tourists don't care about nature and environment. As soon as we have destroyed it, we go somewhere else. We, as host populations, don't care either about our environment. As soon as we have destroyed it, we go for a holiday elsewhere."[1]

The World's Leading Tourism Destination

Fifty percent of international tourism takes place in Europe. Its Mediterranean basin, alpine mountains, thousands of beaches and lakes, and historic cities and towns are the most frequented destinations in the world. Europe offers hundreds of thousands of indoor and outdoor sport and leisure facilities and an endless list of summer and winter tour packages. Tourism and travel is one of Europe's biggest and most rapidly expanding industries and is expected to double over the next decade.

European tourism traces its roots back nearly two centuries to the growth of spa resorts catering to the wealthy and leisure class. Today, Europe can claim to combine a rich diversity of cultures, languages, landscapes, nature, climatic zones, peoples, life styles, and social values together with a high standard of living, an excellent infrastructure, and an expansion of free time for leisure and holiday to the middle and working classes.

This growing interest in visiting cultural, heritage, and natural sites has

187

paralleled the growth in Europe of a high level of environmental consciousness and a willingness to include environmental concerns in the daily
lives of both consumers and host populations. Europe has, for instance,
some half-million accommodations that both impact the environment and
directly depend on the quality of their natural surrounding. Of these, 95
percent are micro or small enterprises with less than fifty employees. Yet,
because they are dependent on their natural location, many of them are
very active and innovative in establishing and maintaining a high level of
environmental performance.

Although the rapid expansion of tourism in Europe has increased environmental threats, the parallel acceleration of technical and management
solutions to environmental problems has created better market opportunities for sustainable products. One of the challenges is to ensure that the
more sustainable products are easily recognized and that the consumer is
offered and then makes the "green" choice in selecting tourism as well as
other types of products. It is here that certification programs can play a vital
role. The dual function of these voluntary initiatives is to help direct travelers to environmentally and socially responsible tourism businesses and to
encourage improvements and set standards within the tourism industry.

Since the 1990s, researchers have identified a remarkable proliferation of
awards, prizes, ecolabels, and certification initiatives given for environmentally sustainable performance. Since 1993, the European Network for Sustainable Tourism Development (ECOTRANS), with its twenty partners in
twelve European countries, has been doing systematic research and monitoring of efforts to set sustainable standards within Europe's tourism industry. Its database, ECO-TIP, contains more than sixty ecolabels and awards
and over 300 examples of "good practice" by tourism businesses.[2]

The diversity of tourism in Europe presents, however, enormous challenges for certification initiatives. In developing an ecolabel, a number of
questions must be asked: Which product group to select? Which services to
include? Which criteria should be mandatory, which optional? What is the
balance between process (environmental management systems) and performance criteria? How to get applicants? How to train and advise them?
How to verify and guarantee compliance with the required criteria? How
to reach tour operators and individual consumers to build demand for
more sustainable products?

In principle, an ecolabel needs a homogeneous product group with clear
and common components or services so that environmental impacts can
be compared and rated. Every ecolabel initiative has to face this diverse
range of products and issues when defining the product group and developing the criteria for a certification scheme. It is argued here—and,
indeed, the rule of thumb for many certification researchers and practi-

tioners in Europe is that the set of criteria for "better environmental performance" has to both go beyond what is required by law (national or
regional) and still be achievable by between 10 and 30 percent of the target group of tourism providers. This is more straightforward for certification programs for which the target group is very specific—tourism on
organic farms, for instance. It becomes a greater challenge when the target
group is the accommodations industry in general, ranging from urban
hotels to seaside resorts to bungalows, guesthouses, and alpine huts. This
can lead to less rigorous, more generalized performance criteria and to the
use of criteria based on process or environmental management systems.

Environmental criteria are the core of every European ecolabel. Some
of these certification schemes do see their role in the wider context of sustainable development and may include some socioeconomic criteria, usually linked to work force and the local community. However, unlike in
developing countries where ecotourism and sustainable tourism are
viewed as important development models (making benefits for and impacts
on communities vital to assess), Europe's relatively high economic level in
most destinations and strong labor rights protections, especially in western
European countries, mean that socioeconomic criteria are viewed as less
critical. Nevertheless, because of the ongoing discussion of the meaning of
sustainable tourism development and of Agenda 21, some certification programs do include at least a few socioeconomic criteria. Typically, these
measure use and consumption of local products, use of organic food, and
employment to support traditional handicrafts and farming and create
other benefits for local communities.

Europe's Many Ecolabels for Tourism

In the 1990s, an increasing number of tourism associations, consumer
groups, and governmental bodies began to pay attention to ecologically
sound tourism. By 2001, there were about sixty environmental certificates
and awards in Europe covering nearly all types of tourism suppliers, including accommodations, beaches, protected areas, restaurants, marinas,
golf courses, tour packages, and various other tourism-related businesses
(see table 6.1). A majority of the ecolabels in Europe—more than thirty—
certify accommodations: hotels and restaurants, campsites, youth hostels,
farmhouses, alpine huts, holiday houses, guest houses, and bed and breakfast lodgings.[3]

The oldest and most successful of these certification schemes is Blue
Flag, which was started in the 1980s by the Federation for Environmental
Education in Europe (FEEE). Blue Flag's main aim has been to better
implement and even exceed the European Community's Bathing Water

Table 6.1. Tourism Certification and Ecolabeling Programs in Europe

Begun	Title	Lead organization	Target area	Product group	Type of criteria	Scope	On-site verification	Number certified
1987	Blue Flag	NGO-E	Europe, South Africa	Beaches, marinas	EM, P	ENV	Y	Total: 2816 Beaches: 2087 Marinas: 729
1988/ 1998	Silver Thistle (Silberdistel/ Qualität Plus Kleinwalsertal)	NGO-T	Austria	Accommodations (all types)	P	ENV, SOC, ECON	Y	
1990	Environmental Snake (Umwelt- schnecke Nord- seeinsel Borkum)	GOV	North Sea Isle of Borkum, Germany	Accommodations (all types), restau- rants	P, EM	ENV	N	111
1990	Blue Swallow (Blaue Schwalbe)	COMP	Europe	Spas, hotels, con- ference centers	P	ENV, SOC	N	118
1991	Green Hand (Grüne Hand)	NGO-T	Saalbach- Hinterglemm, Austria	Accommodations (hotels, private)	P	ENV	Y	65
1991	Environmental Seals for Hotels and Restaurants (Bayerisches Um- weltsiegel für das Gastgewerbe)	GOV, NGO-T	Bavaria, Germany	Accommodations (all types)	EM, P	ENV	Y	200
1992	Environmental Seal of Lungau (Umweltsiegel Lungau)	NGO-T	Austria	Accommodations (several types)	P	ENV	Y	100
1992	Panda Lodging (Gite Panda)	NGO	France	Accommodations	EM, P	ENV, SOC	Y	258
1993	Greener Manage- ment for Hotels and Restaurants (Wir führen einen	NGO-T	Germany	Accommodations (all types)	EM, P	ENV	Y	440

umweltorientierten Betrieb)

Year	Name		Location	Application				
1994	Municipal Eco-tourism Award (Alcúdia-Municipi Ecoturístic)	GOV	Alcudia, Spain	Accommodations (several types), restaurants	P	ENV	Y	17
1994	Green Key (Den Gronne Nogle)	NGO-T	Denmark, Sweden, Greenland, Estonia	Accommodations (all types)	EM, P	ENV	Y	106
1994	Eco-Ibex or Eco-Plus Label for Hotels (Öko-Grischun/Nachhaltigkeits-Zertifizierung für Hotelbetriebe-Label oe-plus)	COMP	Switzerland	Accommodations (hotels)	EM, P	ENV, SOC, ECON	Y	15
1994	Natural Products (Naturprodukt)	NGO	HoheTauren National Park, Austria	Accommodations (all types), other businesses	EM, P	ENV	Y	16
1994	Standards for Countryside Accommodations (Standardy pro ubytovaci zarizeni venkovské turistiky)	NGO	Czech Republic	Organic farm holidays	EM, P	ENV, SOC	Y	120
1994	Environmental Seal Tyrol-South Tyrol (Umweltsiegel Tirol-Südtirol)	GOV	Tyrol in Austria, Italy	Accommodations (all types)	EM, P	ENV	Y	229
1995	Panda Lodging (Gite Panda)	NGO	Belgium	Accommodations	EM, P	ENV, SOC	Y	15
1995	Responsible Tourism System (Sistema de Turismo Responsable)	NGO	Lanzarote, Spain	Hotels in the biosphere reserve	EM, P	ENV, SOC	Y	18

(continues)

191

Table 6.1. Continued

Begun	Title	Lead organization	Target area	Product group	Type of criteria	Scope	On-site verification	Number certified
1996	David Bellamy Conservation Award	NGO-T	United Kingdom	Accommodations (camping, caravan parks)	EM, P	ENV, SOC	Y	429
1996	Ecolabel of Quality for Alpine Huts (Umweltgütesiegel auf Alpenvereinshütten)	NGO-C	Germany, Austria, Italy	Accommodations (alpine huts)	P	ENV, ECON	Y	24
1997	Association of Lodges for Environmental Protection (Alberghi Consigliati per l'Impegno in Difesa dell'Ambiente)	NGO-E	Italy	Accommodations (hotels)	P	ENV, SOC, ECON	Y	127
1997	Austrian Ecolabel for Tourism (Das Österreichische Umweltzeichen für Tourismusbetriebe)	GOV	Austria	Accommodations (all types)	EM, P	ENV, SOC	Y	192
1997	Green Key for Holiday Houses	NGO-T	Moen, Denmark	Accommodations (vacation houses)	P	ENV	Y	54
1997	Eco-Picture (Öko-Pikto)	NGO-C COMP	Europe	Camping and caravan sites	P	ENV	Y/N	500
1997	EcoLabel Luxembourg	GOV, NGO	Luxemburg	Camp sites and other accommodations	EM, P	ENV	Y	21
1998	Guarantee of Environmental Quality (El Distintivo de Garantia de Calidad Ambiental)	GOV	Catalonia, Spain	Camping sites, hostels, hotels	EM, P	ENV	Y	13

Year	Name		Location				
1998	Green Tourism Business Scheme	COMP	Scotland, United Kingdom	Accommodations (all types)	EM, P	ENV, ECON	Y	254
1998	Gold Barometer (Milieubarometer)	NGO, GOV	The Netherlands	Camp sites, holiday parks	EM, P	ENV, ECON	Y	180
1998	Logo for Regional Biosphere Reserve (Regionalmarke Biosphärenreservat Schorfheide-Chorin)	NGO-T	Schorfheide-Chorin, Germany	Accommodations (all types), restaurants, other businesses	EM, P	ENV	Y	20
1998	Environmental Seal (Umwelt-siegel Uckermark)	NGO-T	Uckemark, Brandenburg, Germany	Accommodations (several types)	P	ENV	Y	19
1998	Organic Farm Holidays in Germany (Urlaub auf Biohöfen in Deutschland)	NGO	Germany	Accommodations (organic farms)	P	ENV, SOC	Y/N	143
1999	Guide for Organic Agro-Tourism (Guida Agli Agriturismi Bioecologici)	NGO	Italy	Accommodations (organic holiday farms)	EM	ENV, ECON	Y	135
1999	Green Keys (Les Clefs Vertes)	NGO-E	France	Accommodations (camping, caravan parks)	EM, P	ENV, SOC	Y	49
1999	Nordic Swan (Miljömärkning av hotel)	GOV	Scandinavia, Iceland	Accommodations (hotels)	EM, P	ENV	Y	32
1999	Eco-Proof (Öko-Proof-Betrieb)	COMP	Germany, Spain, Dubai	Accommodations (hotels)	EM, P	ENV	Y	18
2000	Eco-Dynamic Enterprise (Entreprise éco-dynamique)	GOV	Belgium	Accommodations (hotels), other businesses	EM, P	ENV	Y	35
2000	Green Label (Label Vert)	NGO-T	Belgium	Accommodations (several types)	EM, P	ENV	Y	6

(continues)

Table 6.1. Continued

Begun	Title	Target area	Lead organization	Product group	Type of criteria	Scope	On-site verification	Number certified
2000	Environmental Certification for Tourism (Umweltzertifizierung für die Tourismusbranche)	Italy	GOV	Accommodations (several types)	EM, P	ENV	Y	2
2000	Estonia—The Natural Way	Estonia	NGO–T	Rural tourism products and packages	P	ENV, ECON, SOC	Y	15
2001	Committed to Green (Der Umwelt verpflichtet)	Germany	NGO	Golf courses	EM, P	ENV, SOC	Not yet	0
2001	Destination 21	Denmark	GOV, NGO	Destinations	EM, P	ENV, SOC, ECON	Y	?
2001/ 2002	European Charter for Sustainable Tourism in Protected Areas	Europe	NGO	Protected areas	EM, P	ENV, SOC, ECON	Y	15
2001/ 2002	VIABONO	Germany	COMP	Accommodations (several), destinations	EM, P	ENV	N	?
2001/ 2002	Green Globe 21	Worldwide	COMP	Accommodations, tour operators, destinations	EM, P	ENV, ECON, SOC	Y	15
2002	PAN Parks	Europe	NGO	Parks and protected areas	EM, P	ENV	Y	?

Source: ©ECOTRANS, May, 2002. www.eco-tip.org.

[a]Tourism services certified with ecolabels in Europe: ~ 4800 tourism businesses; ~ 2000 beaches; ~ 6800 total in summer 2001.

[b]Lead organization: organization signing the license for the label; NGO: Nongovernmental organization; NGO–C: Nongovernmental organization for consumers; NGO–T: Nongovernmental organization for tourism; NGO–E: Nongovernmental organization for environment; GOV: Governmental organization; COMP: Company a Trade Association.

[c]Type of criteria EM: environmental management or process-based criteria; P: performance criteria.

[d]Scope: ENV = Environmental criteria; ECON = Economic criteria; SOC = Social/Cultural criteria.

[e]Verification on-site—Assessment of compliance with the criteria (verification) takes place on-site: in every case = YES (Y); normally not = NO (N); irregularly, at random = YES/NO (Y/N).

Directive and to combine this with environmental education and aware-ness. Today, about 2,000 beaches and more than 700 marinas are Blue Flag–certified, and the first Blue Flags are waving overseas. Recently, two new certificates have been developed for protected areas in Europe: the EUROPARC Federation has developed the European Charter for Sustainable Tourism Certification for nature and national parks and World Wildlife Fund (WWF) International has created the PAN Park Certification for large national parks (see chapter 7).

Today, regional and national environmental certificates and awards exist in Austria, Germany, Denmark, Luxemburg, England, the Netherlands, Italy, France, Spain, the Czech Republic, and Switzerland. International ecolabels have been developed and implemented in the Nordic countries (Norway, Sweden, Finland, Iceland, and Denmark), and the European Union is developing the criteria for a single Europe-wide ecolabel for accommodations. These programs are intended to stimulate better environmental performance by increasing both competition among suppliers and building consumer demand.

Europe has far more "green" certification programs than any other region of the world. In practice, they represent a rich but often confusing and overlapping array of certification programs. The following is a brief, country-by-country, description.

National Programs

Austria

Austria's Kleinwalsertal Valley introduced the first local ecolabel, the Silver Thistle (*Silberdistel*), in 1988, and it has since become a model for many other regions in Austria and Germany. Developed by the Kleinwalsertal Tourism Organization, Silver Thistle incorporated social and environmental criteria into a preexisting Quality Plus seal. The label covers all types of tourism in this valley, including public transportation, lifts, and ski and snowboarding schools. By 2001, 159 businesses had been Silver Thistle–certified, including 111 for accommodation. This represents 45 percent of the bed capacity in Kleinwalsertal.

Another local initiative is Green Hand (*Grüne Hand*), created in 1991 by the owner of the Hotel Birkenhof in the village of Saalbach-Hinterglemm to cover hotels in the Salzburg area. In 2001, in response to recent European studies about the importance of ecolabeling for sustainable tourism development, Green Hand decided to upgrade its criteria and its verification process.

Also in the Salzburg area is the Environmental Seal of Lungau (*Umwelt-*

siegel Lungau), which was developed in 1992 by Lungau's Eco-Committee in partnership with the local tourism organization, The Holiday Region Lungau. It covers all kinds of accommodations with criteria for energy and water consumption. By 2001, 100 hotels had received this ecolabel.

Yet another locally based ecolabeling program is Natural Products (*Naturprodukt*), which since 1994 has been certifying accommodations, restaurants, manufacturing, and organic agriculture around the Hohe Tauern National Park region in Austria. By 2001, it had certified thirty-seven businesses, including sixteen hotels.

In 1997, the Austrian Ecolabel for Tourism (*Das Österreichische Umweltzeichen für Tourismusbetriebe*) was created as the first government-backed, nationwide ecolabel for tourism services in Europe. Run by the ministries for the environment and for the economy, this Austrian label has been increasingly accepted and may eventually replace other less successful schemes in Austria. Its large number of criteria (135) and its independent auditing and awarding procedures for hotels, inns, guesthouses and mountain huts make it among the most sophisticated certification schemes in Europe. By 2002, 192 accommodations had been certified.

An important regional ecolabel has covered the Tyrol sections in Austria and Italy. The Environmental Seal in Tyrol, Austria, was begun in 1994, and in 1995, it was expanded to cover the neighboring Italian region of South Tyrol. This well-financed and intensely marketed initiative has certified hotels, guesthouses, holiday apartments, farms, camping sites, private accommodations, and pensions. In 1996, this program received British Airways' Tourism for Tomorrow Award. In 1999, it certified eighty-six businesses in Italy and 143 in Austria. However, since then, no certification has been done and the leadership of the Austrian Tyrol program is recommending that businesses apply for the official Austrian national ecolabel.

Italy

The Italian version of this seal, Environmental Seal Tyrol-South Tyrol (*Umweltsiegel Tirol-Südtirol*), was considered too restrictive because it was geared to small-size accommodations. It has been replaced by an ISO 14001 environmental management system, Environmental Certification for Tourism (*Umweltzertifizierung für die Tourismusbranche*), that is being developed in association with the hotelier association. This program has a checklist of requirements that accommodations must comply with, as well as all existing environmental legislation. In 2000, only four businesses participated in this new system and in early 2001, another two were certified.

There are other local ecolabels in Italy. In 1997, Legambiente, a national environmental organization, launched a new label with an awkwardly long name, the Association of Lodges for Protection of the Environment (*Alberghi Consigliati per l'Impegno in Difesa dell' Ambiente*), for hotels in the province of Rimini. Based on Agenda 21 principles, it started first near the Adriatic Sea region and has now widened to other areas, including the Emilia-Romagna region, with hopes of becoming a national scheme.

In 1998, another ecolabel, Guide for Organic Agro-Tourism (*Guida Agli Agriturismi Bioecologici*) was started by the Italian Association for Organic Agriculture (AIAB) in cooperation with WWF-Italy, an Italian tour operator specializing in sustainable tourism, and several other organizations. The purpose of this certification scheme is to evaluate tourism on organic farms to increase customer satisfaction and confidence. By 2000, 135 organic holiday farms had been certified. They are listed in a guide published by New Techniques (*Tecniche Nuove*).

In 2000, given the high importance of tourism throughout Italy and the international character of the market, the National Department for Environmental Protection (ANPA) coordinated the discussion amongst the Italian stakeholder associations to prepare for the possible European ecolabel for accommodation services.

Germany

There are several regional and local certification programs in Germany as well. In 1991, the program Environmentally Conscious Hotels and Restaurants in Bavaria (*Umweltbewusster Hotel- und Gaststättenbetrieb*) was begun by the state government in Bavaria as a pilot project offering three levels of certification (bronze, silver, gold) to hotels, private accommodations, campsites, and holiday apartments. By 2001, about 200 hotels and restaurants in Bavaria had been certified.

In the eastern mountainous area of Germany, the German alpine club of Munich, together with its partner clubs in Austria and Italy, awards the Eco-label of Quality for Alpine Huts (*Umweltgütesiegel auf Alpenvereinshütten*). Begun in 1996, the program has forty-three criteria, all of which are compulsory to obtain certification. By 2001, twenty-four huts had been certified in Germany, eleven in Austria, and one in South Tyrol, Italy. Another program in the Schorfheide-Chorin Biosphere Reserve is certifying accommodations and restaurants, as well as handicrafts, food processing, beekeeping, fishing, forestry, horticulture, and agriculture. This logo for Regional Biosphere Reserve was created in 1997 by the Cultural Landscape Association of Uckermark and began giving awards in 1998.

Most of the other regions in Germany have joined the DEHOGA initiative (German Hotel and Restaurant Association) that has, since 1993, been involved in certification programs. Greener Management for Hotels and Restaurants (*Wir führen einen umweltorientierten Betrieb*) is a national program that seeks to certify and market accommodations, especially small and medium-size enterprises. By 2000, some 500 companies from Mecklenburg-Vorpommern to Baden-Württemberg had been awarded, each based on slightly different criteria.

Local ecolabels exist as well on, for example, the island of Borkum where since 1990 the Environmental Snake certification program has focused on waste management in accommodation services. In 1998, the Brandenburg tourism association developed the Environmental Seal program for hotels and guesthouses in the small subregion of Uckermark/ Brandenburg in eastern Germany. By 2000, only nineteen businesses were certified, and it is likely this ecolabel will cease to exist. In addition, the German automobile association, ADAC, has developed the Squirrel (*Eichhörnchen*) ecolabel, the only certification program for restaurants located on major highways. However, the lack of applicants and consumer interest will probably lead to the demise of this scheme as well.

One highly specialized, Germany-wide ecolabel certifies organic farms that have accommodation facilities. Begun in 1998 by ECEAT (European Centre of Eco-Agro Tourism), this Organic Farms Holidays in Germany (*Urlaub auf Biohöfen in Deutschland*) program seeks to support organic agriculture through soft tourism. A guidebook lists all the certified farms, including a detailed evaluation of each farm's performance. By 2001, 143 farms had been certified.

Another specialized ecolabel still in the planning stage is a certification program for golf courses in Germany. Committed to Green (*Der Umwelt verpflichtet*) was developed by the German golf association with the aim of measuring environmental impacts on golf courses and improving awareness of the need for environmental protection (see chapter 1).

Over the last ten years, several trials have been made in an effort to implement a national ecolabel in Germany. In 2001, DEHOGA and a dozen other leading tourism associations, consumer groups, local governments, and the German environment ministry succeeded in agreeing on a common national brand to measure both quality and environmental standards for tourism. Their intention is to create an umbrella label for all tourism services, including a single logo and specific criteria for each type of product, from small guesthouses to whole destinations. The advantages of such an umbrella label are clear: by means of a single, unified logo, the participants expect not only a higher level of acceptance from customers but also a marked reduction in marketing costs. The brand's name is

VIABONO, which comes from Latin, meaning "the good way" or "path to goodness." VIABONO's website (www.viabono.de) describes its criteria as "demanding, but not impossible." It guarantees tourists "quality, relaxation and experiencing with all senses" and access to not only the natural environment but to regional cuisine, art, and culture. The program has developed different sets of criteria for hotels and restaurants, campsites, and local destinations. In 2001, VIABONO began certifying hotels and has plans to include camping sites and destinations. Its marketing is largely via the Internet. It seeks to become self-financing through charging fees to businesses seeking certification.

In other developments, beginning in 1999, a private German certification company, *TÜV Umwelt Cert Umweltgutachter GmbH*, created Eco-Proof (*Öko-Proof-Betrieb*), an international certification system for environmental management and performance for hotels and holiday centers. Applicants must fulfill 75 percent of the criteria, based on ISO 9000 and 14000 requirements. The company, although concentrating on Germany, is offering certification worldwide. By 2001, eighteen German hotels had been Öko-Proof certified, and several hotels in Spain, Turkey, and Dubai were expected to be certified and receive this label.

Denmark

Between 1994 and 2000, the Green Key (*Den Groenne Noegle*) in Denmark certified over 100 hotels, youth hostels, and restaurants. Run by HORESTA, an industry association, Green Key also certifies conference and holiday centers, camping sites, and holiday houses. In 2001, Green Key expanded its geographical scope and certified a handful of accommodations in Greenland, Sweden, and Estonia.

On the Island of Moen, another ecolabel designed for holiday houses is now cooperating with the Green Key. Known as Green Key for Holiday Houses, this very simple system has only nine criteria. By 2001, fifty-four houses had been certified. This ecolabel is being revamped to bring it into line with the national Green Key program.

Of all the countries in Europe, Denmark was the first country to combine certification of accommodations with ecolabeling schemes for destinations. Over the last few years, tourism associations in Denmark have created Destination 21, a three-stage labeling scheme for local destinations based on ecological, economic, and sociocultural criteria. The initiative is linked to Green Key certification for businesses, with the view that the more Green Key businesses there are in the destination, the better the chances of getting Destination 21 certification.

Switzerland

In Switzerland, a regional green ecolabeling program, Eco-Ibex (Öko-Grischun), began in 1994 to certify accommodations and restaurants in the canton of Graubünden. Supported by industry associations and NGOs, this is one of the most demanding and discriminating programs, with a very detailed set of criteria. Its self-administered questionnaire includes categories on waste, water, air, noise, energy, food products, furnishings, construction, traffic, and surroundings. A commission composed of impartial experts examines and validates the questionnaires and decides whether or not to grant certification. Those certified receive one to five ibexes (an antelope with large curved horns). This is followed by spot audits for businesses receiving one or two ibexes and detailed on-site inspections for those receiving three or more. By 2000, only fifteen companies had been certified. The program also facilitates an exchange of experience and know-how among participating hotels. In 2000, a project team began a complete overhaul of Eco-Ibex's certification process to create even more rigorous performance and process standards. The upgraded program, known as Label oe-Plus or Certification for Sustainability for Hotels (*Nachhaltigkeits-Zertifizierung für Hotelbetriebe*) was then relaunched and made available nationally to eco-hotels throughout Switzerland's alpine region, using the ibex as the symbol. Its immediate goal is to certify fifty hotels by 2002–2003 and to expand into other fields as well.

United Kingdom

Since 1996, the David Belamy Conservation Award, run by this well-known environmentalist and the British Holiday & Home Park Association, audits and certifies holiday parks and caravan and camping sites, as well as holiday villages in the United Kingdom. The program has three levels of certification: gold, silver, and bronze. By 2001, it had certified 429 businesses.

In Scotland, the Green Tourism Business Scheme, begun in 1998, is a very successful certification program, also based on three levels—bronze, silver, and gold. Developed by the Scottish Tourism Board in partnership with SEA Ltd. (Shetland Environmental Agency Ltd.), it covers all types of accommodations, visitor attractions, holiday parks, and other tourism enterprises. By 2001, it had certified 254 businesses in Scotland and was working to develop a national scheme for all of Britain.

France

In 1992, the World Wide Fund for Nature in France, together with the Federation of Natural Regional Parks, created the Gites ("Lodging")

Panda logo to certify accommodations in regional and national parks. To qualify for certification, the lodge owners must conserve the natural beauty and unique features of their property and help educate guests by providing equipment and information, including a kit containing maps, guides to local flora and fauna and other attractions, and binoculars. Both guests and WWF staff assess the lodges, and park staff provide the lodge owners with training sessions on the natural and cultural heritage. Certification is valid for three years. By 2001, 258 lodgings, located in thirty-one regional and three national parks were Gites Panda–certified in France.

A newer program, Green Keys (*Les Clefs Vertes*), is the national ecolabel for camping sites, caravan parks, and bungalow sites in France. The country has some 10,000 campsites or about one-quarter of all the campsites in Europe. In 2000, the French office of the Foundation of Environmental Education in Europe (FEEE) awarded Green Keys to forty-nine campsites. FEEE also collaborates with guidebook publishers such as "Le Guide Suisse" to promote the certified sites. It plans to expand Green Keys to cover hostels and holiday centers.

Spain

Local and smaller regional ecolabeling schemes exist on the Balearic island of Mallorca and on Lanzarote in the Canary Islands. On Mallorca, the municipality Alcúdia has an ecotourism certification program for hotels and restaurants. Started in 1994, its purpose is to promote respect for nature and to help implement environmentally sound measures. By 2001, fourteen hotels and three restaurants had been certified. On Lanzarote, the Responsible Tourism System (*Sistema de Turismo Responsable*) is a certification program with environmental and cultural criteria run by a respected NGO, the Responsible Tourism Institute. It covers hotels in the biosphere reserve on Lanzarote, and its logo includes the phrase Biosphere Hotels— Quality for Life. By 2001, it had certified eighteen hotels and had plans to expand into other biosphere areas in Europe.

In the region of Catalonia, the official government ecolabel is The Guarantee of Environmental Quality (*El Distintivo de Garantia de Calidad Ambiental*), which certifies accommodations. By 2001, nine camping sites, one youth hostel, and three hotels had been certified. The criteria combine environmental management with performance components.

The Netherlands

Since 1998, Gold Barometer (*Milieubarometer*), a project of RECRON, the national association of recreational enterprises, has been certifying campsites and holiday parks in The Netherlands. It has three sets of criteria—general, obligatory, and optional. General criteria require that companies fulfill environmental legislation, have an environmental program and coordinator, and do environmental management assessment. The system's obligatory criteria include energy- and water-saving measures, separation of waste, and use of environmentally friendly cleaning fluids. Optional criteria include use of rainwater, sustainable energy, environmentally friendly paint and construction materials, and recycled paper. The scheme has three levels—bronze, silver, and gold—and requires the fulfillment of a certain number of each type of criteria. By 2001, 180 campsites and holiday parks had been certified. Certified businesses that receive the gold level automatically get certification under the nationally recognized program, Environmental Mark (*Milieukeer*). This national labeling system is now being developed for hotels and swimming pools and the program is seeking international recognition.

The Czech Republic

In 1994, the Czech Republic became the first country in Europe to certify organic farm holidays. ECEAT Czech Republic, a member of ECEAT International (based in Amsterdam), developed the Standards for Countryside Accommodation (*Stanardy pro ubytovaci zarizerni venkovske turistiky*), an ecolabel for rural accommodations. About seventy businesses have been certified at the basic level, and another fifty have reached a higher level. In 2002, ECEAT's criteria and procedures were being developed for additional countries throughout Europe.

Belgium

In 2000, the tourism federation of the small region of Luxemburg Belge started a new ecolabel, Green Label (*Label Vert*), targeting hotels, camping sites, and lodges. During its first year, it certified six accommodations.

That same year, the Department of the Environment and Energy in Brussels created a three-tier ecolabel, Eco-Dynamic Enterprise (*Entreprise eco-dynamique*), which seeks to certify lodges, inns, hotels, and conference centers in the capital. By 2001, it had certified thirty-five companies, including seven hotels.

In 1995, WWF-Belgium started the Gites Panda logo in the Wallonie area for accommodations in rural areas and in national or municipal parks. The program, which has stringent ecological and socioeducational criteria, has certified fifteen lodgings. This program runs parallel to but does not cooperate with the WWF's Gites Panda program in France.

Estonia

One of Europe's newest certification programs, Estonia—The Natural Way, was launched in 2000 by ESTECAS, the Estonian Ecotourism Association, in cooperation with the Estonian Rural Tourism Association and several other environmental, tourism industry, government, and park management institutions. The ecolabel is for tour packages and tourism products in Estonia. As of September 2001, fifteen businesses had joined the ecolabeling scheme.

Luxemburg

Luxemburg, the smallest of the European Union member states, has developed one of the most ambitious certification programs on the continent. The EcoLabel Luxemburg, which certifies all types of accommodations, has become the official national ecolabel program. The purpose of the project is to distinguish environmentally friendly accommodations, including hotels, youth hostels, lodges, holiday apartments, and camping sites. It includes a good mix of performance and process-based criteria and it has an effective marketing program.

This initiative was launched in 1997 by Luxemburg's tourism ministry in cooperation with an advisory group from the ministries of environment and energy, the hotel association (Horesca), the camping association, the Eco-Funds Foundation (*Stiftung Öko-Fonds*), the hotel school, the chamber of commerce, and various cultural and educational centers. Those involved in developing this scheme have learned from other schemes and worked to create a program compatible with other ecolabels and initiatives in Europe. Government ministries have jointly provided Euro 347,000 (US$317,332) to finance the project through 2002.

The Luxemburg ecolabel certification includes ninety-nine process- and performance-based criteria in five fields: water, energy, waste, purchasing, and information. Of these, fifty-four criteria are obligatory and forty-five are optional. To be certified, a business has to fulfill all of the obligatory criteria and at least 50 percent of the optional criteria in each field. The advisory group reviews and revises the criteria every two years.

The Eco-Fund Foundation and partners offer free consultancy services, educational seminars, and training programs to all accommodation businesses, regardless of whether they are interested in applying for the ecolabel. It is highly recommended that business make use of this consultancy before registration for certification. On-site audits, conducted once a year, are carried out by the Examination Commission, which consists of environmental and energy consultants (one from Luxemburg and one from another country), an independent representative of the National

Tourist Office, and a representative of the Foundation. Certification is based on a single level and is valid for two years; additional site visits are conducted only in case of complaints from guests. Guest feedback is the main tool to ensure that an accommodation continues to meet the eco-label's criteria.

The Luxemburg ecolabel is promoted through brochures, folders, press articles, fairs, and special presentations abroad.[4] By mid-2001, twenty-one businesses had been certified.

Multinational Programs

Two Europe-wide certification programs—the oldest, Blue Flag, which started in 1987, and PAN Parks, which began certification in 2001—will be discussed in the next chapter. Several multinational programs in Europe—Ecolable of Quality for Alpine Huts, *Eco-Proof*, and Green Key (in Denmark, Sweden, Greenland, and Estonia)—have been mentioned above. In addition, Green Globe 21 is striving to carry out certification through-out Europe (see chapter 10). There are, however, several other Europe-wide initiatives. One is Blue Swallow (*Blaue Schwalbe*), which was started in 1990 by a private company, Verträglich Reisen in Munich. It certifies spas, hotels, and holiday and conference centers in Sweden, Finland, Germany, Austria, Switzerland, and Italy. By 2001, more than 118 businesses had fulfilled the criteria for certification and were listed in the popular consumer magazine, *Verträglich Reisen*.

Since 1997, ADAC, the German automobile club, also based in Munich, has been labeling camping and caravan sites throughout Europe with a green leaf under the Eco-Picture (*Öko-Pikto*) program. It requires busi-nesses to use at least 30 percent alternative energy sources and to meet at least 30 percent of its water needs with recycled water. By 2001, 500 camping sites had received Green Leaf certification for their environmen-tal initiatives and measures, especially for the use of solar energy. These are promoted in the ADAC's guidebook to camping and caravan sites in Europe, a very popular guide that has sold over 300,000 copies.

One of the most demanding multinational programs is the Nordic Swan (*Miljömärkning av hotel*), the first official ecolabeling scheme for tourism businesses in the Nordic countries—Sweden, Finland, Norway, Iceland, and Denmark—which some experts view as a model for all of Europe. Begun in 1999, it covers hotels, restaurants, conference facilities, and swim-ming pools. It is a very demanding scheme based on both environmental management and performance standards. It is the first to set concrete, per night limits on the consumption of water, energy, cleaning and washing detergents, hazardous substances, and production of unsorted waste. The limits depend on the size, services, and geographical location of the companies. By 2002, it had certified thirty-two businesses.

Between 1995 and 1999, the Federation of Regional Nature Parks in France, or EUROPARC, developed the European Charter for Sustainable Tourism in Protected Areas. The charter has a broad environmental and socioeconomic mandate intended to help protected areas throughout Europe to enhance local heritage, improve the quality of life for local residents, and offer better tourism products to visitors. In 2001, fifteen European parks were certified (see chapter 7).

It is likely that within the next few years a single, official European ecolabel for tourism, the European Flower, will be offered, beginning first with accommodations. In 1999, the European Commission's Directorate General for the Environment commissioned a study to assess the feasibility of the European ecolabel label for tourism services for the eighteen European Union countries.[5] The feasibility study was carried out through a series of workshops organized by the Consultancy and Research for Environmental Management (CREM) in The Netherlands and CH2MHILL in Spain. Their report, *Feasibility and Market Study for a European Eco-label for Tourist Accommodation (FEMATOUR)*, completed in August 2000, found a dozen reasons why a European ecolabel makes sense, including:

- one label makes the environmental performance of European accommodations transparent for tour operators and stimulates use of an ecolabel by tour operators;
- a European ecolabel backed by the European Commission is more reliable than many of the existing (private) ecolabels;
- one ecolabel may reduce consumer confusion about the wide variety of existing certification programs and will increase consumer recognition and consumer demand;
- a single label may serve as a valuable tool for internationally operating tourism service providers;
- a European ecolabel can be an effective tool to enhance environmental improvement and may contribute to sustainable tourism; and
- there is clear market demand for a single ecolabel.

An alternative put forward by several stakeholders who have doubts about a single European ecolabel is that the European Commission develop a framework (guidelines, code of practice, or a "label for labels") for existing labeling initiatives. However, the FEMATOUR study concludes that, "under certain conditions and as part of a wider process towards sustainable tourism . . . the majority of stakeholders might favor a European eco-label for accommodation."[6] Only one major organization, HOTREC, the European confederation of hotels, restaurants, and cafes, representing thirty-seven national associations, was strongly opposed; another, ECTAA, the national travel agents and tour operators association within the European Union, had some reservations.[7]

In terms of next steps, the European Commission is moving forward with the development of criteria and the verification system for a new certification program for accommodation. A final decision about whether to proceed in establishing the European Flower label will be made at the end of 2002. Parallel with this, the European Commission is supporting the VISIT project (see below) which promotes existing tourism eco-labels in Europes.

Effectiveness and Popularity of Ecolabels for Accommodations

Many tourism businesses in Europe have engaged enthusiastically in these environmental award schemes. In 1999 and 2000 alone, over 2,000 hotels, campsites, hostels, and restaurants in Europe were certified and were awarded ecolabels. By combining government, private sector, NGO, legal, and financial instruments, these European ecolabels represent a "soft" approach to regulation of environmental impacts. Businesses voluntarily enroll in certification programs on the assumption that consumers will patronize businesses that have received an ecolabel. Most supporters of these ecolabels argue that compulsory government regulation, whether at a national, regional, or European level, should be avoided as long as these volunteer programs succeed in reducing environmental damage and increasing businesses' commitment to following environmentally sound practices.

These schemes, especially the government-sponsored ones, provide guidelines, checklists, and technical advice for the applicants. However, because most of these programs are only a few years old and have certified only a small number of potential businesses, it is too early to judge whether they are effectively ensuring long-term sustainable practices. There is ample evidence that numerous individual businesses that have applied for ecolabels have successfully reduced their water and energy consumption and waste production, overcome various traffic-related problems, and helped preserve the biodiversity and beauty of the surrounding landscape. For these ecolabels to succeed in meeting the long-term objectives of supporting sustainable development, the criteria and auditing must be rigorous and frequently reviewed to ensure that the award programs have a lasting effect.

Ecolabeling is based on the assumption that there is public demand for green labels. To encourage businesses to take part, there needs to be effective and widespread publicity of both the certification programs and of those businesses and products that have qualified for ecolabels. However, many of these ecolabeling programs have not been very effective in publicizing their programs to consumers. Although a number of guidebooks and magazines promote them, studies have found that the vast majority of holidaymakers are unaware of the existence of the environmental certification schemes in the tourism sector. It is unlikely that any tangible results will be obtained until the major tour operators, tourist clubs, tourist information and reservation networks, and the media publicize ecolabel programs and the individual awardees.

Future of Ecolabels: Growth and Cooperation

The success of tourism ecolabeling in Europe depends upon efforts to increase cooperation and consolidation among the certification programs, including joint marketing activities and a mutual confidence that programs include similar criteria, standards, and auditing practices. The challenges facing tourism industry ecolabeling programs in Europe are largely the same as those facing certification programs in other parts of the world.

In 2000–2001, the World Tourism Organization (WTO) commissioned a global study on voluntary initiatives for sustainable tourism. More than 100 ecolabels, awards, and self-committing initiatives were studied in the first comparative analysis worldwide to assess the history, development, objectives, requirements, procedures, and effectiveness of every initiative.[8] The study found that there are sixty ecolabels for tourism services operating in various parts of the world with largely common goals and catering to an international clientele. Most of them are in Europe. However, the study also concluded that up to now their marketing efforts have been generally poor, there is an enormous lack of coordination in effective marketing approaches, and many ecolabels are struggling to survive and to meet the promises they made to their certified businesses in terms of cost savings and increased consumer demand.

Despite these considerable drawbacks, the history, current strategies, and future plans of tourism certification around the world do show encouraging trends. Programs are moving from:

1) codes and awards to real third-party certified ecolabels;
2) private or public to joint private–public initiatives;
3) covering one type of accommodation scheme to all types of accommodations and tourism services;
4) environmental criteria only to additional socioeconomic criteria;
5) local to national to international target areas;

6) a business approach that emphasizes cost-saving measures to a consumer approach that emphasizes marketing and branding; and
7) individual procedures and marketing to cooperation with other ecolabels and complementary initiatives.

VISIT: A Joint European Initiative

These seven global tendencies of ecolabels reflect the current situation in Europe as well. In Europe, studies show that the consumers are looking for accommodations with high quality and a reasonable price in an attractive landscape. In addition to these basic aspects, consumers are seeking environmentally friendly hotels, camping sites, beaches, or sport facilities. Despite the growth in numbers of programs for environmental quality, most are not well known, by either consumers or tourism businesses. For those who are aware of them, competition and overlap among local, national, and international ecolabels that cover the same product group and have similar criteria can cause confusion. The whole movement toward more sustainable development needs a "green corner" in the European tourism supermarket so that consumers can easily choose certified environmentally sound tourism products.

To achieve this, a joint European initiative was launched in 2001. Cofinanced by the LIFE program of the European Commission,[9] the project, entitled Eco-labels for Sustainable Tourism in Europe, is intended to demonstrate how ecolabels can help move the European tourism market toward principles of sustainability. This project is a partnership among ECOTRANS (European Network for Sustainable Tourism Development, Germany), ECEAT (European Centre for Eco-Agro Tourism, Netherlands), IFN (International Friends of Nature, Austria), the sustainable tourism fair *Reisepavillon* in Hanover, Germany, and ARPA in Italy. In addition, ten and more leading ecolabels in Europe together with about twenty national and international stakeholder associations and the European Environmental Agency (EEA) in Denmark are supporting this initiative. The project will demonstrate how ecolabels can be an effective instrument in moving the European tourism industry and consumers toward sustainability.

This project has set forth four interrelated objectives to demonstrate:

1) how broadly accepted environmental indicators and benchmarks for ecolabels (accommodations and destinations) can contribute to an assessment of environmental effects of various ecolabels and other instruments.
2) how a partnership among ecolabels can be achieved, can lead to common standards, and can contribute to increased transparency, quality, and joint promotion.

3) how products and businesses, especially small and medium ones, that carry ecolabels can be integrated into and marketed alongside other European tourism offerings.

4) how consumer awareness and demand for environmentally friendly tourism can be increased by implementation of a Europe-wide image campaign during the International Year of Ecotourism in 2002 and beyond.

For their promotion and marketing activities, the partners chose the short name VISIT: Voluntary Initiatives for Sustainable Tourism. It is designed to encourage tourism suppliers to coordinate their voluntary efforts and to encourage consumers using the slogan "Your visit makes a difference," to choose ecolabels. The aim is to ensure high quality tourism based on agreed upon basic standards that are readily available in many European countries.[10]

Conclusion

In considering the enormous responsibilities and challenges in trying to build a more sustainable world, the European steps taken thus far may be seen as encouraging but not sufficient. There are many problems, but among the most challenging are how to reduce the number of overlapping and competing labels and how to raise consumer awareness and industry demand. Any Europe-wide label for accommodations is still several years away. Meanwhile, Europe certification programs can benefit from discussions with those running or starting programs in the Americas, Asia–Pacific, and Africa. Perhaps somewhere between 2005 and 2010, these discussions will lead to creation of a global "super label" for tourism products that can certify the mass, sustainable, and ecotourism markets.

Notes

1. Harald Grill, "eigfrorne gmiatlichkeit," passavia, 1982; original text: "so oder so. dene urlauber is unser landschaft wurscht: wenn ses aafgarbat ham fahrns woanders hi. uns einheimische is unser landschaft aa wurscht: wenn ma s aafgarbat ham, fahr ma in urlaub."
2. See ECO-TIP: Tourism and Environment in Europe, Web site: http://www.eco-tip.org.
3. World Tourism Organization (WTO), *Voluntary Initiatives for Sustainable Tourism* (Madrid: World Tourism Organization, 2002). The author was the principle researcher for this study.
4. Consultancy and Research for Environmental Management (CREM), *Feasibility and Market Study for a European Eco-label for Tourist Accommodations*

(FEMATOUR), commissioned by the European Commission (Amsterdam: CREM and CH2MHILL, August 2000); European Union Web site: http://www.europa.eu.int/ecolabel.
5. Ibid.
6. "Conclusions and Recommendations," Ch. 9 in FEMATOUR, p. 99.
7. Ibid.
8. WTO, *Voluntary Initiatives* (2002).
9. LIFE, European Commission, Web site: http://europa.eu.int/comm/life/home.htm.
10. For more on VISIT see, http://www.yourvisit.info.

Chapter 7

Beyond Hotels: Nature-Based Certification in Europe

Xavier Font and Tanja Mihalič

Within the travel and tourism industry in Europe today there are some 5,000 recipients of green certification logos, including a wide range of accommodations as well as tour operators, destinations, golf courses, parks, beaches, and marinas.[1] As discussed in chapter 6, since the 1980s, scores of ecosensitive certification programs in Europe have been developed in a piecemeal fashion by a variety of government agencies, NGOs, and industry associations to cover parts of the mass, sustainable, and ecotourism markets. Both the loose use of terminology and Europe's large number of small, sometimes overlapping, certification systems create customer and industry confusion.[2] Most of the green certification schemes described in the previous chapter measure the environmental impacts or management of a tourism structure or business, such as a lodge or tour operator. This chapter aims to demonstrate that certification programs that measure the quality of natural areas may be more likely to succeed than certification schemes of tourism facilities because they assess aspects of the environment that are more important to both long-term sustainability and the traveling public. This will be illustrated by examining two nature-based certification programs in Europe, the well-established Blue Flag for beaches and the World Wide Fund for Nature's PAN Parks program, which is in its inception stages.

In assessing the significance of these nature-based programs, three factors are important to bear in mind. First, in all certification programs for the tourism industry, "environment" can be understood narrowly as the natural physical setting or as the social and cultural environment within

211

which a business operates.[3] The majority of European schemes focus only on the first, the physical setting, whereas in developing countries, certification schemes (including, as discussed elsewhere in this volume, ones in Africa, Fiji, and parts of Central America and Australia) tend to take into account impacts and benefits to the local community, including financial leakages, labor, stakeholder input, and local participation.

Second, accommodations have traditionally been the target of most tourism quality-assurance programs and, more recently, of environmental certification programs.[4] Although accommodations are certainly a key sector, a hotel's impact is often not among the major threats to the environment posed by the tourism industry.[5] Poor environmental management of a hotel, for instance, might mean greater use of water, energy, and nonrecyclable products, but this is unlikely to have irreversible consequences. In contrast, poor management in a national park can lead to permanent loss of unique vegetation and wildlife and destruction of the quality of natural resources.

Third, research shows that tourists select a hotel not primarily for its internal environmental management practices but for the environmental quality of the destination as a whole. Tourists are therefore more likely to make holiday choices on the basis of, say, environmental quality of beaches, national parks, and rural landscapes, than on the basis of energy or water savings in a hotel. Unspoiled destinations are what tourists want and sometimes are willing to pay more for; the inner workings of a lodge or hotel are not so apparent to guests and therefore typically rate lower on a tourist's want list. Research in both Germany and Italy demonstrates that tourists (excluding business travelers) primarily care about the environmental quality of the destination, while the methods to achieve this quality are not of great concern. In Germany, 60 percent of those surveyed were interested in a destination's water and air quality, while Italians rated the environmental quality of the destination as the top priority in choosing their holidays and ranked environmental management at the bottom of their concerns.[6] Therefore, the evidence indicates that tourists are more interested in ecolabels that measure environmental quality rather than those that measure ecoefficiency.[7]

Criteria for Nature-based Tourism Certification: Green Versus Gray

These differences in certification criteria can be described as "green" versus "gray" environmental indicators. Green indicators are linked to environmental quality of the location, such as cleanliness of the water at a beach or biodiversity within a national park. These indicators are the ones

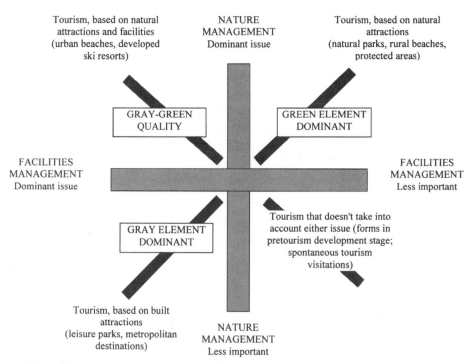

Figure 7.1. Green and gray spectrums of environmental labeling

that are most visible and meaningful to the consumer. In contrast, the environmental management of lodges and other tourism facilities measures impacts linked, most often, to ecoefficiency, such as waste disposal and waste treatment, water and energy use, and environmentally friendly purchasing practices. Although these gray environmental indicators are less visible and less important to tourists, they are, however, both meaningful to the management of the business unit and vital in providing the means to control the impact of that unit on the surrounding environment. Figure 7.1 illustrates the range of green and gray criteria within tourism certification programs.

Gray indicators are typically measured by process-based environmental management systems tailored to the individual business and designed to marry ecofriendly practices with cost-saving measures (see chapter 1). In contrast, green indicators tend to be performance-based criteria or benchmarks that are used to measure all applicants within a particular certification program. Nature-based certification programs that have a greater reliance on environmental quality are typically based more on performance than on process criteria. Yet certification standards do need to take into account region- and site-specific conditions and to encourage continual improvement. In most cases, therefore, it is best to combine a mixture of performance benchmarks modified to fit the geographic areas with management systems and incentives.

Nature-Based Certification Schemes in Europe

Nature-based certification schemes in Europe target tourist destinations and natural or seminatural tourist attractions. There are a variety of certification and ecoaward programs for tourist facilities and attractions that rely heavily on land usage, such as campsites and golf courses. Examples include Environmentally Friendly Campsites and Model Campsites (both in Germany), Committed to Green (Europe), David Bellamy Conservation Award (Britain), the Emblem of Guarantee of Environmental Quality (Spain), and the Scottish Golf Course Wildlife Initiative. These examples blend qualities of the traditional ecolabels for facilities and those for environmental quality of a location because they include both green and gray and performance- and process-based criteria. There are other ecolabels in Europe that are totally dependent on the quality of the business's physical environment. Examples are Destination 21 (Europe), Tidy Britain Group's Seaside Award, the European Charter for Sustainable Tourism in Protected Areas, Blue Flag, and PAN Parks. (In addition, Green Globe 21 is attempting to certify destinations; however by mid-2001, only one had been certified) (see chapter 10). Although these nature-based programs include some process-based environmental management criteria, they primarily contain performance-based benchmarks because the ultimate goal and the message to the consumer is that they can enjoy a healthy and safe environment.

Blue Flag for Beaches

Blue Flag is the oldest and most successful environmental logo for European tourism. The logo includes three ocean waves in a circle that represent a bottle neck and is intended to send a message of the importance of careful environmental management and monitoring of beaches and oceans[8] (see figure 7.2). Blue Flag grew out of a pollution tracking campaign organized by the Foundation for Environmental Education in Europe (FEEE) and was initially based on the idea of "bottle messages." In the early 1980s, environmental activists in France began setting adrift in the ocean bottles containing a message that identified the point of origin. The bottles' courses were then used to track the spread of solid waste in the ocean.

Figure 7.2. Blue Flag symbol *Source*: European Blue Flag, 2000

FEEE was founded in 1981 by environmental educators in France, Denmark, England, and The Netherlands who partnered with the Council of Europe, a non-EU, intergovernmental body of European countries, to establish a separate organization. The Foundation soon became a network of organizations working to promote environmental education through, in addition to Blue Flag, programs such as Eco Schools, Young Reporters for the Environment, and Learning about Forests. Over the years, the FEEE head office moved from The Netherlands to Denmark and then to England, to the offices of Tidy Britain Group, but the Blue Flag coordination office stayed in Copenhagen, hosted by the Danish Outdoor Council.

The Blue Flag campaign for beaches was officially born in 1985 when the first eleven Blue Flags were awarded to municipalities in France that had achieved high standards in bathing water quality and wastewater treatment.[9] In 1986, another forty-three beaches in France were certified. Then, in 1987, during the European Year of the Environment, FEEE presented the Blue Flag concept to the European Commission, the body that handles policy initiatives for the European Union (EU). The EU agreed to launch the European Blue Flag campaign as one of several new environmental activities. FEEE, with financial support from the European Commission, undertook to organize the campaigns throughout Europe.

Beginning in 1987, the Blue Flag concept expanded beyond water quality to include other areas of environmental protection, such as waste management and coastal planning. Besides beaches, marinas also become eligible for the Blue Flag certification. In 1988, FEEE, in cooperation with the Commission of the European Communities,[10] awarded 205 Blue Flags to the beaches in France (87), Ireland (19), Portugal (74), Spain (7), and the United Kingdom (18).[11] A year later, during the 1989 bathing season, the campaign spread to Denmark, Germany, Greece, and Italy, and the number of Blue Flag certifications increased to 391. By 2001, Blue Flag had awarded certification to 2,041 beaches (figure 7.3) in twenty-one European countries. Between the years 1990 and 2001, Belgium, Bulgaria, Croatia, Cyprus, Denmark, Estonia, Finland, Latvia, Norway, Slovenia, Sweden, and Turkey joined the campaign, and Iceland and Lithuania are expected to join in 2002.

In 1996, the United Nations Environment Programme (UNEP) and World Tourism Organization (WTO) joined with FEEE in an effort to

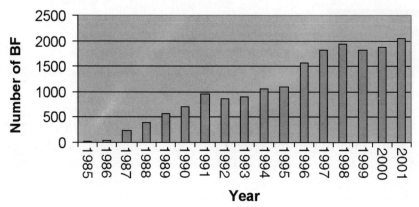

Figure 7.3. Number of Blue Flag beaches in Europe, 1985–2001 *Source*: FEEE-S, 2001

spread the campaign outside Europe. In 2001, after completing a success-ful Blue Flag pilot phase in South Africa, the Wildlife and Environment Society of South Africa (WESSA) became the first non-European mem-ber of FEEE and, in October 2001, began certifying its first beaches.[12] At the same time, pilot phases were planned for launch in the Caribbean.[13] As FEEE became an international organization, it changed its name outside Europe to simply the Foundation for Environmental Education (FEE).

Today, FEE is an umbrella organization with national branches, known as "operators," in every member country. Each FEE national operator has two votes within the FEE general assembly. Before being accepted as members, all operators are vetted to make sure they are reputable NGOs committed to environmental education. When, for instance, the Slovenian National Tourism Board applied to join the Blue Flag campaign in 1993, it was rejected because, as a tourism association, it had not demonstrated a commitment to environmental education. One year later, however, FEE's general assembly accepted as Slovenia's national operator a newly estab-lished environmental NGO that applied to join FEE's Blue Flag and Eco Schools programs. Every four years, the executive board and general assem-bly review the status, organizational structure, financial and activity reports, plans, and recommendations of every national organization. If an organiza-tion shows weaknesses, its status can be downgraded to associate member-ship, with a right to only one vote in the general assembly.

Each national operator is responsible for carrying out the Blue Flag campaign and any other FEE educational campaigns. This type of decen-tralization has contributed to the growth of Blue Flag. It has economic advantages as well because costs in each country are mainly covered by grants from local and national governments, sponsorships by the tourism

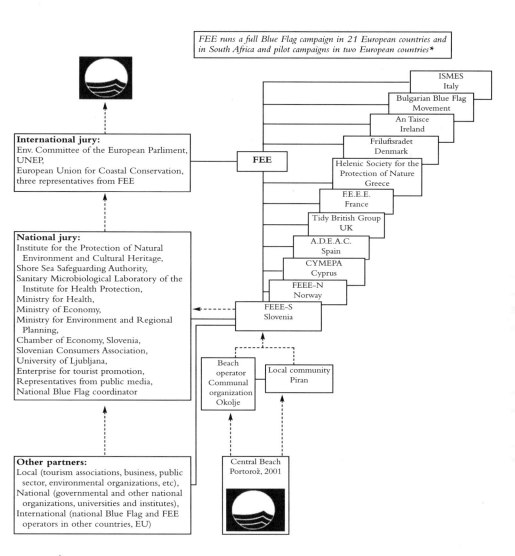

FEE runs a full Blue Flag campaign in 21 European countries and in South Africa and pilot campaigns in two European countries*

ISMES
Italy

Bulgarian Blue Flag Movement

An Taisce
Ireland

Friluftsradet
Denmark

FEE

Helenic Society for the Protection of Nature
Greece

International jury:
Env. Committee of the European Parliment, UNEP,
European Union for Coastal Conservation,
three representatives from FEE

F.E.E.E.
France

Tidy British Group
UK

A.D.E.A.C.
Spain

CYMEPA
Cyprus

FEEE-N
Norway

National jury:
Institute for the Protection of Natural
  Environment and Cultural Heritage,
Shore Sea Safeguarding Authority,
Sanitary Microbiological Laboratory of the
  Institute for Health Protection,
Ministry for Health,
Ministry of Economy,
Ministry for Environment and Regional
  Planning,
Chamber of Economy, Slovenia,
Slovenian Consumers Association,
University of Ljubljana,
Enterprise for tourist promotion,
Representatives from public media,
National Blue Flag coordinator

FEEE-S
Slovenia

Beach operator
Communal organization
Okolje

Local community
Piran

Other partners:
Local (tourism associations, business, public
  sector, environmental organizations, etc),
National (governmental and other national
  organizations, universities and institutes),
International (national Blue Flag and FEE
  operators in other countries, EU)

Central Beach
Portorož, 2001

*Data per July 2001.

Figure 7.4. Blue Flag awarding procedure, 2001: Case of Slovenian Central beach, Portorož *Source*: FEEE-S, 2001

industry, and Blue Flag fees. Funding for the FEE parent body comes from annual membership fees, subsidies, donations, sponsorships, consultancy fees, and sale of products.[14]

As shown in figure 7.4, Blue Flag campaigns involve a wide variety of stakeholders, including government ministries of health, the environment, and tourism; consumer protection associations; and environmental organizations.

Blue Flag Criteria

To be eligible for the Blue Flag award, a beach has to fulfill benchmarks in four separate areas: water quality, safety, environmental education and information, and environmental management systems. These areas include both process and performance criteria. For instance, Blue Flag's standards for the 2001 European bathing season included the following:

- *Water quality:* Water quality must comply with government requirements and standards, such as those of the EU Bathing Water Directive. This directive sets the microbiological standards and physicochemical parameters for bathing water. No sewage discharges may affect the beach area, and the community must be in compliance with requirements for sewage treatment, according to the EEC Urban Waste Water Directive. This last is a new benchmark that FEE started to gradually implement in 2001. It requires that there be no untreated sewage discharged into the beach area from the local community, specifies treatment standards, and sets implementation deadlines depending on the size of the community.[15]
- *Environmental education and information:* These criteria state that information about flora, fauna, and environmentally sensitive areas in the coastal zone must be publicly displayed, along with prescriptions on how visitors should behave and data on bathing water quality. All must be in an easily understood form.
- *Environmental management systems for beach facilities:* These criteria require that there be adequate numbers of trash cans, properly secured and regularly maintained and emptied; safe access to the beach; and bins for recycling materials. The local community must have a land-use and development plan of its coastal zone and must promote sustainable means of transportation in the beach area, such as bicycling, walking, or public transport.
- *Safety and services:* The safety and services criteria require the presence of lifeguards, first aid equipment, and clean drinking water. At least one beach in each municipality must be equipped with access ramps and toilet facilities for people with disabilities.

Some of the twenty-seven criteria contained in these four categories are imperative; others are guidelines. Any new criteria must be confirmed by majority vote at the FEE general assembly. They then become compulsory for all members. Although beach management can fulfill certain requirements, such as providing drinking water and recycling containers, a number of the other criteria (compliance with the EU Urban Waste Water Directive, for instance) require assistance from the local government.

Blue Flag has become more rigorous over time. In 1987, for instance, the European Blue Flag criteria required compliance only with the bathing water quality standards set by either the relevant country or by the European Community, whichever were stricter. After 1990, environmental educational activities became part of Blue Flag's imperative criteria; in 1992, the bathing water quality criteria were changed to conform with the European Community Directive; in 1993, the criteria were strengthened to include maximum counts for fecal streptococci; in 1999, the physico-chemical water standards were added[16]; and beginning in 2001, implementation of the EU Urban Waste Water Directive standards was generally required (see below).

Further, as the Blue Flag campaign has expanded beyond Europe, different geographical and social issues have been taken into account. In 2001, the criteria adopted by Blue Flag in South Africa were somewhat different from the criteria for the European campaign. For example, South African beaches must first apply to run a pilot phase, and only a year afterward can a beach apply for full Blue Flag status. To qualify for a Blue Flag, a South African beach must comply with all criteria in fourteen different areas. Unlike in Europe, these include criteria for visitor security, including that a uniformed guard patrol the beach area twenty-four hours a day.[17]

Blue Flags are awarded for one year at a time. Candidates must meet all the required criteria and be approved by the national jury to be sent to the European jury for confirmation or rejection. During the Blue Flag season, which runs from July to September in Europe, national organizations and the European coordinator conduct site visits.[18] If the inspection team finds noncompliance with one imperative criterion, use of the Blue Flag logo is immediately suspended. The beach is then reassessed within ten days and if the criteria are still not met, Blue Flag certification is withdrawn for the rest of the season. If a site visit reveals noncompliance with more than one imperative criterion, the flag is automatically withdrawn for the rest of the season.[19] During the 2000 bathing season, for example, national operators withdrew about fifteen Blue Flags.[20]

Blue Flag is more than a simple environmental label. Over the years, it has grown into a very complex campaign that aims to increase environmental awareness and responsible behavior within communities. In 1994, the Blue Flag strategy moved from a focus on a single beach to a focus on policies in the surrounding community. Thus, local government became the direct partner in the Blue Flag campaign. In partnership with local organizations, the local authority makes the final decision to apply for the Blue Flag award.[21]

As shown in figure 7.4, in Slovenia, the local government, together with the beach operator, applied for the award. Both are key players in the Blue Flag system. Local government participation is needed because many criteria refer to the environmental management of the local community. For example, the community must have a land-use and development plan for its coastal zone. This plan and the current activities of the community in the coastal zone must be in compliance with planning regulations and coastal zone protection regulations. Although such criteria are of no immediate value to beach visitors, they are vital in laying a framework so that the community undertakes tourism development in conformity with sound environmental practices. Therefore, these criteria contribute over the long run to the quality of the visitor experience. For those beaches that are managed by hotel owners or other tourist firms or associations independent from the local government, a partnership between the beach operator and the local community has to be established.

Building Consumer Recognition and Improving Environmental Standards

Blue Flag has considerable press and public recognition in Europe as a symbol designating clean and healthy beaches. During 2000 and part of 2001, a search of databases[22] revealed, however, that more than 90 percent of the articles in the *Sunday Times, Daily Telegraph, Evening Standard, Telegraph,* and *The Guardian* linked Blue Flag only to water quality, about 40 percent to cleanliness (including physical cleanliness of the beach), 23 percent to general safety (e.g., provision of life-saving equipment, first aid facilities, etc.), and only 15 percent to other, less visible, gray issues, such as implementation of water purification systems. None of these articles referred to Blue Flag's visitor education component, even though this is a key requirement in applications and is strongly promoted by the FEE[23]. One survey[24] among Blue Flag participants in Europe found that Blue Flag certification has helped to improve a beach's environmental image with visitors as well as its physical cleanliness and water quality. For example, in 1995, Dieppe in France spent more than 90 million francs (about $12 million) to improve bathing water quality. In Portovenere in Italy, an environmental education center has been built as a part of the Blue Flag campaign, while in Calvi on Corsica, the campaign led to implementation of an alternative system for disposal of household wastes.[25] In Slovenia, the Blue Flag campaign generated public discussion on seawater quality and public accessibility of environmental quality data.

Despite Blue Flag's strong efforts at environmental education, the logo is primarily viewed by the public, the industry, and government tourism departments as a symbol of clean and safe beaches and bathing water. Many countries have joined the campaign to gain use of this popular logo in hopes of boosting tourism numbers. It is no coincidence, for instance, that it was the Slovenian Tourism Board that first tried to join the Blue Flag campaign by asking for FEE membership. In South Africa, the environmental and tourism ministries have supported Blue Flag as a tool for helping to market South Africa and its beaches internationally.[26] In Germany, the biggest tour operator, Touristik International (TUI), lists Blue Flag–certified beaches in its publications. Wolf Michael Iwand, a marketing expert with TUI, commends Blue Flag for helping TUI to provide "ecological marketing for holidaymakers."[27]

Blue Flag's Main Challenges

One of Blue Flag's ongoing challenges is how to implement new criteria, including more stringent regulations passed by the European Union. For instance, in 2001, Blue Flag found it could not require all beaches seeking certification to immediately adopt the EU's new Urban Waste Water Directive. The directive, which is one of the pillars of EU's legislation on water, seeks to protect against pollution of drinking and bathing waters by requiring that member states collect and treat urban wastewater discharge according to strict standards. The EU-wide costs of the implementation of the Urban Waste Water Directive are estimated at euro 150 billion (about $133 billion).[28] In 2001, many beach candidates were unable to quickly comply with this criteria both because they lacked sufficient technical skills and financial resources and because, in some cases, the source of pollution was outside the control of the beach operator or the local community applying for Blue Flag certification. The situation was further complicated because the European Commission had not yet put in place the directive's general guidelines for ensuring compliance. For all these reasons, the FEE European jury decided to award Blue Flags in 2001 without taking into account these criteria, although in the near future all certified beaches will be required to conform with the EU directive.[29]

This raises several complex and potentially troubling issues. Because Blue Flag, like all current ecolabels, is voluntary, there is a danger that if the criteria become too stringent and too expensive, the industry may withdraw and opt for a more simple and easy to get ecoquality label. The local government may then not have enough power to carry on the Blue Flag campaign without the support of the tourism sector and possibly other stakeholders, including the local community, which looks to the Blue Flag program to help boost visitor numbers. In addition, because wastewater treatment is a gray issue not easily seen by tourists, it may be difficult to build a consumer lobby as a counterweight to industry.

Blue Flag does, however, have the advantage that it is well known and well respected and does not have much competition from alternative logos.

Unlike many of the ecolabels for accommodations, in most European countries there is at present no substitute environmental logo for beaches. The exception is the Seaside Award in the United Kingdom. The Tidy Britain Group, which is also the national operator for the Blue Flag, has developed its own beach environmental logo: a yellow flag with blue flash. Seaside Award water standards are less strict[30] than Blue Flag[31] and cover both urban and rural beaches. This means that beaches that don't comply for Blue Flag certification may be able to get and display a yellow flag ecolabel.

Confusion has also arisen because Blue Flag certification for marinas uses the same sea waves logo as for beaches. The public and press associate this logo with good bathing water, yet Blue Flag–certified marinas do not have to comply with bathing water directive standards because marinas are not bathing places. A lot of public relations efforts have gone into trying to explain that the criteria for marinas are different. Many experts feel, however, that Blue Flag should adopt a distinct logo for its certified marinas.

There have been other problems, as well. Local authorities often want to use the Blue Flag logo to promote tourism on their beaches, even if, in reality, all the criteria have not been met or the Blue Flag award is from a previous year.[32] The campaign must do more to inform visitors that Blue Flags are awarded for only one bathing season and to set in place a system for ensuring that the logo is not used on beaches that did not qualify for certification or where certification has lapsed. More broadly, to continue the Blue Flag success story, the FEE will have to manage and balance the competing demands for environmental education, EU-driven implementation of complex environmental management standards, the interests of the tourism industry, and the public's concern with environmentally clean beaches and oceans.

PAN Parks

Although the PAN Parks project is a decade younger than Blue Flag, it has been recognized at a European level as one of the two most relevant initiatives for Natura 2000, the European strategy for nature conservation.[33] As the World Wide Fund for Nature (WWF) explains, the concept of PAN Parks is "to create a network of parks with an international reputation for outstanding access to wildlife and excellent tourist facilities, combined with effective habitat protection and the minimal environmental impact possible."[34] The target of the label is protected areas, specifically large national parks with outstanding wildlife, such as brown bear, wolf, lynx, moose, and raptors, including the golden eagle. Like Blue Flag, PAN Parks is dealing with sustainability issues for one of Europe's most important tourism sectors. Beaches and protected areas (in the form of national parks and nature reserves) are the two main attractions within nature-based tourism. Environmental quality of these resources is part of their draw, yet the most popular of Europe's protected areas are under increasing pressure from tourism.[35]

PAN Parks was initiated in 1997 through an unlikely alliance between the Dutch tourism and leisure group Molecaten and WWF-Netherlands. Molecaten, a company that develops holiday villages currently hosting some 35,000 people per day in The Netherlands, approached WWF and proposed they form a team. Molecaten's aim is to open new holiday villages in natural areas of Europe, mainly Scandinavia and Central and Eastern Europe. Managing director Cees Slager says he saw that local communities supported this idea but there was resistance from conservationists. He therefore decided to team up with a conservation NGO to ensure that the needs of both groups are met. WWF-Netherlands considered PAN Parks to be a good idea for several reasons: it could benefit the communities near the parks through increased tourism business, it could give the parks some bargaining power in efforts to cut back on illegal poaching and hunting, and it could help protect the parks through improved management. By increasing the benefits of nonconsumptive use of the parks, WWF-Netherlands aims to convince the local population to enlarge the amount of protected land to create a natural north-south corridor in parts of Central and Eastern Europe.

Protected land in Europe is usually in very small units and linked to a single specific scientific interest. Molecaten and WWF decided to concentrate on certifying only those parks that are at least 25,000 hectares. There are only about 100 such parks in Europe, and of these, few are sites with large, free-roaming mammals and therefore of prime importance to PAN Parks. Creating a corridor of protected land is a long-term aim, yet already there are some large pockets of protected lands. In Poland, for instance, one of the current candidates, Bieszczady National Park, together with two adjoining protected areas, covers more than 200,000 hectares—a large space by European standards.

PAN Parks is, in reality, a partnership between Molecaten, WWF, and local park manager, in consultation with neighboring communities and tour operators and others from the tourism industry. Molecaten's contribution has been financial. The PAN Parks Foundation has few staff dedicated full time to the project, relying instead on experts from WWF. The team from WWF had some involvement in the development of the Forest Stewardship Council (FSC) standards but had no previous involvement in tourism certification. PAN Parks is run as a sort of extension of WWF's protected area management and conservation program. WWF provides guidelines and monitoring but is relatively hands-off, thus allowing park management to take ownership of the process. Although it is national park managers who apply for certification, they must work with a variety of local actors (including tour operators) to ensure that the park's plans are coordinated with the needs of the community.

The application process consists of three phases: prospective, candidate, and verified. Parks in the prospective phase receive support from the PAN Parks Foundation in conducting self-assessment exercises against the principles and criteria to see whether they want to move to the candidate status. At the candidate stage, the PAN Parks Foundation and the park work out a strategy to reach the five guiding principles by an agreed date, and the PAN Parks Foundation provides expertise depending on the park's needs. At each phase, the park receives added benefits from marketing and exposure through the WWF dissemination channels.

Each park has to develop its own Executive PAN Parks Organization (EPPO), which serves as a platform for discussion and decision making on issues involving the park and its surrounding areas. This forum and its leader are the direct link between the verified PAN Park and the PAN Parks Foundation. Although the leader is likely to be working at the national park, the EPPO has to be broader, involving as well a wide range of local organizations and businesses. Many park officials had long thought that such an organization was necessary, but PAN Parks has given them the incentive to form it.

PAN Park's Guiding Principles and Criteria

The criteria of PAN Parks were developed with five guiding principles:[36]

1) *Natural values*: PAN Parks are large protected areas representative of Europe's natural heritage and of international importance for wildlife and ecosystems. Each site must be over 25,000 hectares.
2) *Habitat management*: Design and management of the PAN Park aims to maintain and, if necessary, restore the area's natural ecological processes and its biodiversity.
3) *Visitor management*: Visitor management safeguards the natural values of the PAN Park and aims to provide visitors with a high-quality experience based on the appreciation of nature.
4) *Sustainable tourism development strategy*: The national park office and its relevant partners in the PAN Parks region aim at achieving a synergy between nature conservation and sustainable tourism by developing a sustainable tourism development strategy (STDS), committing to it, and jointly taking responsibility for its implementation.
5) *Business partners*: PAN Parks' business partners as legal enterprises are

committed to the goals of the protected area in their region and the PAN Parks organization and actively cooperate with other stakeholders to effectively implement the region's sustainable tourism development strategy as developed by the local executive committee of PAN Parks.

Certification criteria cascade down from each principle, and several indicators are linked to each criteria. The list of benchmarks and indicators is long, ranging from hard, measurable data, such as species counts, to softer management issues, such as community involvement. Although the criteria have gone through little modification since their conception, the indicators have been refined through consultation and pilot projects. Principle one is mostly a list of conditions and thus is unlikely to change, at least in the short term. For principles two to five, the criteria outline the five stages of certification: (1) policy, (2) review, (3) program, (4) operations, and (5) audit and review. For example, under principle (3) on visitor management, the criteria would include having a visitor management plan in which ecological capacity is assessed and measures are taken to address or avoid negative impacts identified as significant by the management body. Under this heading, it is also required to have staff training, a visitor center, and activities for visitors, including methods of visitor education and interpretation.

The indicators linked to criteria—carrying capacity, number of visitor activities, interpretation, and so on—do not have benchmarks at this stage because each park starts at a different level and there are at present no possibilities for providing start-up investment. Although this approach is more realistic in the context of national park management, it does not provide a common denominator for all parks, and it does not guarantee that a minimum benchmark is met. The need for indicators that allow for local conditions to permeate and dictate the priorities on a case by case basis is even more evident on principle (5), the involvement of local business partners, because the willingness of local communities to engage in these discussions is not something that the park can enforce or implement on its own. In addition, because the outcomes of such processes are less measurable in hard terms, benchmarks here cannot be as straightforward as when conducting biodiversity surveys.

Some park officials want additional criteria. For example, Marija Markes of the Triglav National Park in Slovenia has proposed that PAN Parks should include criteria requiring accommodation providers to purchase locally, thereby strengthening economic links and minimizing leakages. Triglav National Park is using its logo as a trade name to support the production of organic cheese and is encouraging the marketing of organic farming in general. However, adopting this as a requirement for all parks will have to wait until PAN Parks criteria are reviewed because parks already have high hurdles to jump in this first stage.

PAN Parks Today and Challenges Ahead

Since 1999, seven parks, or around 7 percent of the target market, have entered the pilot stage toward fulfillment of PAN Parks' criteria, and all have received at least one visit. Of the seven sites—Oulanka (Finland), Bieszczady (Poland), Slovenski raj (Slovak Republic), Mercantour (France), Triglav (Slovenia), Abruzzo (Italy), and Fulufjället (Sweden)—all are national parks except for the last. Fulufjället is a nature reserve, but the EU has decided to grant it national park status in 2002, in part because of its involvement in PAN Parks. (Some other parks that initially expressed an interest in entering PAN Parks then backed away because of other commitments and staff changes.) These national parks applying for certification include a mixture of public and private lands, with their core conservation areas generally being publicly owned. Most parks have a visitor center with some limited facilities. Generally, funds for maintaining the parks come from the public sector, ranging from Oulanka, which is 100 percent publicly funded, to Triglav, where 40 percent of the income is generated from tourism and hunting. Timber extraction is still practiced in some parks, including Slovenski raj.

One contentious issue is the PAN Park certification requirement that a park must increase the amount of tourism within its boundaries. The current controversial proposal is for creation of PAN Park Villages through the lease of land at zero cost to create holiday accommodations and services inside the park or the purchase of land adjacent to the park boundaries. This requirement has been under discussion within the PAN Parks Foundation for some time. Some argue this proposal presents a conflict of interest because the Molecaten group is well positioned to benefit from this requirement. Concerns have been raised that once a park has received PAN Parks certification and the village is built, the foundation has a long-term commitment to the site, thereby making it difficult to withdraw certification. The process is currently going ahead, with Fulufjället as the first park in which a village will be created.[37]

National park authorities and local communities also have reasons to support proposals for increased tourism and accommodations within the parks. Park officials argue that increased tourism in their parks will improve their negotiating power with the local population and help them either to control unsustainable uses of the park or to enlarge the size of the park. Illegal poaching and hunting is common in these parks, and the parks' management does not currently have the resources to police the site. The Swedish community near Fulufjallet, for instance, has accepted limiting the hunting and snowmobiling areas so the nature reserve can apply for national park status because they see this as increasing tourism, which is a more economically beneficial activity.

In addition, park representatives demand concrete benefits from their involvement with this program, especially those in parks with more experience in managing tourism, such as Mercantour in France and Abruzzo in Italy. Those parks with already high visitor numbers and low budgets view PAN Parks certification as a way to balance their books and provide better environmental protection. For instance, Oulanka in Finland has 120,000 visitors a year and no income-generating activities within the park. However, tourists visiting the park generate 30 percent of the revenue in the two local towns. The first challenge for this park has been agreeing on a sustainable tourism development strategy that meets PAN Parks' principles and criteria and is also endorsed by the Finnish Ministry of Environment. The local community hopes that PAN Parks will promote better marketing and increase income from tourism for both the park and the local community.

The assessment and verification processes for PAN Parks certification are being developed by SGS Hungary, part of the SGS group, the largest verification body worldwide, and will be released in the near future. For each park, a team of experts is assigned to undertake a site visit and desk review. These experts will be contracted by PAN Parks when verifications are needed, making this the closest to third-party verification possible within such a small program and consistent with the practices of other sound certification schemes. This avoids outsourcing to an external organization because the small number of applicants makes this financially unfeasible, but the verifiers are provided with training and a detailed verification manual. Costs of verification have not been set, but these will be shared between the PAN Parks Foundation and the individual park and surrounding business partners. The foundation will cover 50 percent of costs for European Union member countries and 75 percent of costs for new EU accession countries. (These latter are mainly in Central and Eastern Europe and, therefore, include several PAN Parks applicants.) Verified partners will be charged a fee to use the PAN Parks logo, but the cost of this fee has not yet been set. Currently, the financial feasibility of the whole program relies on the funding from the Molecaten group, but the program is planned to become self-financing through redirecting a share of the profits from the PAN Park Villages to this purpose. Yet this can be contentious because not all parks that are certified will want to have a PAN Parks Village, and therefore, this will mean cross-subsidizing.

PAN Parks is also serving as an educational tool for parks, helping them to establish management practices and policies to ensure long-term sustainable development. During a workshop in Holland in June 2001, the seven candidate parks and PAN Parks officials devised strategies to lead each park to certification. The workshop adopted a participatory approach and searched for common agreements among participants,[38] with a target of starting the verification progress in January 2002. Each park has had to prioritize needs depending on their local conditions. Oulanka in Finland is currently introducing social and ecological surveys to determine carrying capacities. To reach certification in 2002, Oulanka will also have to work on principle (5), business partners—the principle that most parks currently fail to meet.

PAN Parks is a young program and its impact on the management of national parks in Europe, as well as tourism flows, will not be clear for at least another ten years. Certain changes will take time to show up because some parks have already devised strategies that do not include all the PAN Parks requirements. In the case of Slovenski raj, for example, the forestry plan and the management plan need to be rewritten, but this will not happen until 2006.[39] PAN Parks certification processes do reflect, however, the current philosophy and debates surrounding the methods to assess good environmental management in sites where tourism and conservation need to be made compatible.

Like many other certification schemes, PAN Parks faces competition from another program. The European Charter for Sustainable Tourism in Protected Areas, which targets national parks and nature reserves with similar aims, is a Europarc Federation project supported by the World Conservation Union (IUCN). The program promotes continuous improvement in the implementation of an agreed charter in ten European national parks. Although this is not a certification program in a traditional sense, it does offer tourists a seal of environmental quality of destinations. PAN Parks and the charter are currently discussing areas for collaboration, and the charter is having input in some of PAN Parks criteria to ensure that initiatives are compatible.

Issues Arising from Nature-Based Certification Programs

In evaluating these two nature-based certification programs, it is clear they both have a number of strengths that help them fulfill their two fundamental objectives of assisting tourists in making sound holiday choices and providing a framework for the sustainable management of important natural resources. At the same time, both programs face a number of challenges that may undermine their long-term success.

Certification Goals

There are, as yet, no universally agreed upon principles and criteria for certification programs within the tourism industry. Although many certification programs state that they are following the principles of sustainability established by Agenda 21, the reality is that these principles are very general and do not provide clear guidelines for certification. Rather, tourism certification programs are typically shaped by the mandate and goals of their founding and funding organizations. Both Blue Flag and PAN Parks were founded by environmental NGOs with specific interests and expertise in protecting natural areas, and therefore these certification programs have succeeded in setting rigorous standards for environmental protection. FEEE developed Blue Flag as a means of implementing its goals of ensuring water quality and health and safety standards on Europe's beaches, promoting green education for tourists and local residents, and increasing the participation and responsibilities of local communities, governments, and tourism businesses in the campaign for ecologically sound management of coastal areas. Similarly, the WWF's mandate to protect national parks and other pristine and endangered natural habitats is reflected in PAN Parks' principles and criteria, and WWF experts are helping to ensure that this certification program adheres to high standards.

However, Blue Flag and PAN Parks, like other reputable certification programs, involve a variety of stakeholders who have competing and sometimes contradictory interests and objectives. Tourism businesses, for instance, consider the Blue Flag campaign primarily as a way to improve the image of beaches[40] and thereby increase tourism. Similarly, WWF's conservation goals in creating PAN Parks could at times be at variance with the objectives of Molecaten group, the program's major funding body, which has lobbied for the creation of holiday villages inside certified parks. In addition, both Blue Flag and PAN Parks have been challenged by competing ecolabels that target the same sectors. In Britain, not many beaches were getting Blue Flags and therefore the Seaside Award was created with different, less vigorous water quality criteria and an emphasis on beach cleanliness and safety. Beach managers can apply for either Blue Flag certification or Seaside Award's yellow and blue flag, and customers typically do not know the difference between the two logos. Although PAN Parks and the European Charter for Protected Areas are both in their early stages, parks have opted to pilot one or the other, not both, programs. Parks tend to select the program in which they need to make the fewest efforts to meet the criteria. Currently, these two programs function in parallel to one another rather than in direct competition, but the result is the same as with Blue Flag and Seaside Award: different standards and confusing messages.

Changes in Criteria

As nature-based certification evolves, the performance-based environmental quality criteria and the more visible green elements are being wedded with more or less formal environmental management systems, including more criteria that measure less visible gray areas, such as wastewater disposal. Environmental quality certification is fundamental to these programs first because the quality of a natural attraction is central to the tourism product (a beach or park) itself[41] and second, because customers expect and they implicitly understand[42] green criteria. Success of both Blue Flag and PAN Parks is contingent on their ability to guarantee environmental quality. Blue Flag promises "this is a safe beach," while PAN Parks pledges "this is a good place to see wildlife" or "this is one of the best national parks in Europe." Yet management and improvement of the less apparent gray areas may be equally important. The Spanish island of Majorca, for instance, which receives over 10 million tourists per year, has made the best environmental improvements in Europe in waste treatment and water efficiency.

In addition to the growing recognition of the importance of combining performance and process criteria, there is the increasing recognition that environmental quality criteria need to be tailored to the given geographical area. PAN Parks' biodiversity criteria developed for European parks are not, for instance, rigorous enough to ensure protection and long-term sustainability in South America's biorich Amazon regions or East and southern Africa's wildlife-rich safari parks. Therefore, environmental quality standards need to be put in the frame of environmental management systems that require continuous protection and improvement.

To reiterate, environmental management is a means to ensuring an end—environmental improvement—although environmental quality is ultimately what matters to the tourist. There is a growing consensus that nature-based awards need to include a mixture of environmental quality (based on performance standards) and environmental management criteria (based on process systems) and that the former need to set a minimum threshold, while the latter need to be built in to ensure continuing improvements.

Assessment and Verification

The time frame for application and awarding a logo varies depending partly on the data collection process. Water testing is a crucial issue in Blue Flag, and this is relatively straightforward and cheap to undertake. This is, therefore, done regularly and facilitates the awarding of Blue Flags on an annual basis. In the case of PAN Parks, the application and awarding period is longer and more complex because the criteria are linked both to developing site-specific plans and to their implementation and evaluation. This process is projected to take between three and five years, making awarding of logos much more difficult. In areas such as assessing the impact of tourism on wildlife, the period might have to be even longer, although this could conceivably make the labeling process meaningless.

Impact of Target Size on Operations

The size of the target certification group has an impact on a program's level of standardization and the economies of scale in the application, verification, and awarding procedures. Blue Flag has a large and well-defined target pool: beaches offer very homogenous services and have clearly defined physical boundaries. In addition, the number of beaches and marinas in Europe is easily counted, so FEEE can calculate what percentage has been assessed and certified. However, Blue Flag parameters and criteria need to be precise and self-explanatory because there are many more applicants and verifying agencies. PAN Parks, in contrast, targets large national parks and protected areas, which are far fewer in number and require a long period of two-way contact throughout the application process. These differences in target size and numbers and the amount and type of communication between label organizers and applicants present distinct challenges for each program and increase the difficulty of easily comparing these labels.

Limitations to Environmental Quality Control

Nature-based environmental certification needs to take into account that impacts are not always controllable by the management organization of the destination or natural attraction. The Blue Flag, PAN Parks, and most other nature-based labels certify on the basis of the quality of nature within set physical boundaries, but the management of the site does not have control over external sources of impact from surrounding areas. This is clearly the case in the Blue Flag because the water quality is not only the outcome of the management of the beach, hotels, or even the local community, but it is affected by more widespread sources influenced by water currents and waste disposal practices even long distances away. The same can be said for PAN Parks: the park's management can control only a certain amount of the impact on wildlife and vegetation.

These outside influences demonstrate the need for nature-based labels to include criteria that go beyond site-specific requirements. Both the Blue Flag and PAN Parks recognize the need to link the management of their resources with the broader environment and therefore involve the local community in the planning and decision making, or link, in the case of Blue Flag, to broader management plans. The implementation of the new EU Urban Waste Water Directive is a good example: its link to the quality of the environment is obvious, yet implementation of the directive standards is far beyond the power of either beach managers or local tourism businesses.

Customer Recognition and Acceptance

Blue Flag has reached a stage where it is well established in Europe and its presence or absence on a beach means something to the tourist and to tourism businesses. Although beaches in Europe are expected to attain a Blue Flag, national parks are not yet expected to be seeking the PAN Parks logo. The majority of European ecolabels are, like PAN Parks, only a few years old and have reached only a small share of their target market. Committed to Green, for instance, targets Europe's 5,000 golf courses, but only around one percent of them have sought certification. Ecolabels will only make a meaningful difference in the marketplace when they succeed in reaching the recognition levels of Blue Flag.

Conclusions

Certification based on environmental and in some cases socioeconomic criteria of Europe's nature-based tourism attractions is key to the long-term sustainability of these destinations. Because many travelers in Europe base their decisions on environmental quality, certification is potentially an important voluntary, market-based tool for ensuring the long-term sustainability of these destinations. This chapter has analyzed two different programs to demonstrate the strengths and weaknesses of nature-based certification. On the minus side, both Blue Flag and PAN Parks are facing competition from other ecolabels, which is causing consumer confusion and could in time undermine their credibility and viability. On the plus side, both of these programs have carved out as their role the protection of vital natural resources. In doing so, they have both been assisted by reputable environmental organizations, by support from government agencies ranging from the local level up to the European Union, through buy-in from the tourism industry and local communities, and through relatively generous sources of funding. Finally, both of these programs have reached the conclusion that they need to combine performance-based and green criteria that guarantee environmental quality and meet tourist demands with environmental management systems that monitor gray criteria and establish a framework to guarantee continuous improvement.

Notes

1. R. Spittler and U. Haak, "Quality Analysis of Tourism Ecolabels" in *Tourism Ecolabelling: Certification and Promotion of Sustainable Management*, eds. X. Font and R.C. Buckley (Oxon, UK: CAB International, 2001), p. 214; X. Font, E. Haas, K. Thorpe, L. Forsyth, "Directory of Tourism Ecolabels" in *Tourism Ecolabelling*, eds. Font and Buckley, pp. 271–348;
2. Mihalič and T. C. Kaspar, *Umweltokonomie im Tourismus* (Bern: Paul Haupt, 1996), p. 114.
3. Mihalič and Kaspar, *Umweltokonomie im Tourismus*, 44.
4. C. DeBruyn, "Quality Criteria in Tourism Services," paper prepared for World Tourism Organization, *Tourism Certification Systems and Standards Workshop*, 37th meeting of the WTO's Commission for the Americas (CAM), Oaxaca, Mexico, May 14–15, 2001.
5. European Environment Agency, *Environmental Signals 2001* (Copenhagen: European Environment Agency, 2001).
6. C. Lübbert, Umweltkennzeichnungen für touristische Angebote: Einstellungen deutscher Urlauber-Ergebnisse eine Pilotstudie. Fachtagung "Umweltkennzeichningen im Tourismus," am 29 Oktober 1998 an der Ludwig-Maximilians-Universität München (LMU) (München: Deutsches Wirtschaftswissenschaftliches Institut für Fremdenverkehr e.V. an der Universität München, 1998), pp. 22–31; Agenzia Nazionale per la Protezione dell'Ambiente (ANPA) "Studio nazionale per l'applicazione del marchio europeo di qualita ambientale nel settore del turismo," in *Domanda turistica e qualita ambientale: Indagine realizzata nell'ambito dello* (Rome: Agenzia Nazionale per la Protezione dell'Ambiente, 2001).
7. T. Mihalič, "Environmental Management of a Tourist Destination: A Factor of Tourism Competitiveness," *Tourism Management*, 21 (2000): 67.
8. FEEE, *The Blue Flag Campaign* (Copenhagen: FEEE, 1990).
9. UNEP Industry and Environment, *Awards for Improving the Coastal Environment: The Example of the Blue Flag* (Paris: UNEP, 1996).
10. FEEE, *The Blue Flag Campaign, 1990*.
11. UNEP, *Awards for Improving the Coastal Environment*, 28–29.
12. F. Bolding Thomsen, "FEE(D) Goes Worldwide!" *Blue Flag Newsletter*, FEE (July 2001), http://www.blueflag.org (July 2001).
13. FEEE, *The Blue Flag Campaign, 2001* (Copenhagen: FEEE, 2001), http://www.blueflag.org/news (July 2001).
14. FEEE, "Control Visits," *Blue Flag Newsletter* (July 2001), http://www.blueflag.org (August 2001).
15. Hellenic Society for the Protection of Nature, *The Blue Flag: Guidance Notes to the Blue Flag Criteria for Beaches* (Athens: Hellenic Society for the Protection of Nature, 2001).

16. UNEP, *Awards for Improving the Coastal Environment*, 8.

17. For more about the South African criteria, see http://blueflag.org.

18. UNEP, *Awards for Improving the Coastal Environment*, 12.

19. FEEE, "Control Visits," 2001.

20. F. Bolding Thomsen, correspondence with Xavier Font, June 2001; H. Wals, "The Blue Flag: A Symbol and More," *The European Blue Flag: A Ten-year Contribution to the Improvement of the Management and Protection of Coastal Regions, 1987–1997* (Norwich: FEEE, 1997), pp. 32–33.

21. UNEP, *Awards for Improving the Coastal Environment*, 12.

22. ProQuest database, Web site: http://www.proquest.umi.com/pgdweb (2000–August 2001).

23. G. Ashworth, "Welcome and Opening Presentations," *The European Blue Flag, 1987–1997*, 12–20.

24. P. Kernel, *Survey of Opinions among National Interests about the Blue Flag Campaign* (Copenhagen: FEEE, 1997).

25. UNEP, *Awards for Improving the Coastal Environment*, 9.

26. FEEE, "The Blue Flag Is Official in South Africa (2001)," press release, 2001, http://www.blueflag.org/news/southafrica.htm (July 2001).

27. I. Melahn, "TUI Environmental Award Goes to 'Blue Flag Campaign,'" *TUI Times*, Hanover, Germany, February 2001.

28. European Commission, "EC Directorate General for Environment, Nuclear Safety and Civil Protection (BE)," press release (Brussels: European Commission, 1999), available at: http://europa.eu.int/comm/environment/.

29. FEEE, "The Blue Flag Campaign 2001."

30. S. D'Arcy, "Beach Awards Harder to Earn," *Sunday Times*, London, January 28, 2001, http://www.proquest.umi.com.

31. Tidy Britain Group, "Comparison Between the European Blue Flag and Seaside Award Beaches 2001," Seaside Awards, Web site: http://www.seaside awards.org.uk (July 2001).

32. Wals, *The European Blue Flag, 1987–1997*, 32.

33. *PAN Parks Courier* (Budapest: WWF-Hungary, Summer 2001).

34. WWF, *PAN Parks: Investing in Europe's Future* (Zeist: WWF International, 1999).

35. FNNPE, *Loving Them to Death? The Need for Sustainable Tourism in Europe's Nature and National Parks* (Grafenau: The Federation of Nature and National Parks of Europe, 1993).

36. Z. Kun, "PAN Parks Verification," draft 3, July 13, 2001 (WWF: Budapest, 2001).

37. PAN Parks Supervisory Board, "Resolutions," Meeting of PAN Parks Supervisory Board, September 29, 2000.

38. Statistics from http:// www.panparks.org (July 2001).

39. X. Font and A. Brasser, "PAN Parks: WWF's Sustainable Tourism Certification Programme in Europe's National Parks," in *Sustainable Tourism: A Global Perspective*, eds. P. Williams, T. Griffin, and R. Harris (Oxford: Butterworth-Heinemann, forthcoming).

40. Kernel, *Survey of Opinions among National Interests about the Blue Flag Campaign*, 2.
41. A. Pizam, "The Management of Quality Destination," *Quality Tourism-Concept of Sustainable Tourism Development, Harmonizing Economical, Social and Ecological Interests*, Proceedings of the Association Internationale d'Experts Scientifiques du Tourisme (AIEST), 33 (St. Gallen: Niedermann Druck, 1991), pp. 79–88; E. Inskeep, *Tourism Planning: An Integrated and Sustainable Development Approach* (New York: Van Nostrand Reinhold, 1991); V.T.C. Middleton, "Sustainable Tourism: A Marketing Perspective," in *Tourism Sustainability: Principles to Practice*, ed. M. J. Stabler (Oxon, UK: CAB International, 1997), pp. 129–142; Z. Mieczkowski, *Environmental Issues of Tourism and Recreation* (London: University Press of America, 1995).
42. Lübbert, "Umweltkennzeichningen im Tourismus"; C. Lübbert, "Tourism Ecolabels Market Research in Germany," in *Tourism Ecolabelling*, eds. Font and Buckley, pp. 71–85; ANPA, *Domanda turistica e qualita ambientale: Indagine realizzata nell'ambito dello*; T. Mihalič, "Environmental Behaviour Implications for Tourist Destinations and Ecolabels," in *Tourism Ecolabelling*, eds. Font and Buckley, 65.

Chapter 8

Getting Started: The Experiences of South Africa and Kenya

Eddie Koch, Peter John Massyn, and Anna Spenceley

South Africa and Kenya are two of the many countries on the African continent that rely extensively on tourism to promote economic growth, job creation, and reductions in the high levels of poverty that afflict both nations. The term ecotourism, together with an assortment of other terms—"community-based tourism," "nature-based tourism," "pro-poor tourism," "responsible tourism," "integrated conservation and tourism," "community private public partnerships (CPPPs) in tourism"—is currently being applied to efforts to make the industry respectful of and beneficial to both the natural resources and local people. This chapter looks at these initiatives in general and then, more specifically, at certification programs that are emerging in both Kenya and South Africa to codify and formalize criteria for socially and environmentally responsible tourism. It examines initiatives to provide incentives for government, the private sector, and citizens to abide by these criteria when they develop and operate various tourism enterprises.

The tourism industry in South Africa and Kenya is heavily reliant on Africa's wildlife and the extensive system of national parks in each country. Various types of nature-based tourism form the most strategic sectors within the industry in each country, and for this reason, the certification programs that are being developed draw on practices and standards that have been developed in the ecotourism sector. However, in both these countries, these principles are also being applied and adapted in other sectors of the tourism industry.

Planners and policy makers in both countries are explicitly aware of standards and criteria for responsible tourism that have been developed in other parts of the world, and many of these are being integrated into the plans for certification programs. However, there is also a strong awareness in both countries of the need to devise some home-grown standards specifically in the area of encouraging strong linkages between tourism growth and social development. The South African and Kenyan experiences may, therefore, provide innovative examples of how developing countries can use certification as a tool for linking tourism to an improvement in the quality of life for ordinary people.

The governments in both of these countries have tried to attract foreign investment and make their tourism industries globally competitive. They have partially achieved this objective. There is substantial foreign participation through partial or complete ownership of tourism facilities—in particular the hotel sector—in both Kenya and South Africa.

However, this process of private sector mobilization, promoted as a strategy for economic growth and job creation, has been accompanied by major problems, many of which are typical of mainstream tourism around the globe. One is that foreign ownership substantially reduces the revenues that actually stay in the country. Tourism investments in Kenya and South Africa have highlighted the huge danger of leakages—revenues and benefits that flow out of the local area rather than remaining to improve life for the local populace. Another is the low quality and seasonality of the jobs available to local people. In the town of Malindi, on the Kenyan coast, it is estimated that as much as 90 percent of the local population work directly in the tourism industry. Activities include mostly menial labor in hotels and restaurants; with local construction companies, bus and taxi companies, and local tour operators; and as boat operators and crew, fish sellers, curio sellers, shell collectors, beachboys, prostitutes, thatch-roofing makers, woodcutters, wood carvers, and food growers and sellers. Although this employment pattern suggests good multiplier effects, the downside of reliance on a tourism-driven economy is that in the off-season there is widespread suffering and poverty because there are no alternative sources of income.[1]

Another problem has been the instability of foreign capital. In the latter half of 2001, South Africa began feeling the effects of an exodus of foreign airline carriers from the country. The reasons for this withdrawal are complex and relate to high costs of travel to South Africa and apparently hostile practices by the national carrier designed to protect its own privileged position. Although this controversy is not explored in detail here, it has contributed to a decline—for the first time since 1994 (the year apartheid officially ended and Nelson Mandela became president)—in the number of foreign tourists arriving in South Africa. Private sector leaders and government officials began, as a result, to express concern about relying only on the fickle international market for tourism investment and growth.

Another pervasive concern in both countries is that local communities are generally excluded from decision making in government and private sector development processes. In Kenya, for example, serious political tensions have emerged as the country's policy of "indigenization," which made considerable headway in the 1960s and 1970s, saw Africans being appointed to the top management of companies but being afforded little involvement of local communities in the booming tourism sector (see below). Coastal communities have been forcibly removed from some areas and prevented from gaining access to certain marine and other resources that are monopolized for tourism purposes. In addition, many of the jobs generated by the burgeoning industry have been taken by better educated up-country people who have migrated into the coastal areas because of perceived opportunities created by tourism. The resulting tension between the poor and up-country elite in the coastal tourism belt laid the basis for political clashes in the run-up to Kenya's 1997 elections that left most of the country's coastal resorts looking like ghost towns.

Between 1997 and mid-1998, election unrest, politically instigated ethnic clashes and killings along the Kenyan coast, unusually heavy rains, and a crime wave combined to cause coastal tourism to plummet by two-thirds. By mid-1998, about 50 percent of Kenya's tourist hotels, mostly along the coast, had closed down or reduced their staff, and about 50,000 workers (30 percent of the tourism sector workforce) had been laid off.[2]

An awareness of these and other generic problems associated with an overreliance on conventional tourism to deal with underdevelopment and poverty has led government agencies, the private sector, NGOs, and ordinary citizens in both countries to develop a set of standards for responsible tourism with criteria that seek to protect the natural resource base as well as the interests of poor communities. These approaches—and the way in which they conform to but also deviate from experiments in other parts of the world—form the subject of this chapter.

South Africa

By the early 1990s, South Africa's tourism industry had come to assume a strategic importance in the political economy of the country. The potential of the sector to generate jobs, thus dealing with the single biggest social and economic problem facing the country during its transition to democracy, was highlighted in a 1998 report entitled *Benchmarking South Africa for Labor Intensive Development: International Lessons and Strategic Implications.*[3] Prepared by a group of consultants from Stanford University, the report argued that tourism—especially wildlife, adventure, and sport—had more potential to create new jobs than any other form of economic activity in the country. The Stanford report was designed to feed into the Presidential Job Summit, held in late 1998, so that the South African government and its social partners—organized labor and business—could devise strategies for dealing with unemployment in South Africa.

The study argued that tourism had the potential for creating 450,000 new jobs by the year 2005. The only other sectors with job creation potential were construction (which the report says could create 60,000 jobs by the year 2005), agriculture (50,000 jobs), furniture (30,000), labor-intensive export manufacturing (20,000), and information service industries (10,000). The report thus gave tourism a massive 72 percent of the job-creating potential in South Africa's current economic circumstances. Then, in 1999, the Cluster Consortium (a group of planners and researchers from South Africa, North America, and New Zealand who were appointed by the government to develop an action plan to enhance the performance of the tourism industry) released a report called *South Africa's Tourism Challenge: A Profile of the Tourism Cluster.*[4]

The optimism of The Standard and Cluster Consortium reports regarding job creation was based on data that indicated that South Africa at the close of the millennium was enjoying the longest period of tourism growth in its history. The year 1999 marked the eleventh successive year of increased overseas visitor arrivals, which had grown at a compound rate of over 15 percent per annum during the decade. Recent analysis has shown that much of this expansion was due to above average increases in the number of tourists attracted by South Africa's beautiful scenery and wildlife.

The growth in international tourism came on top of a large, established domestic tourism market worth approximately twice as much as its foreign counterpart. The World Travel and Tourism Council (WTTC) estimated that, in total, South African tourism in 1998 contributed about Rand (ZAR)53 billion (about US$6.6 billion) a year to the economy, and the WTTC expected this to grow at around 12 percent annually, reaching ZAR211 billion (about US$27 billion) by 2010.

Based on the assessment of tourism's strategic role in the South African economy, the post-apartheid government has adopted a range of policies aimed at making tourism one of the lead growth sectors for the country. In 1996, the government approved a tourism White Paper (*White Paper on the Development and Promotion of Tourism in South Africa*)[5] that had a notion of responsible tourism at its core and laid the basis for the development of an extensive set of responsible tourism guidelines (see below). By 1998, tourism had become a key driver of the country's macroeconomic strategy of growth, employment, and redistribution (GEAR). A national tourism council made up of representatives from the private sector and government departments made substantial funds available for a new marketing drive.

Many of the policies were aimed at promoting forms of rural growth and job creation through tourism. A national program of spatial development initiatives (SDIs) (see box 8.1) was set up concentrating on mobilizing private sector investment into parts of the country where there was a

---

Box 8.1. The Spatial Development Initiatives (SDIs) and Community Private Public Partnerships as a Particular Approach to Economic Growth and Job Creation in South Africa

A critical aim of the SDIs is to redress the inequality in the economy that was inherited from apartheid by promoting new entrepreneurs and community involvement in investments. Thus, the SDI program encourages investors to go into partnerships with rural people. A number of SDIs are located in areas that have a rich set of natural resources: forests, dams, the ocean, beaches, wildlife. There are such SDIs in the northeast of KwaZulu Natal, the Cape west coast, the Wild Coast of the Eastern Cape, the Northern Province, and the North West Province.

- Tourism is a major investment sector in these SDIs. The key objectives of the tourism-led SDIs are to:
- Generate sustainable economic growth and development.
- Generate sustainable long-term employment creation.
- Maximize the extent to which private sector investment and lending can be mobilized into the process.
- Change the ownership base of the industry so that men and women previously excluded from the mainstream of the economy by discriminatory practices can play a meaningful role as workers, managers, and owners of new tourism enterprises.
- Exploit the opportunities that arise from new tourism and ecotourism developments for the creation of upstream and downstream business opportunities, especially small businesses owned by previously marginalized groups.

The Department of Trade and Industry has established a Community Private Public Partnership (CPPP) program to facilitate these objectives. The CPPP program aims to revitalize South Africa's rural economies by linking resource-rich communities with appropriate public and private sector investor interests.

Source: G.R.M. De Beer and S.P. Eliffe, *Tourism-led Development, Job Creation and Restructuring the Rural Economy: Lessons Learned and Applied in South Africa's Spatial Development Initiatives*, Special Report on SDIs (Midrand, South Africa: Development Bank of Southern Africa, 1997).

surfeit of natural beauty, landscapes, and wildlife but historically little development. These represent a new economic paradigm aimed at moving away from a protected and isolated approach to economic development under apartheid toward one in which international competitiveness, regional cooperation, and a more diversified ownership base are paramount.

The supply-side response changed substantially from the late 1990s, with the award of concessions in a number of national parks and other concerted attempts to attract new investment into lodge opportunities in other wilderness areas of the country, including the North West Province and the northern parts of KwaZulu Natal. In the past, commercial development in public parks was undertaken almost exclusively by state and parastatal (semi-state) agencies, such as South African National Parks and the Natal Parks Board. The state thus effectively monopolized commerce in most of the country's prime wildlife estate, with private sector development confined to relatively small privately owned reserves (such as the Sabi Sands Game Reserve next to the Kruger National Park) on the margins of the major public parks. As part of the government's broader economic restructuring, state parks and reserves are being opened, for the first time, for private commercial activities.

A number of South Africa's conservation agencies are undertaking programs to commercialize the wildlife estate under their control, thus opening possibilities for private sector investment in lodges and related commercial activities. The lead agency in this regard has been the North West Parks and Tourism Board, which has facilitated the development of private tourism facilities in major provincial reserves, such as Pilanesberg and Madikwe in the North West Province of South Africa. More recently, South African National Parks (SANP), with assistance from the World Bank's International Finance Corporation, has awarded concessions to private developers in a number of the country's national reserves, including the Kruger National Park. Both agencies have increasingly used their procurement practices to advance the economic empowerment of historically disadvantaged South Africans, particularly those residing in the immediate hinterland of the parks. The Greater St. Lucia Wetland Park Authority, a dedicated management institution set up by terms of national legislation in late 2000 to facilitate the commercial development of South Africa's first and largest World Heritage Site, is implementing a similar strategy to promote black economic empowerment.

This approach, which twins commercialization of state assets with a procurement method that favors black South Africans, is in line with recent national legislation on public procurement and employment equity and is likely to be adopted by other state agencies controlling valuable wildlife estate (such as the provincial conservation bodies). If efficiently implemented, it promises to reshape ownership and business practices in the country's wildlife sector, which to date have been dominated by the public and white business sectors. The first round of seven concessions awarded by the SANP in late 2000 provides an early example of the impact of affirmative procurement in the wildlife sector: according to SANP, previously disadvantaged South Africans own, on average, 53 percent of the equity in the successful bidding companies.[6] The conditions under which the concessions were acquired require the new owners to employ local labor, utilize the services of local small businesses, and pay dividends from profits to previously disadvantaged shareholders. New game lodges in these wildlife areas are still being built, and it remains to be seen whether these objectives of commercialization of state assets and black economic empowerment will be successfully realized.

South Africa's land reform program, which aims to create land and resource rights for those who were denied them in the past, has also started transferring conditional ownership of portions of the country's public wildlife estate to groups dispossessed under apartheid. South Africa's magnificent national and regional parks were created during the twentieth century, frequently by forcibly evicting the local people and barring them access to their land. With the end of apartheid, many black communities assumed the Mandela government would dismantle the parks and return their lands to them. The government decided instead to keep most of the parks but to allow communities to file land claims to be adjudicated on a case by case basis. Large sections of South Africa's premier parks are currently under claim, but the restitution program has been slow and heavily contested.

By 2001, there was growing consensus that the landmark Makuleke case offered a model for how to transfer important protected areas to claimants. After a long struggle, the Makuleke people regained title to a prime piece of African wildlife estate in northern Kruger National Park, which lies at the heart of southern Africa's largest proposed transfrontier park. They have decided not to resettle on the land and to leave it as a contractual park within the wider Kruger Park wildlife system. The Makuleke have full commercial rights to their land and have initiated an advanced program for the development of a range of nature tourism lodges and other commercial activities in partnership with the private sector.[7] They are thus relying on a responsible form of nature tourism to alleviate poverty, provide jobs and revenues, and remedy the negative effects that the forced removal had on their livelihoods.

Responsible Tourism and Certification

The South African state has made attempts to promote racial equity, labor standards, and integrated environmental procedures across all industries. It has also encouraged ethical forms of investment into enterprises and companies whose values are inscribed in contracts between companies from the private sector and various groups in civil society. The South African government and the private sector are clearly encouraged by indications that various forms of wildlife tourism are able to bring into the mainstream of the economy some rural people who were previously discriminated against. This is being done either by creating joint ventures between local communities and private investors on communal land or by creating opportunities for small businesses to service a main tourism enterprise. There is also a pervasive belief within government that tourism, unlike the highly damaging mining industry that drove the apartheid economy, can be an industry without smokestacks, that is, one that conserves rather than consumes the natural resources upon which it is based. There are a number of areas of the country where these principles are being implemented.

There are, however, a number of daunting obstacles in the way of achieving these objectives of economic empowerment combined with environmental protection, including the lack of capacity in rural communities, high levels of poverty, and fragmentation of government's ability to implement its own policies. Although the models are too young to assess as being successes or failures at this stage, they are examples of where South Africa is making a new contribution at a policy level to the setting of standards for responsible tourism.

Despite these government initiatives aimed at achieving an ethical and sustainable form of tourism, industry and government were slow in the 1990s to convert the principles of South Africa's tourism White Paper (see below) into a formal system aimed at monitoring and rewarding sustainable tourism practices. By the end of 2001, there were a couple of fledgling efforts by government, parastatals, and/or the main private sector players in the tourism sector to arrive at tourism grading systems that would ensure hospitality levels of quality, health, and safety standards, as well as some ethical environmental and social standards. Some of the larger private sector tourism establishments subscribe to international certification programs, such as Green Globe 21 and ISO 14001-based programs, but to date, very few have applied for such certification.

Qualitour and the Heritage Ecotourism Rating Program

However, in September 2001, Qualitour, a private South African company that runs a small certification program rating service, hospitality, and quality, announced that it was linking up with Green Globe to launch a Heritage Ecotourism Rating Program. Qualitour, which offers a variety of services to both the industry and travelers, has certified less than two dozen hotels, lodges, and resorts using a scale of one to five diamonds. In a press release, managing director Greg McManus explained that Qualitour is partnering with AJA South Africa, the registered Green Globe auditors for the region, to launch a new product designed to "reward establishments and service providers who operate environmentally responsible businesses in the South African tourism industry."[8] The Heritage program is designed to offer certification to businesses throughout the tourism industry but does not contain measurable, performance-based criteria. McManus explained that the Heritage program is based on the International Hotels Environment Initiative, which goes further than Green Globe. He recognized that Green Globe is not wholly suitable to South African realities, especially because it does not work at the community level. However, McManus stated that all enterprises enrolled with the Heritage program will automatically receive Green Globe affiliate status but that qualification for Green Globe certification will take longer (see chapter 10).

AJA South Africa auditors will carry out the environmental assessment and will offer three levels of certification. By early 2002, no hotels had yet been enrolled in the new program, but Qualitour said it planned to announce the first Heritage certifications and Green Globe affiliates at several trade shows and forums leading up to the World Summit on Sustainable Development (WSSD) taking place in South Africa in August–September 2002.[9]

In addition, in May 2002, the Minister for Environmental Affairs and Tourism, Valli Moosa, launched the government's new national guidelines for "responsible" tourism. Although these initiatives remain fragmented and embryonic, they are opening many possibilities to constructively influence a fluid process that is underway in South Africa.

South African Tourism Board Hospitality Standards

In addition to the small Qualitour program, hotels, guest houses, and other types of accommodations in South Africa were, until the late 1990s, governed by a system of grading that awarded stars to the enterprises, primarily for its hospitality standards. This system was administered by the South African Tourism Board (Satour), a parastatal or quasi-governmental body. The code of conduct accepted by members of this scheme emphasized the need to maintain standards of courtesy and quality in facilities and services in hotels and guest houses. There were no environmental standards or social criteria involved in the grading scheme, and the closest the Satour system came to enforcing any kind of social equity was a clause in the code stating that members were required "to ensure that no guest is discriminated against in any manner whatsoever."[10]

With the end of white rule in 1994, the hotel sector in South Africa experienced substantial growth in line with expanding tourism arrivals. Leading local hotel chains, owned by domestic capitalists who had maintained a major presence in the hotel sector under apartheid, along with the big multinational hotel groups who were attracted to the country after the democratic elections, began in the late 1990s to resist the grading system and the levies that went with it. "The big groups argued that their brands were far more effective in the marketplace than the official grading system. They questioned whether it was worth paying for the grading system when it brought them little benefit,"[11] said Mike Fabricius, chief executive officer for Western Cape Tourism.

Thus, a group of owners of the big hotel franchises, local and international capitalists who jointly held some 60 percent of tourism beds in the country, formed an organized lobby called the Hotel Industry Liaison Group. They argued against the grading system, which they saw as outmoded and ineffective, and called for it to be replaced by a more dynamic and effective, in marketing and branding terms, certification program. In the meantime, they relied on their own branding, marketing, and ability to attract consumers. The old Satour grading system was thus abandoned.[12]

Tourism Grading Council Standards

At the same time, the big hoteliers attempted to set up their own private sector–controlled scheme. But this, on its own, did not amount to an effective certification program. In the late 1990s, a Tourism Grading Council, comprising government officials, the major players in the organized hospitality sector, and organized labor, was set up to devise a new grading system primarily to rate hospitality standards, but not socially or environmentally responsible practices.

The new Tourism Grading Council set about conducting a series of discussions and consultations within the tourism sector and within government agencies responsible for tourism management to work out how to implement a new grading system and what criteria to include in it. There were three issues that dominated the debate. These are summarized below:

- How should a system involving a voluntary commitment to a set of accommodation and service standards by all groups in the tourism sector be devised? A key issue of contention, articulated primarily by organized labor, was a potential form of elitism: a set of standards imposed by big global and domestic hotel chains that may create problems for emerging and smaller enterprises in the sector.
- Should there be a mandatory system for businesses to adhere to safety,

health, hygiene, and tax standards in the sector, and if so, what kind of policing/monitoring/auditing body should be set up to administer this system? A major factor favoring a mandatory framework was the fragmented and diverse nature of local government bylaws and municipal regulations then governing these issues. The general consensus in the Tourism Grading Council appears to have been in favor of creating a not-for-profit company to carry out this role.

- Should social, environmental, and equity standards be included, and if so, how should they be worded? Paradoxically, these issues were less prominent within the Tourism Grading Council's deliberations, probably because these factors are seen as being the subject of various government-led programs.[13]

By June 2002, there was a major drive by the Tourism Grading Council to implement a new grading scheme to replace the abandoned Satour system. It will be important to monitor how this scheme unfolds, as it will shed light on the attitudes of large portions of the country's tourism sector (those represented in the Hotel Industry Liaison Group) toward the monitoring of their hospitality standards and possibly also toward the other standards for responsible tourism that are emerging in the country. Early indications are that most sectors of the tourism industry will accept a new grading system but will want this to be simple, effective, and impose minimal cost on tourism enterprises. It is also clear that the big hotel groups will want to participate in the assessment of their hospitality standards and will not feel comfortable if auditing and assessment is conducted by an independent external body.

Conservation Corporation Africa/National Geographic Society Branding Experiment

In part because of this hiatus in Satour's grading system, there was an innovative attempt in 2000 by South Africa's leading nature tourism lodge development and operating company, Conservation Corporation Africa (CCA), to enter into a strategic partnership with the National Geographic Society (NGS). This NGO engaged in negotiations with CCA to establish an alliance between two organizations with similar values and missions. In essence, these revolved around a commitment to various forms of nature and cultural tourism that help protect biodiversity and heritage while at the same time promoting economic growth and development of a type that improves the livelihoods of local residents. A central objective of the alliance was for NGS to certify select CCA lodges with its logo for marketing and branding purposes.

A list of criteria reflecting the shared values of the parties to the proposed alliance was drafted for the purpose of conducting the audits. This list covered a range of issues relating to impacts and performance of the lodges in the following four broad headings: ecology, economy, sociocultural, and a number of factors specific to the interests of NGS members. Although pilot audits were carried out at CCA lodges throughout southern and eastern Africa, the proposed strategic alliance failed to materialize for a number of reasons that had little to do with the content of the proposed scheme. The audits included a qualitatively derived but numbered rating system for environmental and social performance criteria, but in the absence of quantifiable and measurable criteria, it was open to the assessor's own interpretation to determine the score. This is a problem seen in the environmental and social assessment field globally and is not unique to the CCA/NGS scheme.

The branding experiment is mentioned here because it demonstrated a will in some sections of the private sector to adopt for commercial reasons a set of responsible tourism codes that incorporate quality standards as well as environmental, sociocultural, and economic equity criteria. It also indicated the possibility that a well-established and credible (rather than new) global brand, the NGS logo, could be used, especially in the ecotourism sector, to overcome the proliferation of brands that afflicts global certification attempts.[14] CCA is continuing efforts to develop its own assessment methodology, independent of NGS.

Fair Trade in Tourism South Africa

Yet another effort is being spearheaded by the South African chapter of the IUCN (World Conservation Union), which coordinates a Fair Trade in Tourism program. This is linked to the global fair trade movement, which seeks to address North-South inequalities through the creation of fair trade labels, trading partnerships, and ethical trading initiatives (see chapter 3). Fair Trade in Tourism South Africa (FTTSA) has been active since late 1998, when it began to establish a relationship with five small tourism projects in the Northern Province, the Eastern Cape and the Western Cape. The IUCN-South Africa now plans to expand this program primarily for the benefit of community-based tourism destinations and businesses. The project aims to:

• Establish and strengthen the concept of fair trade in tourism in South Africa.
• Promote the implementation of the fair trade principles that are quite well known in Northern European markets.
• Promote and market the tourism activities of FTTSA products (formal or informal tourism enterprises that meet the FTTSA trademark criteria), thus helping to create viable and sustainable businesses that can create employment and wealth.

- Establish a Fair Trade in Tourism South Africa brand and trademark to channel a portion of the country's growing numbers of international arrivals and domestic trips (and tourist expenditures) toward South Africa's disadvantaged communities and population groups.[15]

Blue Flag Certification for South Africa's Beaches

Apart from hotel certification efforts, there has been movement toward protecting South Africa's renowned beaches from pollution and overuse through tourism. In 2001, a nongovernmental organization, the Wildlife and Environment Society of South Africa (WESSA) became the first organization outside Europe to join the Blue Flag certification program (see chapter 7). Although certified beaches must comply with all criteria in fourteen different groups, WESSA tailored the criteria to take into account South Africa's unique geographical conditions and social issues. There are, for instance, additional criteria relating to visitor security, including the requirement that a uniformed official must patrol the area twenty-four hours a day.[16] A South African beach must first apply to run a pilot phase and only one year thereafter may it apply for a full Blue Flag status. Although run by an NGO, the campaign is being supported by the Department of Environmental Affairs and Tourism (DEA&T), which is using Blue Flag status to market South African destinations internationally.

DEA&T's Initiative for National Guidelines for Sustainable Tourism

Concerned with the lack of formal standards in South Africa, the DEA&T began a participatory process of developing responsible tourism guidelines for the South African tourism industry with the aim of promoting these guidelines during the May 2002 International Year of Ecotourism summit in Quebec, Canada. The World Tourism Organization (WTO) was pushing to have some country develop a model set of national guidelines for sustainable tourism, and South Africa, as the host of the World Summit on Sustainable Development in August–September 2002, hoped its emerging set of standards would achieve this status.

As noted, the DEA&T initiative takes as its starting point the South African government's *White Paper on the Development and Promotion of Tourism in South Africa*, published in 1996 after a wide stakeholder consultation process with the tourism industry and wider society. The DEA&T believes that the White Paper contains nearly all the elements necessary to create responsible strategies that can be put into action in each subsector of the tourism industry. However, although the wording of policy is supportive of rural livelihoods and empowerment, there have been major difficulties transferring the aspirations of government policy into practice on the ground. The nature, language, and style of legislative documents often

Box 8.2. Principles and Elements Taken from the 1996 White Paper on the Development and Promotion of Tourism in South Africa

Responsible tourism is the key guiding principle for tourism development. It takes "a proactive approach by tourism industry partners to develop, market, and manage the tourism industry in a responsible manner so as to create a competitive advantage." In addition, this type of tourism "recognises the responsibility of the government and private sector to involve the previously neglected in the tourism industry."

Key elements are to:
• Market tourism that is responsible, respecting local, natural, and cultural environments.
• Involve local communities through meaningful economic linkages and use tourism as "a development tool for the empowerment of previously neglected communities," particularly the empowerment of women in those communities.
• Involve the local community in planning and decision making.
• Assess economic impacts as a prerequisite to developing tourism.
• Ensure that communities are involved in and benefit from tourism.
• Respect, invest in, and develop local cultures, protect them from overcommercialization and overexploitation, and involve local communities in the tourism industry "to practise sustainable development and to ensure the safety and security of visitors."
• Maintain and encourage economic, social, and cultural diversity.
• Be sensitive to the host culture.
• Assess social impacts as a prerequisite to developing tourism.
• Foster "responsibility of both employers and employees in the tourism industry both to each other as well as to the customer," including responsible trade union practices.
• Show responsibility to the environment.
• Maintain and encourage natural diversity.
• Avoid waste and overconsumption.
• Use local resources sustainably.
• Assess environmental impacts as a prerequisite to developing tourism.
• Foster responsibility of tourists to "observe the norms and practises of South Africa, particularly with respect to the environment and culture of the country."
• Monitor impacts of tourism and ensure open disclosure of information.

Source: H. Goodwin, "Notes for Meeting with DEA&T," unpublished document, April 23, 2001. All quotations are drawn from this document.

do not lend themselves to direct translation into action.[17] A number of the key principles and elements from the White Paper are shown in box 8.2.

To implement the policy, both DEA&T and the private sector set out to develop detailed guidelines for implementation and benchmarks against which to monitor and assess progress. International tourism and certification expertise from the British-based Centre for Responsible Tourism (CRT) and the Institute of Natural Resources (INR) in KwaZulu Natal province was used to facilitate the process of developing the guidelines. The British government's Department for International Development provided funding for this process. The criteria for responsible tourism were drawn from a review of international best practices and key economic, social, and environmental objectives in the 1996 White Paper. Thus, by late 2001, a comprehensive set of responsible tourism guidelines had been developed through a series of national workshops and a paper-based consultation process that involved government, the private sector, consultants, academics, and civil society organizations. These new national guidelines for responsible tourism contain a comprehensive set of standards too long to summarize here, but they deal with the "triple bottom line" (economic, social, and environmental) categories agreed to at the 1992 Earth Summit.

DEA&T intends that these guidelines will contain among the most extensive strategies for sustainable tourism development in the world and plans to showcase these during 2002 at the Ecotourism Summit in Canada and, in South Africa, at both the World Summit on Sustainable Development and a special tourism summit meeting. Johann Kotze, an official with the DEA&T, stated that the guidelines are significant due to the way in which they stress human rights, basic labor standards, and social empowerment objectives, along with environmental safeguards. Kotze explained that the guidelines are also unique in that they provide the government with concrete targets against which to cumulatively monitor their progress toward implementing the White Paper policy of responsible tourism. In 2002, DEA&T commissioned the development of a Manuel for Responsible Tourism in order to guide trade associates and tourism enterprises in responsible business practices and in reporting their performance in a transparent way.

Uncertain Future

The South African government is relying on voluntary adherence on the part of industry to the responsible tourism guideline rather than any form of enforcement or set of incentives. Several major private sector groups, including the Federated Hospitality Association of South Africa (FEDHASA) and the Bed and Breakfast Association of South Africa (BABASA), have already initiated discussions to develop specific guidelines for responsible practice for their members in implementing the national guidelines.

In addition, a four-wheel–drive vehicles group called Off-Road Tactix has already drawn up its first draft.[18] These associations have recognized the commercial advantages of implementing responsible tourism, especially in light of new research by Tearfund[19] and the Association of British Travel Agents (ABTA)[20], which clearly shows the importance that British tourists place on environmental and social responsibility in the holidays they choose.

In addition, the members of the British Association of Independent Tour Operators (AITO) have signed on to their own responsible tourism guidelines.[21] These require quantifiable information from destinations to show their clients that they are acting to use responsible ground handlers. Therefore, the members of FEDHASA, BABASA and the four-wheel–drive market will gain significant advantage if they can be the first to conform to these guidelines.

Given the previous reluctance on the part of the large hotel groups to accept a independent grading schemes, it will be interesting to see whether the big players in South African tourism convert in-principle support into real adherence to the set of new sustainable tourism standards. Initial indications are that they will only if there is clear evidence that their occupancies will increase by doing so, if the standards are simple and easy to administer, if they do not involve substantial cost, and so long as industry groups are involved in monitoring and assessing compliance with the standards. Any external monitoring by an independent body is likely to be viewed as interference in internal industry matters. However, in order to encourage and showcase sustainable business practices, FEDHASA has relaunched its Imvelo award in line with the responsible tourism guidelines.

By June 2002, there were no plans for independent monitoring of companies and the scheme did not include a logo or ecolabel. However, these may evolve as the work of developing guidelines proceeds, as well as the forthcoming work of developing subsector guidelines with quantifiable criteria for the land and marine nature-based tourism sector.

Thus, although a number of certification initiatives are now underway and several are hoping to use the International Year of Ecotourism and the pre-WSSD Conference on Repsonsible Tourism in Destinations to gain international recognition, by mid-2002, the reality was that the situation in South Africa remained fluid, and more work appeared to be needed to bring all key stakeholders into agreement behind a single certification program for responsible tourism.

Kenya

History of Ecotourism in Kenya

At independence in 1963, Kenya inherited many of the problems related to neocolonial economies, including reduced investment, capital shortage, and severe unemployment. The government relied from the outset on tourism to promote economic growth, employment creation, private sector investment, and foreign exchange earnings. There was a strong drive to attract private sector investment in the tourism industry. This objective was also supported by easygoing policies on repatriation of foreign capital, profits, and dividends, enabling investors who wished to remit funds to do so without hardships.

The nature-based tourism industry in Kenya is centered around the country's abundant wildlife in protected areas and its scenery, beaches, and coral reefs. The tourism industry has grown significantly from 65,000 tourists per annum at independence in 1963 to 832,000 in 1994. Tourism is a critical national foreign exchange earner and has generated around 150,000 direct and 360,000 indirect jobs.[22]

The Kenyan government allowed the international private sector to purchase land on which they were to develop their hotels. The strategy provided security of tenure that was regarded by both government and the private sector investors as a critical precondition to securing fixed foreign investment. Any benefit flows to the local community from the sale of this land were to be achieved via trickle down effects.[23]

During the 1960s and 1970s, tourism was the second largest sector of the national economy (average 13 percent) after agriculture (37 percent). Although tourism stagnated between 1978 and 1983, it picked up sharply after 1984. It was stimulated by an improved international economic climate and Kenya's economic liberalizations, promoted by the World Bank and the International Monetary Fund, which provided new incentives and tax breaks for foreign investment. By 1987, tourism had become Kenya's number one foreign exchange earner, surpassing coffee and tea (although the agricultural sector as a whole generated more export earnings than tourism). In the early 1990s, no other African country was earning as much as Kenya from wildlife tourism.

But decline set in during the mid- and late 1990s, with earnings dropping 20 percent in 1995 alone. The downturn was caused by a combination of factors: an economic recession, declining infrastructure, increasing insecurity and crime, bad press coverage, excessively recycled tourism products (mainly beach holiday and game safaris and a failure to diversify its range of attractions), poor international marketing, and increasing competition from eastern and southern Africa (particularly Tanzania, Uganda, South Africa, and Zimbabwe).[24]

Post-Independent Indigenization and Ecotourism

In 1966, the recently independent Kenyan government, apparently aware of the potentially adverse effects of foreign private sector dominance of the tourism industry, attempted to counterbalance ownership by foreign and white settlers by creating the Kenya Tourism Development Corporation (KTDC). The main aim was to diversify the ownership of assets and of economic activities and to indigenize the tourism economy. KTDC's mission was to buy shares in foreign-owned tour companies, travel agencies, hotels, and lodges and then sell these shares "to promising Kenyan entrepreneurs on special terms."[25] In practice, KTDC served as a vehicle for using public funds to help handpicked, politically well-connected black Kenyans get a piece of the tourism pie.[26]

During this same period, Kenya also introduced what are often considered to be Africa's earliest experiments with "pro-poor" ecotourism, that is, tourism that is culturally sensitive and economically beneficial to local communities. Kenya established revenue sharing of park fees and tourism profits in several of its most famous game parks. Under an agreement reached in 1961, Maasai Mara, Amboseli, and a few other Kenyan game reserves were to be managed by the local district or country councils rather than the central government, with the aim of channeling earnings into development programs for the local Maasai pastoralists. These innovative programs embodied the principles of local community participation in wildlife conservation and tourism and mixed land use in the buffer zones around the parks. The revenues were intended for local development—schools, water, roads, health clinics, and other basic services—but, after initial successes, these program were undermined by local Maasai leaders who diverted entrance fees and lodge levies into their own pockets. Like the KTDC, these early experiments at local control eventually served largely to enrich a politically powerful elite. By the early 1990s, these game reserves, the local people, and tourism were all suffering from the corruption, land grabbing, diversion of resources, and unplanned and inappropriate investment in both the parks and surrounding areas.[27]

Resentment toward the parks and reserves had, in fact, been building for decades. In Kenya, as elsewhere in eastern and southern Africa, local residents had often been forcibly removed as parks and reserves were created, first for the benefit of trophy hunters and European scientists and later for wildlife camera safaris. Those evicted ended up living on the edges of protected areas and were barred from access to water, grazing grass, and other resources on what had historically been their land. In addition, wildlife tourism was largely for foreigners or local white settlers. Although a substantial amount of money was set aside for overseas promotion, nothing was done to promote domestic tourism in the first decade of independence. This meant that as tourism gained momentum, locals became increasingly distanced and alienated from the parks, hotels, and lodges.[28]

Even when local people have received some income from tourism and the parks, it has been accrued with complications. For example, Arhem noted in the mid-1980s, "From being self-sufficient pastoralists, capable of maintaining a modest but adequate standard of subsistence . . . [the Maasai] have turned into impoverished pastoral peasants, tied to the market and subject to increasing state control." [29] In addition, the Maasai fear that, as Paul Ntiati, one of their leaders in Kenya, put it, "if we designate specific areas within our ranches for wildlife sanctuaries, the government will come along one day and take them from us as they did with Amboseli [National Park], saying that these wildlife areas are a national asset, so the nation must control them." [30] Today, indigenization has brought few sustainable benefits to local communities and rural poor, and wildlife tourism is, by and large, still seen as a luxury activity for rich, conservation-minded foreign tourists. [31]

The growth of tourism has caused ecological deterioration and shortages of vital resources as well. The negative impacts directly attributable to tourism include overuse and overharvesting of sea shells, corals, and precious woods; pollution from sewage, solid waste, and oil; soil erosion in popular game viewing areas; shortages of fresh water; and deforestation. Within the context of Kenya's rapid tourism development, any environmental impact planning, monitoring, and regulation has been, according to various observers, largely haphazard and ad hoc. In practice, no viable and integrated development plan was implemented at the start of the tourism development program, and this situation remained essentially unchanged by the end of the millennium. [32]

Today, there is widespread agreement that both the Kenyan government and private sector must change the tourism industry as a whole if the problems of degradation, decline in tourism quality, decreasing per capita tourist revenues, and inequitable distribution of national tourism earnings are to be addressed. [33] As Kenya's assistant director of tourism Sam Okungu explained at a March 2001 workshop, "tourism today is seen as a set of principles and practices intended to ensure the sustainability to the entire nature-based tourism industry." Okungu went on to list three main objectives of sustainable tourism development in Kenya:

- Improve the quality of life of the tourist host communities.
- Provide high-quality visitors' experiences.
- Maintain the quality of the environment on which the host community and the tourists depend. This encourages understanding of the impacts of tourism on the natural, cultural, and human environment and ensures a fair distribution of benefits and costs. [34]

The philosophy also builds on the work of some conservation NGOs and aid agencies in Kenya that have initiated programs in recent years linking conservation in protected areas with sustainable socioeconomic development in neighboring public lands.[35] As one recent study sums up the current situation, "The (East Africa) region is now poised for progress in community conservation. A number of significant policies are in place, and have been given added impetus and focus by declining government budgets and structural adjustment policies forcing retrenchment. Community arrangements for the management of natural resources are now a necessity, not a luxury."[36]

Setting Standards and Establishing a Certification System

Over the last several years, there has been a growing consensus that the development of a domestic ecorating system will help both to curb destructive and unjust practices and to demonstrate to the rest of the world that Kenya is dealing with its problems.[37] During the late 1990s, calls for a domestic rating scheme were made at various conferences, including the 1997 workshop "Ecotourism at a Crossroads," organized by The International Ecotourism Society (TIES). The TIES forum was attended by a range of national and international NGOs, academics, and private sector representatives and took place as Kenya's tourism industry was experiencing a serious decline, caused in part by government and industry failure to address environmental and social impacts of tourism operations. One of the outcomes of this forum was the endorsement of the need to develop a code of conduct for ecotourism operations in Kenya. Subsequently, a National Tourism Conference, held in July 1998, deliberated over what should be done to improve Kenya's image, including the need to set standards and examine the possibilities of creating a certification system.[38]

Then, in October 1999, the Kenyan Tourism Federation (KTF) initiated a workshop to stimulate support for the development of a domestic certification scheme. This so-called Eco-rating Initiative was aimed at assessing the broader tourism industry (not just the ecotourism slice) with a view toward assisting in the development of a sustainable tourism industry. The workshop was attended and supported by the donor community, tourism associations, conservation organizations, NGOs working with communities, community representatives, and individuals interested in tourism. The workshop participants agreed to move ahead with development of a domestic ecorating scheme.

The Ecotourism Society of Kenya (ESOK) was given the responsibility of developing the ecorating scheme, and a broadly representative steering committee was created to guide the process. This committee is made up of representatives from the industry, government, and NGOs and has embarked on a number of activities aimed at pursuing the ecorating ini-

Table 8.1. Summary Table of Discussions about the Major Ecorating Issues

Issue	Overall Outcome of Discussion
Does the eco-rating scheme have to be Kenyan?	General agreement on the need for a Kenyan ecorating scheme.
What should be the focus of the scheme?	Facilities, services, and locations ultimately need to be included. There was recognition that resource limitations may apply to including all three sectors. In the Mombassa workshop, the overwhelming feeling was that all three sectors were equally important and should be addressed at the same time, therefore the technical committee would need to prioritize.
What approach to assessment would be desirable?	Some minimum performance standards that are measurable should be incorporated. The system should be systematic without being too complex and bureaucratic in order to remain effective.
What sort of criteria should be used?	Criteria need to be developed in a way that enables rating at different levels. Criteria and standards should be reviewed regularly.
Should there be different levels of certification?	The provision of different certification levels, while desirable, will be complex and require additional resources.
How is compliance with the criteria assessed?	As no general agreement was attained, this issue will need to be addressed by the technical committee.
Who should manage the ecorating scheme?	Kenya needs to establish a broadly based management body with a separate independent organization responsible for auditing and awarding of ecoratings. ESOK was identified as an organization that could possibly assume such a role.
What if a company fails the test?	Companies should be given a grace period to meet the criteria. Clear enforcement of the scheme will be necessary.
What sort of support should the scheme offer to companies?	There must be recognition that participating companies will require various levels of support. Smaller companies, for instance, may need considerably more assistance.
Should there be links with other schemes?	Links were seen as beneficial and a way in which duplication could be avoided. For example, it would be counterproductive to develop an alternative system for certifying guides in Kenya.

(continues)

Table 8.1. Continued

Issue	Overall Outcome of Discussion
What resources might be needed for a Kenyan scheme?	A general discussion occurred, but no conclusions were reached, although delegates began to appreciate the considerable resources that will be needed to implement a scheme. The hiring of a consultant was considered essential, and some indication of donor support was provided.
How much would certification cost?	All of the parameters for determining certification charges were regarded as imperfect, although annual profit was perhaps considered the most appropriate.
Is there a process for developing an ecorating scheme?	The proposed process and schedule were accepted as realistic. A general feeling emerged that it was important to develop the scheme as quickly as possible.

Source: Ecotourism Society of Kenya, Nairobi, 2000.

tiative.[39] These have included consultation with the Kenyan tourism industry regarding principles of sustainable tourism and ecorating, a survey of international certification schemes, and organizing two more workshops. In his opening remarks to a workshop held in Mombasa, ESOK chairman Jake Grieves Cook argued that because "some are . . . just paying lip service to the principles of ecotourism as a means of obtaining marketing advantage,"[40] an ecorating system was necessary to help set standards and ensure that tourism businesses that claimed to be acting responsibly were actually adhering to sustainable practices Table 8.1, prepared by ESOK, summarizes the ecorating discussions.

Although some key tourism industry players were absent from the early ESOK workshops, those who were present expressed support of the ecorating initiative and agreed to act as leaders for the process. A technical committee was established that includes both tourism and conservation representatives, and a process and time frame were agreed upon for creating the rating system, beginning in 2002.[41]

In addition to this ecorating scheme, there is a parallel effort to set sustainability standards within a craft closely linked to the tourism industry. The so-called People and Plants Initiative, begun in 1994, is aimed at protecting the hardwood carving industry in Kenya, which produces popular animal and human figures for the tourism market. This US$20 million per year industry supports over 60,000 woodcarvers with an estimated 300,000 dependents, and yet it is based upon a rapidly diminishing timber resource. Just two woodcarving centers at Mombasa and Malindi, for instance, use over 20,000 logs per year. The most preferred species, such as mahogany and ebony, are now in extremely short supply. In addition, some 9,000 of the 20,000 mahogany trees felled each year are hollow. While living, these hollow trees provided shelter for mammals, reptiles, birds, and invertebrates, some of which are endangered species.

With the support of the Mennonite Central Committee, the People and Plants Initiative has brought together all the major stakeholders, including the carvers, traders, concerned NGOs, conservation and forestry organizations, and the United Nations Educational, Scientific and Cultural Organization (UNESCO), in an "inclusive approach" intended to "increase the reliability of the results and raise the likelihood"[42] that its recommendations would be implemented. Kenyan researchers have been working with woodcarvers to record the history, economic value, and ecological impact of the trade. As a first step, the findings were communicated to woodcarving centers in a unique way, using live and videotaped dramatics enacted by woodcarving families themselves. Secondly, they identified additional tree species, including jacaranda, mango, and neem, that are both more available and suitable for carving. The People and Plants Initiative is now working on developing a certification system similar to the Forestry Stewardship Council's for Kenya's carving industry so that consumers can easily identify carvings that have been produced from environmentally friendly raw materials. This certification program will give "Good Woods" ecolabels for carvings from fast-growing, farm-produced trees. In addition, exporters and importers can contribute to tree nurseries run by woodcarvers so that sustainable, cultivated sources of a range of woodcarving species are always available.[43]

Conclusions

Although in different ways, these two African countries are moving toward adopting and implementing best practice standards and ecolabeling programs that draw on the expertise and lessons from other countries considered to have the most responsible tourism industries in the world. In many ways, the emerging certification programs in Kenya and South Africa are similar to CST in Costa Rica, NEAP in Australia, and PAN Parks and Blue Flag in Europe. They include an emphasis on performance standards; involve a range of stakeholders, with a heavy reliance on NGOs; and are heavily focused, at least initially, on evaluating nature-based tourism facilities.

Although the architects of these new African programs are not rein-venting the wheel, they are conscious that the criteria must be tailored to fit the realities of their countries. South Africa's Blue Flag program, for instance, has added criteria for beach security. More fundamentally, the emerging certification programs in Kenya and South Africa are being shaped by debates around wildlife park management and ecotourism as a development tool. They include a number of important innovations and differences in emphasis that reflect the need for African nations to initiate responsible forms of tourism that grapple with conditions of poverty and inequality deriving from a history of colonialism, racial discrimination, and underdevelopment. In South Africa, for instance, proponents of what has been dubbed "pro-poor" tourism argue that poor communities must see tangible benefits from wildlife tourism. Similarly, in Kenya, the ecotourism movement has been propelled by economic equity demands from poor, rural communities that, despite policies of indigenization and community-run conservation, have seen scant benefits from either tourism or national parks. As in Fiji (see chapter 9), issues of economic and social justice are central to discussions of both ecotourism and certification programs.

There is a strong emphasis, especially in South Africa, on building responsible practices into the investment phase of new tourism develop-ments rather than on regulating industry. Thus, there are powerful incen-tives in place for new investors to come up with policies that ensure environmental protection but also bring previously disadvantaged citizens into partnerships with them. With recent research from Britain (mentioned above) showing that there is tourist demand for responsible holidays, trade organizations such as AITO (The Association of Independent Tour Oper-ators) are telling tourists that they offer socially and environmentally responsible tours. They must find operations in South Africa and Kenya that meet these performance standards. In South Africa, new investments are not only aimed at conserving the resource base upon which tourism depends but also at restructuring the economy so that previously disad-vantaged groups are brought into the tourism industry as active partici-pants rather than menial laborers. The investment and procurement policies that apply in South Africa's spatial development initiatives provide a useful example of how the tourism economy can be restructured rather than just regulated in the interests of achieving a responsible and pro-poor set of environmental, social, and economic impacts. In striving to put these worthy principles into practice, South Africa must learn from Kenya's failed efforts at indigenization and work to avoid the pitfalls that derailed its early community conservation experiments in income redistribution.

Today, in both countries there is a far greater stress on pro-poor criteria for achieving responsibility; this differentiates these emerging certification programs from those in more developed countries, such as Australia and Europe, where establishing environmental standards have been more important than economic equity criteria. In Kenya and South Africa, as in the rest of Africa, it is clear that governments do not have the resources to provide effective national social welfare systems of the types that have been developed in Australia, Costa Rica, and Europe. In East and southern Africa, tourism is being asked to play a huge social development role normally handled by the state in more developed countries. This provides an innovative set of challenges and problems, all of which are reflected in the sustainable tourism standards that are emerging in these countries—models that hopefully contain some useful lessons for other underdeveloped countries that also find themselves asking tourism to deal with the challenges of postcolonialism, underdevelopment and free-trade led globalization.

Notes

1. G.R.M. De Beer and B. Wheeller, *Some International Perspectives on Tourism and Socio-economic Development* (Capetown: University of Capetown, 1997).
2. Martha Honey, *Ecotourism and Sustainable Development: Who Owns Paradise?* (Washington, D.C.: Island Press, 1999), 297.
3. Stanford Research International, *Benchmarking South Africa for Labor Intensive Development: International Lessons and Strategic Implications*, unpublished report for Nedlac in South Africa (1998).
4. The Cluster Consortium, *South Africa's Tourism Challenge: A Profile of the Tourism Cluster*, unpublished report for the South Africa Department of Environmental Affairs and Tourism, Pretoria (1999).
5. Government of South Africa, Department of Environmental Affairs and Tourism, *White Paper on the Development and Promotion of Tourism in South Africa* (Pretoria: DEA&T, May 1996).
6. The average shareholding across all seven concessions, either immediately or contractually within three years, was 53 percent. South African National Parks, "Information memorandum on the second round of concession opportunities: Important notice," (SANP, Pretoria, April 6, 2001); Mike Fabricius, chief executive, Western Cape Tourism Board and Paul Bannister, adviser to the Minister of Environment and Tourism, interviews with Eddie Koch, November 2000.
7. Honey, *Ecotourism and Sustainable Development*, 339–385; "The Makuleke Region of the Kruger National Park: Requirements for the submission of bids by interested parties seeking involvement in development projects," undated anonymous paper prepared for the Makuleke Communal Property Association, Kruger National Park.
8. Greg McManus, managing director, Qualitour, interview with Anna Spenceley, January 8, 2002; Ad-Uppe Public Relations, "Qualitour Launches First

Eco-Grading System," Johannesburg, September 27, 2001, posted on South Africa Direct Net News Web site: http://southafricadirect.net/organisations/m/325.html; Ad-Uppe Public Relations, "Qualitour Approved Hotels, Lodges and Resorts" posted on Qualitour Web site: http://www.qualitour.co.za/Qualitour%20Approved%20Hotels.htm.

9. Ibid.

10. Mike Fabricius interview.

11. Ibid.

12. Ibid.

13. Ibid; South African Tourism Media Releases, "Tourism Grading Council Update," Sandton, http://satour.com/media/releases/messages/58.html (March 7, 2001).

14. Mafisa Planning and Research, "National Geographic and Conservation Corporation Africa: Possibilities for branding of CCA lodges through a strategic partnership," draft interim report on twelve CCA lodges prepared for National Geographic (January 2000); Paul Bewsher, Ecotourism Afrika, interview with Eddie Koch, 2001.

15. Jennifer A. Seif, Fair Trade in Tourism, South Africa, "Facilitating Market Access for South Africa's Disadvantaged Communities through 'Fair Trade in Tourism,'" draft paper, prepared for Reispavilion travel fair, Hanover, Germany (January 2002).

16. Thomsen Bolding, "FEE(E) Goes Worldwide!" Blue Flag Newsletter, http://www.blueflag.org (July 2001).

17. White Paper on Tourism, 1996.

18. Dr. Johann Kotze, Department of Environmental Affairs and Tourism (DEA&T), South Africa, interview with Anna Spenceley, January 7, 2002.

19. Graham Gordon, ed. Tourism: Putting Ethics into Practice: A Report on the Responsible Business Practices of 65 UK-based Tour Operators (Teddington, U.K.: Tearfund, 2001).

20. H. Goodwin and A. Spenceley, Unpublished presentation, Final workshop on the draft National Responsible Tourism Guidelines, UNISA, Pretoria, South Africa, 27 November 2001; personal communication with Goodwin.

21. Harold Goodwin, International Centre for Responsible Tourism, interview with Anna Spenceley, November 2001.

22. G. R. M. De Beer and S. P. Eliffe, Tourism-led Development, Job Creation and Restructuring the Rural Economy: Lessons Learned and Applied in South Africa's Spatial Development Initiatives, Development Bank of Southern Africa, Midrand, South Africa, Special Report on SDIs (1997), p. 4; Sam Okungu, "Kenya's Strategy/Programmes for the Development and Management of Ecotourism in National Parks and Protected Areas," paper presented at the World Tourism Organization's Regional Preparatory Meeting for the International Year of Ecotourism, Maputo, Mozambique, March 5–6, 2001, http://www.world-tourism.org.

23. De Beer and Eliffe, Tourism-led Development.

24. Honey, Ecotourism and Sustainable Development, 297; Okungu, "Kenya's Strategy."

25. Perez Olindo, "The Old Man of Nature Tourism: Kenya," in *Nature Tourism: Managing for the Environment*, ed. Tensie Whelan (Washington, D.C.: Island Press, 1991), 29.
26. Honey, *Ecotourism and Sustainable Development*, 295–296.
27. Ibid., 308–321.
28. Okungu, "Kenya's Strategy."
29. Kaj Arhem, "The Maasai and the State," Document No. 52, Copenhagen: International Working Group for Indigenous Affairs, 1985, cited in K. Rao and C. Geisler, "The Social Consequences of Protected Areas Development for Resident Populations," *Society and Natural Resources*, 3, no. 1 (1990), 19–32.
30. Maasai leader Paul Ntiati, quoted in David Lovatt Smith, "Maasai Hopes and Fears," *People and the Planet*, Sustainable Tourism issue 6, no. 4 (1997).
31. Okungu, "Kenya's Strategy."
32. De Beer and Eliffe, *Tourism-led Development*.
33. John S. Akama, "Western Environmental Values and Nature-Based Tourism in Kenya," *Tourism Management*, 17, no. 8 (December 1996), 567–574.
34. Okungu, "Kenya's Strategy."
35. Honey, *Ecotourism and Sustainable Development*, 298–308.
36. D. Roe, J. Mayers, M. Grieg-Gran, A. Kothari, C. Fabricius, R. Hughes, "Evaluating Eden: Exploring the myths and realities of community based wildlife management," Series overview (London: International Institute for Environment and Development, 2000).
37. Judy Gona, Mark Hardy, and Anjali Saini, "Developing an Ecorating Scheme for Kenya: Observations, Issues and Progress," Discussion paper for workshop on "Ecorating: Progressing the Initiative," Nairobi and Mombasa, Kenya, The Ecotourism Society of Kenya, October–November 2000.
38. Ibid.
39. Ibid.
40. Ecotourism Society of Kenya, "ESOK Projects," http://www.esok.org (August 7, 2001).
41. "FSC Certification: A Tool to Make the Kenyan Woodcarving Industry Sustainable," People and Plants Online, http://www.rbgkew.org.uk/peopleplants/regions/kenya/index.html; Anthony Cunningham, "Ecological Footprint of the Wooden Rhino: Depletion of Hardwoods for the Carving Trade in Kenya," People and Plants Online, http://www.rbgkew.org.uk/peopleplants/regions/kenya/hardwood.htm.
42. Message from Robert Höft, People and Plants Initiative, UNESCO, Nairobi to Planeta.com forum on "Ecotourism Certification," http://www.planeta.com (July 2001).
43. Ibid.

Chapter 9

Planning for Ecotourism amidst Political Unrest: Fiji Navigates a Way Forward

Kelly S. Bricker

The dawn of a new millennium arrived with a new commitment to ecotourism, conservation, and sustainable development for the small country of Fiji, located in the heart of the South Pacific. Just one year earlier, in 1999, tourist arrivals to Fiji reached 409,000 visitors and foreign exchange earnings just over US$600 million, making tourism the country's most important industry (see table 9.1). In addition, the country was gaining an international image for responsible, innovative community- and conservation-sensitive ecotourism, on top of its long-standing reputation for traditional beach tourism. Supporting this image and under the guidance of the democratically elected multiracial government, the Ministry of Tourism and Transport had adopted a National Ecotourism and Village-based Policy and Strategy (NEVP). A certification program was to be initiated as part of the policy document.

To facilitate a certification program, the Fiji Ecotourism Association (FETA) was set to launch its first international conference, gaining wide support from industry, government, academicians, and nongovernmental organizations (NGOs). The conference was to focus on how to establish and administer a certification program and how to measure best practices. Experts had been invited from the U.S. and Australia to discuss these topics.

The year 2000 was anticipated to be a banner year for tourism in Fiji. However, in the midst of these efforts, the plight of coral bleaching, uncontrolled and illegal extraction of corals and timber, unusually stormy weather patterns, and other concerns over the degradation of the environment raised to a new level environmental consciousness in tourism and other sectors.[1] The first blow came in March when scientists began recording rising water temperatures and the death of corals. By late 2000,

Table 9.1. Visitor Arrivals 1999–2000 Monthly Comparison

Month	1999	2000	% Change
January	28,950	30,321	÷5%
February	25,263	30,058	÷19%
March	31,589	34,840	÷10%
April	29,082	38,069	÷31%
May	34,203	29,352	−14%
June	38,445	12,066	−69%
July	41,031	12,804	−69%
August	40,680	12,265	−70%
September	36,806	19,867	−46%
October	36,800	24,275	−34%
November	35,180	25,724	−27%
December	31,926	24,429	−24%
TOTAL	409,955	294,070	−28%

Source: Fiji Visitors Bureau, May 2001.

estimates were that coral bleaching, probably caused by global warming, had killed about half of Fiji's coral reefs.

Then on May 19, 2000, Fiji was hit by political calamity: a coup d'état that overnight placed the country on an international tourism blacklist. On that date, a group of seven gunmen, led by businessman George Speight, entered the parliamentary complex in the capital city of Suva and took over the Fiji government, holding twenty-six members of the democratically elected People's Coalition government hostage. The coup caught nearly everyone by surprise, and theories still abound as to the reasons for it and the real behind-the-scenes backers.[2] The coup caused civil unrest in Fiji and nearly halted all tourism traffic for over three months. A majority (18) of the hostages, including deposed Prime Minister Mahendra Chaudhry, were released on July 13, 2000. Several days later, Speight and other rebels were arrested.

Many in the tourism industry breathed a sign of relief, believing that this signaled an end to the political crisis. The Tourism Action Group (TAG), a committee of the Fiji Visitors' Bureau, declared "Ground Zero" to be the date they would launch an international marketing campaign to revive tourism. However, rebel takeovers of various hotels, police posts, and the Fiji water plant, together with roadblocks and other military activities, continued to disrupt the nation, and so the launch date kept being postponed. According to Berno and King, scholars on South Pacific tourism,

Despite the arrest of Speight and many of his rebel supporters on 27 July, travel advisories remained in place. Fiji remained under a state of emergency and many regions were still under curfew. Court hearings for Speight and his supporters (held in Suva) carried with them the potential for further civil unrest. The lifting of travel advisories which [the Tourism Action Group] had initially anticipated did not occur. . . . The benchmark for the launch of the recovery program was shifted to the time at which the travel advisories were downgraded. In a sense this made tourism a captive to external events and actions.[3]

Threats of civil unrest in outlying islands, including Vanua Levu and other small islands, remained. These disruptions, including, but not limited to, police post takeovers and the taking hostage of two New Zealand airline pilots, also spurred locals into action to initiate tourism awareness campaigns so as to thwart further disruptions and emphasize the importance of tourism to Fiji.

However, a year after the onslaught of events at the parliament complex, travel advisories and the impending election in August 2001 continued to have an impact on tourism. The U. S. Embassy, for example, released a public announcement[4] for April through July 2001, which stated, "While the situation in Suva and throughout Fiji is calm at this time, further violent incidents and outbreaks of civil unrest remain possible."[5]

The Canadian government also raised warnings giving the impression that there was potential for further violence,[6] as did the British High Commission. The Australian and New Zealand authorities advised travelers to Fiji to monitor developments and avoid large public gatherings. Needless to say, these advisories had an impact on Fiji's effort to promote the island nation as "the one truly relaxing tropical getaway,"[7] even though many of the reports stated that incidents were isolated to Suva and surrounding areas. However, subsequent takeover of international resorts and other disruptions gave credence to these advisories. Although the status of the advisories was eventually lessened somewhat, they were to remain in place until elections were held in August 2001.

This air of uncertainty continued to affect tourism potential well into 2001. The complex nature of the takeover and subsequent actions that followed left the nation with the enormous task of rebuilding its primary foreign exchange earner: tourism. This chapter explores the initiatives and policy directions for ecotourism that were in place prior to the coup of 2000 and subsequent actions following months of political instability.

Tourism in the Fiji Islands

Fiji is a South Pacific republic of more than 330 islands situated nearly 1,900 miles north of Sydney, Australia and just over 3,000 miles southwest of Honolulu, Hawai'i (see figure 9.1). Nearly one-third of Fiji's islands (approximately 106) are inhabited. The main island of Viti Levu, where Suva is located, encompasses the greatest amount of land (nearly 59 percent). An estimated 75 percent of Fiji's entire population of 772,655 resides on Viti Levu, according to the most recent (1996) census. Vanua Levu (north of Viti Levu) is the second largest island and home to an estimated 18 percent of Fiji's population. The rest of the population is dispersed amongst roughly 100 outer islands. Nearly 60 percent of the nation's population resides in rural areas.[8]

The tourism product in Fiji offers all of the attributes associated with tropical island destinations, the 4 S's—sun, sea, sand, and surf. In addition, Fiji has thrived on an international reputation for friendly service and hospitable locals, with emphasis placed on the Fijian smile.

As a result, the tourism industry in Fiji has grown substantially over the

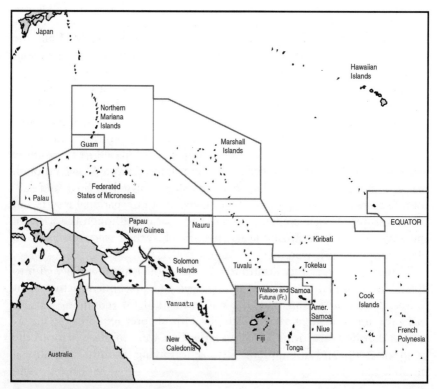

Figure 9.1. Map of the Fiji Islands

past fifty years. In 1999, tourism continued its upward swing, with nearly 410,000 overseas visitors contributing over US$600 million in foreign exchange earnings.[9] As the most important industry in Fiji, tourism is responsible, directly and indirectly, for employment of an estimated 45,000 people. For 2000, all signs had indicated that tourism was once again poised for a record year. According to the Fiji Visitors Bureau (FVB), by the end of April 2000, arrivals were up 16 percent over 1999.

Ecotourism in Fiji

Fiji is a diverse island nation with a wide variety of habitats, including lowland and mountain rainforests, coastal mangroves, inland swamps, mixed grasslands, and an abundance of river corridors that meander from mountain to sea. Fiji is also home to some of the best and most developed reef systems in the southwest Pacific region.[10] Not surprisingly, a range of nature-based activities, such as hiking, trekking, scuba diving, snorkeling, sea kayaking, whitewater rafting, kayaking, rural village stays, caving, and mountain biking—to name just a few—is available to tourists.

The Fiji Visitors Bureau compiles data on visitor arrivals, yet to date has not addressed ecotourism as a separate niche market for research purposes. Part of the difficulty is due to the fact that Fiji does not have any mechanism in place to assess whether or not a nature or culture tour is indeed an ecotourism product, (e.g., operating with key concepts of ecotourism as objectives). Although statistics on ecotourists are not available, FVB data does give some sense of visitors' interests and perceptions. From 1995 to 1998, for instance, 76–80 percent of all overseas visitors went swimming, with 59–65 percent going snorkeling[11], and the most favorable impressions recorded by visitors were of "the people," the "relaxing and peaceful" environment, and "the climate." (The importance of "scenery" has actually declined over the past four years.[12])

Not surprisingly, nature and culture are prominent in the way Fiji is marketed as a holiday destination, and for some time in the 1990s, Fiji was marketed under the banner of "the way the world should be."[13] In 1999, this slogan was replaced by a new brand campaign that labeled the Fiji Islands as "the one truly relaxing tropical getaway."[14] According to Harrison and Brandt, this campaign painted an image of "happy, smiling indigenous Fijian children portrayed against a stereotypical coral atoll."[15]

The fact that Fiji has the resources necessary for ecotourism (i.e., an abundance of natural resources and need for conservation) has been recognized for some time.[16] However, ecotourism had not been central to Fiji's tourism development effort. Nature-based activities were, according to tourism professors Harrison and Brandt, considered to be supplementary to and perhaps less marketable than the "standard tourist attractions of sun, sea and sand."[17]

By 2000, there was, however, a growing awareness of the importance and potential of ecotourism and village-based tourism in government, academic, NGO, and tourism industry circles in Fiji. By recognizing Fiji's diverse cultural and natural heritage, the FVB now acknowledges that "Fiji is distinctive from other sand, sea, and surf destinations—for where else in the South Pacific are waterfalls so prolific, rivers so extraordinary, and seas so pristine?"[18]

Previously, Fiji was simply promoting the "pacific paradise" typical of the demand by mass markets and the "preferred focus on more glamorous and profitable forms of tourism."[19] However, by the late 1990s there was a wind of change in the Fiji Islands. Growing concerns over environmental degradation have led to tourism industry-driven initiatives to promote sustainability in all sectors of development and a new kind of tourism, sensative to the environment and cultural aspects of the country. Through national forums and meetings, Fiji's tourism industry began calling for actions that promote sustainability. Thus, ecotourism has been moved from the depths of "supplemental tourism" to prominence with the FVB promoting ecotourism as an important market to international guests and striving to build true community- and conservative-sensitive ecotourism.

A Strategy for Ecotourism in Fiji: Precoup Initiatives

During the 1990s, continued tourism development and growing concerns over the increased need to import goods and services (e.g., managerial expertise, building materials) to meet the expectations of conventional tourism led to a heightened awareness in ecotourism. Another key factor was government's interest in preventing further rural-urban migration by spreading the benefits of tourism more widely across Fiji. Tourism is typically focused on the western side of the country (see figure 9.2). Thus, ecotourism would potentially maximize the benefits of tourism throughout the country and not just in specific regions.

The ecotourism product in Fiji has the potential of being quite diversified, to include, among other activities, trekking, whitewater rafting, and village visits, resulting in further benefits to rural areas, which are typically undeveloped and traditionally not exposed to the potential rewards of "4-S" tourism development. Throughout the tourism industry, there is a need to promote environmental awareness, conservation, and forms of tourism that minimize negative impacts. Thus, in 1997, the government acknowledged international travelers' interest in ecotourism by disseminat-

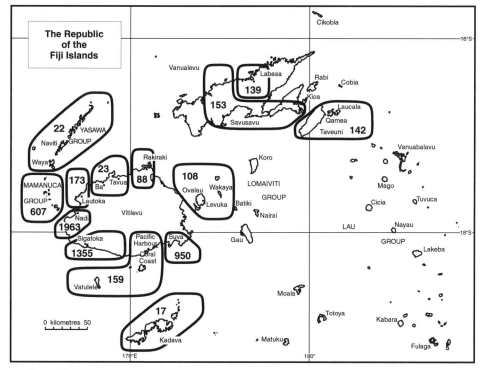

Figure 9.2. Map of Tourism Cites in Fiji

ing a draft of the National Ecotourism and Village-based Policy and Strategy (NEVP) document that effectively resulted in attention to a niche market for ecotourism in Fiji.[20]

The primary objective of the NEVP document was to ensure that sociocultural and environmental impacts were minimized and the quality of tourism products was enhanced or sustained, thereby achieving maximum benefits for rural residents of Fiji. Given that nearly 60 percent of all residents live in rural areas, this document potentially had significant consequences for rural development.

However, the fact that ecotourism was loosely defined in the policy created a lot of confusion for the industry. Prior to the formation of the NEVP, the concept of genuine ecotourism had been hurt by the distribution of lists of ecotourism activities that included virtually anything that occurred in the outdoors or in a village, irrespective of environmental and social consequences. In 1999, the Ministry of Tourism and Transport (hereafter "Ministry of Tourism" or "ministry") clarified its meaning of *ecotourism* by defining it as:

A form of nature-based tourism which involves responsible travel to relatively undeveloped areas to foster an appreciation of nature and local cultures, while conserving the physical and social environment, respecting the aspirations and traditions of those who are visited, and improving the welfare of the local people.[21]

With the principles and definition for ecotourism finally in place, the NEVP moved ecotourism forward by addressing three specific issues related to ecotourism development in Fiji. First, the NEVP recognized that policies must be built upon a genuine commitment to conservation of both the natural and cultural heritage that benefits the people of Fiji. Second, it was agreed that promotion of ecotourism is based on conservation of biodiversity, while enhancing the quality of life for local people. More specifically, different forms of tourism (e.g., ecotourism) and respect for the arts, crafts, and traditions of people in Fiji should be promoted. The government also noted that culture should be promoted congruent to the wishes and aspirations of local communities. Third, government policy for ecotourism supported clarification of land tenure to reduce conflicts and extend incentives to those tourism programs that are principally locally owned and operated and of small scale.[22]

A fourth issue of ecotourism policy addressed quality control within the industry, including the need to carefully consider new ecotourism developments, ensuring diversity in activities and destinations that are strategically located and accessible to tourists. To address these issues, the NEVP recognized the importance of: (1) developing a central register for all ecotourism endeavors, (2) moving toward a nationwide system of best practices or accreditation, and (3) rewarding (i.e., through marketing initiatives) operators who adopt true ecotourism principles.[23] The policy also recognized that implementation requires a national committee to operationalize and support policies of ecotourism and act in an advisory capacity to the Ministry of Tourism. In essence, the NEVP created a foundation from which government, nongovernmental organizations, communities, and the private sector could build a collective understanding of ecotourism.[24]

In May 1999, the Ministry of Tourism began plans to implement ecotourism as defined in the NEVP. The ministry, for example, encouraged various organizations to come together to develop initiatives that supported principles outlined in the NEVP. This was partially accomplished through the reestablishment of the Fiji Ecotourism Association and eventually the creation of a special ecotourism advisory committee to the min-

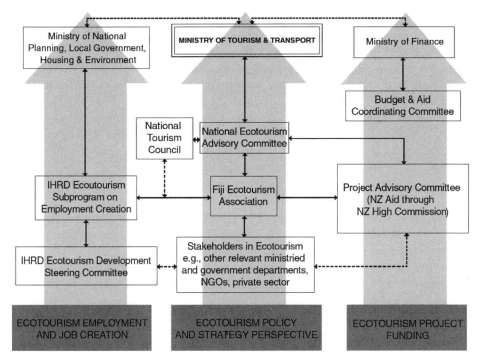

Figure 9.3. Proposed Organizational Framework for Ecotourism within the Ministry of Tourism Fiji Islands. *Source*: K. Bricker in consultation with the Ministry of Tourism and Transport, 2001.

istry. Based on the ambitious policies set forth in the NEVP, coordinating ecotourism initiatives became essential, and the Ministry of Tourism seemed to be an appropriate agency to oversee private, public, and nongovernmental activities (see figure 9.3).

Several organizations are involved in moving the NEVP forward. As indicated by the arrows in figure 9.3, government departments and NGOs, as well as the private sector, help shape and implement ecotourism's three broad areas: job creation and employment, policy and strategy development, and funding sources. With the primary marketing arm, the Fiji Visitors Bureau, under the Ministry of Tourism, government plays a critical role in creating a market for ecotourism in Fiji. However, due to the complex relationship between the private sector, nonprofit associations, and government, cooperation and partnerships amongst the various level of stakeholders is critical. The following section untangles the various government bodies, organizations, and associations that play a vital role in the implementation of principles and policies connected with the NEVP.

Government Initiatives and Ecotourism

Despite the tumultuous political upheavals in Fiji, both pre- and post-coup governments continued to support ecotourism planning efforts, including setting standards and ultimately creating a certification program. What is remarkable is the number of Fijian-driven (as opposed to externally imposed) initiatives that have continued, despite the difficulties. Key officials in the several governments recognized ecotourism as a tool for sustainable development in rural communities, and they saw ecotourism as a way to involve village landowners in the tourism industry.

In May 1999, a newly elected People's Coalition party was in place. By July, the Minister for Tourism, Adi Koila Mara-Nailatikau, addressed the first meeting of the reestablished Fiji Ecotourism Association (FETA). This was a momentous occasion, as it represented the first time outside the NEVP document that the government conveyed its commitment to developing partnerships with village, academic, environmental, and industry organizations. Specifically, the government proposed establishing an administrative framework for sustainable development and ecotourism initiatives that would include natural and cultural heritage enhancement and would develop appropriate infrastructures to facilitate remote village-based and nature-based interests.

During February 2000, parliament was asked to address the Sustainable Development Bill, legislation designed to tackle the creation of codes of environmental practice in all sectors of industry (e.g., tourism, agriculture, fisheries, forestry), as well as environmental impact assessments for new developments. This proposed bill had been inherited from the previous government.[25] When, on February 17, 2000, Parliament convened to debate the bill, Minister Mara-Nailatikau supported several of its aspects. In particular, she called for the tourism industry to adopt a Code of Practice applicable to both resort- and activity-based tourism. She stated that it was important for industry (as opposed to government) to develop a code as a way of demonstrating that it was committed to sustainable development.[26]

Based on discussions with various stakeholders, including the FETA officers, tour operators, and the Fiji Visitors Bureau, the minister publicly advocated putting in place a mechanism assessing whether nature-based tour operations in Fiji were indeed involved in genuine ecotourism. Furthermore, the minister confirmed that the success of ecotourism depended on marketing support by tour operators and airlines, the development of infrastructure to access Fiji's hinterland, and the cooperation of landowners.[27] Additionally, in correspondence with the Ministry of Tourism, FETA requested that the ministry begin to operationalize the definition established by the NEVP at a grassroots level and to support the inclusion of internationally recognized ecotourism best practices.[28]

Minister Mara-Nailatikau announced the establishment of the Fiji Ecotourism Advisory Committee and emphasized the importance of working closely with the Fiji Ecotourism Association to promote increased awareness of principles of ecotourism and development of certification programs.[29] This action gave credibility and national support to FETA and their initial efforts toward developing a certification program for ecotourism. Over the following months, these proposals received some attention through various working groups established by the Ministry of Tourism, including the rejuvenation of the National Tourism Council.

Fiji Ecotourism Advisory Committee

Based on the principles delineated by the NEVP, the Ministry of Tourism established the Fiji Ecotourism Advisory Committee (FEAC) in December 1999. FEAC consisted of members from both public and private stakeholder groups.[30] According to the minister, the primary objectives of this advisory group involved building a strategic management plan for ecotourism; coordinating agencies to ensure that infrastructure requirements were in place; and, most importantly, working with the Fiji Ecotourism Association to address issues identified by all stakeholders in ecotourism and sustainable development. More specifically, FEAC sought to achieve the following:

1) promote ecotourism as a tool for sustainable development and conservation of Fiji's natural resources and cultural heritage;
2) address the importance of considering the values of residents of villages and communities that choose to engage in ecotourism;
3) improve the quality and diversity of current tourism offerings and ensure quality in all future developments;
4) promote the importance of maintaining or enhancing the health of all natural environments at all levels and increasing awareness and appreciation of the diverse natural heritage areas in Fiji;
5) develop training and educational programs for all tour operators to meet the demands of the discerning international tourists; that is, acknowledge that tourists' desire to learn about local culture and natural environments is increasing and Fiji must meet that demand with well-trained, knowledgeable ecotourism employees; and,
6) review the National Ecotourism and Village-based Policy and Strategy (NEVP).[31]

FEAC held three meetings between December 1999 and May 2000. The focus of the meetings was on adopting the above objectives, reviewing and offering preliminary approval for proposed funding for ecotourism projects by New Zealand Overseas Development Assistance (NZODA), and overseeing the development of an ecotourism certification proposal.

To explore ecotourism certification, Tor Hundloe, professor of environmental management, University of Queensland, and chair of the Nature and Ecotourism Accreditation Program (NEAP) of Australia was invited in December 1999 by the Fiji Ecotourism Association to introduce and discuss the highlights of the Australian program with FEAC. From this presentation, FEAC reached consensus on the importance of developing criteria and standards for Fiji's nature-based activities. This represented the first official government call to proceed with building a certification program for ecotourism. It was now time to secure national support, and the timing for the concept of a national ecotourism program could not have been better.

The National Tourism Council

In February 2000, the Ministry of Tourism reconvened the National Tourism Council (NTC) to address issues affecting tourism development. As an advisory committee, the NTC consisted of representatives from government, nongovernmental organizations, and the private sector who were linked to the tourism industry. Because of the various departments and stakeholders represented, the NTC was one of the few places where issues involving all sectors of society—including environmental, law and order, and land tenure—could be addressed.

Members of the NTC took a leading role in creating the Tourism Sector Development Plan, a paper prepared for presentation at the proposed National Economic Summit, as part of the new government's efforts to create a National Development Plan, slated for June 2000. This document was to lay out five-year development plans for thirty-two different sectors.

Several issues documented in the tourism sector plan had considerable relevance to ecotourism development. Within the proposed plan, emphasis was placed on diversifying Fiji's tourism product to include sustainable ecotourism into rural areas so as to enhance the quality of life for local people, including various financial incentives and training programs for village-based projects. Importance was also placed on protecting the environment in all tourism developments and on creating a program that embraced best practices for ecotourism. The document further acknowledged ecotourism as a viable means of conservation of Fiji's natural heritage and biodiversity.

In addition to supporting key areas of the NEVP, the Tourism Sector Development Plan recognized the need for the private sector and government to work in close partnership. Although the proposal outlined strategies and initiatives important to tourism development overall, ecotourism was clearly highlighted and recognized as a means to increase the economic contribution and retention of the tourist dollar, increase the participation of rural resource landowners in tourism, and diversify the tourism product, thereby attracting more visitors.

The tourism sector plan outlined the financial and institutional resources necessary for a national ecotourism plan that moves from theory to practice. Again, infrastructure, training, and education were highlighted; however, the document also emphasized the protection of Fiji's natural and cultural heritage through nationally recognized protected areas, as well as the implementation of licensing and certification programs to ensure quality and diversity of ecotourism products. On May 18, 2000, the National Tourism Council convened to make final adjustments to the Tourism Sector Development Plan and complete the details for presentation to the prime minister. The next day, however, this process was interrupted by George Speight's coup, Fiji's third in thirteen years.

The International Labour Organization Ecotourism Sub-program

Ecotourism in Fiji has involved a number of local and international actors who don't always see eye to eye. This, coupled with political turmoil and collapse of tourism during 2000, has made ecotourism planning, including development of a certification program, difficult. One example of externally imposed involvement took place in 1997 when the International Labour Organization (ILO), the United Nations body that protects labor rights and conditions, put forth an interesting course of action for ecotourism development in Fiji. It proposed, through an initiative called the Integrated Human Resource Development Program for Employment Creation (IHRDP), the creation of 9,950 jobs through an "ecotourism sub-program" (or ESP) between 2000 and 2002.

The ESP was to be integrated with other related entities, including cooperatives and the National Center for Small Business Development, through which ecotourism operators would be able to get government financial and technical assistance to begin new projects. The ILO was to provide Fiji dollars F$357,400 (roughly US$161,000) over the three-year period. By February 2000, a sub-program manager had been hired to carry out an unrealistically ambitious agenda, which included playing a significant coordinating role in certification, inventories, and strategic planning for ecotourism.

From the outset, this ILO initiative was criticized by university experts, NGOs, and the regional tourism marketing organization, the South Pacific Tourism Organization. These critics noted that the proposal was not predicated on a clear definition of ecotourism, as it included coral and pearl farming and bamboo furniture manufacturing as proposed ecotourism activities.[32] Although coral and pearl farming present enormous potential for being ecologically destructive, bamboo furniture manufacturing could possibly be a sustainable endeavor. However, furniture making is not ecotourism, and its inclusion muddies the definition by throwing any village-based economic activities into the pot. Critics noted that this demonstrated the apparent low level of expertise used by the ILO, and many questioned the program's ability to stimulate genuine ecotourism in Fiji. Fortunately, the Fiji Ecotourism Advisory Committee was successful in removing these economic activities from under the ecotourism umbrella and used this incident to further stress Fiji's need for ecotourism standards.

The Fiji Ecotourism Association

In 1995, the first Fiji Ecotourism Association was formed, with the primary objective of bringing together all those with an interest in ecological, cultural, historical, nature-based, and adventure tourism. The association was dominated by mainstream tourism businesses and was focused on attracting ecotourists to Fiji. The initial materials sent to prospective members identified some salient ecotourism characteristics (i.e., benefits to local communities, funds poured back into conservation, environmentally responsible travel), but the association primarily focused on launching itself through the development of a series of booklets about Fiji's natural and cultural environment. Chaired by an inbound tour operator specializing in trekking expeditions, other members included representatives from Fiji Pine Ltd.; the Sheraton Hotel; several airlines, including local carriers Sunflower and Air Fiji; the Native Land and Trust Board (NLTB); and several beach resort hotels. Between its formation and 1999, only one bulletin was issued and the committee met only intermittently. As Harrison and Brandt concluded, "By the end of 1998, it had, in effect, become extinct."[33]

During spring 1999, the Ministry of Tourism called a meeting of tourism industry stakeholders and encouraged the rejuvenation of FETA. The first annual general meeting of this renewed organization was held on July 23, 1999. The revised association not only attracted members from the tourism industry but also included experts from the university, government, and NGOs, as well as private individuals. After the initial annual general meeting, FETA established three regional membership groups: the Coral Coast, western division, and eastern division. The Coral Coast group, located between Nadi in the west and the capital city of Suva, that is, the heart of tourism on Viti Levu, showed little continuing interest, but the other two groups met monthly until May 2000.

The expanded and revitalized membership noted several challenges. These included increasing environmental degradation and competing extractive uses, a lack of knowledge about ecotourism's underlying principles, a need for government and business to develop an operational understanding of genuine ecotourism products, and a severe lack of infrastructure in the hinterland that blocked opportunities for rural ecotourism projects. To address some of these issues, the reconstituted FETA convened, during its first year, two workshops to clarify the particular attributes of ecotourism and how it differed from mainstream tourism offerings. During these workshops, FETA concluded that there was need for a united front in formulating standards for ecotourism operations. During late 1999 and early 2000, a Code of Practice was developed (see box 9.1), which FETA viewed as a preliminary step toward building an ecotourism certification

---

Box 9.1. Fiji Ecotourism Code of Practice

This Code of Practice was adopted by the FETA membership at the annual general meeting, August, 2000.

As a member of FETA, I will do my best to:
 1) Strengthen the conservation effort for, and enhance the natural integrity of, the places visited;
 2) Respect the sensitivities of other cultures;
 3) Practice and promote the efficient use of natural resources (e.g., water and energy);
 4) Discourage importation of harmful/hazardous materials/chemicals and ensure waste disposal (human, organic, inorganic, etc.) has minimal environmental and aesthetic impacts and is properly managed and contained;
 5) Discourage importation of goods packaged in non-recyclable or harmful materials and develop, support, and promote recycling programs;
 6) Support businesses (i.e., hotels, carriers) that believe in and practice conservation of natural and cultural resources;
 7) Keep abreast of current political and environmental issues, particularly of the local area;
 8) Network with other stakeholders (particularly those in the local area) to keep each other informed of developments and to encourage the use of this Code of Practice;

(continues)

Box 9.1. Continued

9) Raise environmental and socio-cultural awareness through the distribution of educational materials and guidelines to consumers and educational institutions;

10) Support ecotourism education/training for tour operations (marine and land-based), accommodations, government, and other tourism industry affiliates;

11) Employ staff knowledgeable and respectful of local cultures and environments;

12) Give clients appropriate verbal and written educational material, interpretation, and guidance with respect to the natural and cultural history of the areas visited;

13) Use locally produced goods that benefit the local community and economy; support sustainable agricultural and fishing practices;

14) Not to buy goods made from threatened or endangered species;

15) Avoid intentionally disturbing or encouraging the disturbance of wildlife or wildlife habitats;

16) Keep vehicles to designated roads and trails;

17) Encourage the development and implementation of the rules and regulations applying to natural areas;

18) Commit to the principles of "best practice" in all tourism activities and programs;

19) Comply with internationally recognized safety standards for all industry activities;

20) Ensure truth in advertising, and,

21) Maximize the quality of experience for hosts and guests with respect to practices outlined in the Fiji Ecotourism Association Code of Practice.

Source: FETA, adapted and revised from the Ecotourism Association of Australia.

program. FETA began working on a national conference to help develop a certification program.

FETA members also felt that it was important to have a voice in government to lobby on behalf of ecotourism operators because the Fiji Hotel Association, the primary lobby for the industry, did not necessarily address the needs of ecotourism development. This objective ultimately led to FETA's involvement in the creation of the ecotourism sector plan for the National Development Plan, originally slated for presentation to parliament in June 2000.

In addition, FETA members stated that they were having difficultly finding information on ecotourism, defining the components of genuine ecotourism, and developing sound ecotourism businesses and products.

Therefore, another FETA objective was to develop a database and library of information for its members, the government, and local NGOs. FETA identified and promoted ecotourism as being nature-based and including the following four principles:

1) providing tourist education/interpretation;
2) being ecologically sustainable and culturally sensitive;
3) bringing benefits to host/local communities; and,
4) promoting conservation of the areas visited.

FETA believed an important step in developing a certification program was that all stakeholders adopt the same principles and understanding of ecotourism. Therefore, to assess the existing state of Fiji tourism businesses that identified themselves as involved in ecotourism, Bricker and Millington inventoried nature- and cultural-based one-day (as opposed to multi-day) tour operations throughout the islands. The primary purpose of this 1999 study was to understand what types of environmental and cultural interpretation and guide training programs were currently underway and to review the standards that existed for ecotourism products in Fiji. Based on forty-three nature- and/or culturally-based tour programs in Fiji, the following findings were deemed pertinent to ecotourism development:

• Visitor reactions to the tours were generally positive (90 percent).
• Most tour operators (87 percent) did not advise their visitors about environmental protocol before departure.
• The majority of tours (80 percent) did not follow an interpretive theme or structure or feature an environmental or cultural message within their program.
• Most tours (almost 95 percent) did not encourage proper disposal of rubbish; only 18 percent helped minimize visitor impacts on the environment through briefings, corrective actions, or literature.
• About half (55 percent) employed local staff in management positions; however, for half of tour operations nearly 90 percent of their employees were from the local area.
• Over half of all programs reported not having guide training programs, and nearly 90 percent of the guides interviewed felt that there was a need for more training.
• Over half of the tour operations are not involved in any type of conservation effort in Fiji.
• All of the tour operation managers surveyed expressed interest in participating in an ecotourism certification program.[34]

Inspired by the Bricker and Millington report, the preferences identified by FETA members, and the guidelines set forth by the NEVP, the eastern division of FETA in Suva, whose members are mainly from NGOs and the university, developed a program for a national conference to be held in spring 2000. The conference was intended to fulfill the following objectives:

- position FETA as a relevant stakeholder of the tourism industry in Fiji;
- heighten the awareness of ecotourism as an important tourism market niche;
- highlight what is occurring in other parts of the world in ecotourism and create a sense of urgency about ecotourism in Fiji;
- establish an ecotourism action group in the South Pacific;
- engage industry leaders in the South Pacific in discussions about appropriate certification development; and,
- demonstrate the relevance of ecotourism and principles of sustainability to the industry at large.

With conference objectives in place, FETA began work to increase its membership and financial base to establish a secretariat and permanent office. By May 18, 2000, FETA had sixty-five members and had established a special Vanua Sponsorship to raise additional funds. Four of the leading luxury resorts—Turtle Island, Vatulele, Tokoriki, and the Jean-Michael Cousteau Fiji Islands Resort—became Vanua sponsors, enabling the first ecotourism office to be set up. NZODA provided additional funds to support FETA's educational workshops and the national conference.

Hoping to learn more about certification, FETA consulted officials from the Nature and Ecotourism Accreditation Program (NEAP) of Australia with the aim of building upon lessons learned in the development of that program. In January 2000, after a series of meetings with NEAP's founding chair Hundloe, FEAC and FETA agreed to set Fiji on a course toward certification for ecotourism. FETA's work with Australia to develop a model for Fiji was to be presented for discussion at the conference in May 2000.

Developments throughout 1999–2000 certainly inspired a lot of momentum for ecotourism and specifically an ecotourism certification program. Between the government's establishment of the NEVP, debate over the proposed sustainable development bill, and the tourism industry's creation of the Tourism Sector Development Plan, FETA was all set for its international conference slated for June 2000. A proposal for government funding to develop the Fiji ecotourism certification program was completed; however, due to the political uprising on May 19, no funds were secured, and FETA was forced to postpone the conference, as well as plans for a certification program.

The New Zealand Overseas Development Assistance (NZODA)

New Zealand has long supported the development of ecotourism in Fiji as a tool to assist in the protection of cultural and natural heritage by providing an alternative to exploitative nonsustainable land uses. In addition to its support for FETA and the Ministry of Tourism, NZODA aided two rurally based ecotourism programs during 1999 and 2000. In Koroyanitu National Heritage Park, field guides and handbooks were completed for trek leaders, the Mt. Batilamu trek was launched, visitor facilities were upgraded, and training was provided for guides and bookkeeping. Additionally, Koroyanitu held a successful Open Day on April 12, 2000, to introduce its programs and facilities to the tourism industry.[35]

In Bouma National Heritage Park on the island of Taveuni, NZODA sponsored ongoing training, along with tourism awareness workshops in five villages. NZODA also assisted in the launch of a dedicated tourist transportation service and a marine park tour, as well as with key interpretive elements of the park's programming, including field handbooks for guides and interpretive signage.[36] NZODA's two-year grant of F$617,093 (US$300,000) for its ecotourism program in Fiji ended on June 30, 2000, just after the hostage taking. Although its funding was halved after the coup, NZODA's work over the previous two years provided a solid foundation for the recovery and development of ecotourism once Fiji regained stability.

Ecotourism and the Coup Aftermath

Following the May 19, 2000, coup and hostage taking, an interim government was put in place, replacing the ministers of the People's Coalition government, including the Minister of Tourism. From the outset, the Fiji Visitors Bureau worked with the tourism industry to develop a recovery plan, including a special unit, the Tourism Action Group (TAG). The TAG called for a "coordinated and collective approach" to the recovery process, via "one voice, one message."[37] But the real challenge was to ascertain when to actually begin a recovery process. According to Berno and King:

> In 2000, the timing of the implementation of the full recovery plan became a major preoccupation. Marketing could not bring about recovery in the tourism industry until the political situation was stable enough to warrant the lifting (or at least the downgrading) of the travel advisories issued by foreign governments. This scenario was unlikely until two key events occurred: (1) the release of the hostages and (2) the return of illegally held arms to the Army. Some foreign governments

warned that any pre-emptive launch of a full recovery campaign before the lifting of the relevant travel advisories would
force them to react, and actively discourage their citizens traveling to Fiji.[38]

On July 27, 2000, the day after coup leader George Speight was arrested,
four men armed with submachine guns ordered two Air Fiji pilots—New
Zealand nationals—out of their aircraft at Savusavu Airport on the island of
Vanua Levu. This was the first time foreigners had been taken hostage, and
it immediately reescalated tensions throughout Fiji. The gang of four held
the pilots overnight in a village while the Tui Wailevu (paramount chief of
the province) and the Savusavu Tourism Association made contact and
began playing a pivotal role in the negotiations. After two days and following a traditional kava ceremony, the pilots were released unharmed without
any demands being made by the hostage takers.

Despite this setback, the efforts of TAG certainly helped the recovery
process in Fiji. As Berno and King summarized,

> The [TAG] campaign achieved some success. Visitor arrivals for
> September and October exceeded the post coup forecasts,
> showing a slow, but steady recovery, particularly in the New
> Zealand market. Australian numbers also increased marginally,
> but the Sydney Olympics, staged in September, had a diver-
> sionary effect on potential travel to Fiji.[39]

Overall, TAG played a significant role in convincing governments to
downgrade travel advisories, in working with the media, and in promoting
a single product branding campaign. "The strategy has ultimately been successful in attracting visitors back to Fiji," concluded Berno and King.[40]

Unfortunately, in many rural communities, the coup had a deeper
impact on local sentiment. Curly Carswell, president of the Savusavu
Tourism Association and longtime resident of the island, realized that as a
result of the takeovers and unruly hostage seizures, there was growing popular resentment toward tourism development. This was fueled by layoffs in
the tourism sector, an insecure and fragile peace, and heightened suspicion
toward villagers who were suspected of sympathizing with the coup plot-
ters. In the heat of the unrest, in July 2000, the Tui Wailevu suggested that
representatives of the Savusavu Tourism Association visit villages in the
province to discuss the importance of tourism to the economy of Fiji as a
whole and Vanua Levu in particular.

Carswell, who was the principle organizer, explained that "the challenges were daunting. This meant visiting forty-five villages—a population
of nearly 6,000—and traveling over a huge area of Vanua Levu. Who would

present and what would be the content?" [41] Yet a number of individuals and organizations responded and contributed sufficient funds. University experts created a training guide of topics to be discussed in village meetings, including the reasons tourists travel to Fiji, the makeup of the tourism industry, the economic importance of tourism, and what tourism needs to be sustainable, i.e., a healthy environment and political stability.[42]

In the villages, members of the presenter team initially found indifference and suspicion, and occasionally, hostility.[43] However, the final outcome was quite positive. In their written evaluations of the workshops, villagers stated that they appreciated that they were being informed (in Fijian vernacular) of tourism's critical role in the economy and its indirect and direct benefits to their villages.[44] The program evaluation indicated that the workshops had fostered a new understanding of the role of tourism, along with a deeper understanding of what villagers need to do to host tourists on their island.

Overall, the workshops were remarkably successful in reaching over 3,000 people living in the villages of the Savusavu region and, most importantly, over 75 percent of all village households in the area. As president of the Savusavu Tourism Association (STA), Carswell pledged that "ongoing contact between the chiefs (leaders of land-owning groups), Tikina Councils (provincial division leaders), and the STA will continue."[45]

This Village Tourism Awareness Workshop Project on Vanua Levu is viewed as an important model for how to build support in rural areas for community and environmentally sensitive forms of tourism. Open discussions with Fijian villagers—the tourism resource owners—were long overdue and served to air issues that have been quite contentious in the country's tourism history. The Fiji Visitors Bureau, Ministry of Tourism, and authors of the teaching materials have pledged to assist in carrying out similar workshops on other islands; this is critical to the foundations of ecotourism certification efforts, which must ultimately be built upon community understanding, cooperation, peace, and stability. Work is moving forward to address not only access and infrastructure, but perhaps more importantly, conservation policies to protect natural resources and provide funding and education programs to enable rural communities to develop quality ecotourism endeavors.

Government Support for Ecotourism Remained Steady

During FETA's annual general meeting in August 2000, the newly appointed interim Minister of Tourism, Jone Koroitmana, again reiterated the government's support for ecotourism development. In his opening address, the minister announced that the marketing budget had been increased by F$4 million (US$2.5 million) for 2000, with ecotourism and implementation of the NEVP being an important new area for development. Enthusiasm for ecotourism was high, and indigenous landowners were encouraged to take an active role in tourism development. Remarkably, despite the political turmoil, the virtual collapse of tourism, and the refusal of other nations to recognize Fiji's interim government, behind the scenes, support for ecotourism continued.

Then, in December 2000, the Ministry of Tourism, the Ministry of Fijian Affairs, the Fiji Visitors Bureau, and the tourism industry initiated a meeting for tourism resource owners. Surprisingly, given the tourism industry's large dependence on lease agreements,[46] it was the first of its kind in Fiji. This gathering passed more than thirty resolutions, including a request that government support ecotourism development. Programs proposed included requests for training of indigenous landowners in cultural and natural heritage conservation, the creation of infrastructure in those rural areas most suitable for ecotourism, and promotion of "sustainability measures" (i.e., monitoring environmental concerns with regard to land, fishing grounds, and culture) for all tourism developments. Once again, it was proposed that the Fiji Visitors Bureau aggressively market ecotourism. In April 2001, Tourism Resource Owners held a second meeting to discuss implementation of these resolutions and to identify funding sources for two upcoming conferences. Consensus was reached regarding the need for government to place greater emphasis on tourism education for rural communities and environmental and cultural heritage conservation. Participants further discussed the need for education to comply with quality standards (e.g., best practices) and for training to be conducted by recognized bodies, such as the Fiji National Training Council, universities, and government training centers.

By May 2001, the Ministry of Tourism leadership had changed for the third time in twelve months. However, once again the new minister, Konisi Yabaki, supported the concept of ecotourism development and rekindled the Fiji Ecotourism Advisory Committee (FEAC), which had been dormant since the coup. The primary aims of this FEAC meeting were to: (1) evaluate the status of programs initiated one year earlier, (2) seek support for the ecotourism certification program, (3) announce a plan for sustainable tourism, and (4) state the ministry's commitment to supporting a regional meeting in 2002 as part of the International Year of Ecotourism. Despite continued uncertainty as to the leadership of the ministry in the coming year, senior tourism officers had begun moving forward (slowly) with these efforts to reestablish the FEAC and push for cabinet support for both ecotourism certification and a sustainable tourism development plan.

FETA Holds On or Barely Survives?

During the months following the May 19 coup, FETA was relatively dormant, with the exception of the executive committee. Many small businesses were quiet due to the lack of tourism and most went into survival mode. Membership renewals came to a halt, dropping 50 percent from the previous year. Despite the downturn in tourism, enthusiasm remained high for the national ecotourism conference, and it went forward as planned in December 2000, amidst continued political uncertainty.

The ecotourism conference, held at the Tanoa International Hotel in Nadi, was the first of its kind in Fiji. It hosted 100 participants from Fiji, other island states, Australia, North America, and New Zealand. There was broad representation of Fijian landowners, village-based projects, individual entrepreneurs, members of the tourism industry, and the government—which led to a range of discussions regarding ecotourism development and certification.

Representatives from the health, environment, and culture ministries noted the importance of both people-centered and conservation-centered developments for the future of Fiji. All reiterated that the model of development must address the needs of the people, social equity, and the provision of authentic depiction of Fijian culture. Additionally, Henry Sanday, representing the regional perspective of the Pacific Islands Forum Secretariat, emphasized the importance of government's role as a catalyst for sustainable tourism and maintaining the region's unique cultural and natural environment.[47]

Unfortunately, the entire conference seemed to be veiled by an underlying concern regarding political stability. Even though political stability is crucial to the growth of sound ecotourism, Fiji's ongoing political crisis was not openly discussed. Perhaps participants were wary and worn out after six months of turmoil, or perhaps they simply needed to look to the future for something positive on the horizon, ignoring the realities of an uncertain political foundation.

From the beginning, members of FETA's executive committee held that all enterprises that claimed to be involved in ecotourism needed to embrace the primary principles of ecotourism. This belief began to evolve into the concept of developing a certification program to set best practice standards for ecotourism endeavors in Fiji.

Following the conference, FETA formed a special task force, consisting of FETA executive board members; representatives from the Ministry of Women and Culture, the Ministry of Tourism and the Fiji Visitors Bureau; and a marine-based environmental educator, to review the Australian NEAP criteria and draft a program for Fiji. This program was modeled

after NEAP, however each criterion was carefully scrutinized for application to the local Fijian context. Several meetings were held to discuss
whether the smallest type of ecotourism operation, often found at the village level, could support the guidelines proposed for certification. Some of
the criteria were eliminated, and most were redrafted to address needs at
the village community level. Because Fiji lacked a solid set of health and
safety laws/guidelines found within Australia and other more developed
countries, the task force addressed this area in detail. A draft proposal was
completed and presented to the public at FETA's annual general meeting
in May 2001. The Ministry of Tourism presented the program to the cabinet for support to further develop and implement the program through
FETA and the tourism industry. Additionally, FETA redrafted a proposal
for funding and in June 2001 presented it to various ministries and funding organizations for support. The FVB has backed the certification
concept and is prepared to work with FETA on promoting the program
internationally. Simultaneously, FETA has been slowly regaining its support
from the tourism industry at large. All of the four original Vanua sponsors
for 2000 again pledged their support for 2001.

Finally, as another step in developing a certification program for ecotourism, FETA helped to organize a regional conference during the
United Nations' Year of Ecotourism in 2002. In this effort, the South
Pacific Tourism Organization, the region's marketing arm, worked with
FETA to establish a regional approach to best practices in ecotourism and
also worked with the World Tourism Organization in organizing the conference, which took place in mid-April 2002.

With continuing support of government and rural land resource owners for ecotourism, FETA will play a critical role in both implementing
standards for ecotourism development on a national scale. However,
although the future holds promise, FETA is highly dependent on membership fees for financial support and any downturn in the stability of the
country does impact both FETA's and the government's ability to reach
rural communities and small operators in remote locations. Additionally,
FETA will need to find ways to finance certification programs that are
affordable to village-based programs and will need to build its membership
in these locations.

Continued International Support for Village-based Ecotourism

Like FETA, rural ecotourism projects have been struggling to survive the
islands' political and economic instabilities. The political turmoil that significantly hurt parts of NZODA's rural ecotourism program, and New
Zealand's contributions decreased by half in the year after the coup.

Because the collapse in tourist numbers made certain activities impractical to run, some funds were redirected to humanitarian and human rights projects. In addition, New Zealand reduced its overall aid in order to protest the coup against a democratically elected government. As tourist numbers started to recover after December 2000, NZODA work focused on finishing off its partially completed ecotourism activities, and assessing its future commitments.

After the coup, the ILO project continued to receive support, but its level was significantly reduced. Due to the enormous decrease in visitor arrivals from the coup, the reformulated goal for creating new products and employment opportunities was radically decreased. The ILO set a new, perhaps more realistic, goal of creating sixty jobs per year via two pilot projects.

These pilot projects opened in November 2000, despite the political crisis. The Nasesenibua ecotourism project includes horseback riding, a visit to a waterfall, trekking, a billi billi ride (indigenous bamboo raft), and a base camp. The approximate number of employees is forty. Second, the Wailotua Caves project has employed twenty villagers, with hopes of expanding into other services, such as trekking. According to the sub-program manager in ecotourism, Viliame Koyamaibole, two additional programs were slated to open in early 2001, creating an additional sixty jobs for indigenous Fijians. However, a review first had to be conducted of twenty-three possible ecotourism projects. As of mid-2001, it remained unclear whether or not the Fiji government was going through with its commitment to implement the full ILO program.

Although there is clearly a commitment to building local employment, there is still confusion as to what constitutes ecotourism in Fiji. Of the two dozen projects briefly outlined in the Ministry of Tourism's Ecotourism Project Inventory-2000, one project is a youth musical group, and others range from financing budget accommodations to water sports activities, without clear criteria for how these actually fit under the auspices of ecotourism. The majority of projects have at least a partial focus on the natural environment; however, there are no guidelines that outline criteria for each of these endeavors. These particular issues have been stalled due to the political instability and lack of consistency in leadership within the ministry. For eight months, between May and December 2000, the Ministry of Tourism has been led by three different ministers. Government officials complained that the Tourism Ministry remained fragmented, with departments working in isolation from on another.

By mid-2002, the ILO objectives as originally constructed were far from being implemented by the Integrated Human Resource Development Program for Employment Creation (IHRDP) through the ecotourism sub-program (ESP). If the ESP has any hope of achieving its objectives, financial support will be crucial. Coordinating efforts should include FETA, so that all bodies are working to establish genuine ecotourism in Fiji. As mentioned previously, ecotourism has become the catchall phrase to include anything village-based (including homestays and budget accommodations)—potentially continuing to "muddle" current efforts.[48]

The efforts of the ESP must also reflect legitimate ecotourism development, focused on nature-based products and fitting within the principles and definition developed by the NEVP. From the current list of sponsored and potential products, the concept of genuine ecotourism is stretched beyond recognizable boundaries (e.g., musical groups, budget accommodations, and water sports). This troubled ESP project is a further illustration why not only a concrete definition but also a sound certification system promoting best practices is needed.

A Way Forward

Despite all the troubles, Fiji has tried to forge ahead with promoting sound ecotourism as the best path for sustainable rural development. Notwithstanding considerable efforts to develop local expertise in ecotourism and to incorporate international expertise such as NEAP into locally created programs, some Fiji government officials continue to be susceptible to outside proposals, such as the ILO program. These programs have seemed especially enticing when they appear to hold out the possibility of outside funding or quick returns. Good ecotourism plans are underway locally, and outside advisors who lack strong connections with these local efforts can be both out of touch and costly. Yet both NZODA and NEAP have certainly developed sensitivities to the local situation, with solid local contacts. They have worked with existing organizations to further empower local expertise and adapt programs sensitive to the cultural and social realities in Fiji.

The Fiji Visitor's Bureau plans to support the creation of an ecotourism certification program for 2002. According to FETA's president and FVB staff member, Severo Tagicakiverata, prior to the coup there was a lack of understanding of the principles of ecotourism within the FVB. Tagicakiverata explains that ironically "the coup acted as a catalyst for ecotourism, specifically to the development and implementation of its policy by government. The expiring leases to farmers, the breakdown in talks over [logging issues], and the return of the land to the traditional owners were just some of the reasons for indigenous resource owners to seek attractive alternatives."[49]

A significant event sponsored by the FVB was the Fiji Tourism Forum held, like the FETA conference discussed earlier, in December 2000. The forum established an environment subcommittee to respond to three of the forum's resolutions on the status of Fiji's natural environment and existing trends in development. The tourism industry representatives concluded that all development proposals involving the exploitation or extraction of natural resources need to be discussed in open forums with representation by all stakeholders, with the outcomes, recommendations, and results of required environment impact assessment (EIA) made public. Presently, law for tourism development projects does not require EIAs. As a result, the industry forum also resolved that Fiji make healthy ecosystems a national priority through:

1) the development of environmental protection laws and policies;
2) environmental education for all stakeholders, with special emphasis in Fiji's schools; and,
3) financial and professional resources for items (1) and (2) above.

What began as a program to pull together stakeholders in a public forum to bring about awareness of environmentally degrading activities (e.g., copper mining) has actually evolved into something much larger. The original intent of the program was transformed to create awareness of the complementary role that tourism and the environment play in sustainable development.[50]

Under this expanded vision, the government's first Tourism and Environment Awareness program covered villages and schools along one of the primary tourist destinations in Fiji, the Coral Coast of Viti Levu. A total of fourteen villages (3,170 participants) and eleven schools (627 faculty and students) were visited. This area was chosen due to its proximity to Suva (economical for staff) and the area's involvement in tourism. According to tourism researchers Batibasaga and Rabici, the content of the program covered social, economic, and environmental issues identified by various stakeholders as negatively impacting tourism.[51] Examples of locally land-based (i.e., logging, agriculture, and improper waste disposal) and marine (i.e., coral harvesting and fishing) activities were addressed. Topics included the direct and indirect impacts of tourism (social, cultural, economic, environmental); law and order issues, including land/fisheries disputes, road blocks, theft, and sexual harassment; coral extraction and unsustainable fishing practices; deforestation, impacts on the watershed and the marine environment, pollution, and other land-based activities that affect tourism and the environment; conservation and beautification issues; and the development of community-based ecotourism to complement mainstream tourism.

The program was well received; community leaders stated that it allowed the village communities to better understand the linkages between tourism and the environment.[52] Additionally, schoolteachers felt that the program was long overdue and should be incorporated into all school curricula in Fiji. According to Batibasaga and Rabici, the Tourism and Environment Awareness program is critical to the tourism industry because it assists in bringing awareness to resource owners of the importance and responsibility of maintaining a pristine environment in order to achieve a sustainable tourism industry.[53]

Overall, the Fiji Visitors Bureau has evolved from a traditional body, promoting a stereotyped image of Fiji, into a proactive organization, demonstrating its ability to influence key stakeholders in understanding the importance of sustaining tourism through the protection of Fiji's natural and cultural resources. However, to continue this commitment, substantial funds must be allocated to campaigns such as this and other ongoing awareness programs aimed at solidifying the linkage between tourism and a healthy environment.

The political crisis of 2000 devastated Fiji's booming tourism industry. Through this tumultuous period, however, ecotourism was recognized as a realistic strategy for developing rural areas and offering new opportunities to rural land resource owners, who have been sidelined by the mainstream tourism industry. Almost miraculously, planning and projects continued to move forward on a number of fronts, including around the need for creating a certification program. The development of the National Ecotourism and Village-based Policy and Strategy provided a platform for country-wide recognition of a sector of tourism typically thought of as secondary to mainstream tourism development in Fiji. The NEVP provided the government with a document from which to further ecotourism implementation. However, political instability took a toll on the implementation process. The Fiji Ecotourism Advisory Committee did not meet again until May 2001, in part because of a lack of consistent leadership within the Ministry of Tourism. Additionally, by mid-2001, the ILO/Ministry of Tourism ecotourism sub-program had not fulfilled its initial aims or made any significant movement toward coordinating its efforts with FETA or the Ecotourism Advisory Committee.

These industry, government, and NGO stakeholders are vital to ensuring national recognition for ecotourism. Yet, on their own, they are not enough to successfully move ecotourism forward in Fiji. From a grassroots level, land resource owners and ecotourism operators must take an active role in establishing guidelines and standards for quality ecotourism delivery. The political crisis has had the greatest impact in this area. Without an integrated plan to promote environmental conservation and halt some degrading and unsustainable economic activities, Fiji's ability to create a culture of ecotourism as exists in some other parts of the world (e.g., Costa Rica, Belize, Australia, and New Zealand) is certainly thwarted. As recognized by the Tourism Resource Owners Forum, ecotourism must be supported through education and training, access and infrastructure, and standards recognized by the international tourism community. Perhaps most importantly, to sustain ecotourism, natural resources must be protected. Fortunately, several grassroots initiatives have highlighted the importance of ecotourism in Fiji and sustained a level of awareness during tumultuous times.

The success, for instance, of the Tourism and Environment Awareness program in Savusavu prompted the Tourism Resource Owners Forum to push for the program's implementation nationwide. This forum has also pushed for principles of environmental conservation and tourism, the certification initiatives of FETA, and internationally accepted principles for ecotourism operations. These efforts, coupled with the government's acknowledgment of the important role of ecotourism, are hopeful signs that ecotourism will move into a prominent place in the future. Campaign speeches in the runup to the August 2001 election included a strong voice for poverty alleviation and sustainable development, so momentum on the ecotourism front looks promising.

Certainly, the changing leadership within the Ministry of Tourism affected the implementation of the NEVP. However, some consistency remains. In July 2001, the Ministry of National Planning stated that the efforts made on the initial May 2000 draft document for the National Development Plan were going forward. The fact that the Strategic Development Plan, which was presented to the newly elected government in September 2001, remains unscathed by the political uncertainty offers reassurance that ecotourism will be an integral component of Fiji's tourism effort. After the elections in September 2001, the Tourism Sector Development Plan, which includes ecotourism, was to be presented in its original draft form as a strategic development document for the next five years. The Fiji Visitors Bureau, urged by the Tourism Resource Owners Forum and FETA, clearly stated their support for the FETA certification initiatives and the International Year of Ecotourism in 2002.

With so many initiatives moving forward, one would certainly question whether or not the coup had any lasting effect at all on the development of sound ecotourism. Yet, for obvious reasons, due to the decline of tourist arrivals, ecotourism operators have been hit severely since May 2000. Some have given up all together; others are looking for ways to hold on until tourism numbers come back up to where they were prior to May 19, 2000. From the outset of the coup through August 2000, losses in tourism revenues reached an estimated F$84.6 million dollars (approximately US$44 million), excluding the losses incurred by the national carrier Air Pacific. Tourist arrivals declined almost 70 percent during these months, and the hotel sector alone experienced a 44 percent reduction in employment. Several major tourism businesses, including for example, Shotover Jet and the Sheraton Royal, were closed as a result of low numbers.[54]

Navigating a way forward for Fiji ecotourism really means first finding a way toward political stability and reconciliation within the country and then regaining the confidence of international tourists. Although the coup and subsequent activities had an enormous impact on visitor arrivals, they also forced several social and political issues to the forefront. Increased indigenous participation in tourism has helped bring further prominence to the role of ecotourism in the country. Therefore, despite numerous setbacks in visitor arrivals, aid programs, and government actions with regard to sustainable development legislation and national development plans, ecotourism has continued to gain momentum in Fiji. As for the development of a certification program that promotes ecotourism best practices, it still awaits full implementation. This can only happen effectively once political stability is completely restored and Fiji regains its international image as a peaceful South Pacific paradise, and perhaps something much more.

Notes

1. M. Bale "Hundreds of forests destroyed daily," *Fiji Sun* (February 2, 2000); S. Kissun, "Concern on reefs," *Fiji Times* (December 11, 1999), p. 4.
2. Some say it was caused by racial conflict, disgruntlement with government leadership, and efforts to secure rights of indigenous Fijians; others charge that the coup was the result of an illegal business deal. Teaiwa analyzed the issues behind Fiji's political conflict by summarizing:

   " . . . the real struggle is among indigenous Fijians, and it is continually masked by the rhetoric of racial conflict between indigenous Fijians and Indo-Fijians. The impoverishment and dissatisfaction of indigenous Fijians is not a result of 12 months of leadership by an Indo-Fijian. It is the result of thirty fraught years of modern indigenous Fijian leadership that have sacrificed the economic and cultural well-being of a people for the advancement of a few." T. Teaiwa, "Fijian Nationalism—Is There Such a Thing?" *Wansolwara* (June 2000), p. 13.
3. T. Berno and B. King, "Tourism in Fiji after the Coups," *Travel & Tourism Analyst*, 2 (2000), 86–92. "Ground Zero" was eventually set to be when the international community (e.g., Australia, New Zealand, and the United States) downgraded their travel advisories.

4. The U.S. State Department uses public announcements as a means to disseminate information about terrorist threats and other relatively short-term and/or transnational conditions posing significant risks to the security of American travelers. They are made any time there is a perceived threat and usually have Americans as a particular target group. Public announcements have been issued to deal with short-term coups, bomb threats to airlines, violence by terrorists, and anniversary dates of specific terrorist events.
5. U. S. State Department, "Travel Warnings and Consular Information Sheets," http://travel.state.gov/travel_warnings.html (April 09, 2001).
6. Canadian Department of Foreign Affairs and International Trade, "Travel Information and Advisory Reports," http://voyage.dfait-aeci.gc.ca/destinations/menue.htm (August 16, 2001).
7. Brand campaign slogan established at the 1998 Tourism Forum by the Fiji Visitors' Bureau, "In-house Statistics" (Suva: Fiji Visitors' Bureau, 1999).
8. Ministry of Information, "Fiji Today 2000" (Suva: Ministry of Information, 2000).
9. Fiji Visitors' Bureau, "In-house Statistics," 2000.
10. V. Vuki, M. Naqasima, and R. Vave, "Status of Fiji's Coral Reefs," Global Coral Reef Monitoring Network, South West Pacific Node, University of the South Pacific, Suva, Fiji. http://www.usp.ac.fj/marine/gcrmn/status/fijiab.htm (June, 2001).
11. Fiji Visitors' Bureau, "International Visitor Survey" (Suva: Fiji Visitors' Bureau, 1998), p. 57.
12. Ibid., p. 69.
13. D. Harrison, "The World Comes to Fiji: Who Communicates What, and to Whom?" *Tourism, Culture and Communication*, 1, no. 2 (1999), 129–138.
14. Fiji Visitors' Bureau, "International Visitor Survey."
15. D. Harrison and J. Brandt, "Ecotourism in Fiji: Making Sense of the Muddle," in *Tourism and Sustainability in the South Pacific*, ed. D. Harrison (Cognizant: New York, 2001).
16. Harris, Kerr, Foster and Company, *Report on a Study of the Travel and Tourist Industry of Fiji* (Suva: Government Press, 1965), p. 2; Belt, Collins and Associates, Ltd., *Tourism Development Programme for Fiji* (Suva: United Nations Development Programme/International Bank for Reconstruction and Development/Government of Fiji, 1973), p. 123.
17. Harrison and Brandt, *Ecotourism in Fiji*.
18. A. K. Mara-Nailatikau, "Ecotourism in Fiji," Opening address presented at the Fiji Ecotourism Association Annual General Meeting, Warwick Hotel, Fiji, July 23, 1999.
19. Harrison and Brandt, *Ecotourism in Fiji*.
20. Ministry of Tourism and Transport, *Ecotourism and Village-based Tourism: A Policy and Strategy for Fiji* (Suva: Ministry of Tourism and Transport, 1999).
21. Ibid., p. 5.
22. Ministry of Tourism and Transport, *NEVP*, 1999.
23. Ibid.
24. Harrison and Brandt, *Ecotourism in Fiji*.

25. M. Gurdayal, "Sustainable Development Council Needed," *Fiji Times* (February 17, 2000), p. 4.
26. V. Evans, "Adi Koila Calls for Codes of Practice," *Fiji Times* (February 17, 2000), p. 4.
27. Ibid.
28. There is general agreement that ecotourism, as opposed to other forms of tourism, minimally adheres to the following criteria: it is nature-based/nature-driven; includes education and interpretation; is ecologically sustainable; includes benefits to the hosts/local communities; is culturally sensitive; and includes benefits/returns to the environment.
29. Evans, "Adi Koila Calls for Codes of Practice."
30. Participation included the following organizations, departments, and agencies: Fiji Visitors Bureau, University of the South Pacific tourism faculty, National Trust of Fiji, Native Land and Trust Board, New Zealand High Commission, Telecom Communications, Ministry of Commerce's Business Development and Investment Unit, Fijian Affairs Board, Fiji Museum, Ministry of Women and Culture, Fiji Ecotourism Association, Fiji Hotel Association, Fiji National Training Council, Department of Environment, and "Keep Fiji Beautiful" Association.
31. Fiji Ecotourism Advisory Committee, "Minutes of the Meeting" (Suva: Ministry of Tourism, December 17, 1999).
32. Harrison and Brandt, *Ecotourism in Fiji.*
33. Ibid.
34. K. Bricker and S. Millington, "A Review of Responsible Practices in Nature and Cultural-Based Tourism Operations, Fiji Islands, 1999," a draft report submitted to the Ministry of Tourism and Transport and the Fiji Visitors Bureau, Suva, Fiji, May 2000.
35. Tourism Resource Consultants, "NZODA Fiji Ecotourism Programme 1997–2000," *Annual Report 1999/2000*, prepared for New Zealand Ministry of Foreign Affairs and Trade, New Zealand High Commission, Communities of Koroyanitu and Bouma National Heritage Parks, October 2000.
36. Ibid.
37. Berno and King, "Tourism in Fiji after the Coups," p. 91.
38. Ibid., p. 83.
39. Ibid., p. 86.
40. Ibid., p. 91.
41. C. Carswell, "The Savusavu Tourism Association," presentation at the 2000 Tourism Forum, Warwick Hotel, Fiji, December 8, 2000.
42. T. Berno and K. Bricker, *Tourism Awareness Workshop Presenters Packet* (Suva: The University of the South Pacific Press, 2000).
43. Carswell, "The Savusavu Tourism Association."
44. Ibid.
45. Ibid.
46. Indigenous Fijians own roughly 80 percent of the land. This land remains under the control of "matagali" or land-owning family groups and cannot be sold. It can be leased, however, and the Native Land and Trust Board acts as

the body that legally assists Fijians with all lease agreements. A small percentage of the tourism plant is actually privately owned, however. This land was deemed freehold during British rule. There is an estimated 20 percent freehold property left in the archipelago.

47. H. Sanday, "Tourism Development in Pacific Island Forum Countries," in *Proceedings of the 1st Fiji Ecotourism Association Conference: Shaping the Future of Ecotourism in Fiji*, ed. K. Bricker (Suva: FETA, 2001), 34–42. The conference was held at the Tanoa International Hotel, Nandi, December 11–42.
48. Harrison and Brandt, *Ecotourism in Fiji*.
49. S. Tagicakiverata, author's personal communication, January 18, 2001.
50. K. Batibasaga and V. Rabici, "Project Proposal: Environmental Education & Awareness Programme (Provinces of Namosi, Serua, Nadroga, Rewa)," prepared for the Fiji Tourism Environment Sub-Committee, Suva, May 1, 2001.
51. K. Batibasaga and V. Rabici, "Tourism and Environmental Awareness Program Progress Report-June 1–22, 2001," prepared for the Fiji Tourism Forum Environment Sub-Committee, Suva, June 28, 2001.
52. Ibid.
53. Ibid.
54. Berno and King, "Tourism in Fiji after the Coups," p. 80.

Chapter 10

Green Globe: A Global Environmental Certification Program for Travel and Tourism

Annalisa Koeman, Graeme Worboys,
Terry De Lacy, Ashley Scott,
and Geoffrey Lipman

Green Globe, the world's only truly global tourism certification program, arose from *Agenda 21*'s principles for sustainable development as they apply to travel and tourism. This important document was signed by 182 countries at the 1992 United Nations Earth Summit in Rio De Janeiro.[1] Green Globe aims to provide the travel and tourism industry with a certification system that responds directly to the major environmental problems facing the planet, including the greenhouse effect, overuse of freshwater resources, destruction of biodiversity, production of solid and biological waste, and social issues.

Green Globe seeks to achieve environmental, social, and cultural improvements at the global, national, and local levels. It encourages and facilitates compliance with national and provincial legislation and accommodates local regulations as required by agencies or authorities. It is attractive to the tourism industry because it targets the achievement of significant savings through an integrated and systematic approach to reducing energy consumption, decreasing waste generation, and lessening the use of potable water.

The certification scheme deals with the entire travel and tourism industry, yet it has developed the flexibility to take into account the specifics of different sectors of travel and tourism operations. It can certify all types of companies used by tourists and travelers, including administrative offices, aerial cableways, airports, airlines, bus companies, hotels, car hires, cruise ships, farmstays, golf courses, exhibition halls, convention halls, vineyards, tour operators, tour companies, marinas, railways, restaurants, trailer parks, and in 2002, protected areas and communities.

Green Globe commits itself to including the latest travel and tourism sustainability research and industry best practices through continual review and improvement. In responding to internal and external critiques, the program has evolved from its inception in 1994 as a process-oriented program to a performance-, compliance-, outcome-, and achievement-based system in 2001. Utilizing its operational experience, Green Globe 21 (the name officially adopted in 2000) has created an upgraded, university-backed certification program that seeks to earn an international reputation for cutting edge quality, credibility, and integrity. It is designed to be rigorous, contemporary, and adaptive. It is, in 2001, for example, being fine-tuned to reflect and accommodate the World Tourism Organization's Global Code of Ethics and regional-national variants, such as the Pacific Asia Travel Association's Asia Pacific Economic Community Code for Sustainable Tourism.

History of Green Globe

Since its inception, Green Globe has undergone two major stages of development. Its evolution has been stimulated by experiences in field testing the program, by internal and external criticism, and by the results of two United Nations forums, the 1992 Rio de Janeiro Earth Summit and the 1999 Commission on Sustainable Development. At the 1992 Rio gathering, the chair of the Earth Summit, Maurice Strong, stated that the tourism industry needed to consider seriously its relationship with the environment and establish a long-term framework for sustainable development. In response, the World Travel and Tourism Council (WTTC), World Tourism Organization (WTO), and Earth Council (the organization created at Rio and headed by Strong) joined together to apply the principles of Agenda 21 to the tourism industry and to develop a program of action. The result was *Agenda 21 for the Travel & Tourism Industry: Toward Environmentally Sustainable Development*, released in 1995.

This Agenda 21 action plan included a number of overall objectives for the industry:

- To contribute to conservation, protection, and restoration of ecosystems;
- To be based on sustainable patterns of production and consumption;
- To make development decisions with the participation of the local population and with recognition of local identity and culture;
- To create employment for women and indigenous peoples;
- To respect international laws protecting the environment;
- To halt or reverse protectionism in trade; and,
- To develop systems to warn nations of natural disasters that could affect tourists/tourist areas.

The plan aimed to convert the objectives into specific targets, naming ten areas in which travel and tourism operations were urged to take concrete action:

- waste minimization, reuse, and recycling.
- energy efficiency, conservation, and management.
- management of freshwater resources.
- wastewater management.
- hazardous substances.
- transport.
- land-use planning and management.
- involvement of staff, customers, and communities in environmental issues.
- design for sustainability.
- partnerships for sustainable development.

In 1994, WTTC, a London-based organization composed of CEOs of major tourism corporations, initiated Green Globe with the aim of providing guidance materials and support to industry members in undertaking activities to achieve sustainability outcomes in the Agenda 21 target areas. Green Globe was originally conceived as a membership-based program whereby travel and tourism companies joined and voluntarily implemented sustainable tourism practices based on Agenda 21 principles. A cross section of about 500 companies (airlines, hotel chains, tour operators, travel agents) joined, and Green Globe quickly gained a considerable profile within the industry.

In its original form, Green Globe was very simple, but it was also the first of its kind for the travel and tourism industry. It required a company to pay an annual fee depending on its size and to develop its own internal environmental management policy and checklist. In return, the company received the Green Globe logo and advisory materials on how to minimize environmental impacts. The logo, which companies were allowed to use as soon as they signed up, was considered a statement of intent to undertake improvement. Companies did not have to meet a uniform set of compliance standards, and Green Globe did not provide for outside auditing.

By the late 1990s, Green Globe was being criticized for allowing less than-green companies to market themselves as green. This highlighted a fundamental flaw in the product at that time—there was no means of authenticating the brand through certified adherence to its principles. Companies signed on to Green Globe, and by simply paying the fee, could use the logo without any requirement that their claims of environmental and social responsibility be assessed and rated by independent third parties. Some companies abused this situation. In addition, the program was focused on process—setting up an environmental management system (EMS)—rather than focusing on the achievement of tangible improvements and outcomes. The program was also criticized for not taking into consideration the variations in travel and tourism operations in terms of scale, type, capital, location, and sector. Although Green Globe, as the tourism industry's first international scheme committed to environmentally and socially sustainable practices, had pioneered an approach, it became clear improvements were needed.

In April 1999, the seventh session of the United Nations Commission on Sustainable Development (UNCSD-7) was focused on sustainable tourism. This UNCSD-7 meeting, held in New York, concluded that to achieve and maintain sustainable tourism, organizations needed to integrate the following fundamental processes:

• build travel and tourism policies on Agenda 21 principles;
• use voluntary mechanisms to regulate sustainable tourism, including certification and industry codes;
• raise awareness of sustainability issues;
• oppose illegal, abusive, and exploitative tourism;
• build capacity;
• conduct integrated planning;
• research impacts on societies, cultures, and environments;
• develop and transfer technology; and,
• assess economic leakage and propose policies to enhance local and indigenous benefit.

Notably, self-regulation was identified at the UN meeting as one of the prime processes required for the achievement and maintenance of sustainable tourism. Green Globe agreed with this approach. It had, since its creation, held the view that if the industry did not "green" itself, it was likely that government-imposed legislation and regulation would force it to do so. At the same time, Green Globe staff came to see the need to turn this voluntary mechanism into a real certification program.

Following UNCSD-7, Green Globe underwent an organizational rearrangement and was relaunched as a certification program based on ISO standards and Agenda 21 principles, which incorporated recommendations from UNCSD-7. The core systems of this new program continue to evolve.

In response to a desire to improve, to move with the times, and to respond to criticisms, in 1999, Green Globe restructured, securing direct investment from WTTC members, and joined partners with the Cooperative Research Center for Sustainable Tourism (CRC) in Australia and the Caribbean Alliance for Sustainable Tourism (CAST) based in Puerto Rico.

This restructuring transformed Green Globe into a credible worldwide certification program. Key to this was the introduction of independent verification of the achievements of an operation and hence its legitimate credentials for certification. A two-logo process was established, whereby the operation could use the logo without a check mark or tick during its path toward certification (to be undertaken within two years) and then could use the logo with a tick once it had been certified by an independent third party.

The scheme had many positive attributes. The quality of the standard—that is, the criteria—had also been substantially improved and included the concepts of benchmarking, continuous improvement, and quantified performance, though performance was not made mandatory. The CRC, with its university-based research capacity, became directly involved in further improvements to the criteria, which were dubbed the Green Globe 21 Standard.

The Green Globe 21 Standard document, which was published in 2000, sets out the requirements needed to meet a level of environmental and social management performance that produces the sustainable development outcomes sought by Agenda 21. The standard recognizes continuous improvement for those participating in the program. It aims to facilitate improvements in the local and global environmental quality, conservation of local heritage, local living conditions, and contribution to local economy.

After 1999, the system of independent assessment worked well, with certification being based on a rigorous process. Training schemes for auditing companies carrying out the on-site inspections reinforced this process. Further improvements were needed though. Green Globe continued to receive some criticism for allowing the logo to be used as soon as an operation is committed to undertaking the certification program. It was argued by some critics that an operation could use the logo without actually acting in an environmentally or socially responsible manner. Green Globe was also criticized at this time for not incorporating the work of other tourism certification programs into the standard and for providing inadequate guidance for participants from some sectors of the industry.

In February 2000, the CRC was delegated the task of enhancing the best features of the 1999 model to upgrade the program. The revised model was to focus an outcome approach to certification through a set of performance criteria. Green Globe would benchmark environmental performance and measure real environmental improvements. The new system targeted nine key environmental and social performance areas. Benchmarking criteria were selected that both worked within a travel and tourism operating environment and achieved real environmental perform-

---

Box 10.1. Green Globe 21 Undertakes Four Main Functions

1) Research and Development
   –Developing cutting edge products
   –Establishing workable benchmarking criteria
   –Implementing ongoing sustainability research programs
2) Customer Services
   –Ensuring quality services for participants
   –Ensuring quality control of all products
3) Sales
   –Expanding the number of participating operations
   –Forging alliances and partnerships
4) Marketing
   –Raising consumer awareness
   –Raising business-to-business awareness
   –Promoting integrity of the brand

---

ance outcomes. Benchmarking criteria have been developed for nineteen company sectors, and by late 2001, work was proceeding on finalizing the criteria for protected areas and communities.

In the criteria developed for hotels, for example, energy consumption—generally the biggest cost after labor—is one of the key performance areas. The indicator used is energy consumed per guest night (or area under roof). This ratio is then analyzed by Green Globe and benchmarked against a derived acceptable normative performance. Details of how the measures work and how they are to be collected and recorded are provided to clients by Green Globe. To be successfully benchmarked, companies must be above a baseline level of performance for nine key performance areas.

In April 2001, Green Globe unveiled its upgraded version of the Green Globe 21 Standard and the "A, B, C of Certification:" affiliate, benchmarking, and certification. As detailed below, a distinction is made between operations that sign on as affiliates to learn about sustainable tourism and the Green Globe program and those who are undertaking benchmarking or certification. The work of Green Globe 21 is divided into four main functions: research, customer services, sales, and marketing (see box 10.1).

Green Globe Organizational Structure

Currently, Green Globe 21 is managed globally by three joint venture partners—Green Globe United Kingdom, Green Globe Asia Pacific (Australia), and CAST (Puerto Rico)—each of which has different roles and

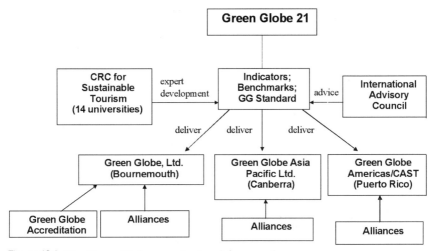

Figure 10.1. The Green Globe organizational framework

functions within the organization (see figure 10.1). Green Globe 21 is headquartered in Bournemouth, England, and this office is responsible for global policy and marketing, as well as for handling certifications in Europe and Africa. Green Globe Asia Pacific, headquartered in Canberra, Australia, oversees research and development of the Green Globe product and organizes certifications in the Asia-Pacific region, while Green Globe Americas, taken on by the Caribbean Action for Sustainable Development (CAST), organizes certifications in the Caribbean and South America. Green Globe United Kingdom has delegated its certification (also covering Europe and Africa) to an independent accreditation company and has created a joint venture partnership with AEA Technologies for the provision of environmental management system support services.[2]

Green Globe Asia Pacific is, in turn, a joint venture between Green Globe and the Cooperative Research Centre for Sustainable Tourism (CRC), based in Queensland, Australia. CRC, whose mandate is to "deliver innovation to enhance the environmental, economic and social sustainability of tourism,"[3] was responsible for developing the upgraded Green Globe 21 Standard and the new benchmarking system. Green Globe Asia Pacific is part of the Australian government's CRC program, which was established to boost collaborative links between industry, research organizations, educational institutions, and relevant government agencies. The CRC for Sustainable Tourism represents fourteen universities, the two major industry associations, all state and territory tourism departments, and over twenty private industry partners. The CRC also provides research on sustainable tourism for the WTTC, and in April 1999, it helped coordinate the travel and tourism industry's contribution to the UNCSD-7 meeting in New York.

In addition to its partnership with CRC, Green Globe has formed various industry alliances. For example, the Pacific Asia Travel Association (PATA) has replaced its Green Leaf program with Green Globe. The Green Key program in the Nordic countries has also worked closely with Green Globe, as has the Green Seal program in the United States. In 2001, the New Zealand Tourism Industry Association's Qualmark, South Africa's Qualitour (see chapter 8), Bali's Greenery, and Australia's NEAP (see chapter 5) certification programs all established formal alliances with Green Globe. In 2002, Green Globe entered into an alliance with a professional tour guides association and the Centre for Environmentally Responsible Tourism (CERT) in Great Britain. In forming partnerships with regional networks and other certification programs, Green Globe is being proactive in initiating the process of building a global brand.

Green Globe receives feedback and advice on the content and quality of its program. This comes from external referees contributing to the benchmarking indicators; consultants, including the National Centre for Tourism in Australia and PA Consulting; attendees to the Green Globe assessor training course; and the twenty-four–member Green Globe International Advisory Council (IAC), which comprises representatives from the travel industry, NGOs, and international agencies. The IAC is supposed to meet approximately twice per year. Following its inaugural meeting in November 2000, it "met" again in 2001 through an e-mail conference in August.

In addition, Green Globe Accreditation (GGA), a company based in Royal Tunbridge Wells, England, supports Green Globe 21 by accrediting certification organizations to undertake audits. GGA gives a training course as part of accreditation, undertakes on-site audits, and conducts independent review audits from time to time to ensure that the standard is maintained. Green Globe 21 has intentionally separated sales and marketing functions from delivery and from the development of the Green Globe 21 Standard.

Green Global Village-Sustainable Tourism Laboratory provides international tourism consulting services and support for Green Globe. It is based at Green Globe 21's offices in Bournemouth, England and provides specialist consulting services in support of sustainable travel and tourism. Green Globe also has established the concept of the Green Globe Foundation[4] to raise funds to reinvest in sustainable tourism projects with a strong ethical and social dimension. This will become increasingly important in the future; it is not yet functioning.

The Green Globe 21 Standard

The Green Globe 21 Standard,[5] which was put in place in April 2001, is considered the heart of the Green Globe scheme. It has evolved and improved through research, analysis, real experience, and application. Initially, it was a standard based on an ISO-style approach involving an environmental policy and a checklist. This process-based system had failings, though. It could easily mean that a company achieved all requirements of the standard but could still be failing to achieve environmentally friendly outcomes. There needed to be a system based on real environmental achievements, a performance-based standard, together with critical processes, such as the development of a policy and an EMS.

The Green Globe's new standard launched in April 2001 provides tourism operations with a framework to benchmark their environmental and social performance, achieve certification, and continuously improve their performance. It also guides operations to achieve continual improvements in several environmental and social performance areas through the implementation of an environmental management system. The result is that the operation both improves its environmental and social performance and saves money through putting in place cost-saving practices and technologies.

The new standard is based on requirement criteria organized in five sections:

1) Environment and Social Sustainability Policy
2) Regulatory Framework
3) Environmental and Social Sustainability Performance
4) Environmental Management System
5) Stakeholder Consultation and Communication

For operations (companies, communities, or protected areas) seeking Green Globe 21 benchmarking and certification, top management must write, adopt, and promote an Environmental and Social Sustainability Policy. This policy commits the operation to making annual improvements in relevant Green Globe performance indicators (described below) as well as in meeting relevant environmental legislation and regulations. It establishes a framework for regularly recording and measuring performance indicators and setting targets. It also commits the operation to give special consideration to employment of local persons and use of local products and services. The regulatory framework states that operations seeking benchmarking must maintain an up-to-date register of relevant legislation, regulations, and other requirements, as well as records of their compliance, and where compliance was not maintained, records of remedial action taken. In addition, the operation must comply with any special guide developed by Green Globe for a particular geographical location.

The standard's framework for benchmarking environmental and social performance specifies that an operation will assess the significance of the positive and negative impacts of its activities, products, and services in each of the key performance areas; establish targets to reduce negative and improve positive impacts; and monitor progress to ensure year to year improvement. Specific indicators for sectors help companies with their benchmarking process.

Development, implementation, and maintenance of an environmental management system is an integral part of the standard.[6] A senior executive in the operation is to be responsible for the implementation of the EMS and is to ensure that staff receive training in the EMS. This executive should also assess the possible environmental impacts of planned, accidental, and emergency situations and develop ways to mitigate negative impacts as well as to undertake regular reviews of the EMS. The Green Globe benchmarking report is designed to ensure that operations achieve a minimum significant improvement in relevant performance areas.

Finally, the standard deals with stakeholder consultation and communication, stating that the operation will regularly communicate its environmental and social performance resulting from participation in Green Globe to customers and stakeholders and will determine the significance of its impacts through consultation with and feedback from stakeholders. The standard states that the operation should inform customers (i.e., tourists) about sensitive local customs, ways of life, natural areas, environmental issues, and how best to contribute to the local economy.

The ABC of Green Globe 2001

The Green Globe program is open to all travel and tourism industry sectors and sizes and types of operations, including companies, communities, and protected areas. Participants are referred to as operations. Tourism operations are able to enter the program at any of three levels, namely, affiliate, benchmarked, or certified levels (see figure 10.2). Operations at the benchmarked and certified levels are able to use the Green Globe logo without tick and with tick, respectively. Travel and tourism operators committing to certification are automatically required to undertake benchmarking. Affiliates are encouraged to move to benchmarking or certification after 12 months. This is dubbed the ABC of Green Globe.

At each of the three levels, there is a clear protocol in place dictating the eligibility of an operation to use the Green Globe logo. For example, there is a distinction made between an operation's registration for benchmark-

Figure 10.2. The "ABC" of Green Globe 21

Table 10.1. Green Globe Vital Statistics, January 2002

Category	Global Fee*	Participants	Symbol
AFFILIATES:		550	Flag
Companies	$100		
Communities	$1000		
BENCHMARKING:			Globe without tick
Companies	$200–$1000	11	
Communities	$3000–$5000	1	
CERTIFICATION:			Globe with tick
Companies	$200–$1000	49	
Communities	$3000–$5000	4	
Awaiting classification		171	

* Reference price only when there is no stated regional fee scale.

ing or certification and the successful benchmarked or certified status of an operation. The Green Globe logo may be used only after the successful completion of the process, at which time a certificate is issued that has a unique serial number, a date, and has an expiration date. Green Globe has developed a set of web-based and CD-ROM materials for the three levels of the Green Globe program in support of its participating businesses.[7]

The cost of enrolling in Green Globe 21 differs depending on the size and type of operation, ranges from $100 for affiliate companies up to nearly $5000 for a community seeking certification (see table 10.1). Those enrolled in any of the three levels are listed in a single Membership Index on the Green Globe 21 Web site. By the end of 2001, there were 781 companies and communities. The directory designates the status of members with an A, B, or C and provides links to company web sites. In early 2002, 171 members were awaiting designation.[8]

A = Affiliates

At the introductory stage, affiliate, the global fee is $100 for a tourism company. Regional and national Green Globe fees may vary from this global fee; Web sites provide information on regional and national (usually lower) fee levels. This is currently the most popular level of the upgraded Green Globe system. By the end of 2001, there were 550 affiliate companies and communities listed on the Green Globe 21 Web site. The affiliate category, however, is really not part of the certification scheme. Rather, it enables companies and communities to learn about Green Globe and encourages them to take some action, including the development of a company environmental policy, and research into the Green Globe process.

Affiliates have a separate Green Globe flag and cannot use the green circle logo that is widely identified with the program. In addition to listing on the Green Globe Web site and use of the affiliate symbol for marketing purposes, they receive Web-based access to information on benchmarking, certification, the standard, and performance indicators. They also have access to the list of Green Globe–registered environmental management consultants and accredited assessor or auditing companies.

Although any company or destination can remain as an affiliate for longer than a year, Green Globe encourages them to enroll in the benchmarking or certification process and to take practical steps to improving their sustainability performance. Higher fees in the second year and regular reminders by Green Globe and others assist in the process of encouraging upgrading.

B = Benchmarking

The newest feature in the April 2001 version of Green Globe 21 is benchmarking. The brand new process was fully operational by the end of 2001; eleven companies were actively being benchmarked and one community had already completed the benchmarking process. This level is intended to enable measurement of real environmental performance of operations. Because it is applicable for operations worldwide, it provides an internationally comparable performance standard. Companies may opt either to just undertake benchmarking or they combine it with advancing to the next level, certification. Companies, communities, or protected areas that are successfully benchmarked receive the Green Globe logo without the check or tick. Green Globe has established a global fee of $200–$1000 for benchmarking, depending on the size of the operator. Fees are negotiated with the largest companies. Regional and national fees may vary from this global fee, with Web sites providing information on regional and national fee levels.

Green Globe has benchmarking guides to assist operations in nineteen different travel industry sectors, and further guides are being developed for other sectors as well as for destinations (communities and protected areas).[9] These guides assist operations through the steps to achieve benchmarking.

They include key performance areas, indicators, and measures specifically determined for each sector. Guides have been developed for the following sectors:

administrative offices
aerial cableways
airlines
airports
bus companies
car hires
convention centers
cruise ships
exhibition halls
farmstays
golf courses
hotels
marinas
tour companies
tour operators
trailer parks
railways
restaurants
vineyards

The benchmarking form is provided on a CD-ROM or in hard copy at the end of the published benchmarking users guide. The benchmarking form is straightforward and may be filled out by operations, or operations may wish to hire professional consultants for this. The process involves operations collecting, on an annual basis, measures of indicators for the following key performance areas:

greenhouse gas emissions
energy conservation and management
freshwater resource use
ambient air quality protection
wastewater management
waste minimization, reuse, recycling (including of hazardous substances)
ecosystem conservation and management (including biodiversity
   impact, particularly on habitats)
environmental and land-use planning, particularly in areas of high
   social and environmental value
local social, cultural, and economic impact, in particular, respecting
   local culture and generating maximum local employment.

These results contribute to the preparation of an annual benchmarking assessment report for the operation. It is similar in logic to the generation of an annual financial performance report. This benchmarking report summarizes the environmental performance of a company or destination for the previous year. Within each key performance area, Green Globe has carefully researched and selected the performance criteria (called benchmarking indicators), and these are designed to be as practical and easily measured as possible. In addition to the core set of indicators for the nine key performance areas, Green Globe recommends that operations select optional indicators that are specific to their circumstances. Green Globe works with operations to choose the best measures for their situation and has trained travel and tourism professionals to support this process. Operations may seek a recommendation from Green Globe as to the type of professional support required, or operations may utilize the Web-based register directly. Companies providing these services do so at a competitive rate.

The measurement of the overall energy consumption for a hotel, for example, uses the annual electricity, gas, diesel, and other fuel bills as the source of information. Green Globe benchmarking uses such information in the form of pro rata data. It also assists with the calculation of a common unit of measurement. For energy, it is gigajoules. A compact disc is supplied for benchmarking operations. When energy data are entered into a form provided, the CD automatically calculates the information in gigajoules. When the energy usage is combined with hotel occupancy figures (total number of guest nights), the result is calculation of the hotel's fossil energy use per guest night. Such pro rata information deals with the differences in the scale of operations and allows for growth or contraction of operations over time. (If Green Globe customers do not have access to a CD-ROM drive, Green Globe also supplies a user's manual that includes a paper copy of the form to be completed.) For a tourist railway, a similar calculation could produce an energy figure per passenger kilometers.

Other examples of indicators and measures for the hotel sector include:

• The freshwater management indicator might be measured by liters of potable water used per guest night, with the objective of minimizing water consumption. It includes as well calculations for other activities, such as washing, recreational facilities, gardens, and surface cleaning where potable water is used for these purposes. Many hotels are located in regions where freshwater is a concern, so overall reduction (lowering demand and increasing reuse and recycle) in use of this resource will be a significant contribution to the local environment and the long-term sustainability of the operation.

- Local social, cultural, and economic impact might be measured by efforts to respect (where appropriate) local traditions and customs, purchasing (where possible) local goods and services, and participating in local committees and organizations. The benchmarking indicator to monitor is the portion of all employees that has a primary address within approximately twenty kilometers (or appropriate agreed distance) of the operation. This encourages local employment and minimizes environmental impacts due to personnel transportation.
- Energy conservation and management is calculated by measuring consumption/guest night per year (or area under roof, using conversion factors supplied by Green Globe). Consumption includes all forms of energy—grid electricity, natural gas, gasoline, diesel, and liquefied propane gas. Green Globe acknowledges that many operations are making significant efforts to utilize energy from renewable sources (e.g., wind, solar, hydro), thereby conserving resources and minimizing greenhouse gas emissions. This can be recognized through adoption of an optional indicator that highlights the percentage of renewable energy consumed each year.
- The solid waste reduction indicator might be measured through the volume of waste landfilled per guest night per year (or area under roof). Reductions can be achieved by cutting down on quantities of materials consumed (including packaging), reuse, or recycling. Consideration should be given to the options that have the best local environmental impact. For example, recycling may not always be feasible (e.g., no local facility), and on-site waste to energy systems may be a better route, obtaining both energy and a reduction in the volume of waste disposed (measured either as uncompacted or mechanically compacted material).

In addition, each applicant is encouraged to list at least one other indicator that it considers particularly relevant to its operation and its environmental impact. This may be operation- or locality-specific and will reflect its commitment to improving local issues (e.g., water quality, endangered species, habitat preservation, cultural heritage, community development, etc.). Examples of possible supplementary indicators include:

- renewable energy consumption per year/total energy consumption per year.
- monetary contributions made to sponsor conservation and/or local community.
- area used for habitat conservation/total property area.

The information collected by an operation is recorded on the benchmark form supplied and then sent to Green Globe. No matter at which office it is received, it will be forwarded (under present arrangements) to the Asia Pacific office. It is checked for completeness and then forwarded to an independent CRC office in Brisbane for analysis. The CRC analyzes the information for each key performance area, and an aggregated reporting index will be provided in the future. To achieve the index, each of the individual scores for each performance area will be summed. For the interim, advice will be provided if an operation is above or below baseline or above best practice level. All of this information is printed onto a single attractively designed sheet known as a benchmarking assessment report. Green Globe also produces benchmarking report notes for the operation, which indicate its current standing and provide advice on where appropriate and worthwhile improvements may be made.

Green Globe has established a baseline level of performance and a best practice level of performance to illustrate where an operation's performance is placed within the industry. It allows comparison with industry best practice, and it allows improvements in performance to be tracked annually. How is the Green Globe baseline determined? The CRC is developing a unique database from 240 countries. It contains extensive information on domestic and individual resource consumption and conservation and social activity. In large countries (e.g., United States, Canada, Australia, France, Spain), subdivisions are introduced at a regional (e.g., state, province) level. This database provides the guidelines for the level of baseline and best practice for each country or province. Where information on a country (or province) does not currently exist, a neighboring region with a similar geographic, climatic, and economic profile is used as a proxy. Information has also been compiled on baseline and best practice for individual tourism sectors (e.g., hotels, restaurants, etc.) found in individual countries and provinces. The travel and tourism industry values are tagged to the average domestic and industrial consumption/production/activity of the region. In this way, baseline practice and best practice numbers are established for the benchmarking indicators for each sector in each country or province. As developed and verified, the baseline benchmark will be made available to Green Globe participants.

To be able to use the Green Globe logo without the tick and receive a benchmarked certificate, the measures in all key performance areas must be above the Green Globe baseline level and the operation must have an environmental policy. (Note: some flexibility is provided in the first 12 months of benchmarking for one of the nine criteria.) The measures of key performance area must also be maintained above the baseline level each year for an operation to maintain its benchmarked status. If an indicator's measure is above the Green Globe baseline but below Green Globe best practice, the operation will be encouraged to make annual improvements for

Box 10.2. Registering for Green Globe Benchmarking means:

- An operation registers and pays a fee for benchmarking.
- The operation receives a Web access number and is eligible to use the Green Globe affiliate flag.
- The operation receives a compact disc and a Benchmarking User's Guide.
- The operation collates basic data required for benchmarking.
- The operation inserts information into the files on the CD and prints the completed document.
- The senior manager of the operation signs off on the prepared document.
- The operation forwards the document to Green Globe.
- Green Globe analyzes the information and forwards the operation a benchmarking assessment report.
- For those who achieve above the baseline level for all measures for each key performance area, a benchmarked certificate is presented. Use of the Green Globe logo without tick is allowed.
- At the end of the first year, the operation documents its annual benchmarking measures and forwards them to Green Globe. The measures are assessed and a benchmarking assessment report provided. If successful, a benchmarked certificate is provided. In subsequent years, this process is repeated, with the Green Globe logo being used if the performance continues to be above baseline.
- Spot audits of benchmarked information are made from time to time.

that indicator. The CEO or executive manager of an operation must sign off on the benchmarking figures before they are sent to Green Globe. There is a potential audit of figures supplied by an operation, and Green Globe may instigate this at any time. Compulsory audits are not required for benchmarking. Operations undertaking benchmarking are encouraged to proceed directly to full certification and the compulsory audit that accompanies this. The data supplied for benchmarking are checked during full certification. Operations regularly undertaking benchmarking without an audit will be subject to surprise audit checks (see box 10.2).

Once best practice is achieved for all key performance areas, Green Globe encourages operations to maintain this level of performance. At this stage, an operation should select supplementary performance indicators to maintain continuous improvement. Although a key issue in defining environmental performance benchmarks is that they must reflect above baseline to be credible, they must also be achievable by reflecting local conditions and the type of activity being certified. The benchmark for the amount of energy consumed per guest night per year, for instance, must be tailored to the climate in particular geographic areas. Similarly, benchmarks for purchasing local goods, hiring local people, and using renewable energy sources will vary depending on the level of production, labor supply and skills, and availability and cost of alternative energy technologies in a particular country or region. The intention of Green Globe is not to discourage the industry by setting standards that only a few can achieve but rather to encourage, through its services and support, widespread adoption of the principle of continued improvements that provide tangible benefits toward achieving a sustainable travel industry. The baseline level determined will be environmentally responsible and transparent.

Benchmarking: A Focus on Greenhouse Gases

The greenhouse gas issue, intimately linked to energy consumption and environmental sustainability, encompasses both fixed and mobile assets, and transcends local and international boundaries. Green Globe believes that it provides the most high-profile international environmental performance currency by which to gauge and benchmark performance on a like-for-like basis.

Not only is the greenhouse gas issue considered urgent within the environmental sector, but it also has particular relevance to the travel and tourism industry because it consumes significant amounts of fossil fuels. This is why Green Globe has decided to ask its participants to concentrate on this area for improvement, with the major focus being reduced energy use per customer. Thus, greenhouse gas emission reductions can be measured collectively through:

• reduction in energy use.
• reduction in the primary consumption of raw materials.
• reduction in the energy required for potable water transmission.
• reduction in the use of energy required for water treatment and cleanup.
• sequestration of carbon through habitat conservation.

This analysis is achieved through Green Globe's current benchmarking indicators. The benchmarking CD automatically calculates the greenhouse gas contributions.

Green Globe recognizes that the long-term solution to reducing greenhouse gas production by the travel and tourism (and all other industries) is to tackle it at source by introducing more efficient equipment and procedures that use renewable energy sources. However, application of this cleaner production or ecoefficiency approach will take time. Additionally, many operations in the industry are already energy-efficient and/or further significant reductions in energy from fossil fuel sources may for operational and commercial reasons not be feasible.

Therefore, Green Globe recognizes that an optional indicator may be carbon sequestration through habitat conservation. Under the Kyoto Protocol, the international treaty on greenhouse gas emissions, carbon sequestration has been designated as an acceptable mechanism to offset net carbon emissions. Growing forests naturally remove carbon dioxide (CO_2) from the atmosphere and convert the carbon into new tree biomass, resulting in carbon storage (sequestration) in both wood and soils. Under the Kyoto agreement, companies can receive credit toward compliance by purchasing forests for conservation purposes. However, carbon sequestration will be credited only for trees planted after January 1, 1990.

For Green Globe participants, the issue is to evaluate the total amount of carbon dioxide (CO_2) generated through all the operation's activities and to offset as much as possible by purchasing land to protect natural tree growth. Involvement in carbon sequestration can be through large-scale national and international programs, as well as by direct actions in promoting local tree planting schemes.[10]

A key long-term objective of Green Globe is to stimulate initiatives for tackling noncompliance in meeting emissions targets, in particular, capacity building in developing countries (such as transfer of climate-friendly technologies) and establishing the Kyoto Protocol's market-based mechanisms—emissions trading, carbon trading, joint implementation and clean development.

C = Certification

There are a number of important aspects of Green Globe certification for companies and communities. It is based on a standard that has global application. The Green Globe 21 Standard is based on Agenda 21 and uses an ISO-style environmental management system. In focusing on sustainable travel and tourism, it provides strong support for the World Tourism Organization's Global Code of Ethics.[11] It requires companies applying for certification to:

• develop a sustainability policy.
• benchmark environmental performance.
• involve stakeholders.
• be independently audited prior to certification.

Operations can register with Green Globe to immediately undertake the certification level, but since April 2001, they are required to go through the benchmarking step as part of the certification process. At the end of 2001, the Green Globe 21 Web site listed forty-nine certified operators, most of them hotels in Barbados, Egypt, Jamaica, and the United Kingdom.

318   PART II. CASES

Many of these never went through the benchmark level because they received certification prior to April 2001. Instead they have been grandfathered into the upgraded Green Globe 21 program. However, their certification must be renewed annually, and they must meet the requirements of the new system by the end of 2003. Certified operations use the Green Globe logo with the tick in the center.

Operations currently seeking full certification must be benchmarked above the baseline level of performance. This means that companies and communities have actually demonstrated a minimum standard of environmental performance prior to certification. Operations registering for certification automatically receive the same benefits as those registering for benchmarking.

Operations seeking certification pay Green Globe a global fee ranging from $200 to $1000, depending on the size of the company. This does not include the cost of the on-site audit. Regional and national fees may vary from this global fee; Web sites provide information on regional and national fee levels. Operations receive a Web access number that provides a directory of Green Globe–approved assessor companies and, by mail, the benchmarking CD-ROM and user's guide, which gives guidance for certification. The operation initiates work on the requirements of the Green Globe 21 Standard in preparation for certification assessment. Environmental management professionals may provide guidance on the EMS as well as on customizing performance criteria. Assessor companies may participate in a preassessment of environmental performance. To be awarded the Green Globe logo with the tick, all operations are required to undergo an on-site third-party assessment against the Green Globe 21 standard.

The operation can undertake a self-assessment against a Green Globe specially designed checklist. This is an aid only and is not used in the formal assessment. It is based on the assessor's checklist and helps operations to order their information and to streamline the actual assessment. This reduces costs. When the operation considers it is ready for certification, it requests Green Globe to organize a certification assessment. Green Globe then assigns the certification task to an accredited certification firm and recommends how much time the assessment process should take. Fees are based on a rate negotiated between the operation and the firm and are additional to the fee paid to Green Globe. Typically, an assessment of a small operation takes between four and eight hours to complete. The assessor e-mails the completed certification assessment checklist to Green Globe and authorized Green Globe personnel approve or reject certification based on the advice of the assessor.

If the operation is approved, a formal certificate is presented and the operation may use the Green Globe logo with the tick. The logo carries a year date of issue, and each certificate has a unique registration number. The logo must be updated and renewed each year based on a successful annual environmental performance report.

Green Globe will withdraw the right to use the brand for matters of non-compliance or where the use of the brand has been abused. A dispute process has been instituted, based on ISO certification guides and involving independent assessment of the dispute. For a company to keep its logo, Green Globe will require rectification—both immediate and longer term corrective action. Green Globe has also sought to put in place systems for quality control. All certification organizations and environmental management organizations involved in assessing participants are required to undertake Green Globe training and to update their Green Globe qualifications every three years. Training systems and standards have been designed to match the requirements of the Green Globe 21 Standard. Assessors are trained by Green Globe and must work for an accredited certification organization. Independent checks of audits will be conducted. Green Globe will not issue a certification certificate unless it has been signed by an accredited assessor. In using a network of facilitators and in operating training programs globally, the initiatives help to build capacity for sustainable tourism. Green Globe will also undertake quality control checks of its process through spot checks of operations to ensure that the integrity of the standard is maintained.

Benchmarking and Certification for Destinations: Communities and Protected Areas

Many communities and protected areas are actively seeking recognition for their environmental performance achievements. Green Globe is currently evaluating the concept of certifying entire communities and protected areas as sustainable tourism destinations and is working on finalizing a certification program for both. In 2001, pilot studies were begun at Douglas and Redlands Shires in Queensland, Australia, and Kaikoura on the South Island of New Zealand. By the end of 2001, Green Globe listed four communities—Cumbria and Bournemouth in England, Jersey in the Channel Islands, and Vilamoura in Portugal—as certified and another sixteen communities spread around the globe as "a few of the communities currently working toward Green Globe 21 Certification."[12]

Green Globe believes that travel and tourism destinations are an appropriate scale for considering sustainable tourism management, planning, and development. Effective planning generally occurs at the destination level, usually through local governments, and new tourism products are developed within a destination's particular image and brand. Tourists choose holidays based on a destination's perceived attractions or experiences.

In keeping with the fundamental Green Globe principles, a destination will be required to demonstrate environmental performance according to the principles of Agenda 21. Upon certification, it must demonstrate continuous improvement. Beyond this, a Green Globe destination must encourage cooperation between the tourism industry, government departments, NGOs, and communities at a local level. Local political, cultural, and social conditions will be considered in order to create a realistic, achievable program of action that is flexible enough to suit a location's various attributes. A key result of destination certification will be the increased involvement of the private sector in environmental action, which will, in turn, provide the opportunity for Green Globe and the destination to heighten community and consumer awareness through the destination brand.

The annual global fee range for a community to be benchmarked or certified is between $3,000 and $5,000 for registration and the annual fee, depending on the size of the community. In some cases, national fees differ from this global fee and they are listed on the respective Web sites. This does not include the cost of doing the independent audit.

Benchmarking criteria for protected areas are also being finalized. The concept of benchmarking of protected areas will apply to the whole of a protected area and will include an assessment of the lead agency and the performance of other operations within the area. Pilot studies will be completed before the concept is made available as a product. By late 2001, four protected areas in China were registered with Green Globe to undergo benchmarking and certification.

The developing Green Globe destination and protected areas programs require the involvement of a lead organization that can deliver on both sustainable tourism development and environmental regulation. This is usually an agency that has authority to implement actions and coordinate stakeholders. It also requires detailed research on developing clear indicators, benchmarks, and targets, as well as new approaches from third-party auditing companies. The Green Globe destination concept is a complex one, but it has enormous potential to harness and drive the environmental sustainability of communities and protected areas.

Benefits of Benchmarking and Certification

Green Globe believes that there are many benefits for companies and destinations that are involved in its environmental certification. Benchmarking and certification facilitate a competitive advantage in an increasingly ecoconscious market. Various studies have shown that a majority of travelers are inclined to support green travel companies and pay more for the services of environmentally and socially conscious companies.[13] Green Globe is promoting its benchmarked and certified companies on its Web site and through media exposure and encouraging certified or benchmarked companies to maximize awareness of their achievement. This is designed to help increase consumer awareness of the program.

By the same token, Green Globe believes that its brand demonstrates improved environmental performance to the community, regulators, shareholders, and employees, and to investors who are increasingly looking for ethical standards. The certification process establishes quality performance. The Kandalama Hotel at Dambulla, Sri Lanka, for instance, was proud to be the first Green Globe–certified hotel in Asia, and its on-ground environmental performance is very high. The Melia Bali Villa and Spa resort of Bali, Indonesia, has embarked on an ambitious series of actions to enhance its environmental and social performance. It advertises its Green Globe qualifications throughout Europe (Russia, Spain, England, and France) and the Asia Pacific as part of its marketing campaign. Linus Bagley, manager of the Binna Burra Lodge in Lamington National Park, Queensland, Australia, said at his certification acceptance speech in August 2001 that Green Globe certification was the best step his company had taken in its overall aim to improve its environmental and social management performance. In Great Britain, all sixteen Marriott Hotels have elected to become certified, not only for the substantial cost savings but also for its appeal for the growing green market. At the World Travel Market in November 2001, CAST produced a booklet extolling the values of certification for fifteen hotels certified in the Caribbean.

Benchmarking and certification also directly contribute to improvements in the efficiency of operations through the use of fewer resources. Savings are achieved through reduced energy consumption, reduced waste generation, reduced use of potable water, and enhanced efficiency arising from treating such issues in an integrated, systematic manner. Green Globe believes that participating in its benchmarking and certification process can also help to improve staff commitment, increase productivity linked to clear environmental policies and programs, and improve knowledge and awareness of sustainability issues through targeted environmental training and on-the-job implementation. In addition, Green Globe offers the potential for improving relations between tourism operations and their local communities. Operations are actively encouraged to work with local communities through transparent and participatory consultation and communication activities, as well as incorporation of buy local and employ local strategies where feasible and appropriate.

The Green Globe approach has the strength that it can be adopted by any tourism operation in any location. Yet, despite this adaptability, it also retains rigor. It can be especially useful in countries where tourism bodies or governments have established their own certification programs. Alliances can be established to achieve the dual advantage of an international program and a local certification scheme being applied in a country. These alliances may also include quality assurance programs.

Green Globe also targets mainstream tourism businesses that may have a lower level of environmental awareness and less motivation to adopt sustainability programs. This can help provide positive examples to the mainstream tourism market and can help raise the bar on sustainable practices. Finally, the program places environmental management within a consistent framework that can, theoretically at least, be used by any tourism business anywhere in the world to systematically monitor environmental performance in tourism.

Improving the Green Globe Model

Maintaining the integrity of the brand is critical to the future of the Green Globe concept. As of April 2001, with the release of the upgraded Green Globe program, improved measures have been put in place to ensure that this happens. This will include the systematic phaseout of the old certification system by the end of 2002. Some measures and systems will be introduced immediately. Others will be introduced progressively. The upgraded Green Globe 21 scheme is global. All operations that are currently involved will be systematically encouraged to undertake the new scheme. The target date for the phase in of the upgraded scheme exclusively is the commencement of 2003.

The International Advisory Council, which ideally meets every six months, provides crucial peer review of the Green Globe 21 Standard and the sector performance indicators. In further steps intended to help maintain the impartiality and integrity of the process, there is a clear separation of functions between the certification assessors and the environmental management advisors/consultants who are available to operations to help them prepare for benchmarking and certification. Green Globe has also separated the sales and marketing functions of the organization in England from the research and development arm spearheaded by the CRC in Australia. Experience gained through implementing the scheme, including feedback from customers, consumers, and the community, is fed directly to the CRC and helps ensure Green Globe's system of continuous improvement. Finally, Green Globe declared itself an open system in 2001, recognizing that local, regional, or even global sectoral activities can reach the quality and responsible standards established by Green Globe and as such can be incorporated into Green Globe benchmarking and certification.

Conclusion

Green Globe has developed a new suite of environmental and social performance measures that can be used extensively by the travel and tourism industry to significantly improve environmental and social performance. Its benchmarking and certification levels and logos are providing a new and improved service to tourism. At a time when increasing numbers of global and regional codes for sustainable tourism and ethical tourism are being launched, this new service can help operations to achieve the highest standards of performance. The service is equally applicable to the smallest companies as it is to large communities and protected areas. Green Globe 21, through its benchmarking and certification systems, has introduced travel and tourism into the world of actual environmental performance accountability. It is at the cutting edge. It is what is needed to ensure a sustainable travel and tourism industry in the future.

Notes

1. United Nations, *Agenda 21: The United Nations Program for Action from Rio* (New York: United Nations, 1992); World Travel and Tourism Council, World Tourism Organization, and Earth Council, *Agenda 21 for the Travel and Tourism Industry: Toward Environmentally Sustainable Development* (London: WTTC, 1995).
2. "EMS Support Services," Green Globe 21, http://www.greenglobe21.com/refs/ems.htm (September 2001).
3. Cooperative Research Center, http://www.crctourism.com.au/.
4. Green Globe Asia Pacific, http://www.ggasiapacific.com.au/.
5. "The Certification Standard," Green Globe 21, http://www.greenglobe21.com/refs/standard.htm (September 2001).
6. See http://www.greenglobe21.com for details on various resources available to Green Globe members.
7. Green Globe 21, http://www.greenglobe21.com. See, for instance, "EMS Support Services," www.greenglobe21.com/refs/standard.htm (September 2001).
8. Green Globe 21, "Membership Index," http://www.greenglobe21.com (September 2001).
9. Green Globe 21, "Good Practice Indicators," http://www.greenglobe21.com/refs/standard.htm (September 2001).
10. "Global Warming: Green Globe Takes a Stand," http://www.sustravel.com/html/ggm_html/ggm1100/AG-12PAG.ENE.pdf (September 2001).
11. World Tourism Organization, "Code of Ethics Presented at UN," News Release, November 19, 2001, http://www.world-tourism.org/newsroom/Releases/more_releases/November2001/un_codeofethics.html; World Tourism Organization, Code of Ethics, http://www.world-tourism.org/projects/ethics/principles.html (September 2001).

12. Green Globe 21, "Certified communities" and "Current participants," www.greenglobe21.com/ (September 2001).

13. MORI, *Business and the Environment* (London: MORI, 1995); MORI, *Public Views on Travel and the Environment* (London: MORI, 1998); MORI, *Business and the Environment: Attitudes and Behaviour of the General Public–Trends 1989–1999* (London: MORI, 1999); Tearfund, *Tourism–An Ethical Issue. Market Research Report* (Middlesex, United Kingdom: IPSOS-RSL, 2000); Travel Industry Association of America, *Survey Results* (Washington, D.C.: Travel Industry Association of America, 1997).

Chapter 11

Accreditation: Certifying the Certifiers

Ronald Sanabria

One central issue confronting every certification program is credibility. As ecotourism and certification expert Amos Bien states, "There is an indispensable requirement for all certification systems: *credibility*. A system without credibility does not have a market; it does not convince clients and it does not demonstrate anything."[1] According to United Nations Environment Program official Jacqueline Aloisi de Larderel, "*Credible* ecolabels promote sustainable consumption patterns by providing concise and accurate information to consumers to help them identify those products and services which incorporate a good level of environmental performance."[2]

Ultimately, the credibility of both certification programs and the certifying agents (the certifiers or auditors) could be determined and measured by an accreditation body. *Accreditation*, in its simplest conceptualization, is the process of qualifying and endorsing entities that perform certification of companies, products, or services. Being accredited works as a "license" to perform certification based upon agreed principles and standards (see also definition in introduction). Through accreditation, certification entities can demonstrate their capacity to undertake certification and thus, build credibility around their systems. Based only on this conceptualization, accreditation could be seen as a bureaucratic, regulatory system. However, if accreditation is seen as only one of the components of a stewardship system, it could become a vital complement to certification programs.

Stewardship systems or councils have been implemented in several industries as "multi-stakeholder partnerships designed to provide a forum in which various [entities] with different interests in the targeted sectors can engage in collaborative solution-oriented dialogue to their mutual advantage, and create market-based incentives to stimulate the production and consumption of certified sustainable products."[3] Stewardship councils accredit certifiers based on their performance and help ensure that certification is being conducted through objective and transparent mechanisms. This chapter outlines the effort by the Rainforest Alliance, an international environmental NGO, to investigate the possibilities for creating an international accreditation body for sustainable tourism and ecotourism certifiers. This project is known as the Sustainable Tourism Stewardship Council (STSC), and it represents a leading example of an NGO playing a significant role in developing industry standards and a framework for sustainable development (see chapter 3).

For the purposes of this chapter, an *accreditation body* is understood as playing this stewardship role. Done properly, accreditation bodies have numerous advantages. They can build credibility and transparency because they strengthen stakeholder involvement. For instance, the Forest Stewardship Council (FSC), an accreditation body for certifiers of sustainable forestry, engages "a diverse group of representatives from environmental and conservation groups, the timber industry, the forestry profession, indigenous peoples' organizations, community forestry groups and forest product certification organizations from twenty-five countries."[4] Figure 11.1 illustrates the links between an accreditation system and the different stakeholder groups.

Accreditation bodies can also facilitate international and regional recognition. Using the same example, the FSC engages in worldwide campaigns to promote the use of certified woods (see chapter 3). Some of the mechanisms FSC uses include retail postcards[5] (see an example in figure 11.2), brochures, press releases, and the Internet, all of which give exposure to accredited certifiers at the industry, consumer, and retail levels. FSC also lists in its public documentation all the accredited certifiers so timber companies interested in certifying their operations can contact these certifiers.

Furthermore, accreditation bodies allow for better organization and harmonization of policies, procedures, and standard setting among accredited certifiers. Because they measure the same criteria across different certification programs for the same type of product, they also permit economies of scale for promotion and research.

Accreditation bodies represent forums for continuous improvement and conflict resolution. They can help certification programs stay abreast of changing international laws. They attract political and financial support and protect consumers and certifiers against false claims. Through international accreditation, certifiers demonstrate their environmental and social commitment to consumers. In many countries, the boom in the nature-based tourism movement has allowed "free riders" to emerge: companies that claim to provide ecoservices when in reality they follow only superficially sound ecotourism principles and practices. Accredited certification schemes can help mitigate this effect by recognizing only those operators

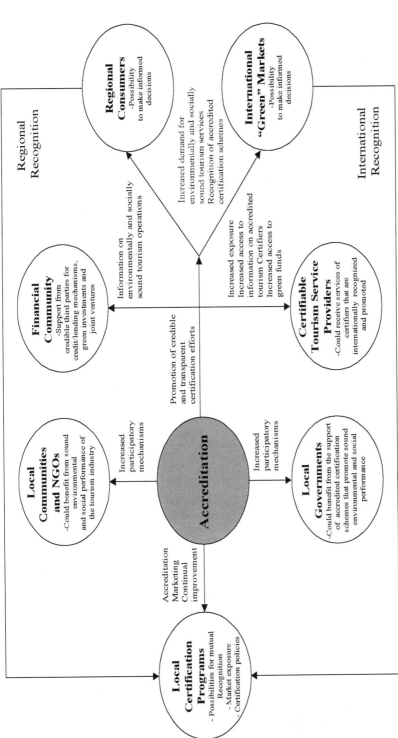

Figure III.1. Simplified links between accreditation and stakeholders. *Source:* Adapted from Rainforest Alliance (RA), World Wide Fund for Nature (WWF) and The Nature Conservancy (TNC), "Protected Areas and Environmentally and Socially Sound Products Program," a proposal to the United States Agency for International Development (USAID) for expanding market access for environmentally sound products and services (Washington, D.C.: TNC, 2001), p. 17.

Figure II.2. FSC retail postcard: an example of promotion that benefits accredited certifiers

that comply with internationally agreed upon criteria. Travelers can then make informed decisions. Environmentally and socially concerned tourists are typically well-educated professionals who have a good grasp of technology, such as the Internet, and usually rapidly learn of and recognize quality products. Therefore, credible certification schemes will have market advantages.

Aside from the FSC, other examples of performance-based stewardship councils are: the Marine Stewardship Council for certifiers of sustainable fisheries, the International Federation of Organic Agriculture Movements for certifiers of organic foods, and Social Accountability International for certifiers of social responsibility standards.

Since 1993, the FSC has been supporting "environmentally appropriate, socially beneficial and economically viable management of the world's forests."[6] Today, through FSC-accredited certifiers, 55.3 million acres of well-managed forest in thirty-five countries have been certified globally, 1,485 certificates have been awarded to industrial operations that use wood from certified sources, and over 20,000 products use FSC–certified wood worldwide.[7] Consumers purchasing products carrying an FSC label can be assured that their purchase comes from a forest that has been responsibly managed. Although the forestry and tourism industries may differ significantly on the ground—for instance, in tourism, single products are not easily identified and there is a greater number of stakeholders involved—the success of sustainable forestry certification and the experiences, achievements, and limitations compiled by accreditation bodies such as the FSC make developing a similar model for tourism well worth considering. Although there has never been an accreditation system tailored to the tourism industry and the significant challenges that such a system would need to overcome are undoubtedly complex, the potential benefits for the tourism industry, governments, certifiers, NGOs, and travelers led the Rainforest Alliance (RA) to initiate an eighteen-month feasibility study to develop a stewardship council for tourism.

The Sustainable Tourism Stewardship Council (STSC) project's goal is to analyze whether or not an accreditation system is feasible and, if so, is it to determine the most appropriate organizational structure, the necessary steps for implementation, and recommendations for accreditation criteria. The Rainforest Alliance sees a potential STSC as an entity that could help guide the tourism industry toward a more environmentally and socially sound future by using credible certification programs as a tool to measure and compare environmental, sociocultural, and economic impacts and promote positive change within the tourism industry.

Background on the Rainforest Alliance

The Rainforest Alliance[8] is an international nonprofit organization dedicated to the protection of endangered ecosystems and the people and wildlife that live within them by transforming land-use management, business practices, and consumer behavior. The work of the Rainforest Alliance is guided by these core values: (1) respect and concern for natural environments and local peoples, (2) dedication to pioneering pragmatic means for enabling socially and environmentally responsible action, (3) belief that success is achievable only through collaboration, and (4) unwavering commitment to integrity in its activities.

Since its founding in 1987, the Rainforest Alliance has played a leadership role in entrepreneurial conservationism, identifying new opportunities and acting as an innovator and a catalyst for change. Based on its experience, the Rainforest Alliance believes that only through "collaborative sustainability"—partnering with business, workers, scientists, and local community leaders—is it possible to develop socially and environmentally responsible as well as economically viable best management practices (BMP) for using our natural resources sustainably. Its goal is to improve the management of natural resource-based extractive activities in areas of high biodiversity. Certification is seen as a tool to hold companies accountable, to enable consumers to make informed choices, and to help advance human commitment to living responsibly with nature, protecting biodiversity, and providing economic equity to populations in need.

In 1989, the Rainforest Alliance became the first organization to conceive of forest certification and the first to issue a certificate for sound forest management, helping forestry certification become a worldwide movement. Its SmartWood program was the first forest management certification program of its kind, operating in all forest types worldwide. SmartWood has certified nearly 500 operations, and demand for certified lumber from these operations is increasing rapidly. Products crafted from certified SmartWood now include furniture, musical instruments, flooring, and picture and window frames. The international FSC, whose establishment was supported by the Rainforest Alliance, has accredited SmartWood for its certification of forestry operations. SmartWood has also worked with a worldwide network of regionally based conservation organizations to implement certification services in tropical, temperate, and boreal regions. Additionally, this program has developed the innovative SmartWood Rediscovered Program, which certifies salvaged or recycled wood that is being laid to waste or rescued from rivers or streams and from buildings that are being demolished.

The Rainforest Alliance was also the first organization to tackle the certification of sustainable agriculture in the tropics, helping the banana industry transform its land-use and business practices. The Rainforest Alliance's Conservation Agriculture program, winner of the 1995 Peter F. Drucker Award for Nonprofit Innovation, transforms the social and environmental impacts of tropical agriculture, including bananas, coffee, cocoa, oranges, flowers, foliage, and other export crops. The Rainforest Alliance and its partners throughout Latin America formed the Sustainable Agriculture Network (SAN), a coalition of independent, nonprofit conservation groups that work with farmers to develop social and environmental guidelines for sustainable agriculture. Food products from Rainforest Alliance–certified farms are distinguished in the marketplace by ecolabels, giving consumers a way to show their support for responsible farmers. As of June 2000, this coalition had certified over 225 tropical farms representing more than 125,000 acres of land by using certification standards that promote the conservation of wildlife, reforestation along waterways and roads, and a safe, healthy environment for workers and their families.

SmartVoyager, Rainforest Alliance's newest certification program, is a joint effort of Conservación y Desarrollo (Conservation & Development), a nonprofit conservation group in Ecuador, and the Rainforest Alliance to certify responsible management of tour boats in the Galapagos Islands. The SmartVoyager seal of approval gives travelers the assurance that they are supporting operators who care about the environment, wildlife conservation, and the well-being of workers and local communities.

These certification programs help protect biodiversity, local communities, and human health while allowing companies and workers to produce coffee, harvest lumber, and conduct ecotours, among other activities. Through these pioneer programs, the Rainforest Alliance has developed an international reputation for credibility in the development of BMPs and certification. By sharing expertise and understanding each other's needs and constraints, NGOs, producers, and other stakeholders can achieve practical, on-the-ground solutions to complex social and environmental problems. Some key lessons about certification include:

- Certification can provide powerful incentives and guidance for socially and environmentally responsible business practices.
- Protection of wildlife and threatened ecosystems does not have to come at the expense of production and profits.
- All resource-based production activities can be improved. Even intensely managed monocultures such as bananas can be managed in ways that greatly reduce environmental impacts and increase community benefits.
- It is not possible to separate environmental and social concerns. Workers and businesspeople themselves depend on a clean and productive environment, and consumers are increasingly interested in purchasing environmentally and socially responsible products.
- Both conservationists and companies have to be careful not to expect too much too soon, as organizational structures and motivations can be very different.
- All stakeholders should be included from the outset—not just industry representatives. This is critical to the credibility and effectiveness of a certification program.
- For the sustainability of certification programs, particularly those that target small operations, it is necessary at this stage to implement a combination of financial mechanisms that includes grants and donations as well as certification fees paid by the applicants.
- An accreditation system can help strengthen certification programs, just as the FSC accreditation has helped SmartWood and other certifiers

develop sound certification systems and open markets for sustainable timber.

The Need to Explore Accreditation in the Tourism Sector

In discussions with government officials, tourism professionals, and other conservation groups, the Rainforest Alliance has pinpointed the following as the principal reasons to explore the development of a tourism accreditation system:

Conserving Biodiversity

The Rainforest Alliance and many conservation leaders, from the presidents of major NGOs and foundations to the chiefs of Amazon tribes just entering the cash economy, recognize the potential of ecotourism as one of the few options that conservationists can offer to rural people who want to conserve their forests, coastlines, coral reefs, wetlands, other ecosystems, or social and cultural structures while accruing economic benefits. Ecotourism is one of very few industries that, at least in theory, depend on protecting rather than exploiting natural resources. It potentially offers numerous local community benefits, including education, employment, and respect for traditional ways of life.

Over the last two decades, a handful of lesser-developed countries, such as Costa Rica, have joined the ranks of developed nations, largely due to nature-related tourism. Nature-based tourism has become one of the top industries in that country, surpassing coffee and banana production. Costa Rica is not the only example. The tropics are dotted with tens of thousands of enterprises that now depend on tourism. Conservationists can also point to dozens of world-class attractions that were "saved" by tourism, from national parks in Africa, to the Galapagos Islands, to the cloud forests and turtle beaches of Costa Rica, to Khao Yai National Park in Thailand. But most conservationists, village leaders, and governments have also learned that tourism, including much that calls itself ecotourism, has pitfalls, some hidden and some obvious. For example, when a natural area is transformed into miles of concrete and steel, clearly tourism can be labeled as destructive as other development activities, such as slash-and-burn farming, unsustainable logging, oil drilling, and mining. Tourism, the industry without smokestacks, requires infrastructure—hotels, roads, parking lots, trails, restaurants, and other services. Success and profit breed more development, which can quickly overwhelm a vulnerable natural area. Improperly managed tourism causes pollution and erosion, disturbs wildlife, kills delicate plants, mars scenery, and brings undesirable influences to once isolated cultures.[9]

Governments are critical in determining what types of operations are built and promoted, but few governments have demonstrated sufficient resolve and consistency to guide tourism development. Ideally, carefully planned tourism should represent an integral part of a country's development strategy for promoting conservation and improving the well-being of local communities. Nonetheless, once an area has chosen the mass tourism option, it forever forfeits the chance to develop a more sustainable and ecofriendly tourism business. Some state and national governments have surrendered to the economic lure of mass tourism, choosing visitor volume over quality of experience and abandoning other conservation and social goals in the process. Cancun, much of the Caribbean, and large parts of the Mediterranean are infamous examples of mass tourism with negative impacts. There are many examples around the world where tourism has spawned crime, drug use, and prostitution. Many indigenous and rural community leaders often have good ideas and the best of intentions but neither the political power nor the access to international markets to implement them.[10] Certification of environmentally and socially sound operations through accredited programs can support governmental, nongovernmental, and private initiates for conserving biodiversity.

Fairness to Consumers

The international community needs a tool to address the fragmentation of certification schemes that currently exist to help sustainable tourism suppliers and conscientious consumers truly and effectively contribute to biodiversity conservation and social welfare. With the dramatic growth in the number of travelers looking for nature-related experiences, tourism operations are seeking ways to differentiate themselves and appeal to these environmentally and socially conscious consumers. Certification represents a viable tool for achieving such differentiation and promoting positive changes in the field. However, the lack of stakeholder participation in the definitions of certification standards, lack of transparency about who will set these standards and how they will be implemented, lack of clarity about the evaluation and monitoring systems used, the absence of harmonization and mutual recognition among certifiers, and manipulation of the terms "sustainable" and "ecotourism" diminish the potential benefits of certification and may lead to consumer confusion. Meanwhile, many natural areas have been pushed beyond capacity by tourism operations that are masked behind green propaganda. For example, hotel enterprises often include statements on their brochures highlighting their so-called environmental consciousness when in reality the only green thing these hotels may have is their gardens. Consumers deserve to know that a nature lodge that calls itself green or a mountain trek that claims to be environmentally sensitive truly is.

Equitable Access

Some certification experts argue that although an international certification program could be easier to market and win consumer support, local certifiers have the advantage of personal knowledge of the environmental, social, political, and economic realities of their countries. However, local certifiers often are unable to promote their certification schemes because they have limited access to financial and technical resources and information, as well as a lack of networking and marketing experience. In addition, many local certification programs are not compatible, leading to consumer confusion.

An international accreditation entity could establish generic criteria for ecotourism and sustainable tourism, accredit the certifiers, guide the definition of local standards for each country or region, guarantee stakeholder participation, promote the accreditation system and standards on an international level, perform random audits of certifiers and certified companies, and thus, increase credibility of certification schemes. Certifiers and operations that perform environmentally and socially sound activities in the tourism arena deserve to be recognized by a truly independent third party. An accreditation body could provide its services to large and small certification programs in nations with sophisticated tourism industries as well as in countries just beginning to invest in tourism. In addition, an accreditation body for sustainable tourism could raise the environmental and social standards for all sectors of the tourism industry worldwide. The Rainforest Alliance has reached these conclusions through a two stage process of, first, studying the possibility of creating an accreditation system for sustainable tourism, and then, second, launching a formal feasibility study.[11]

Certification: Initial Research Findings

Concerned about the unplanned and unchecked growth of tourism development in Latin America, during summer 1999, the Rainforest Alliance explored the subject of ecotourism certification in this region, with the initial objective of analyzing the possibility of expanding the organization's certification activities to areas where certification might help mitigate negative environmental and social impacts of the growing mass tourism industry. This initial study concluded that as the exploding international tourism industry increasingly affects developing countries, as tourists become more environmentally sensitive, and as the tourism industry becomes more aware of the economic benefits of ecotourism, certification via a credible, voluntary, independent, third-party mechanism is vital. Capturing this new tourism market presents a window of opportunity for local communities to secure the long-term financial viability of their ecotourism operations.

The Rainforest Alliance found that despite the growth of nature-related travel and the number of conscientious travelers in Central America, this region has faced significant constraints in the development and marketing of environmentally and socially sound tourism operations. Certification could play a valuable role in boosting the market for legitimate sustainable tourism operations by creating a link between destinations and green markets.

The existence of several local certification or endorsement efforts in this region, as well as other developing external initiatives, calls for the creation of appropriate mechanisms for small tourism operations. To date, the most consolidated program is the Certification for Sustainable Tourism (CST) run by the Costa Rican Tourism Institute (ICT)[12] (see chapter 4). In principle, this program targets large, international hotel accommodations as well as small operations.[13] Apart from CST, there are a number of other smaller initiatives led by Central American NGOs to develop standards and codes of conduct for ecotourism.[14] Amos Bien, owner of one of Costa Rica's first nature lodges and a certification consultant, explored the feasibility for expanding the Costa Rican system for Certification of Sustainable Tourism (CST) to other countries in Central America. Bien concluded that one of the limitations for implementing the CST in other nations is the lack of an accreditation scheme.[15] The situation gets even more complicated in other regions, such as Western Europe, where many more certification programs exist.

The Rainforest Alliance's (RA) initial study also concluded that the lack of a global accreditation body has led to markedly different definitions of sustainable tourism and ecotourism, and thus to false claims and confusion. Although the use of certification mechanisms to green the tourism industry at large is valid and important, there is a strong need to distinguish certification schemes that certify sustainable tourism and ecotourism from those that target mainstream tourism. In addition, RA found that the fragmentation among the current myriad certification schemes is contributing to consumer confusion.

Based on these findings, the objective of the Rainforest Alliance's initial research shifted from looking at the possibility of expanding its certification activities to ecotourism in Latin America to the need to take a closer look at the possibility of contributing to the establishment of an international accreditation body for ecotourism certifiers. An initial group of nine advisors[16] was established to guide the process of documenting a proposal to conceptualize the project and begin the fundraising efforts.

Although the Rainforest Alliance was conducting this study, several other experts and organizations independently concluded that there is a need for an accreditation body in tourism. Justin Woolford, who was working for the Tourism, Business & Consumption Unit at the World Wide Fund for Nature (WWF) in the United Kingdom, submitted one of the most thorough academic studies that provides valuable information in understanding accreditation of sustainable tourism. In his master's of science thesis for the University of Kent, Woolford found that an accreditation agency in the tourism sector similar to the FSC in forestry has "a significant part of applicability and opportunity" not only in terms of its "theoretical and conceptual feasibility, but also in the degree to which stakeholder attitudes produce a positive response."[17]

Similarly, international consultant John Shores published an article called "The Challenges of Ecotourism" on a nature tourism Web site (www.planeta.com) in which he stated: "It is in the best interest of local communities, the travel industry, and protected area practitioners that 'green' stamps and labels be adopted."[18] However, Shores added that it is necessary for these labels to "have precise requirements, that the requirements be respected, and the public be informed and motivated to insist on compliance."[19] Even though Shores does not mention accreditation in this paper, he does identify problems that could be solved if an accreditation body were in place. Travelers need to be able to distinguish among different advertising claims. Green labels or seals could help, but without a set of accepted criteria, independent monitoring, and consumer information, labels or seals will not have any meaning. "The time has come for establishing criteria that focus on the conservation of the resources, both cultural and natural. The standards must be clear and defined in steps or phases so that travelers can make rational choices among tours and operators."[20] Establishing such requirements and promoting consumer awareness are clear responsibilities of an accreditation body, as is checking the quality and accuracy of the monitoring.

In their essay evaluating ecotourism certification, Megan Epler Wood, president of The International Ecotourism Society (TIES), and Elizabeth Halpenny, former projects director at TIES, write that problems are becoming more apparent with the fragmentation caused by many different certifiers. With no international accreditation system to monitor tourism labels and with no "international standards for ecotourism certification, there is a greater possibility of opportunism, graft and corruption, and profit-making approaches."[21]

Several United Nations (UN) agencies have also demonstrated awareness and involvement in these issues. "Ecolabels and voluntary schemes in
tourism should serve to stimulate the continuous introduction of sustainable practices,"[22] said Eugenio Yunis, chief of the sustainable development
of tourism at the World Tourism Organization (WTO). In a 1998 study on
ecolabels in the tourism industry, the United Nations Environment Program (UNEP) concluded that there is "a need for internationally recognized standards for environmental labels."[23] Later, Epler Wood and
Halpenny also pointed out that in the 1999 meeting of nongovernmental
organizations at the UN Council on Sustainable Development (UNCSD),
many participants agreed on the need for a worldwide standard for tourism
labeling to diminish consumer confusion. Participating NGOs recommended that the UNCSD "invite public, private, and NGO certification
initiatives to join in an evaluation process to determine [and distribute]
what are the best procedures for tourism certification and monitoring."[24]
Furthermore, at the November 2000 Ecotourism and Sustainable Tourism
Certification Workshop organized by the Institute for Policy Studies and
held in New Paltz, New York, participants agreed that more efforts should
be devoted to investigating the possibility for establishing an accreditation
body for sustainable tourism certifiers.[25] During 2001, WTO undertook a
study to assess the effectiveness of voluntary certification programs and
their contribution to the sustainability of the tourism industry.

Opportunities and Challenges in Accreditation

Accreditation mechanisms can provide opportunities for governments and
NGOs concerned about the negative impacts of unsustainable tourism
activities to diminish such impacts through credible voluntary certification
schemes that complement governmental legislation. Accreditation could
also provide opportunities to certifiers seeking international exposure
and validation of their systems; to tourism service providers looking for
credible certification services; and to tourism operators concerned about
the type of tourism services they promote. This section looks at some of
these opportunities as well as some of the challenges of accreditation. The
following are some of the opportunities the Rainforest Alliance has identified:

• *Growing market:* The size and reach of the existing green market and the
  expected growth of ecotourism clearly present an opportunity for industry and NGOs to become players in this field[26] (see introduction and
  chapter 1). This growth raises concern among NGOs and governments
  that want to ensure that the tourism services being sold as ecologically

and socially sound actually do comply with the necessary regulations and deserve participation in this market.

• *Need for more regulation*: The need for more regulation is coupled with insufficient governmental capacity to monitor compliance with such regulations. "Independent evaluations of inbound tour operators as well as lodges and other facilities . . . may help ensure adherence to the principles of ecotourism."[27] Ecolabels are "one of the many voluntary instruments that can provide an effective complement to formal regulation by national authorities." [28] To date, all tourism certification programs are voluntary and, given the governmental limitations and the lack of means for law enforcement in many nations, it seems to make sense to have an accreditation system also be voluntary. However, the most suitable type of agency to house a sustainable tourism accreditation system is still under exploration by the Rainforest Alliance initiative.

• *Need to measure certification programs against common standards*: Several certification and award schemes currently operating have been criticized by NGOs, academics, and activists for various reasons, including their nonindependent nature (i.e., many are created and run by the tourism industry with no participation from other stakeholders), nonparticipatory process for defining standards, costs that limit access to certification services to large and/or upscale tourism operations, lack of flexibility to adapt certification systems to small enterprises, inaccessibility for remote operations, lack of monitoring to ensure compliance, and the possibility to acquire certificates simply by paying a fee and without an audit. As an example, at the 1999 UN meeting of the Commission on Sustainable Development, there was opposition from NGOs regarding the endorsement of the Green Globe tourism certification program as the international label.[29] "Tasks that are essential to the credibility [of this program like] the convening of the international multistakeholder advisory panel have slipped. . . . The number of times the program has been rebranded and launched has caused considerable confusion about its precise requirements."[30] Having a third-party accreditation system in place could help measure certification schemes against each other and thereby clarify concerns about credibility.

• *Need for an independent, third-party evaluator*: There is no independent accreditation body to coordinate tourism certification efforts.[31] "The problem with evaluation and accreditation remains the fact that there is no 'third party' we can turn to . . . yet." Certification always calls into question who will accredit the certifiers. "This topic is just in its infancy."[32]

• *Need for international exposure*: Certification schemes that are general enough to cover a large part of the industry across several countries may not be meaningful to small and remote ecotourism operations, which are often exactly the operations that conservation NGOs want to distinguish, promote, and protect. But small, precise, localized certification programs are difficult to promote due to lack of resources in implementing marketing strategies. An ecolabel must be known, recognized, and credible to be effective.[33] As Amos Bien puts it, "when the objective of a certification program is to open external markets, the recognition and credibility must exist in the target markets. Local certification systems serve to improve the quality of the product and to assure minimum norms, but they do not manage to attract external clients or to convince governments as far as preferential tariffs or permissions for specific labels. . . . In tourism, local certifications do not generally have the recognition of the clients. By consequence, they cannot increase sales and therefore, do not stimulate entrepreneurs to improve their performance."[34] An accreditation system may increase international recognition of small, sound certification schemes through the implementation of international marketing campaigns that will benefit accredited certifiers. For example, Green Deal continues its efforts to grow local support in the Peten region in northern Guatemala, despite modest marketing resources; how much support Green Deal–certified operations may be getting from, for instance, European tourists traveling to the Peten and outbound operators selling trips to this region is questionable. Through accreditation and the marketing activities of a potential international accreditation body, Green Deal may be able to increase its international exposure.

• *Mutual recognition (reciprocity) among certifiers*: Certifiers that offer services for very specific sectors of the tourism industry may have the opportunity to partner with other certification programs to complement their activities and save critical resources. Accreditation may provide a forum for certifiers to exchange information and create alliances based on mutual recognition of certification criteria. An accreditation program based on internationally accepted criteria could help ensure that all sustainable tourism certifiers comply with a set of universal components. However, each program may then have to be adjusted to fit the local needs and conditions. Through mutual recognition, larger certification schemes could partner with local, accredited programs and make certification accessible to operations that could fulfill certification criteria but may not have the means to pay for international certification fees. For example, the Costa Rican CST is currently looking at ways to regionalize its certification activities throughout Central America. Assuming CST and the Guatemalan Green Deal are both accredited programs that comply with universal accreditation criteria, a partnership between these programs may facilitate the access of small, remote ecotourism operations in

Guatemala to a joint certification program. Thus, the geographic scope of the certification efforts could be enhanced and the environmental and social benefits of certification would have been brought to operations that otherwise may not have been able to apply. Mutual recognition between certifiers could then facilitate purchasing decisions among informed consumers. Through these partnerships and mutually support-ing marketing efforts, consumers/travelers may be able to compare, for instance, lodges certified by the Horizons certification program in Saskatchewan, Canada with those certified by Green Key in Denmark.

• **Promotion through joint projects:** Conservation groups can influence tourism trends and impacts by working with one or more leading travel arrangers, as Conservation International (CI), a U.S.-based international environmental organization, is doing with G.A.P. Adventures (a Canada-based tour operator) and the Rainforest Alliance with the International Galapagos Tour Operators Association. NGOs could help travel agencies and tourism operators prioritize the destinations (countries, parks, lodges, in-country operators) that meet the certification standards of accredited, credible certifiers. Smaller NGOs could work with just one or more tourism agencies (domestic and/or foreign) that send visitors to the areas where those NGOs are working.[35]

Equally important are some of the challenges that accreditation efforts will need to face:

• **Public awareness:** A pillar for the success of sustainable tourism is having a more informed public.[36] Despite the growth of the green markets, mil-lions of travelers have little or no reliable information about the places they choose to patronize. To illustrate the need for a strong information campaign, an ecotourism entrepreneur in Costa Rica said: "I can count on two hands the number of guests who ask about eco-ness in a year. And, those few who do ask, ask once they've gotten here, not as part of the buying decision."[37] There is a rather underdeveloped public demand for green travel that must be triggered by more information, thus taking advantage of the fact that 83 percent of travelers claim to support green travel companies and to be willing to spend more for their services.[38] In Europe, where certification programs have been around for longer peri-ods and are better marketed, there is a stronger tendency to look for certified products. Therefore, a parallel process for raising consumer awareness and providing education must accompany accreditation. The rise of ecolabels worldwide in areas such as forestry and agriculture and the creation of accreditation agencies to endorse credible certification schemes and promote environmental and social consciousness among consumers in these sectors show that this task is achievable.

- *Multidisciplinary and multisectoral approach*: "Ecotourism, as a logical component of sustainable tourism, requires a multidisciplinary approach, careful planning and strict guidelines and regulations that will guarantee sustainable operations."[39] In accreditation matters, this multidisciplinary approach represents a necessity and a challenge. Some may consider that in the definition of performance-based accreditation guidelines, ensuring participation from different sectors and disciplines may place an obstacle to achieving quick results. Nevertheless, this may be the only way to have a solid accreditation system that takes into consideration what different sectors and disciplines believe is necessary to guarantee sound tourism certification systems.
- *Ever changing technologies*: "There are so many [technological] possibilities and the number of options will be increasing every day."[40] Certifiers must be well informed of the technological advances in this industry and adapt best management practices and certification guidelines accordingly. For example, the SmartVoyager tourist boat certification program in the Galapagos Islands encourages desalination of seawater to reduce the consumption of potable water from the islands. SmartVoyager staff should then stay abreast of technological developments regarding desalination units for maritime operations. Another example: Energy efficiency is one of the standards that Green Globe 21 monitors. Thus, directors of this program must be aware of the latest developments in energy saving devices to ensure that their standard continues to reflect a commendable and achievable practice. It is not always possible, especially for those certifiers with limited resources, to stay informed about technological improvements in all the areas in which certifiers may be working. An accreditation agency could facilitate access to this information by organizing seminars and gathering, distributing, and promoting the exchange of experiences and information among certifiers.
- *Consumer education*: Apart from having true ecotourism enterprises, some entrepreneurs argue that it is necessary to "provide very good service to have satisfied guests. You can't generate money to save wilderness areas unless you have happy guests who leave monies behind, and you can't get happy guests unless you meet or exceed expectations."[41] The challenge lies in the fact that tourists may feel more comfortable or better served with air conditioning in the Amazon, for instance, but need to understand why this would not be appropriate. This represents a costly effort that a single certification scheme may have a hard time addressing. On top of that, in terms of the marketability of environmentally and socially responsible tourism services, it is difficult to establish a threat of a consumer boycott because these businesses are so diffuse, unlike timber products, bananas, or coffee. An accreditation body could support con-

sumer awareness campaigns that will help tourists understand the implications of unsustainable tourism, particularly around fragile ecosystems.

But perhaps the immediate challenges in moving toward a credible and effective accreditation system lie in (1) the need for a highly participatory approach that involves all stakeholders and (2) the need to answer some remaining questions regarding market demand, financial sustainability, and appropriate organizational structure and governance of an accreditation agency. The following sections deal with these issues.

A Change in the Scope: From Ecotourism to Sustainable Tourism Certification

The scope of the feasibility study initially proposed by the Rainforest Alliance was later modified to encompass not only ecotourism but also sustainable tourism certifiers, as explained in this section.

Tourism certification programs can be classified based on their geographical scope, the type of operations they certify, and their methodology (performance- or process-based). However, in the context of this chapter, another classification becomes relevant. As mentioned in the previous section, the Rainforest Alliance concluded that it is necessary to differentiate certification schemes that certify sustainable tourism and true ecotourism from other mainstream or conventional tourism certification, award, and endorsement mechanisms (see chapter 2).

In this regard, the participants of the Ecotourism and Sustainable Tourism Certification Workshop in November 2000 agreed that in any certification scheme, the criteria used for sustainable tourism certification should address at least minimum standards (see appendix). Additionally, in any ecotourism certification program, the standards should address the same areas as for sustainable tourism certification plus at least minimum standards in the following aspects:[42]

- Focus on personal experiences of nature to lead to greater understanding and appreciation;
- Interpretation and environmental awareness of nature, local society, and culture;
- Positive and active contributions to conservation of natural areas or biodiversity;
- Economic, social, and cultural benefits for local communities;
- Fostering of community involvement, where appropriate;
- Locally appropriate scale and design for lodging, tours, and attractions; and
- Minimal impact on and presentation of local (indigenous) culture.

Simply put, certification programs for ecotourism must positively and proactively contribute to both conservation and local community well-being; simply doing no harm or mitigating negative impacts is not enough.

Based on this differentiation, the participants at this certification workshop endorsed the Rainforest Alliance's proposal to initiate a "Feasibility Study, Organizational Blueprint and Implementation Plan for a Global Sustainable Tourism Stewardship Council (STSC): An Accreditation Body for Sustainable Tourism Certifiers." The study was designed to explore the possibility of establishing an international STSC that could serve not only ecotourism certification programs, as initially envisioned, but also a larger audience, namely, sustainable tourism certifiers.

Moving Toward Accreditation: The STSC Project

In August 2001, the Rainforest Alliance officially began coordinating the Sustainable Tourism Stewardship Council (STSC) Project. This study is taking place over an eighteen month period and seeks to overcome the immediate challenges in moving toward a sound accreditation system, as previously stated: (1) the need for a highly participatory approach that involves all stakeholders and (2) the need to answer some remaining questions regarding market demand, financial sustainability, and appropriate organizational structure and governance of an accreditation agency. The activities proposed in this project have a global scope because the objective is to design a worldwide accreditation system. The proposed activities are aimed at obtaining the following:

- The needs assessment of the different stakeholders to identify what is required from an accreditation system.
- An assessment of the demand for accreditation services and the credibility of current certification schemes.
- The feasibility of defining minimum international principles and standards.
- The financial feasibility of establishing and maintaining an accreditation organization.
- The marketing potential of this organization.
- A complete organizational blueprint.
- An outline of the steps that need to be taken to implement this accreditation agency.

The rest of this section delineates some guidelines on how the STSC Project has proceeded in encouraging stakeholder participation around accreditation discussions and the market, financial, structural, and implementation questions that this project is trying to answer through

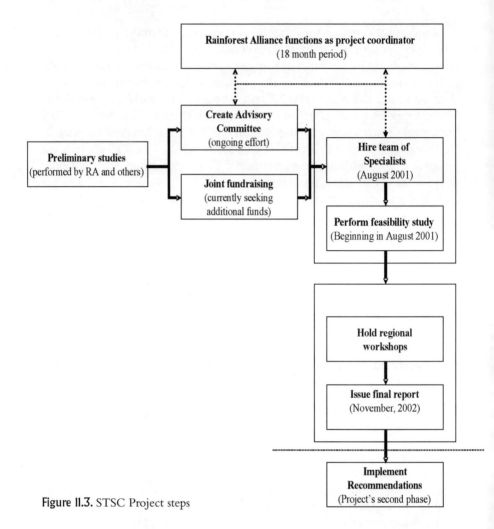

Figure 11.3. STSC Project steps

stakeholder participation.[43] The components of this project are also shown schematically in figure 11.3.

Project Supervision

The original group of nine advisors that helped conceptualize the project and document the initial proposal was later enhanced with representatives from a coalition of organizations, as listed in box 11.1. This group contributes expertise in areas such as conservation, certification and accreditation, sustainability of tourism enterprises, indigenous cultures, and environmental education, as well as contributing to the understanding of

Box 11.1. STSC Project Advisors

STSC PROJECT ADVISORS★
(Listed alphabetically)

Executive Advisory Committee:
- Kelly Bricker, formerly with the Fiji Ecotourism Association
- Andrew Drumm, The Nature Conservancy
- Herbert Hamele, European Network for Sustainable Tourism Development
- Oliver Hillel, Ecotourism Specialist
- Martha Honey, Institute for Policy Studies
- Judith Kepher-Gona, Ecotourism Society of Kenya
- Eddie Koch, South African Tourism Specialist
- Fergus Maclaren, The International Ecotourism Society
- Oswaldo Muñoz, Ecuadorian Ecotourism Specialist
- Abigail Rome, Ecotourism Specialist
- Greta Ryan and Seleni Matus, Conservation International
- Michael Meyer, Ecological Tourism in Europe (ETE)
- Sergio Salvati, World Wide Fund for Nature (Brazil)
- Bob Toth, Certification Specialist
- Brett Tollman, Wildlife Tourism Specialist
- Tensie Whelan, Rainforest Alliance
- Justin Woolford, World Wide Fund for Nature (UK)
- Eugenio Yunis, World Tourism Organization

Core Consultation and Advisory Committee:
- Mary Altomare, The Natural Step
- Trevor Axford, Accreditation Specialist
- Amos Bien and Rodolfo Lizano, Costa Rican Certification for Sustainable Tourism
- Saul Blanco Sosa, Asociación Alianza Verde
- José Luis Cabada, Sunny Land Tours, Inc.
- Crist Inman and Lawrence Pratt, the Central American Institute of Business Administration
- Coralie Breen, Oceans Blue Foundation
- Guy Chester and Alice Crabtree, Australian Nature and Ecotourism Accreditation Program
- Angela Kalisch, Fair Trade in Tourism, Tourism Concern
- Antonio Compagnoni, representing the International Federation of Organic Agriculture Movements
- Ruud Klep, Sustainable Tourism Experts and Partners
- Sarath Kotagama, Ecotourism Society of Sri Lanka
- Alice Tepper Marlin, Social Accountability International
- Kelly Robinson, Caribbean Alliance for Sustainable Tourism
- Peter Scott, Marine Aquarium Council
- Michael Seltzer, Business Enterprises for Sustainable Travel
- Scott Wayne, SW Associates
- Arthur Weissman, Green Seal
- Graeme Worboys, Green Globe 21

★Important note: There is an ongoing effort to strengthen these committees to ensure participation from the industry and other stakeholders. The people listed hereby have accepted the invitation to become members of the Executive Advisory Committee as independent specialists as of January 2002. This does not necessarily mean an official endorsement by the STSC organizations they work for.

the political, economic, cultural, social, and environmental elements inherent in the tourism industry (see figure 11.3).

In addition, the STSC team decided it needed direct participation from persons with established major certification schemes and the tourism industry who have firsthand knowledge of some of the problems and obstacles with certification programs and issues specific to the tourism industry. By the end of July 2001, STSC advisors were structured into the following two committees:

- *Executive Advisory Committee* consisting of individual experts and representatives from the different stakeholder groups, including environmental and social NGOs, private sector associations and intergovernmental agencies. The Executive Advisory Committee is responsible for the overall supervision of the project, making decisions by consensus or majority vote, approving public statements, and providing guidance in fundraising efforts.
- *Core Consultation & Advisory Committee* consisting of representatives from independent tourism companies, tourism certification schemes, and organizations associated with specific certification programs. This group of advisors represents the main source of information and feedback for the team of specialists developing the study.

All advisors in both committees have the following responsibilities:

- Represent their organizations.
- Nominate other organizations and individuals that should become part of this effort to ensure representation of all stakeholders.
- Evaluate project's progress (updates and final results).
- Respond periodically to queries by consultants.
- Provide advice on potential new directions for the study.
- Allow use of names and affiliations on publications.
- Represent the project to their constituents, staffs, and members.
- Participate in quarterly discussions via Internet to evaluate project's progress.
- Participate in a minimum of two and a maximum of four advisors' meetings or conference calls.

Consultation with these advisors was vital to finalizing the project's proposal, to hiring a team of specialists to carry out the study, and to getting it underway.

Project Development

The Rainforest Alliance's Sustainable Tourism Division functions as the project's coordinating body. The Rainforest Alliance was viewed as well suited for this role because it is an international, independent, nonprofit organization with expertise in certification, accreditation, and consultation processes as well as a balanced understanding of conservation, sociocultural issues, and economic objectives. Rainforest Alliance's objective is only to coordinate this feasibility study, not to house a potential accreditation agency in the future.

The Rainforest Alliance, with supervision from the committees, hired a team of specialists formed by Xavier Font, Margot Elizabeth Sallows, and Morten Frederiksen from the Centre for the Study of Small Tourism and Hospitality Firms at Leeds Metropolitan University, the Centre for Responsible Tourism at the University of Greenwich, and Abel Projects, respectively, to carry out the study. It is expected that this team will also receive support for specific activities related to the project from other specialists around the world. The project's objectives and deliverables have been grouped in four clusters, as described in the following sections.[44]

Cluster No. 1: Stakeholder Participation

In *The Opportunity for a Tourism Stewardship Council: Applicability of the Model and Stakeholder Attitudes,* Justin Woolford noted that without "willingness and mutual cooperation, an operational tourism stewardship council is not possible."[45] In moving toward accreditation via the STSC project, consensus building through an open, transparent process is vital. Therefore, this cluster has the following objectives:

1) Identify and recruit stakeholders, including representatives from NGOs, certifiers, multilateral funding agencies, governmental entities, and members of the tourism industry to participate in discussions concerning the viability of a sustainable tourism accreditation body.
2) Ensure that the project involves all the stakeholders, maintains an open and participatory approach, and performs the necessary actions to ensure good participation.
3) Document and prepare reports of recommendations based on the outcomes of stakeholder meetings. Equally important is to ensure the involvement of representatives from different geographic regions and with different interests. Thus, this cluster includes the development of at least three participatory workshops in different regions.

The following activities are being undertaken in an effort to help integrate as many stakeholders as possible in this process:

• Document and implement a strategy to ensure adequate participation from different stakeholders. This should include a list of participants and the appropriate recruitment procedures. This strategy includes:

Organization of physical or virtual meetings with tourism certifiers.

Identification of the most efficient communication mechanism to ensure participation of an extended audience that will include representatives from all stakeholders.

Consultation with other accreditation organizations, either through meetings, interviews, or participation in workshops.

Meetings with specific key individuals to ensure involvement and endorsement.

Consultation with ministries of tourism in host countries through WTO.

Consultation through national accreditation bodies.

Consultation through national standardization and normalization offices.

Creation of online feedback mechanism.

Use of popular tourism electronic list servers.

- Organize participatory workshops in coordination with local organizations as tools for facilitating stakeholder participation and incorporating their feedback into the project process. At least three participatory workshops—one each in Africa (most likely in Kenya) and Asia Pacific (most likely in Australia) and two in Latin America (most likely in Belize and Ecuador)—are planned. The final locations and venues for these workshops will be defined based on the available resources and the possibilities to:

  Include as much regional and multistakeholder representation as possible.

  Maximize representation not only of ecotourism experts, but also representatives from the larger tourism industry.

  Ensure participation from more than one certifier (hopefully from different countries and different types of certification services).

  Piggyback on other relevant tourism-related events. It is then necessary to ensure that the STSC discussions are compatible with the objectives of such events.

- Coordinate with UN agencies to incorporate the topic of accreditation into discussions taking place at regional meetings within the framework of the UN decision to declare 2002 as the International Year of Ecotourism. For example, the Rainforest Alliance has allocated funds to include a session on accreditation matters in the ecotourism regional meetings organized by UNEP and TIES; materials are also being distributed among collaborators and advisors attending the WTO regional meetings to present the STSC Project when appropriate.

In addition to ensuring that an international accreditation system for sustainable and ecotourism certifiers is developed through a transparent consultation process, this project must also address a series of issues before proceeding. In an effort to answer some of the pending questions, the team of specialists has been organized into three additional clusters:

Cluster No. 2: Market Demand

The objective of this cluster is to assess the demand for accreditation services, analyze the causes that are affecting the demand, and determine what the different stakeholders—consumers, tourism operators, certifiers, and ultimately, countries and regions—need from an accreditation system to achieve the greatest possible market penetration.

The following are some of the activities that are being undertaken to help determine market demand:

• Research market demand and marketing strategies of international accreditation agencies, including the following four performance-based agencies: International Federation of Organic Agriculture Movements, Forestry Stewardship Council, Marine Stewardship Council, and Social Accountability International.
• Perform a needs assessment and determine willingness to pay of different stakeholders for an accreditation system at three levels: a) certifiers, b) industry, and c) governments, and answer the following questions:

  What is the need for such a unified system?

  Are beneficiaries willing to pay for maintaining an accreditation agency?

• Analyze the effectiveness of certification at the consumer level and its link with accreditation.
• Prepare a research paper analyzing market demand for accreditation, including an analysis of the effectiveness of certification at the consumer level. This paper will be distributed to all interested parties.
• Document the marketing parameters and propose a marketing strategy for a potential sustainable tourism accreditation agency, answering at minimum the following questions:

  Is it possible to achieve worldwide recognition of a single seal for accredited sustainable tourism certifiers? This question does not refer to a single certification seal. It refers to an accreditation seal for certifiers.

  Are there compelling reasons for a single worldwide certification mark/label or would regional and local marks/labels of accredited certifiers suffice?

Who should do the marketing: the accreditation body or the industry?

Who should be the target markets?

Who should be the target audiences of any marketing campaign?

Cluster No. 3: Financial Sustainability

In moving toward accreditation, it is essential to undertake a benchmarking study of other financial models implemented by relevant accreditation agencies, as well as to study the financial feasibility and recommend a financial model for establishing and maintaining an accreditation organization.

The following are some of the activities being undertaken to help understand the financial feasibility:

- Interview staff at key international accreditation agencies (including the ones mentioned in the previous section) to perform a benchmarking study of different financial models and scenarios and to recommend a financial model that takes into consideration previous experiences.
- Analyze the market data, potential expenses, and other financial data to determine the financial implications of creating and maintaining an accreditation body.
- Complement the research paper that analyzes market demand for accreditation by documenting the financial feasibility of establishing an accreditation body.
- Distribute this information to the interested parties.

Cluster No. 4: Organization and Implementation

Finally, it will be necessary to produce a report on the most effective organizational structure and financial model with the necessary timing and staffing implications for a sustainable tourism accreditation body. The steps for its implementation, as well as a study on the feasibility of defining minimum international accreditation standards, will also be covered.

The following are some of the activities that can help determine the most appropriate organizational structure and answer some of the most important questions that remain:

- Interview staff at a minimum of ten key international accreditation agencies (including the ones mentioned in the two previous sections) to design an organizational model that takes into consideration previous experiences.
- Issue a complete organizational blueprint that takes into account the results of the regional participatory workshops and answer the following questions:[46]

1) Planning:

What will be the mission, goals, and objectives of the accreditation body?

Will it seek UN or other credible endorsement?

What is the general perception of the success/failure of an accreditation entity?

Where should an accreditation agency be housed (including potential geographic location)?

What will be the most appropriate marketing strategy?

2) Accreditation process:

Should the sustainable tourism accreditation body define its own accreditation standards or adapt others' standards?

What existing standards and protocols, if any, are appropriate for adoption or adaptation by a potential accreditation body?

Should the accreditation body define protocols for setting certification standards?

Should the accreditation body establish protocols to ensure that certifiers have adequate stakeholder involvement and transparency?

3) Criteria and standards:

Should the accreditation body set minimum performance criteria for certifiers?

What are the recommendations for accreditation criteria per region?

Is it possible to define international accreditation criteria utilizing the regional inputs?

Should the accreditation system be targeted to certifiers of accommodation providers, transporters, operators, agencies, guides, products, etc. or to all of the above?

Is it necessary to have international standards for each application, (e.g., accommodations, operators, transportation, etc.) or are local or regional standards appropriate for each type of application?

4) Organizational structure:

What kind of structure should the organization have?

What type of governance should the organization have?

What are the necessary timing and staffing implications that the accreditation body should take into account?

Should it be a membership or a nonmembership organization?

5) Finances:

What is the expected budget to create and maintain such an organization?

Should it be a self-financed organization or rely on donations and selling of services?

The study team is documenting recommendations for accreditation criteria based on the results of the participatory workshops and a thorough analysis of current accreditation criteria from other accreditation agencies. The preliminary recommendations are contained in the Mohonk Agreement (see appendix).

STSC's Conclusion, and Beyond

Isolated, desk-oriented research without stakeholders' participation cannot result in an accurate assessment of the feasibility for creating an accreditation body and a complete implementation plan. It is essential to advance at a pace that will allow for the incorporation of input from all key stakeholders, including NGOs, community leaders, certifiers, government representatives, and members of the tourism industry. A participatory approach will create a solid foundation for any accreditation effort.

The Rainforest Alliance acknowledges the fact that the Sustainable Tourism Stewardship Council feasibility study is an ambitious project and given the time frame and resources currently available, this effort may not answer all questions regarding accreditation. However, this project represents an important step toward creating an accreditation system that will benefit all stakeholders and strengthen certification as a viable tool for promoting sound sustainable tourism development. It is foreseen that one of the main challenges a potential sustainable tourism accreditation agency will encounter is developing public awareness to strengthen the demand for sustainable tourism services.

Another challenge will be the need to maintain a multidisciplinary and multisectoral approach, rather than one focused more narrowly on environmental issues. In addition, there is a need to maintain a system to monitor technological advances to ensure that continual improvements are always encouraged among certifiers and, through them, among tourism operations.

It is the aim of the organizations involved in this project to provide the international community with the results of this project during 2002, the UN International Year of Ecotourism. It is hoped that this study will lay a firm foundation and set out a path for forming and financing a global accreditation program with wide stakeholder participation and strong support from existing certification programs.

Notes

1. Amos Bien, "Los Sellos Ambientales y de Calidad en el Sector Turismo: Principios generales de certificación" in "Taller Internacional de Ecoturismo: Aciertos y debilidades en casos concretos," Universidad de Cooperació Internacional, San Jose, Costa Rica, 2001, p. 2. This was a privately circulated document.

2. Jacqueline Aloisi de Larderel, "Forward" in *Tourism Ecolabelling: Certification and Promotion of Sustainable Management*, eds. X. Font and R.C. Buckley (Oxon, UK: CAB International, 2001), p. xv.

3. Justin Woolford, *The Opportunity for a Tourism Stewardship Council: Applicability of the Model and Stakeholder Attitudes*. MSc. and/or DIC dissertation. (London: Imperial College of Science, Technology & Medicine, Centre for Environmental Technology, University of London, 1998), p. 5.

4. Forest Stewardship Council (FSC), "About FSC: What is The Forest Stewardship Council?" http://fscus.org/html/about_fsc/index.html (August 2001).

5. Forest Stewardship Council, retail postcard used with authorization from Meme Lobecker, FSC, U.S. National Initiative http://www.fscus.org/html/press_center/press_kit/index.html (August 2001).

6. M. G. Wenban-Smith, T. J. Synnott and J. R. Palmer, "The Mission, Status and Activities of FSC" in *FSC Accreditation Manual* (Oaxaca, Mexico: Forest Stewardship Council A.C., 1998), p. 2 of Part 1, Section 1; Forest Stewardship Council (FSC), "About FSC: What is The Forest Stewardship Council?"

7. Forest Stewardship Council, "Results/Impact: Facts and Figures" http://fscus.org/html/results_impact/index.html (August 2001).

8. Rainforest Alliance, *2000 Annual Report* (New York: Rainforest Alliance, 2001); Tensie Whelan, *New Directions at the Rainforest Alliance* (New York: Rainforest Alliance, 2001); http://www.rainforest-alliance.org (August 2001). For more information, write to canopy@ra.org.

9. Chris Wille in Ronald Sanabria, "Exploring Ecotourism Certification: Creating a Conceptual Framework for the Rainforest Alliance," Summary, Final Report, JP Morgan Internship (New York: Rainforest Alliance, 1999), p. 5.

10. Rainforest Alliance, "A Proposal from the Rainforest Alliance as Coordinator of the 'Feasibility Study, Organizational Blueprint and Implementation Plan for a Global Sustainable Tourism Stewardship Council (STSC), An Accreditation Body for Sustainable Tourism Certifiers'" (New York: Rainforest Alliance, 2001), p. 8.

11. Ibid.

12. Certificación para la Sostenibilidad Turística (CST), "El Certificado para la Sostenibilidad Turística" http://www.turismo-sostenible.co.cr/ES/entrada.shtml (August 1999).

13. Certificación para la Sostenibilidad Turística (CST), "Hoteles Aprobados por Tamaño" http://www.turismo-sostenible.co.cr/ES/directorio/estadisticas/hotel_eval_tam.shtml (August 2001); "CST Integrando Otro Sector de la Actividad Turística," Archivo de Boletines http://www.turismo-sostenible.co.cr/ES/boletin/docs/20010817.00021.htm (August 2001).

14. Other initiatives in Central America include *Service Best* by the Federación de Cámaras de Turismo de Centroamérica (FEDECATUR); *Sello Verde* or *Green Deal* by Alianza Verde; *La Guaria* by the Cámara Nacional de Microempresarios Turísticos (CANAMET); *Criterios de Afiliación* by the Consorcio Cooperativo Red Ecoturística Nacional (COOPRENA); and *Estrategia del Programa de Calidad* by the Centro Ejecutor de Proyectos Económicos y de Salud (ACEPESA). For information on these initiatives, see: Damaris Chaves, ed., *Sesión de Trabajo: Iniciativas Centroamericanas de Sellos y Certificaciones en Turismo. Material Informativo* (Guatemala: Mercadeo Pro Ambiental, PROARCA/CAPAS, 1999).

15. Amos Bien, *Diagnóstico Institucional y Estructural Regional para el Programa de Certificación de Sostenibilidad Turística (CST) en Centroamérica* (San Jose: PROARCA/CAPAS, 1999), p. 4-5, 10, 35.

16. The initial group of advisors includes the following specialists: Andrew Drumm, The Nature Conservancy; Martha Honey, Institute for Policy Studies; Michael Kiernan and Chris Wille, Rainforest Alliance; Greta Ryan, Conservation International; Lawrence Pratt and Crist Inman, Central American Institute of Business Administration (INCAE); Abigail Rome, ecotourism specialist; and Arthur Weissman, Green Seal. The names of the organizations these advisors work for are included only for reference; this does not imply an official endorsement from these organizations.

17. Justin Woolford, *The Opportunity for a Tourism Stewardship Council: Applicability of the Model and Stakeholder Attitudes*, p. 113.

18. John N. Shores, "The Challenge of Ecotourism," Planeta.com. http://www2.planeta.com/mader/planeta/0295/0295shores.html (December 1999), p. 3.

19. Ibid.

20. Ibid., p. 4.

21. Megan Epler Wood and Elizabeth A. Halpenny, "Ecotourism Certification and Evaluation: Progress and Prospects" in *Tourism Ecolabelling: Certification and Promotion of Sustainable Management*, eds. X. Font and R.C. Buckley (Oxon, UK: CAB International, 2001), p. 124.

22. Eugenio Yunis, "Preface" in *Tourism Ecolabelling: Certification and Promotion of Sustainable Management*, eds. X. Font and R.C. Buckley (Oxon, UK: CAB International, 2001), p. xix.

23. United Nations Environment Program, *Ecolabels in the Tourism Industry*, Industry and Environment Technical Report No. 29 (Paris: UNEP, Industry and Environment, 1998), p. 41.

24. Council on Sustainable Development. "NGO Dialog Speech. Industry Initiatives for Sustainable Tourism," (New York: CSD-7 on Sustainable Tourism, 1999), quoted from Megan Epler Wood and Elizabeth A. Halpenny, "Ecotourism Certification and Evaluation: Progress and Prospects" in *Tourism Eco-*

labelling: Certification and Promotion of Sustainable Management, eds. X. Font and R.C. Buckley (Oxon, UK: CAB International, 2001), p. 125.

25. Martha Honey and Abigail Rome, "Mohonk Agreement" on Institute for Policy Studies Web site http://www.ips-dc.org (August 2001).

26. Travel Industry Association of America, "Travelers Expect Environmental Responsibility," press release, March 17, 1995, quoted from Martha Honey, *Ecotourism and Sustainable Development: Who Owns Paradise?* (Washington, D.C.: Island Press, 1999), p. 19.

27. Martha Honey, *Ecotourism and Sustainable Development: Who Owns Paradise?*, p. 75.

28. Jacqueline Aloisi de Larderel, "Forward" in *Tourism Ecolabelling: Certification and Promotion of Sustainable Management*, p. xv.

29. N.R. Otte, personal correspondence, The International Ecotourism Society. July, 1999.

30. World Wide Fund for Nature, UK, *Tourism Certification: An Analysis of Green Globe 21 and Other Tourism Certification Programmes* (London: WWF-UK, 2000), pp. 48–49.

31. Ronald Sanabria, "Exploring Ecotourism Certification: Creating a Conceptual Framework for the Rainforest Alliance," p. 33; Damaris Chaves, personal correspondence, USAID-PROARCA. July–August, 1999.

32. Ron Mader, personal correspondence via Green Travel, green-travel@peach. ease.lsoft.com (January, 1999).

33. Chris Wille in Ronald Sanabria, "Exploring Ecotourism Certification: Creating a Conceptual Framework for the Rainforest Alliance," p. 35.

34. Amos Bien, *Los Sellos Ambientales y de Calidad en el Sector Turismo: Principios Generales de Certificación*, pp. 2–3.

35. Chris Wille in Ronald Sanabria, "Exploring Ecotourism Certification: Creating a Conceptual Framework for the Rainforest Alliance," p. 34.

36. Martha Honey, *Ecotourism and Sustainable Development: Who Owns Paradise?*, p. 25.

37. Michael Kaye quoted in R. Bangs, "Meet the Godfather of Ecotourism. Michael Kaye of Costa Rica Expeditions Comes Clean on Truly 'Green'." EXPEDIA/MSNBC. April, 1999, Web site: http://www.msnbc.com/news/256379.asp?cp1=1.

38. Travel Industry Association of America, "Travelers Expect Environmental Responsibility."

39. Héctor Ceballos-Lascuráin, "Ecotourism As a Worldwide Phenomenon" in *Ecotourism: A Guide for Planners & Managers*, eds. Kreg Lindberg and Donald E. Hawkins (North Bennington, VT: The Ecotourism Society, 1993), p. 13.

40. V. Kuska, personal correspondence via Green Travel, green-travel@peach. ease.lsoft.com (January, 1999).

41. Michael Kaye quoted in R. Bangs, "Meet the Godfather of Ecotourism. Michael Kaye of Costa Rica Expeditions Comes Clean on Truly 'Green'."

42. Martha Honey and Abigail Rome, "Mohonk Agreement" on Institute for Policy Studies Web sit: http://www.ips-dc.org (August, 2001).

43. Rainforest Alliance, "A Proposal from the Rainforest Alliance as Coordinator of the 'Feasibility Study, Organizational Blueprint and Implementation Plan for a Global Sustainable Tourism Stewardship Council (STSC): An Accreditation Body for Sustainable Tourism Certifiers,'" p. 13–20.

44. These sections were written based on several documents: Rainforest Alliance, "A Proposal from the Rainforest Alliance as Coordinator of the 'Feasibility Study, Organizational Blueprint and Implementation Plan for a Global Sustainable Tourism Stewardship Council (STSC): An Accreditation Body for Sustainable Tourism Certifiers,'" p. 13–20; Rainforest Alliance, "Request for Proposals. Project: 'Feasibility Study, Organizational Blueprint and Implementation Plan for a Global Sustainable Tourism Stewardship Council (STSC): An Accreditation Body for Sustainable Tourism Certifiers'" (San Jose, Costa Rica: Rainforest Alliance, 2001), pp. 3–10; Xavier Font, Margot Elizabeth Sallows and Niels Riis Jensen, "Feasibility Study, Organizational Blueprint and Implementation Plan for a Global Sustainable Tourism Stewardship Council (STSC): An Accreditation Body for Sustainable Tourism Certifiers," Proposal submitted to the Rainforest Alliance (London: Centre for the Study of Small Tourism and Hospitality Firms at Leeds Metropolitan University and the Centre for Responsible Tourism at the University of Greenwich, 2001), pp. 7–20.

45. Justin Woolford, "The Opportunity for a Tourism Stewardship Council: Applicability of the Model and Stakeholder Attitudes," p. 113.

46. These questions were designed based on Rainforest Alliance, "A Proposal from the Rainforest Alliance as Coordinator of the 'Feasibility Study, Organizational Blueprint and Implementation Plan for a Global Sustainable Tourism Stewardship Council (STSC): An Accreditation Body for Sustainable Tourism Certifiers,'" p. 17; Rainforest Alliance, "Request for Proposals. Project: 'Feasibility Study, Organizational Blueprint and Implementation Plan for a Global Sustainable Tourism Stewardship Council (STSC): An Accreditation Body for Sustainable Tourism Certifiers,'"; Coopers & Lybrand, "Marine Stewardship Council: Organizational Blueprint and Implementation Plan" (London: Coopers & Lybrand, 1996), pp. 3–12.

C h a p t e r   1 2

Conclusions

Don't Reinvent the Wheel

Although tourism certification measuring quality, safety, and hygiene for lodgings and restaurants goes back a century, sustainability criteria within tourism certification programs are a relatively new, but rapidly growing, phenomenon. Most of these programs—more than 100 worldwide—have sprung up within the last decade in the wake of the 1992 Earth Summit. However, the underpinnings and impetus for socially and/or environmentally responsible certification schemes can be traced to the global environmental and ecotourism movements begun in the 1970s. Certification marks a logical step in a series of initiatives to green the tourism industry. Certification is not a substitute for other efforts, but rather an important instrument in the mix that, along with other tools, rules, and regulations, seeks to reshape tourism toward sustainable development principles and practices. Further, as Robert Toth explains, certification is one component of a broader assessment and standard-setting process that serves to verify that a business or product meets a specified level of quality, health and safety, and sustainability standards (see chapter 2). Certification, as a voluntary, multistakeholder process predicated on consumer demand, is uniquely suited to the current age of economic globalization in which the authority of governments has been diminished and circumscribed by the new international trade and investment institutions and structural adjustment policies (see chapters 1 and 3).

As outlined in chapter 1 and detailed in a number of the case studies, certification methodology is, broadly stated, either process-based or performance-based. Process-based programs, using environmental management systems (EMS) such as ISO 14001, help management conduct baseline studies and award a logo based on the creation of systems for ongoing monitoring of environmental targets. In contrast, performance-based certification schemes involve awarding logos based on achievement of a set of specific environmental and, usually, social and economic equity criteria, benchmarks, or standards against which all applicants are measured. Although this process-performance distinction is useful in analyzing the different methodologies governing certification programs, these schemes can also be divided into three basic categories that encompass more than methodology: (1) conventional tourism certification uses environmental management systems created by or for the particular business, focuses on internal procedures and innovations that are both green and cost-saving, emphasizes continual improvement, and usually offers a logo once the EMS is in place; (2) sustainable tourism certification is achievement-based or combines process and performance methodologies, is drawn up in consultation with a variety of stakeholders, includes criteria to measure both internal and external impacts, and offers logos based on environmental and some sociocultural and economic equity criteria; and (3) ecotourism certification covers businesses that are located in or near protected or fragile ecosystems and/or indigenous communities. Ecotourism certification programs utilize criteria similar to those for sustainable tourism, but they weigh internal and external impacts of the business as equally important, and they require that businesses provide tangible benefits for conservation and the local community (see chapter 1).

Today, there is growing recognition that in creating new certification programs, it is not necessary to reinvent the wheel. There are now ample models of solid tourism certification programs, as well as examples of effective responsible certification programs in other industries, including timber and coffee (see chapter 3). Although programs, such as those under discussion in South Africa, Kenya, and Fiji, should be tailored to local conditions, they can adopt their framework and main components from existing programs. An important step toward formulating a framework and guidelines for a two-tiered sustainable tourism and ecotourism certification program is the so-called Mohonk Agreement (see appendix). This document was drawn up and endorsed at the Ecotourism and Sustainable Tourism Certification Workshop held at Mohonk Mountain House in New Paltz, New York, in November 2000. The workshop was attended by experts from twenty countries who represented many of the best-known global, regional, national, and subnational sustainable tourism and ecotourism certification programs. In the Mohonk Agreement, the workshop participants defined the common components that constitute the "spokes" or framework that should be used in constructing any sustainable tourism and ecotourism certification program.

It was the consensus of that workshop that a sustainable tourism certification program—rather than a weaker, process-based conventional tourism certification or a more rigorous but more specialized ecotourism certification program—usually offers the best model. However, in areas where travel involves visiting natural, pristine, or fragile ecosystems (parts of Costa Rica, Guatemala, Kenya, South Africa, Fiji, Australia, New Zealand, Nepal, and Kenya, to name a few), an ecotourism certification system might well exist alongside or as a distinct level within a sustainable tourism certification program. This will help to evaluate and distinguish those enterprises that identify themselves as being involved in ecotourism, will better serve consumer needs, and will help to set higher standards that can, hopefully, raise the bar for the broader tourism industry. In some highly fragile areas, such as Ecuador's Galapagos Islands or Amazon region, the only appropriate certification system is one based on ecotourism principles and standards. Ideally, if tourism is to become an industry truly grounded upon sustainable development, it must all be based on ecotourism principles and practices. But we are, of course, far from this reality. Therefore, a more attainable but still enormously important step is to promote worldwide adoption of sustainable tourism certification programs.

Toward a Sustainable Tourism Certification Program

Within this framework, there are some other ingredients that are desirable as part of any internationally recognized sustainable tourism certification system:

- *Award achievement, not just process*: Certification programs based only on environmental management systems, that is, on process or commitment, are insufficient, by themselves, to measure and guarantee sustainable tourism practices. EMS-based programs grant certification for setting up acceptable environmental procedures, not for implementing them. Any credible certification program must include publicly stated performance standards and benchmarks. Increasingly, certification programs are combining performance criteria with an environmental management system to help with implementation. Both NEAP in Australia and CST in Costa Rica, as well as a number of the European schemes (see table 6.1), contain process and performance criteria, and Green Globe 21 has moved away from an exclusively ISO-based system to incorporate some performance benchmarks (see chapter 10). Given the time and expense of setting up an environmental management system, it is recognized, however, that this may not be feasible or necessary for smaller enterprises.
- *Independent assessing and auditing*: Although some of the earliest green programs, such as NEAP, gave certification based only on a written ques-

tionnaire filled out by the business, it is now widely accepted that self-assessment is far too open to abuses and lacks credibility with the public. In addition, there is growing recognition that there can be a conflict of interest when a certification program also handles the recruiting of applicants and the auditing and awarding of logos, as has been the case with CST. Today, the trend is toward independent third-party assessment. Some programs still use a written prescreening application form as a first step in the certification process and then move to on-site, third-party audits and/or spot checks and follow-ups, usually after one or two years. There are an estimated 200 agencies certifying industries around the world, most of which are for-profit companies. Some have been recognized by a national accreditation body; others have not. To help set uniform global standards for sustainable and ecotourism certification programs, it is important to create an accreditation body along the lines of that being designed by the Rainforest Alliance (see chapter 11).

• *Control and integrity of the logo*: As the most public symbol of certification, the logo should only be used after a company has met the criteria. Logos should be dated, issued for a specific period (usually one or two years), and then withdrawn if a company or product fails to meet the standards or to renew. In addition, it is often useful to have several levels of logo so as to encourage on-going improvement. Green Globe, for instance, which over the years has been through a number of reforms, has faced a series of problems with its logo. Initially, companies that paid a modest enrollment fee could immediately begin to use the logo, based on their statement of intent rather than proof of compliance. Today, the certification logo (the green globe with a check in the middle) is only awarded when companies have been assessed by a third-party auditor and found to comply with Green Globe 21's criteria. However, there is an ongoing problem of "loose logos"—companies that continue to display the emblem even though they have not been certified under Green Globe 21 standards. There is at present no enforcement mechanism for withdrawing these logos. In addition, Green Globe has incorporated or made alliances with a number of other certification programs, and this has raised concerns that its logo is being used by businesses that complied with standards set by other programs. Under the direction of the Cooperative Research Centre for Sustainable Tourism, a well-respected scientific research institution in Australia, Green Globe is now working to, as Graeme Worboys states, "ensure that the integrity of the logo is maintained."[1] This includes a systematic phase-out by 2003 of its old certification system, the institution of a dispute mechanism, and a clear commitment to withdraw a company's right to use the logo on grounds of noncompliance.

- *Act locally, think globally*: Certification programs seem to work best if they are implemented on a country by country or, in some instances, state by state basis. This cuts down expensive travel by consultants, permits involvement of a variety of local stakeholders in the certification scheme, and allows criteria to be tailored to fit particular geographical, political or economic conditions. Both Green Globe and ECOTEL certification, for instance, are relatively expensive, in part because they operate globally and often use foreign consulting or auditing firms. Over the last couple of years, Green Globe has taken the sensible step of setting up regional operations, but its three main offices still cover large geographical areas. It is preferable that auditors be locally based to help keep down costs and ensure that they interpret their findings with the utmost sensitivity and knowledge, thereby minimizing the possibility that false or misleading applications are approved. In a tiny country like Costa Rica, for instance, it is unlikely that the owners or managers of a lodge who have volatile relations with the surrounding community could conceal this information and win a high CST rating.
- *Promote improvements within the tourism industry*: Programs should include a consultative process to encourage continual improvement. This is best facilitated by both providing technical advice to businesses that sign up for certifications and awarding different levels of ecolabels, not simply a single, "winner-takes-all" award. In Australia, NEAP officials have found that many businesses sign up for certification because they want to go through the self-assessment process so that they can learn how to improve their environmental and socioeconomic performance (see chapter 5). According to Guy Chester, EAA Vice President and an experienced environmental consultant, "Having undertaken a number of audits of both NEAP certified ecotourism accommodations and other tourism accommodations, it is apparent that a savings of at least 20 percent in energy usage can be achieved by implementing the NEAP guidelines. For a new property designed by NEAP criteria, the energy savings can be as high as 50 percent."[2]
- *Backward/forward and horizontal linkages*: Sustainable tourism certification programs can expand their effectiveness by forming alliances with certification programs for different tourism sectors, accommodation, restaurants, transport, tour operators, guides, etc. They can also encourage, reward, and highlight links to other environmentally and socially responsible certification programs in other industries. The sustainable tourism programs can do this by including in their criteria points, for instance, for accommodations that are built with certified wood, use renewable sources of energy, or purchase organic foods, certified coffee,

and sustainable and "fair trade" handicrafts. These kinds of alliances and purchases help to strengthen other certification programs.

- *Ensure transparency in methodology:* All steps in the certification process should be clearly and publicly laid out, and results of audits should be made public (except for certain proprietary information) so that consumers and other stakeholders can make more detailed comparisons and informed decisions. The CST program in Costa Rica (see chapter 4) has set a good example by posting the results of surveys on its Web site (even though the site itself is rather difficult to locate and the survey numbers are not easy to interpret).

- *Multiple criteria:* A sustainable tourism certification system needs to combine green and gray environmental criteria that measure both external and internal impacts, that is, impacts on the wider community (such as amount of trees cut down to build the lodge) and within the hotel (such as electricity usage). Although tourists are concerned with green issues that they can easily see, sustainability also depends heavily upon compliance in less visible gray environmental areas such as waste disposal and energy consumption (see chapter 7). In addition, although the criteria should include environmental measures that are cost-saving, they should not shy away from measures that are essential to protect the environment but may be more costly, at least in the short run. At a minimum, the criteria and standards should meet and preferably go beyond compliance with government regulations. A sustainable tourism certification program must measure as well environmental, sociocultural, and economic equity issues connected to the community and geographical area in which the business operates.

- *Broad-based stakeholder involvement:* Although identifying the appropriate stakeholders to be involved in formulating and implementing a certification program can be complex, there needs to be clear recognition that a credible program must involve a wide range of the interested parties.

- *Effective branding and good marketing strategy:* The aim is to avoid both consumer and business confusion. Consumers must have clarity as to what an ecolabel promises. Certified businesses need to know that if they invest time and money to earn an ecolabel, they will gain both information on how to improve performance and market advantage. It is now widely recognized that a sound marketing strategy must be built into any successful tourism certification program. It is not true that if a good program is built, consumers will automatically come.

Areas of Ongoing Debate

Although the framework and principles for sustainable and ecotourism certification programs are largely in place, debate continues around a number of issues. A vibrant and interactive certification debate has been taking place since January 2000 as a part of on-line discussion hosted by Planeta.com.[3] In this and other forums, two of the most hotly debated issues surround consumer (and industry) demand and what can be termed as the North-South divide.

Consumer Demand

Everyone agrees that certification will only work if tourists want and support green and socially responsible enterprises. It is clear, however, that so far, the marketers of certification programs in the tourism industry have not reached the majority of consumers. Testimony by an operator in Australia indicates that even where sound ecotourism and sustainable tourism programs are up and running, consumer awareness remains low. "As an ecotourism owner/operation, I have never been asked if I have advanced ecotourism accreditation [certification] by a consumer," wrote Lee Etherington, manager of Local Focus Nature Tours in the Planeta.com workshop.[4]

In fact, there is considerable debate and uncertainty among experts as to the depth of consumer demand for sustainable tourism, especially if it costs more. Some recent studies indicate that although tourists may say in theory that they would select an environmentally sensitive alternative, in practice, they are influenced by a wide range of factors, including their personal knowledge of a destination; its cost and reputation; safety and security issues; logistics, such as flight availability and transportation schedules; political, social, or environmental conditions of the destinations; and need for visas and immunizations.

However, the 2000 FEMATOUR report cites studies done in several European countries showing that tourists are concerned about environmental conditions in destinations they chose. In a decade-long study, the German tour operator TUI found that environmental quality is "very high on the list of holiday essentials."[5] These data reveal that consumers are concerned about positive environmental dimensions of their tourism travel, but they don't necessarily convert that into a deep appreciation of environmental characteristics of tour facilities. An Italian survey showed overwhelming support (94 percent) for adoption of environmental protection measures by hotels and accommodations. Tourists rated an accommodation's "proximity to zones of environmental interest" (76 percent) as just about as important as the price (78 percent). Yet a slightly older Dutch study, done in 1996, found that most respondents were not willing to pay extra for environmentally sound tourism unless environmental aspects were an "integral part of a better quality of accommodation or vacation."[6]

Surveys also reveal that in choosing an accommodation, tourists are more concerned with green environmental aspects, that is, those that they see, and with health and safety conditions (clean water and air) than they are with gray ones, that is, those that are less visible. Therefore, criteria for ecoawards and ecolabels that link gray environmental measures (related to energy savings, water savings, etc.) to green ones (clean natural surrounds) seem likely to have more consumer appeal (see chapter 8).

Recent studies done by Tearfund, a British Christian relief and development agency, are among the strongest in showing consumer demand for environmentally and socially responsible tourism. A January 2000 Tearfund survey done in Great Britain found clear evidence that "the majority of tourists want a more ethical tourism industry, and would be willing to pay more for it."[7] In January 2001, a Tearfund study concluded that responsible tourism makes good business sense: "The tourism industry is highly competitive and tour operators are under increasing pressure to differentiate their products. Research suggests that once the main criteria for a holiday are satisfied (location/facilities, cost and availability), clients will make choices based on ethical considerations such as working conditions, the environment, and charitable giving. Clients are also looking for increased quality and experience in their holiday. "In this climate," the study proposes, "companies would do well to differentiate their products according to consumer demand, i.e. based on ethical criteria."[8]

Although none of these surveys focused solely on the question of certification, several did ask consumers about tourism ecolabels as part of a more general questionnaire on consumer demand for environmental qualities. The Italian study is one of the clearest endorsements for certification. It found that 90 percent of those interviewed favor creating a European ecolabel focusing on the environmental quality of accommodations. The TUI study also found that respondents are confused by so many labels and in favor of one uniform ecolabel.[9]

These surveys indicate that there are at least three consumer-linked factors that present obstacles to success of certification.

• Most tourists are unaware of the existence of tourism certification programs. It is estimated that probably less than one percent of consumers know of programs.[10] The TUI study found, for instance, that although most German domestic tourists are familiar with consumer product labels, far fewer are familiar with German ecolabels in the tourist sector. For instance, only 3.3 percent said they know of Blue Flag, one of the most well-established certification programs.

• Tourism certification has been hurt by a lack of credibility. Market confusion has been created in part because one of the most prominent schemes, Green Globe, has gone through several metamorphoses and in part because there is not yet an internationally accepted framework against which to measure certification programs.[11] As Amos Bien aptly puts it, "[T]here is an indispensable requirement for all certification systems: credibility. A system without credibility does not have market, it does not convince clients and it does not demonstrate anything. When the objective of a certification [logo] is to open external markets, the recognition and credibility must exist in the target markets."[12]

- The plethora of ecolabels serves to confuse consumers, thereby undermining certification programs. In a number of countries, there are several competing and overlapping certification programs, making it difficult, if not impossible, for consumers to distinguish among them or for businesses to prove their legitimacy.[13] In Costa Rica, for instance, at least four programs—CST, *New Key*, ECOTEL, and Best Practice Guideline for Ecotourism in Protected Areas—have all set standards for environmental performance (see chapter 4).

Tourism certification programs face an additional challenge. Although responsible certification programs in timber and coffee have used consumer protests and advocacy to drive change within their industries, tourism certification proponents have not done so. Rather, consumer support for green and socially responsible tourism is relatively passive. It is measured and noted in surveys, but no one has organized campaigns to aggressively promote certified companies and products and boycott those that are not. One likely reason is that to date, none of the large international environmental organizations have used their memberships and their media clout to support sound certification programs. Several, however, appear to be on the cusp of taking a significant step forward into the arena of certification and accreditation:

- World Wildlife Fund/UK has completed its major study of Green Globe and other certification programs and is discussing a global accreditation program, while WWF offices in Europe (chapter 7) and Brazil are involved in helping to create new certification programs[14];
- Rainforest Alliance has set up Smart Voyager, a small certification program for "floating hotels" (boats) in the Galapagos and is coordinating a feasibility study for a global accreditation program for sustainable tourism (see chapter 11);
- Conservation International is running a pilot certification program in the Peten, Guatemala, and its ecotourism department has expressed interest in getting more deeply involved in certification programs (see chapter 4);
- The National Geographic Society is discussing a plan to use its formidable marketing and membership reach to brand sustainable tourism projects (see chapter 8).

There is, as well, the potentially positive role of the travel media, including magazines such as *National Geographic Traveler*, *CondeNast*, and *E*, tour guides, and newspaper travel sections. The *New Key to Costa Rica* was the first to promote a sustainable tourism survey; today other guidebooks and magazines are moving in this direction. As Jonathan Tourtellot, an editor of *National Geographic Traveler*, wrote in the Planeta.com discussion on certification, "Consumers cannot demand what they do not know exists. This is where the travel media comes in. Many of us would love to be able to cite reliable accreditation or sustainability ratings (as well as using them to guide our own decisions about places to publicize)."[15]

A promising strategy, at least in the short run, may be positive campaigns organized by environmental NGOs and backed by the more enlightened travel media, to encourage their members, readers, and the broader swath of responsible travelers to patronize certified business. Gradually, once positive alternatives have gained wider popular attention, it may be possible to mount campaigns and consumer boycotts against cruise lines; sun, sand, and surf hotel chains; casinos; theme parks; and other icons of mass tourism.

North-South Divide

A second broad issue currently being debated in international forums and on-line discussions is often described as the "North-South divide." Many, particularly those in the global South, are concerned that certification may be used to further enfranchise the most powerful tourism companies rather than to help level the playing field by protecting and bolstering locally owned companies. Although both sustainable and ecotourism certification programs are more sensitive to the concerns of poorer countries and local communities, voices of the disenfranchised tend to be fainter as certification discussions move higher up the ladder within corporations and international financial and political institutions. Some government officials from poorer countries, NGOs, environmentalists, and community activists are raising concerns that international environmental standards and certification programs can be used to favor the wealthy and powerful and exacerbate rather than help alleviate the economic divide within and across countries.

With the imposition of structural adjustment policies in the 1980s and the push toward privatization and open markets in the 1990s, governments in much of Africa, Latin America, and Asia have lost income (from taxes and tariffs), as well as economic and political power, as government assets are sold off and national policies are increasingly circumscribed by international trade and investment rules. For instance, as a study by Worldwatch Institute details, under the General Agreement on Trade in Services

(GATS), a 1994 international trade agreement aimed at liberalizing service industries, "member countries must give equal market opportunity to service providers from other signatory nations—including foreign tourism businesses like hotels, restaurants, travel agencies, tour operations, and guide services. GATS requires governments to remove subsidies and protections on local enterprises and makes it considerably easier for foreign businesses to establish franchises, transfer staff, and repatriate profits."[16] The World-watch study further notes, that another relatively new trade measure, the Agreement on Trade Related Investment Measures (TRIMS), "makes it harder for governments to require foreign companies to use local materials and inputs."[17]

These and other international globalization rules and institutions make governments in the global South less equipped to enforce strong environmental, workplace, and social equity standards. At the same time, locally owned businesses typically do not have the capital, level of training, or access to technology needed to make many environmental and other workplace reforms. In an open letter calling for "a fundamental reassessment of the International Year of Ecotourism," a group of mainly southern activists wrote, "As supranational institutions such as the World Bank, the IMF, and the World Trade Organization are pressuring developing countries toward trade and investment liberalization, national and local governments are increasingly disabled to plan and manage tourism—and ecotourism—on their own terms."[18]

This has meant that in a number of countries where the tourism sectors had been owned largely by either government or nationals—Costa Rica, Cuba, South Africa, Kenya, Tanzania (and Zanzibar), Nepal, to name a few—there was an enormous influx of foreign capital and the takeover of much of the industry, or at least the more high-end businesses, prime urban real estate, beachfront property, and private reserves by foreign companies and investors. Oftentimes, local regulations, licenses, and taxes give preference to foreign over local capital. Not infrequently, urban bureaucrats in government ministries, under pressure from international lending agencies and out of misguided conceptions that foreign investment is necessary for development, set policies that tend to bar local communities and businesses from tourism projects. Although an influx of foreign investment may have helped create a tourism boom, there are serious questions about whether foreign ownership and mass-tourism projects are contributing toward the country's long-term sustainable development. Within this context, many in poorer countries tend to look with suspicion on international efforts to set environmental and socioeconomic standards for tourism (and other businesses). They fear that such regulations will give unfair advantage to both more-developed countries and international corporations. Rather than helping to lift standards around the globe, certification can, in practice, be used to penalize poorer countries and locally owned businesses that cannot subscribe to the standards or meet, at least in the short term, the criteria.

Even in Costa Rica, which has an international reputation for sound ecotourism and enlightened environmental and social policies, the North-South, big-small, and urban-rural divides have been evident in its tourism policies and its certification program. Since 1985, the policies of the Ministry of Tourism (known as the Costa Rican Tourism Institute or ICT), including licenses, tax breaks, duty-free imports, and other incentives have given preference to foreign investors and larger businesses.[19] Although the ICT's certification program, CST, has gained wide recognition internationally, it has also been criticized for its bias against smaller operators (see chapter 4). In 2001, for instance, the ICT drafted a decree proposing new standards for certification of naturalist guides, including that they speak two languages, have a high school education, and take a training course in the capital, San José, among other requirements. Conceived as a response to a number of deaths in high-risk adventure tourism, such as whitewater rafting and canopy riding, the proposed new rules seek to establish rigorous certification criteria for other types of guiding, not just high-risk adventure activities, and the requirements go well beyond safety standards. Carol Cespedes, a small U.S.-based ecotourism operator, noted that this law sets "expensive and unattainable requirements" for many guides from rural communities who "are often some of the best guides." In an on-line discussion about certification, Cespedes wrote, "I'm all for CPR and basic first aid but the other requirements will make small-business guides and independent guides in the rural areas illegal." She continued, "The people most in need of tourism income and the closest to the parks and forests are the ones that will not be able to meet the requirements. We need these local people, with their enthusiasm for the natural history, to help inspire the other locals to stand behind conservation efforts. If we put them out of business and take away their economic incentives we will be doing the forests great harm. . . . Once more the short-sightedness and uninformed thinking of ICT."[20]

Amos Bien says that although "the industry itself, especially the more responsible adventure operators, wanted to put the fly-by-night white-water and canopy operations out of business,"[21] the broad sweep of the proposed decree caused a storm of protest. In an effort to protect their reputations, in mid-2001, more than a dozen of the larger, mainly foreign-owned canopy tour operators sought certification under the international standards of the Association for Challenge Course Technology (ACCT) which designs, builds, and audits high rope courses. Companies seeking certification pay ACCT a $500 fee, plus any cost of modifying their course to fit the safety criteria. Small local operators, of course, found such protection too expensive.

In the wake of the Costa Rican standards controversy, enactment of the ICT decree was stalled, and then the implementation rules were redrafted to set standards for guides involved in adventure and so-called "adrenaline tourism" that requires risk and physical endurance. At present, the decree requires annual certification by designated Costa Rican institutes based on health, safety, and environmental criteria for operators offering activities such as whitewater rafting, kayaking, bungee jumping, canopy walks, and rope climbing. Bien states that the decree is now reasonable except that it still includes simple horseback riding and small kayaking operations, which are generally not risky and are run by microenterprises.[22]

Such concerns have created lively debates over certification within Planeta.com's online certification discussion group as well as at the series of regional meetings sponsored by the World Tourism Organization, United Nations Environmental Programs, and The International Ecotourism Society in preparation for the May 2002 World Ecotourism Summit. As ecotourism expert Juergen Gnoth noted, "Economic, cultural and other socio-demographic variables may well generate ethical dilemmas and unfair situations. In other words, destinations in Europe can possibly afford more stringent requirements for an eco-label than Tanzania or Thailand."[23]

There are, clearly, no easy solutions to the deep and widening chasm created by unchecked economic globalization. But it is, as indicated earlier, not going unchallenged. By the late 1990s, citizen movements around the world were protesting globalized capital's "race to the bottom" and demanding that free trade be replaced with a fairer trade that provides worker and environmental protections. Certification schemes, as well, can address the North-South divide by building in some buffers. Certification programs and auditors can, for instance, charge less for auditing smaller and newer companies, give more weight to locally owned businesses and those that actively support community and conservation issues, and can provide technical assistance to businesses to train staff and adapt reforms to comply with certification standards. Most importantly, certification programs, although adhering to a framework of principles that have wide international acceptance, must tailor the specifics of a certification program to the local needs and realities. As Epler Wood and Halpenny ask, "The Maasai in Kenya, the Aborigines in Australia, and the Amazonian peoples of the rain forest are all stakeholders in the development of ecotourism. Are international certification systems really capable of incorporating these sensitive sociocultural concerns?"[24] A first step in doing so is to ensure that local communities, NGOs, and domestically owned tourism businesses play a strong role in helping to create programs in their region.

By 2002, the scattered tourism certification efforts around the world had begun to gel into a more unified movement. There is increasing clarity and agreement among practitioners and proponents about what should be the basic framework and ingredients for sound sustainable tourism and ecotourism certification programs. There was progress in completing a sound feasibility study for an international accreditation system. The difficult and contentious issues were being debated and some creative solutions were beginning to emerge. Most fundamentally, a growing number of experts, analysts, practitioners, and travelers were coming to view sounder certification programs as important tools for helping to measure and promote sustainable development and to distinguish genuine ecotourism from the lite and greenwashing perversions. As Michael Conroy has concluded, "Certification is a type of insurance against social and environmental damage, not totally foolproof, but far better than running unprotected."[25]

Notes

1. Author's correspondence with Graeme Worboys, January 2002.
2. Author's correspondence with Guy Chester, April 2002.
3. The Ecotourism Certification Workshop, Planeta.com Web site: http://groups. yahoo.com/group/ecotourism_certification, various occasions, January 2000–2002.
4. Web site: http://groups. yahoo.com/group/ecotourism_certification/message/ 74, July 2001.
5. Chapter 3, "Consumer Demand Regarding Tourism and Environment," Consultancy and Research for Environmental Management (CREM), *Feasibility and Market Study for a European Eco-label for Tourist Accommodations (FEMATOUR)*, commissioned by the European Commission (Amsterdam: CREM and CH2MHILL, August 2000).
6. Ibid.
7. Cited in Graham Gordon, "Overview," *Tourism: Putting Ethics into Practice* (Teddington, Middlesex, England: Tearfund, January 2001), p. 3.
8. Ibid.
9. FEMATOUR, 2000.
10. FEMATOUR, 2000.
11. Synergy, "Tourism Certification: An Analysis of Green Globe 21 and Other Tourism Certification Programmes," Report prepared for WWF-UK (London: Synergy, August 2000); author's communication with WWF-Brazil, April 2002.
12. Amos Bien, "Estrategia de Centificaciones Turisticas en Centroamerica," FODESTUR-GTZ (Fomento al Desarrollo Sostenible Mediante el Turismo en Centroamerica–Gesellschaft fur Technische Zusammenarbeit), Managua,

2000, on FODESTUR Web site: http://www.geprotur.com.ni/download/
estudio.abin.zip.

13. Synergy, 2000.

14. Synergy, *Tourism Certification: An Analysis of Green Globe 21 and Other Tourism Certification Programmes*, Report prepared for WWF-UK (London: Synergy, August 2000); author's communication with WWF-Brazil, April 2002.

15. Web site: http://groups.yahoo.com/group/ecotourism_certification/message/87, July 2001.

16. Lisa Mastny, *Traveling Light: New Paths for International Tourism*, Worldwatch Paper 159 (Washington, D.C.: Worldwatch Institute, December 2001), p. 23.

17. Ibid., p. 24.

18. Anita Pleumarom, letter calling for "a fundamental reassessment of the International Year of Ecotourism," Third World Network, et al, October 2000.

19. Martha Honey, *Ecotourism and Sustainable Development: Who Owns Paradise?* (Washington, D.C.: Island Press, 1999), pp. 132–135.

20. Web site: http://groups.yahoo.com/group/ecotourism_certification/message/349, July 2001.

21. Author's email communication with Amos Bien, March 2002.

22. Correspondence with Amos Bien, January 2002; Decree number 29421-S-MEIC-TUR, Gaceta Nol 77, April 23, 2001, received from Bien; Chakris Kussalanant, "Adventure-Tourism Companies Get Extended Safety Deadline," *The Tico Times*, July 20, 2001; David, Boddiger, "Canopy Tour Safety Eyed," *The Tico Times*, August 24, 2001; Chakris Kussalanant, "Confusion Persists over New Tourism Law," *The Tico Times*, June 15, 2001, available on Web site http://www.ticotimes.net.

23. Cited in Megan Epler Wood and Elizabeth Halpenny, "Ecotourism Certification and Evaluation and Prospects," in X. Font and R. C. Buckley, *Tourism Ecolabelling: Certification and Promotion* (Oxon, UK: CAB International, March 2001).

24. Ibid.

25. Michael E. Conroy, Senior Program Officer, Ford Foundation, "Certification for Natural Resource Management: Processes, Participants, and Critical Challenges," PowerPoint presentation to Trustee Assets Committee, Ford Foundation, September 27, 2000.

Appendix: Mohonk Agreement

A Framework and Principles for the Certification of Ecotourism and Sustainable Tourism

Background

This document contains a set of general principles and elements that should be part of any sound ecotourism and sustainable tourism certification programs. This framework was unanimously adopted at the conclusion of an international workshop convened by the Institute for Policy Studies with support from the Ford Foundation. It was held at Mohonk Mountain House, New Paltz, New York on November 17–19, 2000.

Participants came from twenty countries, and delegates represented most of the leading global, national, sub-national, and regional sustainable tourism and ecotourism certification programs (including Blue Flag, CST★, Green Globe Asia Pacific, CAST★, QTC★, NEAP★, TIANZ★, ISO★ 14000, Kiskeya Alternativa, Green Deal, PAN Parks, Smart Voyager, and Saskatchewan), new certification initiatives (Brazil, FEMATOUR★, Kenya, Peru, South Africa, Sri Lanka, Fiji, and Vermont), organizations involved in certification (including UNEP★, EAA★, ECOTRANS★, FETA★, Imaflora, Mafisa, Oceans Blue, TIES★, CREM★, PROARCA/CAPAS★, Rainforest Alliance, WWF/UK★, Conservation International, Ecotrust Canada, and SOS Mata Atlantica), and academics, consultants, business leaders, and others (including BEST★, CEC★, Ecoresorts/African Ecolodges, Lindblad Expeditions, Rainforest Expeditions, R.B. Toth Associates, Environmental Training and Consulting International) with expertise in tourism and ecotourism certification and environmental management.

Workshop participants recognized that tourism certification programs need to be tailored to fit particular geographical regions and sectors of the tourism industry but agreed that the following are the universal compo-

---

★ See Acronym list.

nents that must frame any ecotourism and sustainable certification program.

1) Certification Scheme: Overall Framework

Basis of Scheme

- The objectives of the scheme should be clearly stated.
- The development of a certification scheme should be a participatory, multistakeholder, and multisectoral process (including representatives from local communities, tourism businesses, non-governmental organizations, community-based organizations, government agencies, and others).
- The scheme should provide tangible benefits to tourism providers and a means for tourists to choose wisely.
- The scheme should provide tangible benefits to local communities and to conservation.
- The scheme should set minimum standards while encouraging and rewarding best practice.
- The scheme should include a process to withdraw certification in the event of noncompliance.
- The scheme should establish control of existing/new seals/logos in terms of appropriate use, an expiration date and, in the event of loss of certification, a procedure to withdraw the logo.
- The scheme should include provisions for technical assistance.
- The scheme should be designed such that there is motivation for continual improvement—both of the scheme and of the products/companies to be certified.

Criteria Framework

- Criteria should provide the mechanism(s) to meet the stated objective(s).
- Criteria used should meet and preferably exceed regulatory compliance.
- Criteria should embody global best practice in environmental, social, and economic management.
- Criteria should be adapted to recognize local/regional ecological, social, and economic conditions and local sustainable development efforts.
- Criteria should be subject to a periodic review.

- Criteria should be principally performance-based and include environmental, social, and economic management process elements.

Scheme Integrity
- The certification program should be transparent and involve an appeals process.
- The certification body should be independent of the parties being certified and of technical assistance and assessment bodies (i.e., administrative structures for technical assistance, assessment, and auditing should avoid conflicts of interest).
- The scheme should require audits by suitably trained auditors.
- The scheme should require consumer and local community feedback mechanisms.

2) Sustainable Tourism Criteria

Sustainable tourism seeks to minimize ecological and sociocultural impacts while providing economic benefits to local communities and host countries.

In any certification scheme, the criteria used to define sustainable tourism should address at least minimum standards in the following aspects (as appropriate):

Overall
- Environmental planning and impact assessment considering social, cultural, ecological, and economic impacts (including cumulative impacts and mitigation strategies);
- Environmental management commitment by tourism business;
- Staff training, education, responsibility, knowledge, and awareness in environmental, social, and cultural management;
- Mechanisms for monitoring and reporting environmental performance;
- Accurate, responsible marketing leading to realistic expectations; and
- Consumer feedback.

Social / Cultural
- Impacts upon social structures, culture, and economy (on both local and national levels);

- Appropriateness of land acquisition/access processes and land tenure;
- Measures to protect the integrity of local communities' social structure; and
- Mechanisms to ensure that rights and aspirations of local and/or indigenous people are recognized.

Ecological

- Appropriateness of location and sense of place;
- Biodiversity conservation and integrity of ecosystem processes;
- Site disturbance, landscaping, and rehabilitation;
- Drainage, soils, and storm water management;
- Sustainability of energy supply and minimization of use;
- Sustainability of water supply and minimization of use;
- Sustainability of wastewater treatment and disposal;
- Noise and air quality (including greenhouse gas emissions);
- Waste minimization and sustainability of disposal;
- Visual impacts and light;
- Sustainability of materials and supplies (recyclable and recycled materials, locally produced, certified timber products, etc.); and
- Minimal environmental impacts of activities.

Economic

- Requirements for ethical business practice;
- Mechanisms to ensure that labor arrangements and industrial relations procedures are not exploitative and conform to local laws and international labor standards (whichever are higher);
- Mechanisms to ensure that negative economic impacts on local communities are minimized and preferably that there are substantial economic benefits to local communities; and
- Requirements to ensure contributions to the development/maintenance of local community infrastructure.

3) **Ecotourism Criteria**

Ecotourism is sustainable tourism with a natural-area focus that benefits the environment and local communities and fosters environmental and cultural understanding, appreciation, and awareness.

In any ecotourism certification scheme, the criteria should address standards (preferably, mostly best practices) for sustainable tourism (as per above) and at least minimum standards for:

- Focus on personal experiences of nature to lead to greater understanding and appreciation;
- Interpretation and environmental awareness of nature, local society, and culture;
- Positive and active contributions to conservation of natural areas or biodiversity;
- Economic, social, and cultural benefits for local communities;
- Fostering of community involvement, where appropriate;
- Locally appropriate scale and design for lodging, tours, and attractions; and
- Minimal impact on and presentation of local (indigenous) culture.

Glossary of Terms

Accreditation is the procedure by which an authoritative body formally recognizes that a certifier or certification program is competent to carry out specific tasks. In other words, an accreditation program certifies the certifiers. In Australia, New Zealand, Canada, Fiji, and some other places, accreditation has been used synonymously with certification, but in this book, they have distinct meanings.

Adventure tourism is nature tourism that involves a degree of risk taking.

Assessment is all activities related to the certification of business or entity to determine whether it meets all the requirements of the specified standard necessary for granting certification.

Audit is a systematic, documented, periodic and objective evaluation and verification of how well a particular entity (company, product, program, individual, destination, etc.) is doing compared with a set of standards.

Benchmarking is the process of comparing performances and processes within an industry to assess relative position against either a set industry standard or against those that are "best in class." Benchmarking is not synonymous with baselining which establishes the existing level of performance within an operation.

Best practice(s) is used to designate highest quality, excellence, or superior practices by a tourism operator. The term is widely used in many award and certification programs, as well as academic studies, to designate the best in a particular class or a leader in the field. "Best," however, is a contextual term. There is no set standard of measurement, and the term is often loosely or ill-defined.

Biodiversity means biological diversity in an environment as indicated by the various plants, animals, and microorganisms, the genes they contain, and the ecosystems they form. Biodiversity is usually considered at four levels: genetic diversity, species diversity, community diversity, and ecosystem diversity.

Certification is a voluntary procedure that assesses, monitors, and gives written assurance that a business, product, process, service, or management system conforms to specific requirements. It awards a marketable logo or seal to those that meet or exceed baseline standards, i.e., those that at a minimum comply with national and regional regulations and, typically, fulfill other declared or negotiated standards prescribed by the program.

Community is people living in one place, district, state, or country.

Conventional, mass, or mainstream tourism are terms commonly but loosely used to refer to popular forms of leisure tourism pioneered in southern Europe, the Caribbean, and North America in the 1960s and 1970s. This typically involves the movement of a large number of people on nominally standardized packaged tour holidays to resorts, theme parks and on cruise ships.

Conventional (or mass) tourism certification covers companies within the mass market or conventional tourism industry. These programs, which tend to be dominated by industry, are based on setting up environmental management systems (often ISO 14001 or their derivatives) and focus internally on the physical plant, product, or service. They are the narrowest and least effective of the certification models: they can lead to some green innovations, but they are insufficient to ensure sustainable development.

Cultural tourism is travel for the purpose of learning about cultures or aspects of cultures.

Culture is the sum total of ways of living by a group of human beings that is transmitted from one generation to another.

Degradation is any decline in the quality of natural or cultural resources or the viability of ecosystems that is caused directly or indirectly by humans.

Ecolabeling describes a scheme in which a product, company, service, or destination may be awarded an ecological label on the basis of its "acceptable" level of environmental impact. The acceptable level of environmental impact may be determined by consideration of a single environmental hurdle or after undertaking an assessment of its overall impacts. Ecolabeling sometimes refers to the natural environment only; sometimes it takes into account social and cultural environments as well. An ecoquality label marks the state of the environmental quality, such as water quality for beaches or quality of wildlife in national parks.

Eco-Management and Audit Scheme (EMAS) is a voluntary European Union regulation created for businesses interested in certification to an environmental management system. It helps them evaluate their programs and work toward continuous improvement in environmental performance. It calls for businesses to establish and implement environmental policies, programs, and management systems and to periodically evaluate the performance and provide environmental performance information to the public.

Ecotourism is "responsible travel to natural areas that conserves the environment and improves the welfare of local people," according to The International Ecotourism Society. A more comprehensive definition is travel to fragile, pristine, and usually protected areas that strives to be low impact and (usually) small scale. It helps educate the traveler; provides funds for conservation; directly benefits the economic development and political empowerment of local communities; and fosters respect for different cultures and for human rights.

Ecotourism certification programs cover businesses, services, and products that describe themselves as involved in ecotourism. Because these tourist activities are located in or near fragile, pristine or protected ecosystems and, often, near indigenous communities, they require, in addition to the sustainable tourism certification criteria, a set of criteria to ensure benefits for and protection of both conservation and local communities. The goal is to improve or at least have near-zero impact on the areas in which they are located.

Ecotourism "lite" involves a business adapting sensible but small, cosmetic, and often cost-saving practices that are typically marketed as major innovations.

Environmental impact assessment (EIA) is a process of predicting and evaluating the impacts of specific developments or actions on the environment. Associated with the development planning process and found in most countries, the purpose of an EIA is to prevent degradation by giving decision makers better information about the likely consequences that the action could have on the environment. The EIA process involves reviewing the existing state of the environment and the characteristics of the proposed development; predicting the state of the future environment with and without the development; considering methods for reducing or eliminating any negative impacts; producing the environmental impact statement for public consultation that discusses these points; and making a decision about whether the development should proceed at the proposed site, along with a list of relevant mitigation measures.

Environmental impact statement is the report resulting from an environmental impact assessment.

Environmental management system (EMS) is part of the overall management system that includes the organizational structure, responsibilities, practices, procedures, processes, and resources for determining and implementing the environmental policy. An environmental management system includes tools such as environmental impact assessment, environmental auditing, and strategic environmental assessment.

Greenwashing is a term used to describe businesses, services, or products that promote themselves as environmentally friendly when they are not.

International Organization for Standardization (ISO) is a world federation of national and regional standards bodies founded in 1946 and based in Geneva. Its goal is to develop voluntary standards designed to facilitate international manufacturing, trade, and communications. It covers all fields except electrical and electronics, which are covered by the International Electrotechnical Commission.

Interpretation is a means of communicating ideas and feelings that help people enrich their understanding and appreciation of their world and their role within it. Common interpretation techniques used in ecotourism include commentary on guided tours, presentations and discussions, dramatic and musical performances, brochures, signs, displays, and audiovisual presentations.

ISO 9000 is the international series of standards for quality management systems.

ISO 14000 is the international standard series for environmental management systems that includes five elements: 1) an environmental policy; 2) an assessment of environmental aspects and legal and voluntary obligations; 3) a management system; 4) a series of periodic internal audits and reports to top management; and 5) a public declaration that ISO 14001 is being implemented.

ISO 14001, the cornerstone of the ISO 14000 series, is a prescriptive document against which the company will be benchmarked and receive certification.

ISO 14001 Plus seeks to address some of the limitations of the ISO system by including requirements for public participation, corporate disclosure of environmental statements, and compliance with government regulations.

Life-cycle assessment is a variant of an EMS that evaluates the environmental burdens associated with a product, process, or activity from "cradle to grave." It does so by identifying and qualifying energy and materials used and wastes released to the environment and by evaluating opportunities for reducing the impacts of these processes. In the tourism industry, this process assesses the use of resources and social and environmental impact during three phases: (1) departure and return travel, (2) stay at the destination, and (3) activities at the destination. For accommodations, the three-phase life cycle can be analyzed as: (1) construction, (2) operation, and (3) demolition.

Mohonk Agreement is a framework for creating a certification program for both sustainable tourism and ecotourism that was written and adopted at an international conference held at Mohonk Mountain House in New Paltz, New York, in November 2000. Under this plan, ecotourism is a restricted subset of sustainable tourism; that is, to be classified as an ecotourism business, a company must first comply with the basic requirements for sustainability and then comply with additional requirements.

Monitoring is an ongoing review, evaluation, and assessment to detect changes in the condition of the natural or cultural integrity of a place with reference to a baseline condition.

(The) Natural Step (TNS) is a nonprofit environmental education organization working to build an ecologically and economically sustainable society. It offers a framework that is based on science and serves as a compass for businesses, communities, academia, government entities, and individuals working to redesign their activities to become more sustainable.

Nature tourism is travel to unspoiled places to experience and enjoy nature.

Performance-based programs use a set of externally determined environmental and usually sociocultural and economic criteria or benchmarks to measure companies, services, products, individuals, and attractions seeking certification.

Process-based programs use environmental management systems to measure companies seeking certification.

Production and process methods (PPMs) refer to the way products are produced. Under the terms of the World Trade Organization, governments cannot exclude imports on grounds of concern about production and process methods. This has made voluntary certification programs an increasingly important tool for setting standards.

Recognition is the process of evaluation and designation, usually by a government entity or prominent NGO, that an accreditation program is competent to carry out its activities.

Small and medium enterprises (SME) are generally companies that employ more than ten but less than 250 individuals. Companies employing less than ten people are generally referred to as microenterprises.

Stakeholders are, in the context of this book, environmentalists, park managers, tourism industry representatives, consumers, local governments or communities, NGOs, academics, and any others who have an interest in a particular tourism project or certification program.

Standard is a technical specification or other document available to the public, drawn up with the cooperation and consensus or general approval of all interests affected by it. A standard is based on the consolidated results of science, technology, and experience, aimed at the promotion of optimum community benefits, and approved by a body recognized on the national, regional, or international level.

Stewardship councils are multistakeholder partnerships designed to provide a forum in which various actors with different interests in the targeted sectors can engage in collaborative solution-oriented dialogue to their mutual advantage and can create market-based incentives to stimulate the production and consumption of certified sustainable products. Stewardship councils accredit certifiers based on their performance and help ensure that certification is being conducted through objective and transparent mechanisms. An "accreditation body" is understood in this book as a stewardship council.

Sustainable development is that which "meets the needs of the present without compromising the ability of future generations to meet their own needs," according to *Our Common Future*, the 1987 United Nations' document commonly referred to as the Brundtland Report. It entails using, conserving, and enhancing the community's resources so that ecological development processes, on which life depends, are maintained and the total quality of life, now and in the future, can be sustained.

Sustainable tourism is, according to the World Tourism Organization, "envisaged as leading to management of all resources in such a way that economic, social, and aesthetic needs can be fulfilled while maintaining cultural integrity, essential ecological processes, biological diversity, and life support systems."

Sustainable tourism certification assesses companies, products, and activities for their environmental and socio-economic impacts, based on a set of performance and often process-based criteria.

Tourism is travel undertaken for pleasure.

Tourism certification programs typically measure quantity, service, and price which are the areas deemed most important to conventional travelers. Today, many programs also measure the environmental, socioeconomic, and cultural impacts of tourism businesses. These programs can be divided into three broad categories: conventional tourism, sustainable tourism, and ecotourism certification programs. All such programs are based on criteria that are either process- or performance-based or a combination of the two, and they may involve first-, second-, or third-party verification or auditing.

Voluntary initiatives (agreements) within the tourism industry are not legally required or binding and are usually focused on achieving environmental benefits beyond what the law requires.

WTO stands for the World Tourism Organization, a quasi-UN institution based in Madrid that collects data on tourism and lobbies on behalf of the industry. Founded in 1975, its members include national governments and more than 325 affiliates, representing tourism-related businesses.

WTO also stands for the World Trade Organization which is comprised of member countries who are voted in and was founded in 1995 to regulate international trade.

List of Contributors

Amos Bien, owner of Rara Avis, Costa Rica's original ecolodge, has been directly involved in certification programs in Central America and has written widely on them. Trained as a population ecologist, he helped establish Costa Rica's carbon trading mechanism for private reserves and developed innovative mechanisms for rainforest conservation. He teaches and audits environmental management systems for small tourist businesses, has worked in building construction, and is currently a member of Costa Rica's National Commission for Biodiversity.

Kelly S. Bricker is an assistant professor of recreation, parks, and tourism resources in the Division of Forestry at the University of West Virginia. Until mid-2001, she taught in the Tourism Studies Program at the University of the South Pacific and served as president of the Fiji Ecotourism Association. She holds a Ph.D. in leisure studies from Pennsylvania State University and has published dozens of articles on nature-based tourism, ecotourism marketing, and sociocultural impacts of tourism development. She serves on the board of directors for The International Ecotourism Society.

Guy Chester is a founding member and vice president of the Ecotourism Association of Australia and has been instrumental in the development of NEAP, including an audit protocol. He was manager of environmental services with GHD, a major Australian consulting firm, where he specialized in tourism and other assessment, management, and audit projects. He is an experienced environmental consultant and is currently director of EcoSustainAbility in Queensland.

Michael E. Conroy is a senior program officer in the environment and development field at the Ford Foundation, where part of his work has involved supporting the development of advocacy-led certification systems as market-based mechanisms to encourage and reward superior corporate social and environmental performance. Prior to joining the Ford Foundation in 1994, Dr. Conroy taught economics at the University of Texas at Austin for nearly twenty-five years. His principal areas included regional and urban economics, Latin American political economy, and the global economics of sustainable development.

Alice Crabtree holds a Ph.D. in aquatic zoology/ecology and has worked in the marine tourism industry in the United Kingdom, Cyprus, and Australia. She was a founding member and office holder of the Ecotourism Association of Australia and has played a key role in the development of NEAP and the complementary EcoGuide Program. She works as a guide, guide trainer, writer, and independent consultant specializing in training, accreditation, and licensing issues.

Terry De Lacy is chief executive, Co-operative Research Centre for Sustainable Tourism in Australia. Previously, De Lacy was dean of the Faculty of Land and Food Systems at the University of Queensland, where he continues to hold a chair in environmental policy. He is the author of four recent books on environmental policy and sustainability topics and has extensive research experience in Asia, in particular China.

Xavier Font is senior lecturer in tourism management at Leeds Metropolitan University (UK) and member of the PAN Parks Advisory Board. He has coauthored and coedited four books, including *Tourism Ecolabelling: Certification and Promotion of Sustainable Management* (Oxon, UK: CAB International, 2001), and undertaken research and consultancy for the European Union, WWF, UNEP, WTO, and Rainforest Alliance's Sustainable Tourism Stewardship Council.

Herbert Hamele is a German economist and president of Ecotrans, a European network of experts in sustainable tourism development. Since 1997, he has managed the on-line database ECO-TIP, the leading information service for ecolabels and good practices in European tourism. Hamele's extensive research and publications include serving as a chief consultant for the WTO's *Voluntary Initiatives for Sustainable Tourism* (Madrid: World Tourism Organization, 2002).

Martha Honey is director of the Ecotourism and Sustainable Development project at the Institute for Policy Studies in Washington, D.C., where she also co-directs the Foreign Policy In Focus project. She lectures and writes widely on ecotourism and certification issues, and her publications include *Ecotourism and Sustainable Development: Who Owns Paradise?* (with Abigail Rome, Washington, D.C.: Island Press, 1999) and *Protecting Paradise*

(Washington DC: Institute for Policy Studies, October 2001), a report on sustainable and ecotourism certification programs. She worked for twenty years as a journalist in Africa and Central America and holds a Ph.D. in history from the University of Dar es Salaam, Tanzania.

Eddie Koch is a South African environmental writer who consults for rural communities, NGOs, and the private sector in the area of community-based tourism. He is co-director of Mafisa Research and Planning, which is dedicated to creating partnerships between rural people and the private sector in the area of nature tourism.

Annalisa Koeman works on world heritage monitoring and reporting for the IUCN, based in Australia. She previously worked as an advisor for the IUCN on sustainable tourism in Vietnam, for CARE in Croatia and Vietnam, and with Timor Aid in East Timor. She has worked for Green Globe Asia Pacific, holds a master's degree in environmental management from the Australian National University, and is the author of multiple papers.

Geoffrey Lipman is chairman of Green Globe, based in Great Britain, and deputy chairman of Green Globe Asia Pacific. As former president of the World Travel and Tourism Council, he championed sustainable tourism and the creation of Green Globe. He serves on the boards of CAST Caribbean, Agenda 21, and the Great Canadian Railway Company.

Peter John Massyn is a co-director of Mafisa Research and Planning in South Africa. He is the principal tourism planner and adviser to the Greater St. Lucia Wetland Park and the Lubombo Spatial Development Initiative. He has extensive experience in the economics of the African game lodge industry.

Tanja Mihalič is a professor in tourism economics and management at the University of Ljubljana, Slovenia, where her research focuses on environmental policy measures in tourism. She has published many articles on environmental labeling in Slovene, German, and English journals and is author of *Environmental Economics in Tourism* (in German, with Claude Kaspar; Bern: Paul Houpt, 1991). She brought the Blue Flag campaign to Slovenia and is the Slovenian president of the Foundation for Environmental Education in Europe.

Ronald Sanabria is manager of the Rainforest Alliance's Sustainable Tourism Program, based in Costa Rica. He also teaches in the Faculty of

Engineering at the University of Costa Rica. Since 1992, he has worked in certification efforts and helped establish the Smart Voyager Boat Certification program in the Galapagos Islands. A Fulbright scholar, Sanabria holds a degree in industrial engineering from the University of Costa Rica and a master's in sustainable international development from Brandeis University.

Ashley Scott is the executive director of the Great Lakes Institute for Environmental Research at the University of Windsor, Ontario, Canada and a fellow of the Institute of Engineers in Australia. His areas of expertise include industrial sustainability, life-cycle assessment, and tourism and travel environmental benchmarking. He has done consultancies for over forty international companies, state and local governments, and NGOs. He played a leadership role in the development of the Green Globe benchmarking criteria.

Anna Spenceley is a consultant and researcher specializing in sustainable nature-based tourism at the Institute of Natural Resources in South Africa. She is currently researching for her doctorate at the Centre for Responsible Tourism (UK) by developing a practical framework to assess the environmental, economic, and social sustainability of nature-based tourism operations in transfrontier conservation areas in southern Africa.

Emma Stewart is a Ph.D. candidate in environmental studies at Stanford University, where her current research focuses on policies regarding the sustainable development of tourism in Cuba. She did her undergraduate degree in human sciences at Oxford University and was a researcher at the Environment and Development consulting group in Oxford. She is also active in modern dance and performs around the West Coast.

Robert Toth is an engineer who has earned an international reputation for applying modern management techniques to standardization, certification, and accreditation. He has consulted for the Costa Rican Tourism Institute (ICT) on aspects of its Certification for Sustainable Tourism (CST) program. Since 1981, his company has provided consulting services to small enterprises, global corporations, NGOs, and international organizations, including the World Bank. Toth is the author or editor of eight books and more than fifty articles and technical papers.

Graeme Worboys is chief executive officer of Green Globe Asia Pacific and a principle consultant to the Cooperative Research Centre for Sustainable Tourism. He is director of Jagumba Consulting and has worked in

environmental management for thirty years, including as executive director with the New South Wales National Parks and Wildlife Service. He has
worked as an environmental management consultant in China, Solomon
Islands, Thailand, Nepal, New Zealand, Canada, and Australia and is an editor of *Protected Area Management, Principles and Practice* (Oxford University
Press, 2001).

Index

AAA (American Automobile Association), 17, 34–35, 81, 143
Aborigines, 369
Acceptance/recognition of certification/accreditation programs, 77, 90–94, 220–21, 232, 326
Accommodations, *see* Hotels/accommodations
Accor, 12, 43
Accreditation:
  biodiversity, conserving, 332–33
  credibility as central issue, 325
  criticisms, 87–88
  defining terms, 5–6, 326
  ecotourism to sustainable tourism certification, 342–43
  equitable access, 334
  fairness to consumers, 333–34
  Green Deal, 145
  improvement, continuous, 326, 328
  International Electrotechnical Commission, 88
  International Organization for Standardization 9000/13000/ 14000, 77, 88
  opportunities and challenges, 337–42
  peer review, 88–89
  Rainforest Alliance, 329–32
  reasons for exploring tourism, 332–34
  recognition, regional, 326
  research findings on certification, 334–37
  standards used by accreditors, 89–90
  stewardship systems/councils, 325–26, 328
  third-party systems, decentralized, 88
  training, auditor, 84–85
  see also Australian Nature and Ecotourism Accreditation Program; Forest Stewardship

Council; Sustainable Tourism Stewardship Council
Achievement *vs.* process, certification and rewarding, 359
Acronyms, xv–xvii
Activism/consciousness, rising global, 39, 51, 105
ADAC, 204
Adventure tourism, 1
Adventure Travel Business, 21
Advocacy and NGOs' attraction to certification programs, global, 119–21
Advocacy-led standard-setting processes, 106–7, 126
  see also Fair trade certification movement; Forest Stewardship Council
AENOR, 153
Affiliates, Green Globe, 309–10
Africa:
  airlines, 13, 14
  Conservation Corporation, 247–48
  consolidation within tourism industry, 12
  growth of tourism, 10
  history behind tourism, 2
  North-South Divide, 366, 367
  pitfalls/benefits of tourism, 332
  regulations, government, 66
  see also Kenya; South Africa
Agenda 21, 4, 299, 300–301
Agreement on Trade Related Investment Measures (TRIMS), 367
Agriculture, sustainable, 330–31
Air Afrique, 13, 14
Air France, 13
Airline Reporting Corporation (ARC), 16
Airlines, 12–14, 16, 39–40
Alaska, 16, 42
Alianza Verde, 144
Alliances, improbable, 107–9

393